An East St. Louis Anthology:

The Origins of a River City

Charles L. Lumpkins, Ph.D.
Pennsylvania State University
Editor

East St. Louis Sesquicentennial Series

2

SERIES EDITOR: Andrew J. Theising, Ph.D., SIUE Institute for Urban Research

VOLUME EDITOR: Charles L. Lumpkins, Ph.D., Pennsylvania State University

MANAGING EDITOR: Victor O. Hicks, SIUE

DIGITAL IMAGING: Virginia Stricklin, SIUE

IUR STAFF:
Andrew J. Theising, Ph.D., Director
Hugh Pavitt, Senior Research Fellow
Rhonda Penelton, Senior Research Fellow
Carrie Smolar, Office Support Specialist, 2011
Julie Eudy, Office Support Associate, 2012

SOUTHERN ILLINOIS UNIVERSITY AT EDWARDSVILLE
INSTITUTE FOR URBAN RESEARCH
Box 1246
Edwardsville, Il 62026-1246

BOOK DESIGN: Ben Pierce

Virginia Publishing Company
PO Box 4538
St. Louis, MO 63108
www.STL-Books.com

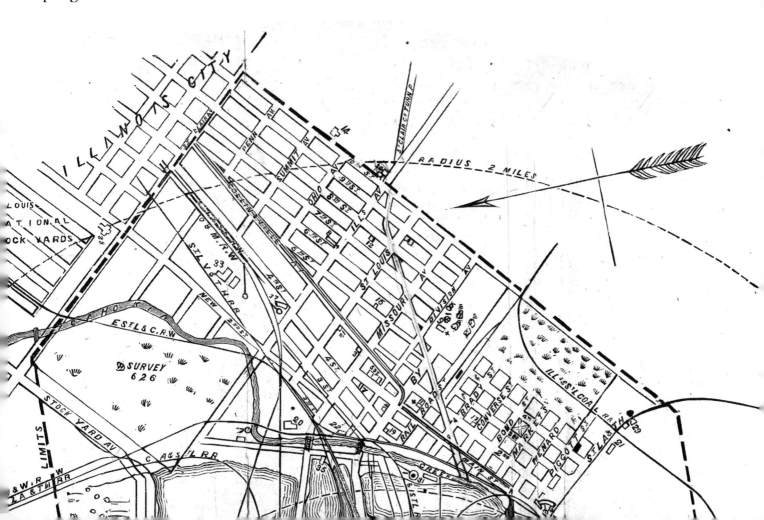

4

Acknowledgements

The Institute for Urban Research at Southern Illinois University Edwardsville acknowledges the hard work of many people who have made this volume possible. The volume and series editors are grateful to all of these people, and have attempted to provide a complete list. For any omission or error, the editors extend their heartfelt apology.

Dr. Charles Lumpkins spent many hours reviewing thousands of pages of archival material, and winnowing down the collection to the gems contained in these pages. It was long and difficult work, but Dr. Lumpkins showed his skill as writer, editor, and historian. He was an outstanding choice for this work. Victor Hicks served as managing editor of the volume. His task was to assemble image collections, manage content creation and flow, prepare files for the publisher, and assist Dr. Lumpkins in his work. He was a tremendous asset to the project. Dr. Andrew Theising provided editorial guidance and proofing.

Carrie Smolar managed contracts and payments, and provided administrative support for the project. University support was provided through the leadership of Dr. Jerry Weinberg, Dean of Graduate Studies and Research.

Dr. Steve Kerber, university archivist, and Virginia Stricklin, digital imaging specialist, provided access to and digital images of the vast material held in the Bowen Archives of SIUE. Jeff Fister of Virginia Publishing provided considerable technical and administrative guidance.

Finally, to the good people of East St. Louis past and present, the editorial team extends its admiration and appreciation. Happy sesquicentennial anniversary, East St. Louis!

...a place called East St. Louis

It was April Fool's Day, and the people went to the polls... again. They had just gone there a month before to approve a new charter for the place that had been known as Illinois Town. They had settled on a new government. They had new boundaries. Now, they were deciding on a new name. A few different choices were discussed, but "East St. Louis" was the name that was ultimately put forward, and the people approved it by a vote of 183 to 89. So, on April 1, 1861, there was a new place on the map—a place called East St. Louis. In the 150 years that have passed since that day, much has happened. It has been a place of boom and bust, of triumph and tragedy, of joy and pain. From its ranks have risen global beacons of sound, and song, and dance, and motion.

The centennial celebration of that event, held in 1961, was an occasion to remember. Many alive at that time recall it as the city's finest hour. It was a double celebration because, in 1960, the place called East St. Louis was honored with *Look Magazine*'s All-America City designation. There were flags and banners, beautification campaigns, and lots of media attention.

That celebration melded right into the year of centennial celebrations, where there were parades and contests. Men grew beards and women wore bonnets. The newspaper published the local history and many businesses took the opportunity to document their own histories in the place called East St. Louis. (There is a fine collection of ephemera from this event in SIUE's Bowen Archive.)

Southern Illinois University Edwardsville, which traces its beginning to classrooms in the old high school building in East St. Louis, is pleased to recognize the 150th anniversary of a place called East St. Louis by sponsoring a series of books over the course of the sesquicentennial year. *The East St. Louis Sesquicentennial Series* will release several volumes (both digital and print) that examine the city's impact over 150 years, document and preserve its history, and provide meaningful reference for historians to come. Dr. Charles Lumpkins continues the series with this anthology of historical works. The history of East St. Louis is long and interesting, but it is sorely lacking in resources. Many historical items have been scattered and lost.

Preserved here, though, are words and images of a city in its youngest years. We possess hindsight today that allows us to see the outcomes of decisions and understand the influences of global society. However, these pieces were written when the city had more years in front of it than behind. It was then a place of dreams and a place of hope. In some ways, it still is.

Andrew J. Theising, Ph.D.
Series Editor
Institute for Urban Research
Southern Illinois University
Edwardsville

Introduction

**Charles L. Lumpkins, Ph.D.,
Editor**

A number of scholarly and popular studies have focused on East St. Louis, Illinois, a small city whose population has been in a steady decline since the 1960s. Historically, East St. Louis has always been a small city; its population never topped 100,000 inhabitants. Many of these studies look at political corruption, decades of economic dependency on regional and national corporations, racial tensions, rapid and massive deindustrialization during the 1960s and 1970s, poverty, crime, an expanding welfare relief population, white flight to the suburbs, transition to an overwhelmingly black city, and other issues. *(1)* The published inquiries comment on the city mired in seemingly intractable social problems. Some cite historical patterns to explain the presence of current problems; other publications dwell on contemporary issues. Some of the studies reached an array of conclusions about East St. Louis, especially the post-1960s municipality, of which two are mentioned here. One conclusion is that post-1960s East St. Louis has become a classic case of a modern American city locked in a decline toward its possible demise as an incorporated entity. Another conclusion is that East St. Louis is a "failed" city, the result of over one hundred years of political and fiscal mismanagement. The many studies of East St. Louis look only at a slice of the historical record to discuss contemporary concerns, but the historical record is deeper and more varied than one may realize.

Primary sources—the very historical records themselves—are the building blocks of historical narratives and interpretation, and the extent and availability of such materials affect the soundness of understanding the past and present political, economic, social and cultural life of East St. Louis. Whereas the primary source documents about medium- and larger-size cities, for example, Atlanta, Chicago, Detroit, New York City, St. Louis and Seattle, are extensive and relatively easy to access, the primary sources about East St. Louis are very limited in extent and availability. For example, most studies of East St. Louis make use of recent materials that have not been lost to time or older, archived materials that are accessible with little effort. In practice, monographs tend to fixed their inquiry either on the wide range of recent problems that have characterized the city since the early 1960s, or the voluminous collection of archived materials that discuss the East St. Louis race riots of 1917.*(2)*

Since the mid-1990s, East St. Louis studies have seen works steeped in the historical perspective not bound by the 1917 race riots and post-1960 issues. The newer monographs draw in part from earlier titles and of course mainly from numerous primary sources. *(3)* The popular layperson books by Bill Nunes, Ruben L. Yelvington, and other local writers are reminiscences that make heavy use of personal stories and photographs. *(4)* The books by these local authors, some of whom were East St. Louisans, attempt to show the other side of life in East St. Louis. That side dramatized black and white residents' pride in their neighborhoods and city and their spirit to forge a good life in what nonresidents frequently depicted as a grimy, industrial suburb. The titles by Andrew Theising, Malcolm McLaughlin, and Charles Lumpkins are geared for concerned laypersons and scholars. Although these monographs explore the historical reasons for city's political, economic and social turmoil, at the same time they show East St. Louisans engaged in a range of pursuits, sometimes at cross-purposes to shape and reshape politics and life in the river city. Whether popularly or scholarly oriented, both categories of publications have aimed to plumb the historical record and in the process open new paths to available primary source materials. Nonetheless, East St. Louis studies need more additions that must connect to a wider variety of primary sources.

An East St. Louis Anthology has for its main purpose the task to bring a sample of primary source documents to the attention of concerned laypersons and scholars. As part of the *East St. Louis Sesquicentennial Series*, *An East St. Louis Anthology* also informs readers that mammoth collections of digitized primary source materials exist at the Lovejoy Archives on the campus of Southern Illinois University Edwardsville.*(5)* The anthology contains a small number of samples that the editor considers representative of the collections that contain hundreds, if not thousands, of print and digitized pages and images. The book looks at several works that were published between 1870 and 1910. *(6)* Some of them have materials that the anthology places in two or more categories.

These five chapters are mere scratches on the tip of the proverbial iceberg of primary source documents that await lay and scholarly researchers who seek to widen the knowledge about East St. Louis. Chapter 1, Early Histories of the City, discusses the coverage of the primary sources that are historical narratives or that contain historical accounts of mainly pre-twentieth-century East St. Louisans. Chapter 2, Maps of a Growing City, highlights the importance of maps as historical documents that show the city's political and economic development. Chapter 3, Biographical Sketches of Prominent Citizens, looks at the vignettes of well known, if not leading, personalities in the life and culture of East St. Louis. Chapter 4, Directories and Miscellany, shows that city directories functioned not only as street guides and as listings of businesses and professional services, but also as a device for advertising and communication. Finally, Chapter 5, Ordinances and Statutes, demonstrates that many of the ordinances embodied city leaders' bold visions for a prosperous future for East St. Louis that would rival that of Chicago. *An East St. Louis Anthology* accomplishes its modest task of alerting people to the wealth of primary source documents, and it dramatizes that the need exists to extend the chronological coverage of the five chapters and to expand the number of relating to East St. Louis for future anthologies.

An East St. Louis Anthology reinforces the viewpoint made by historian Mark Abbott that "East St. Louis may be the most 'American' city in America." *(7)* The anthology takes its place among other works that collectively show that East St. Louis is an iconic American city.

Endnotes:

(1) For example, Graham Romeyn Taylor, *Satellite Cities: A Study of Industrial Suburbs* (New York: Appleton, 1915); Dennis R. Judd and Robert S. Mendelson, *The Politics of Urban Planning: The East St. Louis Experience* (Urbana: University of Illinois, 1973); Jonathan Kozol, *Savage Inequalities: Children in America's Schools* 1st ed. (New York: Crown, 1991);

(2) The voluminous collection on the East St. Louis race riots is U.S. Congress, House, Special Committee to Investigate the East St. Louis Riots, *Transcripts of the Hearings of the House Select Committee That Investigated the Race Riots in East St. Louis, Illinois, 1917* (Washington, D.C.: G.P.O., 1918).

(3) For example, Elliott Rudwick, *Race Riot at East St. Louis, July 2, 1917* (Carbondale: Southern Illinois University Press, 1964); Clementine Hamilton, *The Ebony Tree* (East St. Louis, IL: privately printed [1971?]); Sheryl H. Clayton, *Black Women Role Models of Greater St. Louis* (East St. Louis, IL: Essai Seay Publications, 1982).

(4) Bill Nunes, Coming of Age in '40s and '50s East St. Louis (Glen Carbon, IL: [s.n.], 1995) and Illustrated History of East St. Louis (Dexter, MI: Thomson-Shore, 1998); Ruben L. Yelvington, East St. Louis: The Way It Is (Mascoutah, IL: Top's Books, 1990).

(5) *An East St. Louis Anthology: Origins of a River City* is the second title in the *East St. Louis Sesquicentennial Series*.

(6) Robert A. Tyson, *History of East St. Louis, for Resources, Statistics, Railroads, Physical Features: Business and Advantages* (East St. Louis, IL: John Haps, 1875); L.U. Reavis, *Saint Louis, the Future Great City of the World: With Biographical Sketches of the Representative Men and Women of St. Louis and Missouri* centennial ed. (St. Louis, MO: C.R. Barns, 1876); *History of St. Clair County, Illinois, with Illustrations: Descriptive of Its Scenery, and Biographical Sketches of Some of Its Prominent Men and Pioneers* (Philadelphia, PA: Brink, McDonough & Co., 1881); *Ordinances of the City of East St. Louis, St. Clair County, Illinois: Published by Authority of the City Council in Pursuance of a Resolution Adopted June 10, 1884* (East St. Louis, IL: H.D. O'Brien, 1884); *Directory* (East St. Louis, IL: Herald Publishing, 1887); *Directory of the City of East St. Louis, St. Clair County, Illinois, for 1893: Giving an Alphabetical List of All the Inhabitants, with Their Residence and Occupation: Also an Index to the Advertisers and Business Houses Represented in This Book, Together with a List of the Officers of the Government Since Its Incorporation in 1859, Besides Other Historical Data* (East St. Louis, IL: East St. Louis Directory Co., 1893); *East St. Louis Directory; Standard Atlas of St. Clair County, Illinois: Including a Plat Book of the Villages, Cities, and Townships of the County* (Chicago: George A. Ogle & Company, 1901); Newton Bateman and others, *Historical Encyclopedia of Illinois and History of St. Clair County* (Chicago: Munnell Publishing Co., 1907).

(7) Mark Abbott, ed. *The Making of an All-America City: East St. Louis at 150* (Edwardsville, IL: Southern Illinois University, Edwardsville, 2010), 1.

Chapter 1: Early Histories of the City

A general history of East St. Louis, Illinois, should properly begin with at least an acknowledgement of the Native American Mississippian civilization that flourished in the region for hundreds of years before 1492, when Christopher Columbus made his first voyage westward and found lands unknown to Europeans. The Mississippian civilization built cities and earthen mounds, big and small. The largest of the Mississippian cities was the Cahokia complex, which also was the largest pre-Columbian urban area north of Mexico. This urban entity stretched from its center in modern-day Collinsville, Illinois, to East St. Louis, and to St. Louis on the Missouri side of the Mississippi river. Cahokia merits in-depth treatment, but the earliest books that discussed the history of East St. Louis started much of the narrative with stories of European and European American settlers of the seventeenth, eighteenth, and nineteenth centuries. *(1)*

The four earliest monographs containing extensive or providing sole historical coverage of East St. Louis are Robert A. Tyson, *History of East St. Louis* (1875); Logan Reavis, *Saint Louis, The Future Great City* (1876); the *History of St. Clair County, Illinois* (1881); and Wilderman and Wilderman's *Historical Encyclopedia of Illinois* (1907). *(2)* These monographs focused on the white settlers who developed East St. Louis and its environs. Twenty-first-century Americans might wish the books were not boosterish in style and had mentioned people of color and more about women making their contributions to the history and development of East St. Louis. Unfortunately, the books were published at a time when many Americans eagerly charted the origins and rise of their cities from lowly beginnings to mighty industrializing entities. East St. Louisans certainly believed that their city was poised to outdistance St. Louis and perhaps even Chicago as the premier industrial giant and railroad freight node of the Midwest. The books celebrated the founders and the political and economic movers and shakers of East St. Louis in context of the zeitgeist when city boosters worked tirelessly to promote the city's geographical, political, and economic advantages in order to entice financiers and industrialists to invest in the city.

Although those four titles were celebratory in tone and drew information from some of the same sources, they have their differences. Tyson's *History of East St. Louis* is the most research-oriented among the four histories, obtaining information from private and public institutions and sources. *(3)* Tyson saw the interests of East St. Louis as identical to those of St. Louis. He received endorsements from prominent East St. Louisan leaders, including Mayor Samuel S. Hake, retailer John B. Sikking, and attorney Maurice Joyce. The volume reproduced here was the personal copy of James W. Kirk, longtime editor of the city's most prominent newspaper. His signature appears on the title page. Reavis's *Saint Louis, The Future Great City*, is actually focused on the city across the river, but dedicates a lengthy appendix to East St. Louis. Of particular interest here is that Reavis turned to John B. Bowman, founder of the city, to ghost-write the city's story. Bowman presented a traditional historical narrative of East St. Louis, discussing the significance of the Mississippi River, early pioneers, the Eads Bridge, and other topics in context of the future greatness of St. Louis and East St. Louis. Bowman believed that the river's advantages are inherent on the Illinois side and "bound to play a conspicuous part of the development and maturing of St. Louis as the greatest inland city of the globe." In addition, Bowman saw the Eads Bridge as a symbol uniting the two cities in their quest for prosperity and world importance. The 1881 *History of St. Clair County* focused on the pioneers who prominently shaped the politics, economy, and social life of the county and East St. Louis. The authors clearly informed readers about how the facts were gathered and checked, stating that the "many facts depend[ed] on the recollections of individuals." They further indicated their concern about being careful with the facts with statements about consulting French and English language manuscripts and other writings, including American State Papers and reports filed by the Jesuits. Wilderman's *Historical Encyclopedia of Illinois and History of St. Clair County* preserves the stories of pioneer men and women who settled St. Clair County in the eighteenth and nineteenth centuries. Compared to the other titles, the encyclopedia placed much of its historical coverage of St. Clair County and East St. Louis in the extensive vignettes of biographical sketches. Thomas Fekete, a prominent citizen at the time, wrote the East St. Louis portion of this work.

The four documents prove useful to scholars and laypersons for several reasons. They reflected East St. Louisans' intentions to build and sustain an industrial city of great importance to the nation. They operated like advertisements and announcements from the local chamber of commerce to encourage economic growth. Most importantly, the four histories preserved the stories of colonizers and settlers of East St. Louis.

HISTORY

OF

EAST ST. LOUIS

ITS

RESOURCES, STATISTICS, RAILROADS,

PHYSICAL FEATURES

BUSINESS AND ADVANTAGES.

BY

ROBERT A. TYSON,

Professor of Rhetoric—Howe Literary Institute.

WITH ILLUSTRATIONS.

EAST ST. LOUIS:
Printed by John Haps & Co., National Stock Yards.
1875.

PREFACE.

In the execution of the object of showing the History and Resources of East St. Louis, I have relied mainly on knowledge obtained at first hand, having personally visited the several public and private institutions of our enterprising city and conversed with their owners. The courtesy of these gentlemen is hereby acknowledged.

Among the works consulted I hereby acknowledge the assistance derived from "Peck's Western Annals," "Melnotte's Valley of the Mississippi," Shea's "Discovery and Explorations of the Mississippi by Marquette, LaSalle, Allouez, Membre, Hennepin and Douay," "Smith's Railway Celebrations of 1857," "Ford's Illinois," "History of St. Louis and Missouri," by E. Shepard, and various pamphlets and papers.

I have in my possession a mass of historical data, including a fac simile of a map drawn in 1763, by James Marquette, of the Mississippi river and Illinois country, that was unavailable for the present object, which is, as stated in my original prospectus, to illustrate and exhibit the great natural resources of East St. Louis. In a future publication I design utilizing this data, and also add to the historical value of this work by means of such emendations, corrections and additions as may be suggested by friends, and which properly belong to the permanent History of East St. Louis.

THE AUTHOR.

Howe Literary Institute, October 4, 1875.

Original Prospectus, June, 1875.

HISTORY OF EAST ST. LOUIS.

ITS RESOURCES, GROWTH AND ATTRACTIONS

The subscriber respectfully directs the attention of the public to the above work. It is intended to supply a want felt by all for a sketch of the progress and present standing of East St. Louis among other western cities.

The plan is to present a view of important events which have occured from the earliest records to the present time.

Information is solicited; all that is available will be drawn from the records existing and from persons still living who have been eyewitnesses of the city's growth, of

"Scenes which they saw,
Part of which they were."

The work will be issued in pamphlet form, in order that public spirited citizens may send it at small outlay to their friends. By thus showing in a convenient form this view of the social and business advantages of the place, citizens may at a day near at hand have the satisfaction of causing a large number of enterprising people (including their friends and kinsfolk) to move here to share the general prosperity.

Authentic anecdotes connected with the subject will be admitted. As the work will be circulated freely far and near among reading people, who will read its advertisements to get a true view of the business enterprise shown here, it thus becomes a first-class means of bringing together seller and buyer. Hence such advertisements will be admitted, at cheap rates, as will give a just idea of the enterprise of the young city. The first edition of three thousand copies will be published in paper covers for general distribution.

The interests of East St. Louis are identical with those of St. Louis. Their interests are one and the same by nature, situation, language and common pursuits. Community of interests interlace and lock them together in the friendly bonds of prosperous brotherhood. Their interests are as nearly related as those of mother and child. The pursuits of manufacturing, commerce, science, art and literature are alike open to both. The development of the great natural resources of each, of excellence in the above pursuits, and as the grand result of these the development of noble character in the individual citizen, that he may be public spirited, wise, far-seeing, patriotic, fraternal and progressive, is the aim alike of the best classes in both the elder and younger St. Louis. To this end may he adopt as his motto these noble sentiments of the world's poet:

"Corruption wins not more than honesty;
Still in thy right hand carry gentle peace,
To silence envious tongues. Be just and fear not;
Let all the ends thou aim'st at, be thy Country's, God's, and Truth's."

As an effort looking toward this end, the above work is undertaken by the author. Application for copyright has already been made.

ROBERT A. TYSON,
Howe Literary Institute, East St. Louis.

We, the undersigned, heartily endorse the above work of Prof. Tyson. We promise him our assistance and patronage, and respectfully urge every public spirited citizen to do the same.

Samuel S. Hake, Mayor; Maurice Joyce, P. W. Vaughan, John Benner, Christ. Rohm, John Doyle, John Niemes, John V. Tefft, Nicholas Colgan, Councilmen. Ernest W. Wider, Wm. C. Ellisor, Luke H. Hite, Marcus Finch, Harry Elliot, John W. Renshaw, L. M. St. John, J. Phillips, Prop. St. Louis Hotel, Henry Schall, Dry Goods and Clothing, Vital Jarrot, Banker; Jasper & Koeling, Dry Goods and Clothing, J. B. Sikking, P. M; Henry Jackiesch, J. D. Manners, Arch'd Beatty, James H. Campbell, Thomas Quick, Geo. W. Brackett, J. B. Messick.

COUNTY DIRECTORY.

CIRCUIT COURT—JUDGE, WM. H. SNYDER.

First term, first Monday in January; Second term, third Monday in April; Third term, third Monday in September.

COUNTY COURT—JUDGE, F. H. PIEPER.

Probate Matters—Third Monday of every month. County Court—Common Law Jurisdiction—Second Monday of March, July and December.

COUNTY OFFICERS.

Louis C. Starkel, County Clerk; George W. Sieber, Treasurer; Charles P. Knispel, Attorney; Charles Becker, Circuit Clerk; James P. Slade, Superintendent Schools; G. F. Hilgard, Surveyor; Hermann G. Weber, Sheriff; Phillip Schildknecht, Coroner.

COUNTY COMMISSIONERS.

Augustus Chenot, C. L. Emmerich, Frederick C. Horn. The Board meets on the first Monday of each month.

CITY DIRECTORY.

COURT OF RECORD—JUDGE, DANIEL M'GOWAN.

CITY COURT—JUDGE, J. B. MESSICK.

CITY OFFICERS.

Mayor. S. S. Hake; Treasurer, B. Franz; Clerk, Wm. O'Neill; Collector, J. M. Sullivan; Assessor, T. J. Canty; City Attorney, ..., City Counsellor, J. B. Bowman.

ALDERMEN.

First ward—Maurice Joyce. P. H. Vaughan; Second ward—John Niemes, John Benner; Third ward—Christian Rohm, John V. Tefft; Fourth ward—John Doyle, Nicholas Colgan.

BOARD OF HEALTH.

Michael Higgins, First ward; Alexander Fekete, Second ward; Michael Flynn, Third ward; Patrick Hennesey, Fourth ward· Meet in Council Chamber.

Officers in the Board—Alexander Fekete, President; J. W. Benedict, Clerk.

OFFICERS OF THE LIBRARY—1875–6.

John B. Bowman, President; Charles C. Shuetz, Vice President; Wm. O'Neill, Secretary.

DIRECTORS.

John B. Bowman, Henry Elliott, Luke H. Hite, Wm. G. Kase, E. L. McDonough, Wm. O'Neill, Chas. C. Schuetz, John M. Sullivan, P. M. Sullivan.

Janitor Public Offices—Daniel Sexton.

CHAPTER XI.

CHAPTER XII.

CHAPTER XIV.

CHAPTER XV.

APPENDIX.

Mr. Wm. E. Putnam, Missouri Car and Foundry Works, 137. Missouri Car and Foundry Co., 138. Canfield's Beef Refrigerator, Masonic Lodge No. 504, Turnverein, Saengerbund, 139. Treubund, Officers of Douglas School, Made Land, Fires of 1872, 140. St. Clair County Turnpike, 141.

ERRATA.

At page 63, in the 17th line, "on" should be "out."

At page 67, line 34, "have" should be "having."

At page 70, 7th line, "Hinly" should read "Hinkley."

At page 76, the name of "Hyer" should be "Heyer."

At page 77, "Kindly" should be spelled with a small "k."

At page 80, in the last line, "varities" should be "varieties."

At page 78, "260" should be 360 barrels of water an hour.

At page 97, "James" West should be Benjamin West.

At page 103, "Cahokia" should be Centerville, and after blacksmithing the statement, "he was for some time engaged in civil engineering," should be inserted.

At page 107, 28th line, "Barbara" should be "Bavaria."

At page 118, last line, "Lumrix" should be Sumrix.

At page 119, the first sentence should end with the words, "by Hon. J. B. Bowman, who has owned it from the first." In the same article the sentence, "the ownership then vested in a Stock Company," should be omitted.

At page 128, in ex-Mayor Bowman's address, "the bank" should be "the right bank."

At page 106, 7th line, "George" should be "Charles."

At page 140 "Freubund" should be Treubund.

At page 140, "as," the first word of the article on "Made Land," should be "It."

At page 129, 17th line, "is" should be "are."

HISTORY OF EAST ST. LOUIS.

CHAPTER I.

It has been said that God made the country, and man made the town.

This was however a hasty utterance. When we consider the natural causes that conspire to give importance to given situations on the globe; where commercial advantages are great; and agriculture, the great mother of all temporal interests, has rich and open fields; when mines are over-running with riches and ready to pour their cornucopias of wealth at the bidding of busy man, we see the power, and hear the fiat of God as much in the creation of the town, as in that of the country.

Indeed the town is the crown of the country; the spot most favored of all the country. Its markets are fed by the agricultural and mineral products; and its very life-blood and healthy vigor assured by the vigor of the outlying country; by the replacement of men of failing health and fortune in the rushing town, with men of strong physique, bounding blood, and intact coffers from the quiet country.

So, as it is a general truth that God made the country, that truth includes the other, that he also made the country's most important part the town.

These principles which were taught to Alexander the Great by the greater Aristotle led the former to the site of Alexandria, where he built a city whose hygienic, commercial and literary advantages were unsurpassed in the Ancient World. These principles led Romulus to the site of Rome. By these were founded other cities of the classic age. And so we may remark of Paris, London and Vienna.

In our own country, in modern times, the same reasons in 1729 piloted the fleet of Lord Baltimore to the head of Chesapeake Bay, where he laid out Baltimore; the ships of William Penn, in 1682, to the confluence of the Delaware and Schuylkill rivers for the founding of Philadelphia; induced Peter Minuits, of the Dutch West India Company, in 1625, to pay twenty-four dollars to the Indians for the Island of Manhattan, between Hudson River and Long Island Sound, and establish there the City of New York; led Bienville in 1718 to found New Orleans, near the Gulf of Mexico, on a Crescent of the Mississippi; caused two Franciscan Missionaries, in 1776 to found San Francisco, on that Bay, and open the Golden Gate of America to the riches of the Indies; drew the first white man, Father James Marquette, to the site of Chicago; founded and prospered many other cities like pearls in a crown. And which in 1764, led Pierre Laclede Liguest and Colonel Auguste Chouteau, to plant the good city of St. Louis, at the confluence of the Illinois, Missouri and Mississippi rivers, like a central diamond in the crown of Columbia.

The original site of East St. Louis was forest and prairie agricultural land.

Up to the year 1764, when the Future Great City of the World was planned and laid out on the high lands on the West side of the river and named St. Louis, for the reigning king of France, Louis XV, these lands possessed no more importance than any others which the great Father of Floods, in the wild rage of his annual overflow, tossed from side to side along his course.

As that city grew, the produce from Illinois naturally sought there a market. To reach St. Louis then, as now, it had to be landed first on the site of East St. Louis. From here it was crossed by ferry.

The Indian canoe styled "pirogue" was probably the first means of crossing from side to side, when skins, powder, lead and whisky were the chief articles of freight. One of the first established means of crossing worthy the name of Ferry was originated by Captain James Piggot, who, living on the Illinois side visited the Governor of St. Louis, Zenon Trudeau, and sought the privilege of a regular landing at the wharf of that city. He was very cordially received. His petition not only was granted but he was made a citizen of St. Louis, and clothed with further powers and privileges.

Among these he was permitted to put his west side ferry house on the Place d'Armes, near the east end of Market street, St. Louis. The landing now is at the foot of Spruce street.

The Illinois landing was nearly opposite where the Belleville round house is. The consideration for this privilege, it is said, was a certain amount of domestic fowls and wild game to be paid the Governor by Captain Piggot. The shore on this side was then heavily timbered. The solid land extended all the way back eastward from the river bank to Cahokia Creek and beyond.

Then before the time of the steamboat, or locomotive, if science had been as advanced as was the enterprise of Captain Piggot, the *Piggot* Bridge would have spanned the Mississippi. As it was it only spanned Cahokia Creek.

He worked, sometimes alone, for three years, from 1692 to 1695, and erected a bridge over Cahokia Creek on the Illinois road leading to St. Louis. The most of the trees he cut down with his own hands; his rifle, meanwhile, leaning near, ready for instant use, against an Indian foe. The bridge was a few feet north of the one now at the east end of Trendley street.

FIRST HOUSES IN EAST ST. LOUIS.

Having built the bridge as stated, he built two log cabins and a ferry boat for crossing teams, in the year 1797. This boat was a simple platform surrounded by railing and floated on Indian pirogues. These were probably made of the largest trees. Pirogues were made by hollowing trees of various sizes by cutting and burning out the inside till nothing but the sides of the canoes thus shaped were left. The ferry boat was poled or paddled with long sweeps handled by creoles. The houses above named were probably the first houses erected on the present site of East St. Louis.

THE FIRST FERRY

at this point was thus established also in the year 1797. We can in imagination look back and see the beginning of this important city, also the prosperity of St. Louis greatly increased by the patient, wise and heroic will of Captain Piggot. We see the young mart of St. Louis then but thirty years old; the river, the primitive ferryboat, the timbered Illinois shore, the blue smoke curling upward from the two log cabins, the first road, Cahokia Creek, the Piggot bridge: and beyond all these the great country of Illinois. These early scenes should be worthily painted and adorn the walls of every citizen who feels a thrill of gratitude to the brave man who may be considered the founder of the city of East St. Louis.

After the establishment of the Piggot ferry, successive attempts were made to establish towns which bore various names. Some of these were laid out immediately on the shore of the river, and as there were no paved levees to protect the banks, the river kept constantly encroaching upon the land and the towns were washed away.

The first was named Washington. It was situated on the Illinois shore, eastward and opposite to the St. Louis Grain Elevator. It consisted of a tavern owned by Mr. Samuel Wiggins and four or five dwelling houses. A gentleman now living near Belleville, once Clerk of St. Clair county, relates an incident that occurred to him during the time when Washington was gradually washing away. He states that he had been to St. Louis with produce from his father's farm, 15 miles eastward. He says, "One night I slept in Wiggins' tavern. It was pretty close to the shore. A big sycamore tree stood eight feet from the house on the bank. Along about midnight I heard water. It seemed from the sound to be under the house. I thought it must be the river. I partly dressed, as quickly as I could, and ran out shoreward. Wiggins and every body else that was in it ran out too expecting the house to go. The big sycamore was gone. It had taken with it a piece of ground from under the house, and the river was running under the outer wall. But it stood till morning, I got breakfast there, when they moved it back further from the river. Subsequently all of the town of Washington was washed away.

A gentleman of this city holds a deed to a lot in the town of Jacksonville, one of the quasi towns of the olden time, whose sands long since ran out—and down the river.

CHANGE IN THE MISSISSIPPI.

The Mississippi in 1797 ran by St. Louis with a strong current seventy-five feet deep. It was therefore comparatively narrow. So that persons wishing to cross from either side could easily make Captain Piggot, on the other, hear the old time shout of "O——ver!" An island existed at the above date near the Illinois shore below the site of this city.

1800—FORMATION OF BLOODY ISLAND.

Below Bissell's Point in 1800 near the Illinois shore a small sand bar lifted its head above the surface of the river. This was the first appearance of Bloody Island. A portion of the water passing between the Island and the Illinois shore being directed against the latter with some force began wearing it away. This wholesale destruction continued for twenty-five years aided by nature and unhindered by art.

Large trees growing near the water, were undermined. This expanded the channel shoreward until in 1825 half the Mississippi flowed on the east of Bloody Island. As in all such river changes where there is a wash there is a corresponding fill, so while this shore was thus fearfully washed the Island was filled.

In 1825 its breadth had become greatly increased. This was especially the case near the middle of the Island. When the channel so largely increased the upper end of the Island was washed off.

Yet large deposits of sand were filled in at the lower end increased by each flood, for which the river was more famous in those days than in these, until in 1850, the western side of the Island was on the site of the main shore of Illinois in 1797 and 1800.

OTHER ISLANDS.

The strong current of water thus deflected against the Illinois shore, fairly struck the other small island near it, below this site and carried it away.

What was afterward known as Arsenal Island was formed. Duncans Island formed directly in the former deep original channel of 1797 and 1800. Bars appeared at various places in the river. These impeded navigation. Boats grounded in front of the city. All growing from the one little sand bar of 1800 below Bissell's Point.

CONCLUSION OF HISTORY OF THE FERRY,

Captain Piggot enjoyed the fruits of his important enterprise but two years. He died in 1799, having continued his ferry till his death. The ferry subsequently was owned by Mr. Day, who in 1817, sold it to Samuel Wiggins. The means of crossing when Mr. Wiggins bought it were the same as originally, except the addition of a small horse-power boat.

In 1820, however, Mr. Wiggins built a larger ferry boat which he ran by horse-power. Horse-power boats were used till 1828. Their names were "Serpent," "Rhinocerous," and "Reindeer," succeeding each other.

FIRST STEAM FERRY BOAT.

Mr. Wiggins in 1828, started the first steam ferry boat. It was named the St. Clair. It landed at two places in St. Louis, at Market and Morgan streets. On this side near the foot of Trendley street. The "Ibex" was the next boat, put on the line. This occurred in 1832. In the same year when the "Ibex" was built Samuel Wiggins sold the ferry to eight persons: Bernard Pratt, Sen., John O'Fallon, Adam S. Mills, Samuel C. Christy, Charles Mullikin, William C. Wiggins and John H. Gay. Mr. Andrew Christy bought an interest from Colonel John O'Fallon in 1834.

The descendants of these owners are yet the principal possessors of the ferry property. From 1832 the ferry was conducted by the above company. In 1844 the boat "Icelander" was burned, date of building unknown. In 1852, a charter was obtained from the State of Illinois, and the property consisting of boats and real estate valued at one million of dollars, was represented by share stock issued for that purpose.

The next boat built was the "Ozark" in the same year when the charter was obtained. The following steam ferry boats were afterwards added to the line: "Vindicator," "Wagoner," "Grampus," "Illinois," "Wiggins," "St. Louis," "America," "New Era," "John Trendley," "Illinois No. 2," "Samuel C. Christy," "Charles Mullikin," "Cahokia," "Belleville," "Edward C. Wiggins," "East St. Louis," "Springfield," "Edwardsville," "Ram," "Louis V. Bogy," the tugs "H. C. Crevelin," "S. C. Clubb," "D. W. Hewitt." Several disasters occurred. The "St. Louis," blew up on the 21st February, 1851, and the "Vindicator," was wrecked in 1871. In 1875, the "S. C. Clubb," took fire and nearly burned. Since then it has been repaired.

The fact that through all these years the entire river front of East St. Louis has been owned by the same interest, has greatly conduced through unity of action in public improvements to the prosperity of both cities.

The Company has expended one million of dollars in revetting the shore next to St. Louis. This is a striking instance where private interest operates to benefit the public. This magnificent stone wharf, after the above expense, contains 6,000 front feet. The value of each front foot is $250. Hence the wharf alone is worth $1,500,000. The Company own the river front of East St. Louis for four miles. Their lands here are worth several million dollars. They are all suitable for manufacturing purposes.

The same natural causes which in the time of Captain Piggot, led commerce to this point, and caused the eastern lines of wagon travel to terminate here, in the era of steam travel operated with a much more potent sway to fix here the termini of the railroads. The time-honored ferry company moved by the same farseeing principles of sagacity that influenced its founder, granted to the railway companies suitable grounds for tracks, depots, warehouses, yards and machine shops. Thus they greatly aided eastern commerce to reach the Mississippi, where nature designed it should; establishing and opening wide the Eastern Gate of the city, to the royal highways of eastern trade.

This old Ferry Company is entitled to a large share of credit for the creation of the City of East St. Louis, which as we have seen, from two log cabins, erected in 1797, has grown, since the advent of steam travel to an established city of many thousands of inhabitants.

Manufacturing interests have as a rule, been liberally dealt with by this company. And now as this the chief interest of East St. Louis requires fostering care they feel that in adhering to their generous traditions relating to great public interests in the disposal on liberal terms of lands for manufacturing purposes, they are still benefiting the city which they have from the first endeavored to build up.

Colonel L. V. Bogy, at present United States Senator, associated with the commercial and mining interests of St. Louis and Missouri for a third of a century, was the President of the Ferry Company for eighteen years. Captain John Trendley has served the company continuously in various capacities since the 7th of May, 1825, which comprises a period of half a century. He is still engaged in active duty.

The present officers are as follows:

N. Mullikin, President.   F. M. Christy, Vice-President.
S. C. Clubb, Gen. Superintendent. Henry Sackman, Asst. Supt.
                    John Trendley, Agent.

First Grade Directors.—N. Mullikin, F. M. Christy, S. C. Clubb, J. H. Beach, Earnest Pengnet.

APRIL 2, 1860, SECOND ELECTION.

There were 119 votes cast for the officers elected. Daniel Sexton. was elected Police Magistrate without opposition.

For Town Marshal—E. D. Walker, received 58 votes; Geo. L. Johnston, received 58 votes.

For Town Trustees—W. J. Enfield, recived 39 votes; R. C. Bland, received 65 votes; B. B. George, received 91 votes; Timothy Canty, received 77 votes; S. W. Toomer, received 37 votes; Henry Jackeisch, received 4 votes; Richard Herman, received 45 votes; B. F. Sikking, received 9 votes; Frank Karle, received 1 vote.

There were four Trustees to be elected, those of the candidates who received the four highest numbers of votes cast were declared elected. It appears the Police Magistrate was also President of the Board.

Daniel Sexton was qualified April 28, 1860, for the above offices and took the place of Mr. Jackeisch, President *pro tem.* On the 14th of April, the latter was elected Treasurer. April 16, 1860, E. D. Walker, was qualified as Marshal.

THIRD, FOURTH AND FIFTH ELECTIONS,

August 30, 1860, Andrew Wettig, was elected Town Treasurer. He held this office until the organization of the City of East St. Louis. October 13, 1860, Richard Hennesey resigned his office as Trustee, which he probably held in place of some one resigned.

On the 20th of October, 1860, an election was held, at which Frederick Fye, was elected to fill the vacancy. He received 70 votes. His opponent H. Jackeisch, received 40 votes.

The Fifth Election was held on February 21, 1861.

NEW CHARTER, TOWN OF EAST ST. LOUIS.

In the spring of 1861, at a session of the Legislature, (see Private Laws of 1861). a new Charter was granted increasing the boundaries of the Town. from what they had been under the name of Illinois Town upon a vote of the people, 174 for, and 95 against the adoption of the New Charter, March 11, 1861.

SEVENTH ELECTION.

On April 1, 1861, an election was held for or against changing the name to East St. Louis, and for town officers. For changing the name 183, against 89.

OFFICERS ELECTED.

For Police Magistrate—highest number of votes to elect. J. B. Bowman, 185 votes; D. Sexton, 100 votes.

For Town Marshal—highest number of votes to elect. John Hennesey, 185 votes; Samuel Hender 95 votes; Thos. D. Burke, 7 votes.

For President Town Council—highest number of votes to elect. Samuel W. Toomer, 235 votes; R. C. Bland, 51 votes.

For Town Council—Four Councilmen to be elected, four highest numbers to decide. Candidates—John Monaghan, 185 votes; Florence Sullivan, 192 votes; Frank Karle, 139 votes; Samuel G. Walker, 124 votes; B. B. George, 111 votes; Jas. Hazen, 103 votes; G. B. Sikking, 65 votes; Wm. Quitzow, 45 votes; Wm. E. Rose, 30 votes; Henry Jackeisch, 10 votes; Peter Richter, 10 votes; —— Beatri, 1 vote; J. Herron, 1 vote; A. Lincoln, 1 vote. Some warm friend of Lincoln probably thought he was running for all the offices in the Union.

The new Council was organized on the 22d of April, 1861. Florence Sullivan and John Monaghan, drew the long terms, two years; Frank Karle and Samuel B. Walker, drew the one year term. Samuel M. Lount, was appointed Clerk. F. R. Hinze, Assessor. John Hennesey, Collector.

At a subsequent meeting on the 25th of April, Louis A. Delorme and Edmond D. Walker, were appointed assistant Assessors.

THE EIGHTH ELECTION.

For two members of the Town Council, on the 7th of April, 1862. Louis A. Delorme, 122 votes; John O'Connell, 103 votes; Samuel B. Walker, 15 votes. The two first were elected.

HENNESEY'S RESIGNATION.

July 7th, 1862, John Hennesey resigned the office of Marshall of the town.

NINTH ELECTION.

An lection was ordered for a new Marshall, and for one Trustee to be held the 1st Monday of August, 1862. Henry Jackeisch was elected Trustee to fill the vacancy caused by the retirement of John Monaghan. Timothy Canty was elected to fill the vacancy caused by Hennesey's resignation.

FIRST PLANK SIDEWALK.

Twenty-seventh of August, 1862, this was ordered; consisting of two planks six inches wide, laid paralled, six inches apart, on south-east side of Collinsville Avenue, between Broadway and Illinois Avenue.

TENTH ELECTION, 25 OF APRIL, 1863.

Ninety-eight votes polled, to elect the President of the town Council and one member of the same. H. Jackeisch polled 46 votes for President; Nicholas Spanagel, 32 votes; S. W. Toomer, 5 votes. Henry Oebike was elected member of Council without opposition. He received 97 votes.

resolved that the local representative, in the legislature of the State, convening in January, 1865, viz: Hon. A. W. Metcalf, of the Senate, and Hon. Messrs. Nathaniel Niles and John Thomas, of the House, be requested to oppose and endeavor to prevent the passage of any law authorizing the said company without the concurrence of this town, to extend their road any further into this town, than is now the case. Henry Jackeisch, Esq, was commissioned to visit Springfied and convey a copy of the resolutions to the said representatives, explaining to them the cause which prompted them, and solicit their attention to the desired amendments to the Town Charter, also to assure them of the deep felt gratitude, with which the citizens of the town would witness their kind action in all laws which may come before the legislature, affecting the present and future prospect of our promising town.

CITY CHARTER.

On the 17th of January, 1865, the Council appointed a committee of four, consisting of the president, and three others, Messrs. Oebike, Bowman, Kase and Millard, to draught a City Charter. The Council at this session, also ordered that the census of the town be forthwith taken. A committee to take the census was appointed as follows: Messrs. Kase, Feigenbutz, Canty and George.

The Charter Committee were instructed to report at the next meeting. They did so. After some debate of their report, their draught of the new city charter was approved.

A motion was lost that with the adoption of a new charter, the name of the town be changed to St. Clair. J. B. Bowman, on the 20th of February, gave a brief, but interesting history of the passage of the city charter through the legislature.

The Draft Fund.—On the 8th of February, 1865, the Council appropriated one thousand dollars ($1000) for draft purposes.

First Census of Bloody Island.—This was ordered by the Council on the 20th of February, 1865, to be taken. At the Council meeting on the 6th of March, the census report from that portion of the city (the Island) was shown to be about eight hundred.

In 1865 at the First Election for Mayor, Hon. J. B. Bowman was elected for two years. This was ordered for, and occurred on April the 3rd, 1865. The following named officers were elected: John B. Bowman, Mayor; Wm. G. Kase, City Judge; John O'Connell and Michael Murphy, Aldermen of the First Ward; Henry Schall and James Hazen, Aldermen of the Second Ward; John Trendley and John B. Lovingston, Aldermen of the Third Ward.

Installation of Mayor and Council.—This occurred in the Council Hall on the 10th of April, 1865.

CHAPTER IV.

The official oaths of the Mayor and Aldermen, as required by the City Charter were submitted, approved of, and ordered on file.

On motion the Clerk was instructed to prepare official commissions, properly executed and issued to said Mayor and Aldermen, pursuant to the provision of the City Charter. The new Council being found duly qualified and prepared to enter upon their duties, after some parting remarks of the president to the old Board of Town Trustees and of welcome to the new Board of City Aldermen, on motion, the Board of Trustees adjourned *sine die.*

ORGANIZATION OF THE CITY GOVERNMENT.

Mayor Bowman immediately called the City Council to order and delivered an inaugural address and recommended that a speedy organization be effected.

The first motions were by J. B. Lovingston, who moved that Mr. John O'Reilly be appointed Clerk *pro tem*; that Mortimer Millard, Esq., be appointed city attorney *pro tem*, and that a committee, to consist of the Mayor, Mr. Millard and three others be instructed to draft by-laws and ordinances.

These were carried; the last with an amendment by Mr. Hazen, that the three persons not named on said committee should consist of one appointed by the Mayor, from each Ward. The Mayor appointed from First Ward, Mr. Murphy; from Second Ward, Mr. Schall; from Third Ward, Mr. John Trendley. According to the City Charter the Aldermen then divided themselves by lot into two classes, for one and two year terms.

Complimentary resolutions were passed, expressing to the old Board the thanks of the public and of the new officers for their faithful discharge of public duties. The Mayor then appointed a committee to consult with the different railroad companies on the subject of police regulations, in connection with the city.

ADOPTION OF BY-LAWS.

The special committee on By-laws and Ordinances reported through Mr. Millard at the next meeting of the Council, on the 17th of April, 1865.

Three Ordinances were read. Two were passed by Sections One relating to City Clerk and one to City Treasurer. The one relating to City Marshall was laid over till next meeting. Mr. Bowman from the same committee reported a series of by-laws for the government of the City Council. On motion of Mr. Lovingston, they were unanimously adopted.

STATED MEETINGS OF THE COUNCIL.

At the above session, the committee on ordinances were instructed to report at the next meeting an ordinance, fixing the 1st Monday in each month, at 3 p. m., as the time for the stated meetings of the Council. Mr. John O'Reilly was appointed City Clerk.

APPOINTMENT OF STANDING COMMITTEES.

At the meeting of the Council on the 24th of April, 1865, the Chair appointed the following standing committees, viz: Of ways and means; on claims; on streets and alleys; on revision and unfinished business; on engrossed and enrolled bills; on harbors; on police; on market house and public buildings; on fire department, and on Council.

The Ordinance fixing stated meetings of Council, was passed, also one concerning the city seal, and one relating to licenses.

Francis Wittram was appointed City Treasurer, and Timothy Canty City Marshall.

The question of the constitutionality of the establishment of the city court, was ordered to be submitted to Messrs. Underwood, Koerner and Snyder, of Belleville. In case they decide it to be unconstitutional, the Mayor was authorized to request the County Court to order an election under the general law for Police Magistrates.

At this session, also on motion, it was agreed that the city subscribe $250 towards establishing a

PUBLIC SQUARE.

The fencing of this square was discussed.

On the 19th of June, 1865, John O'Rielly having resigned as City Clerk; M. Millard, Esq., was appointed to that office. Timothy Canty was appointed calaboose keeper. A complimentary resolution was passed and transmitted to Mr. O'Reilly, attesting efficiency and faithfulness as an officer of the Council.

GRADING AND PAVING STREETS AND ALLEYS.

This important matter received the attention of the Council in March, 1866. Resolutions were passed authorizing the same to be done.

DRAM SHOPS—MONEY FOR SCHOOLS.

One-half of the money collected for licences and fines from

the dram shops was ordered to be paid over to the School Trustees.

PREVENTION OF OVERFLOW.

Mayor Bowman at the meeting of the Council, August the 6th, 1866, presented a communication on overflows. It was referred to the City Engineer and himself as a special committee.

CHOLERA.

In August, 1866, this dread scourge having appeared, the Mayor and Council took precautionary measures against it. The Mayor was authorized to establish a hospital in the Third Ward, and procure disinfectants.

EAST ST. LOUIS GAZETTE.

This paper having succeeded the Sunday Herald, issued its first number on June 28, 1866. The city printing was awarded to its publishers, Macauly & Straub.

CITY CLERKS.

Mr. M. Millard, as City Clerk, gave place on December 10, 1866, to William O'Neil.

Petition to Legislature For and Against Amendments to the City Charter.—A petition to the legislature for certain amendments to the City Charter, having been made in 1867, by parties whose landmarks were changed by the new survey, ordered by the City Government, for the relocation of streets, the Council *en masse* presented a cross petition against the amendment asked for.

East St. Louis Gas Light and Coke Company.—This company having been established by the charter in 1865, the city, as by law enabled, took stock therein to the amout of five thousand dollars. A warrant for two hundred dollars of this sum was ordered February 18, 1867, to be drawn on the City Treasurer, in favor of the Treasurer of the Gas Light and Coke Company.

POLICE FORCE.

Mr. Lovingston having presented a resolution establishing a Police Force, the same was unanimously passed. The Mayor was authorized to employ such police force as he deemed necessary for the city's safety.

CHARGES AGAINST THE MAYOR.

Charges of misapplication of city street labor, by the Mayor in causing his own lots to be filled up, having appeared, he requested the Council to investigate said charges. This they did by the appointment of a committee. Having appointed the 12th of March, 1867, in the City Council Chamber, and published the same in the East St. Louis Gazette, as the time and place of investigation, the committee took the evidence under oath of the parties making the charges, and exhonorated the Mayor from all knowledge of or blame in the matter. Their report was unanimously adopted.

Second Municipal Election—J. B. Lovingston elected.—The Second election for Mayor was held on April 1st, 1867. It resulted in the election of Mr. J. B. Lovingston. By the first Charter the Mayor's term of office was two years. In 1867, however, amendments to the Charter reduced the time to one year. This, therefore, was the duration of Mayor Lovingston's term of office.

The Metropolitan Police movement was put on foot during the latter part of Mayor Bowman's and the first part of Mayor Lovingston's administration.

A BOARD OF HEALTH.

This Board was established June 3rd, 1867. Improvements in various parts of the city, and efforts toward amicable adjustment by arbitration of different interests marked the remainder of the administration of Mayor Lovingston.

Third Municipal Election—J. B. Bowman elected.—On April 6th, 1868, J. B. Bowman, Esq., was re-elected by a decided majority to the Mayoralty.

CONTRACT FOR MARKET HOUSE.

On the 18th of October, 1868, a contract between the Mayor and committee with Messrs. Niemes and Mathews, for the building of the market house, for $14,450 was ratified and confirmed by the Council. A competent architect was appointed November 16th, 1868, to superintend its erection.

FILLING OF STREETS.

Front and Third streets were in 1869, filled by contract of the city with Joseph Brown. Front street was filled from Dyke avenue to Christy avenue and Second street from Dyke avenue to the south part of Bogy street. The contract was to fill them to the highest grade of Dyke avenue.

Fourth Municipal Election—Vital Jarrot elected.—On April 6th, 1869, there was an election for Mayor and Aldermen. Vital Jarrot, the successful candidate, having received a majority of the votes cast, was declared elected. The Council now consisted of Messrs. Doyle, McCormack, Murphy, Ryan, Stack and Vaughan.

As all the city officers had been vacated at expiration of terms by the new charter, which went into effect March 26th, 1869, Mayor Jarrot, by the consent, and with the concurrence of the Council, appointed new officers to fill the vacancies not filled by election.

FUNDING THE CITY DEBT.

On June 25th, 1869, Ordinance No. 97 was passed in the Council, by which was funded the floating debt of the city of East St. Louis.

BOWMAN'S DYKE.

August 19th, 1869, the Council instructed the Engineer to advertise for bids for grading this important causeway. Bids were received, but all rejected. The Street Inspector, under the direction of the City Engineer, was ordered to level said dyke so as to make it passable.

Enlarged Improvements, Grade.—Mayor Jarrot communicated a paper to the Council, September 6th, 1869, recommending that a permanent grade be established, and an enlarged system of improvements be carried on.

American Bottom, Lime, Marble and Coal Company.—On the 28th of June, 1870, an election was held to vote for and against the city taking fifty thousand dollars of the stock of the above company. The votes stood, for subscription 236, and against subscription, 143 votes.

Another election on the same subject, held on August 4th, 1870, resulted in the following: 565 votes for subscription, and 76 against. The stock was accordingly taken.

RETRENCHMENT.

An Ordinance was adopted in the Council September 27th, 1870, fixing the salaries of the city officers, and reducing the expenses of the city government, and to abolish certain offices therein named. The resignation of Mayor Jarrot took place also on September 27th, 1870.

Mr. Murphy, Acting Mayor.—September 29th, 1870, upon the meeting of the Council, four ballots were taken to determine who should be acting Mayor. At the fourth ballot, Mr. Murphy having received a majority of all the votes cast, was declared to have been duly elected acting Mayor. A resolution instructing the Clerk to give notice for the election of a Mayor was lost. In reconsidering the vote accepting Col. Jarrot's resignation, and that appointing Mr. Murphy, acting Mayor, however, the Council instructed the Clerk to notify Col. Jarrot of their wish, that he withdraw his resignation. This was accordingly done and the Colonel, at the next meeting, again graced the chair.

Fifth Municipal Election—Dennis Ryan elected.—The candidates for the Mayoralty at the election held on the 4th of April, 1871, were Dennis Ryan, Anton Cramer, Geo. W. Brackett and Edwin R. Davis. All these gentlemen received a fair share of votes. But the number required to elect, were cast for Dennis Ryan. He was, therefore, declared Mayor, and placed at the head of city affairs.

The new government comprised, beside the Mayor's appointees, Messrs. J. B. Bowman, Davis, Doyle, Gilchrist, McMullan Scullen, Tefft and Vaughan. An inaugural address was delivered by the Mayor to the Council, upon its first meeting after the election.

Cahokia Creek.—The bridge approaches and embankments on this ancient stream, formerly named by the French Riviere a l'Abba, being threatened with removal by the washings of high water, Mr. Vaughan introduced in the Council on the 2nd of January, 1872, a resolution ordering the same to be secured. It was passed.

Public School Libary.—Hon. J. B. Bowman serving the city as Alderman, sat on foot in the Council the movement which culminated in the fine Libary in East St. Louis. He introduced a resolution on February 15th, 1872, providing room for a public school libary in the office of the City Attorney, Hon. L. H. Hite. This resolution was unanimously adopted. The School Board, however, failed to establish the Libary then for the schools.

Sickness of Mayor Ryan and appointment by Council of John McMullan, Acting Mayor.—When the Council met March 23rd, 1872, Mayor Ryan was absent by reason of sickness.

On motion of Mr. Bowman, Mr. Scullan was appointed Chairman pro tem.

The Council then proceeded to ballot for acting Mayor. Messrs. Bowman, Doyle and McMullan, were nominated. Mr. Bowman positively declined acting even if elected. Nevertheless, his name was continued in nomination. Two ballots were taken. The last narrowed the choice to him and McMullan. It stood two for Bowman, and three for McMullan. The latter was declared appointed.

this city may enjoy like privileges by filing like bond and paying the sum of three dollars.

Sec. 2. The privileges granted in consequence of filing the bond mentioned in the preceding section may be revoked, at pleasure, by the Library Board, or the security.

Sec. 3. Each person entitled to draw books from the Library must produce his or her card whenever a book is taken, returned or renewed. If a card is lost, the person to whom it was issued shall notify the Librarian thereof, and two weeks from such notification the Secretary shall issue a new card to such person.

Sec. 4. Books may be retained two weeks, and may be once renewed for the same period. Application for renewal must be made within the first fourteen days. Books of recent purchase, labeled "Seven day book," cannot be retained more than one week, and cannot be renewed.

Sec. 5. A fine of three cents a day shall be paid on each volume which is not returned according to the provisions of the preceding rule.

Sec. 6. If any person shall lose or injure a book, he or she shall make the same good to the librarian; and if the book lost or injured be one of a set, he or she shall pay to the Librarian—for the use of the Library and Reading Room—the full value of said set; and may thereupon receive the remaining volumes as his or her property.

Sec. 7. No person shall be permitted to receive a book from the Library until he or she shall have paid all sums due by him or her to the Library and Reading Room, and make good all damages and losses which he or she may have occasioned; and no person shall receive a book until the one previously loaned be first returned.

Sec. 8. Any person abusing the privileges of the Library or Reading Room, by unbecoming conduct, or by the violation of any of the by-laws or regulations, by defacement of a book, pamphlet, periodical or paper, by writing in or on it, or in any other way, shall be reported to the Directors as soon as may be, and by them excluded from the Reading Room or Library, for a time, or permanently, according to the nature and degree of the delinquency or default; but in case of any gross offense the Librarian, Acting Librarian, or his assistant or assistants or representatives shall act summarily in the matter, and cause the offender to be at once excluded from the building, or take such action as the case may require, reporting the same to the Directors as soon as possible, for their final decision.

ST. LOUIS NATIONAL STOCK YARDS.

At the Council meeting on July 17, 1872, covenants of mutual advantage were given and received by the city and the above company.

The company agreed to construct a magnificent hotel of stone and brick, to cost not less than one hundred thousand dollars, and to construct Stock Yards to exceed in importance, magnitude and completeness any like institution of the kind in this country; the hotel to contain broker's offices, commission offices, telegraph office, post office, and all modern conveniences for living and for transacting business.

And the city covenanted to abstain from infringing, by constructing streets, avenues or any city improvements, or otherwise, upon the survey of land No. 627, owned by said company, and devoted by them to the purposes of a truly great National Stock Yard.

In testimony of the above covenants, both parties thereto, the city of East St. Louis through Acting Mayor John B. Bowman and Wm. O'Neil, City Clerk, under an order from the City Council to that effect, given on the seventeenth day of July, 1872, attested by the City Seal, and the St. Louis National Stock Yards aforesaid, acting through Archibald M. Allerton, their Manager and Attorney in fact, on the day aforesaid, interchangeably executed duplicate originals thereof.

FIRST CITY AUDITOR.

Mr. James W. Kirk was elected to the office of Auditor on the 17th of July, 1872.

FIRE DEPARTMENT.

A Babcock Hook and Ladder Truck, costing $975, was contracted for by Mayor Bowman, and ratified by the Council, January 22, 1873; said Extinguisher to have 500 feet of hose and two tongues—one for men and one for horses.

CITY CLERKS.

John O'Reilly was appointed, April 10, 1865, Town Clerk, and held the office till 3d July, 1865.

Mortimer Millard was appointed Clerk on 3d July, 1865. Removed on 3d December, 1866.

Wm. O'Neil was appointed 3d December, 1866, and holds it at the present writing.

CITY MARSHALS.

Timothy Canty was appointed 24th of April, 1865; held office till 1st April, 1871, when he was removed.

John Hogan was appointed on the 1st of April, 1871, to fill the vacancy.

Michael Walsh was elected April 29, 1871, and has held the office to the present time.

CITY TREASURERS.

Francis Wittram was appointed City Treasurer 14th April 1865. Having removed to St. Louis, his office was declared vacant July 8, 1869.

On that day Benedict Franz was declared Treasurer, and he still holds the office.

EAST ST. LOUIS FIRE CO. NO. 1.

A resolution (No. 302) ordering the purchase of a lot and building of a house for this company was adopted January 22, 1873.

BUYING EARTH.

This became necessary in May, 1873, and was authorized by resolution.

THE ST. LOUIS BRIDGE COMPANY

Was bound to East St. Louis on July 1, 1873, in the sum of sixty thousand dollars, to reimburse parties in East St. Louis whose land should be damaged by the building of the eastern approach to the Eads bridge, by the payment to the authorities of East St. Louis, for the use of the owners of such damaged property, a sum equal to its value.

In consideration of this bond the Council of East St. Louis granted the right of way over Crook and other streets. Therefore the eastern approach of the Eads bridge was accordingly located where it now is.

COLLECTOR AND ASSESSOR.

These offices were filled at this same session of the Council, July 1, 1873, by the appointment of John M. Sullivan to the first named, and of Patrick M. Sullivan for City Assessor.

PERMANENT GRADE AND SEWERAGE.

Mayor Bowman presented to the Council at its session, on July 1, 1873, a lengthy and forcible paper containing recommendations for the establishment of a public park—a public breathing place, as he happily termed it—and for the making of several other public improvements. This paper shows great depth of reflection and wise foresight into the future needs of the city. He also recommended means whereby these improvements could be made. The most important of these measures was that of fixing a permanent grade for streets, assuring forever the health of the city, by placing the grade above the highest water marks, and establishing a grand and economical system of sewerage, well fitted to rapidly remove all filth and causes of disease from the city. He presented an elaborate scientific report upon the Grade and Sewerage of East St. Louis, with estimates of their cost by Messrs. Flad and Whitman.

The figures and arguments adduced by the Mayor and by the scientific minds of the Messrs. Flad and Whitman upon this all-important subject, on which so many others impinge, afford conclusive proof that regarding the interests of the future, as well as of the present, the joint system of Grade and Sewerage thus recommended were correct. The report showed that to inaugurate this grand public work would involve grading Christy avenue and Missouri avenue from the river to the St. Clair county turnpike. Grading Broadway from the creek to Collinsville plank road. Grading Collinsville plank road from Broadway to city line. Grading St. Clair avenue from Collinsville plank road northwest to city limits.   Building a bridge over the railroads on Missouri avenue.   Carrying St. Clair avenue under the railroads between the Collinsville plank road and the Stock Yards.   Construction of the main sewer commencing at the river on Trendley street, through by Vaughan's dyke to Main street, to Broadway, to Collinsville plank road, and through this road to St. Clair avenue.   The sewer to be constructed of brick, and furnished with all necessary man-holes, street basins, and house lateral connections.   The length of the sewerage would be about 10,000 lineal feet.   The scientific report estimates the total cost of this great work, lying at the foundation of the prosperity of the city, as follows :

We estimate the total amount of filling required to grade the streets mentioned as being :

Three hundred thousand cubic yards, at 35 cts. per yard.................$105,000
Ten thousand lineal feet of brick, sewer complete, at $9 00 (average)
    per foot   90,000
Cut at St. Clair avenue   10,000
Bridge on Missouri avenue (iron)..   24,000
                                                                               $229,000

   If the bridge be of wood it will be $12,000 less.
Total cost of improvement $217,000
   Thus bringing the cost to less than a quarter of a million dollars.

   Mr. Henry Flad, of the above firm of engineers, furnished the calculations for the construction of the Eads bridge across the Mississippi river.   This was a gigantic triumph of scientific knowledge on the part of Henry Flad, joined to the engineering skill of James B. Eads, which in reality, at this point on the great river, binds the East to the West with "hooks of steel," and literally rivets their bands of union.

   The reports of the Mayor and Engineers were adopted by the Council.

   Subsequently the Council passed a resolution announcing that they were ready to proceed with the work, by advertising for bids, etc.   At this point, however, an injunction was obtained from the Circuit Court restraining the city from executing these plans for the present.   So here the history of this vast work rests. It is proper to state that Mayor Bowman for six years as Mayor and Councilman has labored earnestly to place the city upon the above firm foundation.   East St. Louis, however, has this year not been troubled, while towns on the Ohio and elsewhere have been submerged by high water.

   In the territory of Holland the dykes there surround the parts exposed to the sea.   Inside of these are great surface sewers into which the country is drained.   At proper points on these outer drains are immense reservoirs, where the great drains convey their surplus water in the spring.   These are emptied over the walled dykes into the sea, the means employed being pumps which are run by the wind.   Steam might be used.   This method of surface draining having proved economical and effective in the old world, might, with profit, be applied in the new, where localties are in danger of inundation.

CHAPTER VII.

The sun is the source of heat and light. The heat of our coal was at first derived from the sun when the vegetation was growing which formed the coal. It has been latent heat for ages, and now, when freed, gives light and heat—the sun's light and heat—to our parlors.—[Prof. Mitchell.

THE FIRST COAL IN THE UNION WAS FOUND IN ILLINOIS—HEAVIEST BED OF COAL CLOSE TO EAST ST. LOUIS.

The State of Illinois is all—except the extreme north, the west edge, and the southwest part—underlaid with coal. Nowhere is the supply greater nor more convenient than in the Belleville district. The first discovery of coal in the United States was made at Ottawa, Illinois, by Hennepin, in the latter part of the 17th century. St. Louis obtains its principal supply of bituminous coal from what is known in coal regions as the Belleville district, in St. Clair county, Illinois. It is brought to East St. Louis by the St. Louis and Illinois, commonly known as the Pittsburg Railroad. This Railroad is only 12 miles long, from East St. Louis to Belleville, but it intersects the western boundary of the coal measures at Centerville, six miles out from East St. Louis, and runs six miles through the coal field. St. Clair county contains 450 square miles of coal, or three-fourths of the county, embracing all the central and eastern portions, with a thickness of about 300 feet of the lower and most productive of the coal measures, embracing five coal seams, only two of which, however, appear to be of economical value at this time.

In 1871 there were transported by this railroad, from Belleville and Centerville to East Louis 361,630 tons. The last United States census reports the coal production of St. Clair County at 798,810 tons. This is, therefore, by far the most productive, and, in that respect, the most important coal region in Illinois. The thickest coal seam out-crops in the river bluff and along the western borders of the coal measures in the southwest portion of the county. The dip is very moderate, not more than five or six feet to the mile, and is in an easterly direction, or a little north of east, and in consequence the coal lies deepest below the surface in the eastern portion of the county, and crops out to the surface near East St. Louis. The Belleville coal seam, No. 6, is the principal one worked, and it was probably the first ever worked in the State. Its natural out crop along the bluffs, in such close proximity to St. Louis, called attention to its value at an early day. Its general thickness in this county ranges from five to seven feet, and it has a solid limestone roof, so that it can be worked with safety and in the most economical manner.

This coal is generally quite regularly stratified, and the two upper layers, which vary in their aggregate thickness from 16 to 24 inches, are much the purest in quality. It is usually separated from the lower coal, and sold at about three cents per bushel higher, as a blacksmith coal; thus: heating coal, six cents; blacksmith coal, nine cents per bushel.

The lower coal contains more sulphuret of iron, but the quality varies somewhat in various mines, and no general description would be applicable to every locality. Sometimes there is a foot or more of bituminous shale above, and a thin bed of clay shale below, but sometimes both are absent, and it is by no means uncommon, either in this or the adjoining counties, to find coal directly enclosed between two beds of limestone origin, containing fossil shells in abundance, which is a very unusual occurrence elsewhere. The main coal seam, No. 6, has been opened at many points about Belleville, and the river bluffs back of the out crop. It is reached by twenty-five shafts, sunk to the depth of from 50 to 150 feet. In Alma shaft the coal was found at a depth of 170 feet below the surface, and the seam is seven feet thick. It is the same thickness at Mascoutah, at 132 feet deep, and 6½ feet thick at Urbana or Freeburg, and about the same depth below the surface.

In the southern part of the county the Belleville coal is opened at many places along its out crop, and retains its full thickness of about seven feet. Everywhere it seems to be from six to seven feet thick.

It will be seen that the coal measures underlie all the highlands in the county of St. Clair, except a narrow belt from three to five miles wide across the southwest border, and the land is also among the most productive agricultural lands in Southern Illinois. The analysis of the Belleville coal shows the following results:

	Specific gravity	Loss in coking.	W't of coke.	Moist use.	Vol'e. matter	Carbon in coke	Ash.	Carbon coal.
Caseyv'e mines..	1.304	39.8	60.2	6.0	33 8	55.2	5.0	55.3
Pfeifer's mines...	1.293	44.3	55.7	8.5	35.8	51.2	4.5	57.5
Bellevillemines..	1.293	45.0	55.0	5.5	39.5	49.6	5.4	54.6
Dill & Knapp's..	1.340	42.51	57.49	4 43	38.8	44.48	13.9	54.28
Churchill mine..	1.315	45.40	54 60	6.00	39 40	45.70	8.90	52.63
Belcher mines....	1.296	44.66	56.34	8.10	35.56	47.74	8.60	54.50

Prof. Worthen says that from the analysis, the Belleville coal will compare favorably with the average of bituminous coals from other localities either of this or adjoining States.

CHEAP COAL IN EAST ST. LOUIS.

Coal is cheaper in East St. Louis by the cost of transportation across the Mississippi. It is brought in wagons and cars on a down grade, six or eight miles from the out crop in the bluffs to East St. Louis. The process at the mines is as follows:

After the coal is mined the cars are drawn horizontally up grade into the mine by a mule. The mule is detached; the cars filled, started out of the mine by hand, and carried down grade by their own weight to a trestle at the entrance. Here they are dumped. Coal cars receive the falling coal. These are standing ready to receive it. When full the coal train starts and moves a considerable distance down grade, unaided. Engines are then attached, which complete the transportation to East St. Louis.

ORIGIN OF COAL AND METHOD OF ITS FORMATION.

The opinion now held by Geologists is that the vegetation from which coal of the carboniferous age originated was similar to that of the peat bogs now found in nearly all parts of the world. The examination of coal does not afford evidence of its having been produced from the flattened trunks or more solid parts of trees, but it abounds in fragments of the leaves and occasionally extremities of branches and fronds, or leaves of the kind which retain the stalk when they fall off. In anthracite coal, the process of liquifaction and carbonization, or perhaps it should be called crystalization, has obliterated all traces of the original vegetable matter; but, as we go farther westward, we find some kinds of bituminous coal which appear to be composed of minute leaves and fibres matted together. This vegetable matter was of fresh water species. A large part of the vegetation of the coal era or age of the world is composed of ferns of incredible size, sometimes measuring 60 feet in height. Therefore, as to the composition of the coal slates (next the coal) you must disbelieve the evidence of your own eyes, to deny the presence of vegetable matter, where they had their origin, for you see in them the daguerreotyped likeness of plants, leaves, roots, trunks and branches. But as to the coal itself, the evidence to the naked eye, of its vegetable nature, is not apparent, as it does not show impressions of plants like the slate rocks. The slate found in coal is supposed to have been mud.

"Coal, it may be easily demonstrated," says Prof. Newberry, "has been derived from the decomposition of vegetable tissue, which represents one of the different steps in the formation of coal. Peat is bituminous vegetation, generally mosses and other herbaceous plants, which, under favorable circumstances, accumulate in marshes called peat bogs. Lignite mineral coal, retaining the texture of the wood from which it was formed, and burning with an empyreumatic odor, is the production of a similar change effected in woody tissue, and, because it retains to a greater or less degree the form and structure of wood, has received the name it bears.

Peat is the product of the present period, and lignite is found

CHAPTER XV.

ORIGIN AND PRESENT STATUS OF THE NATIONAL LIVE STOCK INTEREST.

On the extreme northeast side of the city of East St. Louis are the National Stock Yards, a particular description of which is elsewhere given. They comprise 656 acres, enclosing 100 acres, and have 60 acres shedded. The trade in live stock now culminating there was originally transacted at a point near by, in East St. Louis, called Papstown, or New Brighton. It was called the former from the founder, a Mr. Condit, who built and kept the first house as a tavern. People called him "Pap," and the place Papstown. He was an Englishman. His descendants are now among the most prominent citizens of Centralia, this State, Hon. E. S. Condit, "pap's" son, having been a long time Mayor of that place, and now President of the First National Bank. Brighton is a noted cattle mart in England. Hence the name New Brighton was very appropriately applied to this great western cattle market. Mr. Wettig, a former Postmaster of East St. Louis, also kept tavern at Papstown. He kept the first Bank in East St. Louis in an old trunk. Sometimes he had $10,000 in it. A stock man would come in and say, "Wettig, here, take this, and keep it for me; I have no place to put it." Mr. Wettig would say, "well, I'll keep it for you." He also relates, "I gave no receipt, and took no note; yet I never lost a cent." "I tell you that Papstown was a money-making place." "Condit made lots of money." "He used to treat it like rags."

Once he missed six hundred dollars. They hunted for it high and low. Finally Condit remembered that he had put it in a straw bed. This bed had been emptied in the barn yard some time before. They looked there among the dirt and straw, and found it. "Pap" Condit's first house here he built of grub plank from the rafts. Here he sold spruce beer, which he made himself. Now the great Brewery of the Messrs. Heim Brothers is built on the opposite side of the street from this site, which is on the corner of Tenth street, Illinois avenue and St. Clair turnpike.

Jacob Strawn, the celebrated Illinois stock drover, used to stop with his droves for St. Louis with Condit. The life of Strawn was of thrilling interest and full of incidents. Once the buyers of St. Louis refused to give him his price. He compelled them to do so by making a corner on beef by stationing his men around St. Louis and buying all the incoming supplies. Prices advanced to his figure, and he sold out to suit himself. He was immensely wealthy. He had a farm, yet owned by his widow, in Morgan county, comprising thousands of acres, having many tenants upon it, whom he employed to raise corn and feed his cattle. Mrs. Strawn lives near Jacksonville, and is known as the dispenser of charities far and near.

The old time traditions of the St. Louis cattle trade, and the prestige of Strawn and other active dealers have culminated in these truly grand National Stock Yards. Indeed, this immense interest is only second to the great steam interests of the nation.

THE NATIONAL STOCK YARD COMPANY,

Originally consisted of President A. M. Allerton, of the firms of Allerton, Dutcher & Moore, and National Drove Yard, New York; Treasurer and Assistant Secretary, R. M. Moore, of New York; Azariah Boody, President Toledo, Wabash and Western Railway, New York; Augustus Schell. the attorney of Commodore Vanderbilt, and Vice President of the Lake Shore and Michigan Southern Railroad, New York; J. B. Dutcher, New York Central and Hudson River Railroad, New York; T. C. Eastman and A. M. White, capitalists, New York; H. H. Huston, of Pennsylvania Railroad, Philadelphia; I. N. McCullough, President of the Pennsylvania Company, Pittsburgh; Oscar F. Townsend, Cleveland, Columbus and Cincinnati, and Indianapolis Railroad, Cleveland; John B. Bowman, East St. Louis; and Andrew Pierce, of the Atlantic and Pacific Railroad, New York.

There have since been added the following additional stockholders: Hon. W. H. Vanderbilt, heir of the Commodore; Vanderbilt's son-in-law, Horace F. Clark, now deceased; Hon. J. B. Dutcher, Vanderbilt's confidential agent; Hon. Thomas Scott, President of the Erie and other Roads, and Hon. J. H. Banker.

The present officers are: Hon. Isaac H. Knox, Banker, of New York, and resident in St. Louis, President: Col. R. M. Moore, Secretary and Assistant Treasurer; Superintendent, Joseph Mulhall; Assistant Superintendent, J. Green Cash; Hon. J. B. Bowman, Attorney.

The land originally was four hundred acres adjoining the northeast side of the city. It was bought of Messrs. Bowman and Griswold. Two hundred and fifty-six acres have since been added. The covenants with the city, noticed elsewhere, were fulfilled, and the National Stock Yards formally opened to the world in October, 1873.

The distinguished men at the head of the Company cannot fail to command the respect of all, nor to absolutely control at this point the vast cattle trade of the west. The result of this cannot but be beneficial to the two classes of the public who supply and consume the beef and pork. Here sellers and buyers are brought face to face, and the supply and demand in the leading markets of the East and of the world being constantly known here by means of the telegraph, values are nicely graded to the actual needs of consumers.

The Company have constructed at their own expense a large sewer to the Mississippi river, whence is conducted under ground all ordure from the yards.

The following figures show the amount of business done here in one year, 1874:

Cattle received, 233,829 head.

Hogs   "   492,471   "

Sheep   "   40,608   "

Horses and Mules received, 2,534 head.

This statement was kindly furnished the writer by Colonel Moore.—[ED.

Connected with the National Stock Yards is Messrs. Richardson's Packing House. This was built in 1873–4. Its cost was $125,000. Its capacity is to slaughter 6,000 head of hogs per day.

Beside the hogs killed and packed in 1874, they killed, packed and shipped to New York 5,000 head of cattle. They made 4,000 tierces of lard of 300 lbs. each. They can kill and pack 200 head of cattle per day. Messrs. Richardson & Co. desire to extend to both St. Louis and East St. Louis facilities to do all their butchering at their packing house, instead of, as now, compelling every butcher to run his own shop, and his horned cattle through the streets to the endangering of the lives and limbs of passers.

This is a humane proposition, as numbers of persons have been gored to death by reason of the existence of irresponsible driving of single cattle, frightened, wild and maddened, by separating from their fellows. The cost to the butcher would be no more if killing at the National Stock Yards, and perhaps would be less, as the facilities are better. Two men can keep clean this great house for their accommodation at much less cost than the 500 butchers of the city can keep their 500 private slaughter houses, thus costing each butcher less than now.

This question was settled at Paris by the first Napoleon, in favor of a general slaughter house. He established the Parisian Abattoir, in the Forest of Borgne, near Paris, where he caused the butchers to take all their stock and prepare their meat for market. Such an abattoir the National Stock Yard Company, through Messrs. Richardson, desire to establish for the cities of St. Louis and East St. Louis. It is a great move looking toward the health, safety, profit and convenience of all.

North of the great brick Packing House stands a large white house with no windows, to which we now repair. This contains the

WATERWORKS OF THE NATIONAL STOCK YARDS.

They were built in 1873, by William Bement, engineer, who has had them since in charge. The building is seventy feet high.

and return. Of these river trips, the moonlight excursion, with a band of music, and your best friends for company, is a favorite at this season of the year.

THE SURROUNDINGS OF EAST ST. LOUIS

Are of the deepest interest. These places as objects for drives or journeys are almost numberless. Beside St. Louis, full of splendor, we will mention a few: Commencing with Kaskaskia on the south, some sixty miles distant; we remember its history as older than Philadelphia. Its founding unknown. in 1675, when visited by Marquette, it had been for generations the chief village of the Kaskaskia Indians. It remained for years the chief town of the west. It was headquarters successively of the French, the English, and the Americans. There is old Fort Gage, built upon scientific principles. There Gen. LaFayette visited his friend, Gen. Edgar, on the 29th of April, 1825. The glad people spread their carpets for him to walk on from the Kaskaskia landing to the door of Gen. Edgar. The remains of the old house are not yet gone. This was the first capital of Illinois.

Nearer we remember Cahokia, an old French village. Here Pontiac, the great Indian Chief, was killed, and the High Court of Sessions of Northern Illinois was held. A few miles below East St. Louis, and now out in the river, was the site of Fort Chartres. This was a beautiful specimen of military skill. The walls were white, turreted, bastioned, and pierced with port holes. Its shape toward the river was circular, like the outer edge of a ladies' fan. In it resided with his soldiers, Gen. St. Ange de Bellerive, last French Governor of Illinois, and first Governor of Missouri.

Not far from the city is Monksmound, an elevated piece of land, where there was a monastery, wherein lived some forty monks at the beginning of this century. They allowed no woman to enter their precincts. Col. Jarrot relates that when a boy, his father, Nicholas Jarrot, one of the wealthiest merchants of the west in early times, visited them on business. He took his son and wife along for the enjoyment of the ride. The monks refused her admittance, therefore she waited in the buggy till the business was concluded.

A few miles from East St. Louis is the Cantine, a French hamlet, around which cluster a world of interesting recollections.

HIGH-GRADE BUILDING—ABOVE THE FLOOD OF 1844.

An event which marks a new era in the growth and prosperity of this city, took place at 10 o'clock, on September 10th, 1875. This was the laying of the corner stone, with appropriate ceremonies, of the new three-story brick erected for a bank and office building, by Mr. Louis Weiss, on the corner of Fourth street and Broadway. It was viewed as a gala occasion by a majority of the citizens. Quite a number of St. Louisians participated.

Hon. John Niemes, the contractor and builder, was master of ceremonies. There were present, among others, Hon. S. S. Hake, Mayor; Ex-Mayor John B. Bowman, and other dignitaries, beside a number of gentlemen representing the press of both cities, and Mr. Martin Zike's Silver Cornet Band.

As is the custom upon the erection of important structures, in this corner stone were deposited articles of interest to future generations; when the envious tooth of time shall have destroyed that which the hands of men have builded. These articles were a package deposited in a glass jar by His Honor Mayor Hake, containing copies of all the important documents and records pertaining to the city; among them were a copy of the city charter, of the high grade ordinance, a list of the city officers list of the standing committees of the city council, a copy each of the first and last report of the Library and Reading Room. This jar was hermatically sealed by Hon. John Niemes, who deposited some coin. Two watches were deposited by Messrs. Guinin and Wuille, a silver badge by Dr. Winton, and a cigar by Mr. Epstein.

The stone was laid by His Honor Mayor Hake and Hon. John Niemes. The National Banner was flung to the breeze, while the band gave forth music in keeping with the time.

When the crowd had been regaled with music, His Honor the Mayor made an address, which was to the point and well received. Ex-Mayor Hon. John B. Bowman was then introduced by the Mayor, and followed in a forcible speech, of which the annexed is nearly a complete report, taken at the time by Mr. H. D. O'Brien, of the "Press:"

EX—MAYOR BOWMAN'S ADDRESS.

"Fellow Citizens:—But for this occasion I would not be present, as I am sick, and have just arisen from my bed in order to be here.

"We are present to celebrate the laying of the corner stone of the first building which is to be built on the grade of 1844. Mayor Hake has not said all. Under this corner stone has been buried the East St. Louis of the past, and on it will be built the city of the future. Under the old system the resources of East St. Louis could not be properly developed. Long before Tom Benton pointed to the west and said, "Westward the star of empire takes its way," the people came to this point and located here in preference to St. Louis. At that time the merchants of that city purchased at Cahokia their wares and merchandise, but on account of the low foundation on which the town rested, and from the calamities resulting from high water, its progress was prevented. I say, and defy the future to contradict my statement, that here we are located on the banks of the Mississippi river, where the soil is fertile and abounds in coal, without which civilization would be a dead body. Coal molds the iron, without which no civilization can exist. East St. Louis, with this advantage, is to be the Birmingham of America. Without machinery, we would go without the clothes upon our backs. When manufactories are numerous labor will flourish and will be plenty when our buildings are built upon the foundation of high grade, which is the only thing will save East St. Louis and the American Bottom. Now there is a bright future before us of which we cannot reasonably form a proper conception. This building inaugurates a new era in the history of East St. Louis. We will no longer have to beg for money on account of insecurity, but can secure it at low rates of interest. We can have no credit with low grade, and we must have credit, as business cannot flourish without it. There are millions of dollars locked in the vaults of the country to-day ready to loan on proper security, which we can get if the proper course is pursued. We cannot have credit abroad unless we carry out the high grade project—this will bring it; nothing else will.

"It does me double pleasure to be with you fellow citizens upon this occasion, for the reason that beneath this stone is deposited the poll lists which show conclusively that the people are no longer to be humbugged by those who have no interest in the welfare of the city. Injunction or no injunction, East St. Louis must be built up. The returns of the polls are deposited beneath this corner stone. Every stone which shall be laid in the walls of this building will be a monument to the enterprise of those who advocated and defended the high grade movement."

"Tracts were distributed to the people and they were advised by one of the papers of this city to throw high graders out of the windows. But in spite of their machinations we have triumphed. The people of East St. Louis have decided to march forward, and you are here to celebrate the laying of the corner stone of the first building to be erected on the high grade basis. It was unpopular to speak of this at one time, and it is a gratification to come here in the broad light of day and speak my sentiments."

"Fellow citizens. I say in conclusion, this is the corner stone of the future East St. Louis, just as dismal as has been the past just so bright will be its future. No longer will our laboring men go abroad to look for work, but for fifty years to come they will find plenty to do here in this city. I cannot close my remarks without referring to the gentleman who has undertaken this work, Mr. Louis Weiss. He was opposed to high grade, but eventually became convinced that the old ideas which he had so long entertained were wrong, and he repudiated them. When all the other buildings which are to be built in the future shall have been erected then he will be more honored and complimented than now. He is the pioneer, the first man to risk his money to back his faith in this new enterprise. I propose three cheers for Mr. Louis Weiss."

The Ex-Mayor's speech was loudly applauded during its delivery, and he received three cheers and a tiger at its close.

I

INDEX TO BUSINESS.

Daily Journal

, MARCH 12, 1931

MEMBER AUDIT
BUREAU OF CIRCULATIONS

TWELVE PA

Dies from Stroke

John Hubert

JOHN HUBERT;

Capt. R. A. Tyson, Author of First History of City, and War Vet, Dies in West

Word has been received here of the death of Captain Robert A. Tyson, prominent and widely known Civil war veteran of Napa, Cal., a former resident of East St. Louis and author of the first history of this city, who passed away on February 25 last, following a major operation at the Victory hospital of Napa.

Captain Tyson would have reached his 90th birthday on April 19. His family moved from East St. Louis to California 56 years ago.

Captain Tyson was an officer in the 47th Indiana Volunteers in the war between the states. Chaplain of the Napa Post of the Grand Army of the Republic, Captain Tyson remained active in veterans' affairs until very recently when he was overtaken by ill health. The operation which he underwent proved a severe shock and although he battled valiantly his strength gradually ebbed.

The civil war veteran had resided in Napa for five years, removing there from Calistoga, where he had been a resident for seven years. Prior to establishing his home in Calistoga, he had been in business in Spokane, Wash. He was a native of Pennsylvania.

Surviving are his widow, Mrs. Samatha Tyson; two daughters, Mrs. Amy Mourer of North Dakota and Mrs. Elizabeth Dayton of Spokane; five sons, Robert E. Tyson of Napa; Dr. William E. E. Tyson, Detroit, Mich.; Fred Tyson, Grass Valley; Charles Tyson, Tekoa, Wash., and Homer Tyson, Honolulu.

Interment was made in the Veterans' Home cemetery at Yountville, Calif.

SAINT LOUIS:

THE

FUTURE GREAT CITY

OF

THE WORLD,

WITH

BIOGRAPHICAL SKETCHES OF THE REPRESENTATIVE MEN AND WOMEN OF ST. LOUIS AND MISSOURI.

BY L. U. REAVIS.

"Had ST. LOUIS been destined to remain a village, her history might
have been dispatched in a few lines; but future generations
will inquire of us all that concerns the origin of
the 'River Queen,' the destined Queen
of the Western Empire."—*Nicollet.*

CENTENNIAL EDITION.

ST. LOUIS:
C. R. BARNS, 215 PINE STREET.
1876.

East Saint Louis.

ITS PAST HISTORY—GROWTH—PRESENT STATUS AND FUTURE PROSPECTS.

ON the eastern bank of the Mississippi river, directly opposite the city whose future greatness and prosperity we have heretofore predicted, and which prediction is fast becoming a reality, stands the young and thriving city of "East St. Louis."

Up through the floods and soft alluvial soil she has risen—little by little—each year overcoming barriers and difficulties that were considered almost insurmountable; and now having gained the mastery, stands as a powerful adjunct and ally of the great city on the western bank of the river. So intimately associated are the two cities, and so necessary to each other's existence and prosperity, that we cannot do full justice to the one without mentioning the other. Indeed, we cannot truly prognosticate the growth and future greatness of the older and larger of the two, without also calling attention to the younger and less pretentious city, through which, as an *entrepot*, much of its trade and commerce must flow.

We have known the place hitherto, as simply a terminus for the railroads.

The few restaurants, saloons and boarding-houses at the depots were deemed the natural appendages of the railroads, but for many years no one thought of warehouses, elevators, iron mills or manufacturing establishments or a Continental stockyard. If a thought was given to the place where the railroads terminated, beyond the interest mentioned, it was of an historical character; for, as "Bloody Island," it was known far and wide, and the tragic scenes enacted on its soil were the themes of frequent discourse, by old residents of St. Louis and strangers in transit. The character of this neighboring "province" is not yet clearly understood by the busy inhabitants of St. Louis, nor have they noted the many improvements going on constantly in the new city.

Be it known then to all, that the old lines are wiped out;—the familiar haunts for fishermen and sportsmen are no longer to be found; the localities known as "Bloody Island," "Illinoistown," "Papstown," and by whatever other names they may have been known, are the centers of trade and manufactures, now crossed and recrossed by wide and handsome streets bearing christian names. The old names have passed into history. And the history of East St. Louis must be valued more for the narration of early incidents and facts connected with its foundation and first years of existence, than to subsequent and later events in its growth. The reader of to-day will peruse with more than usual interest the written facts and narration, about the topographical character of the locality where East St. Louis now stands, and the early history of those who pitched their tents on the site, long before the village or city was dreamed of.

Since the first white man traversed the shore where the city now stands, the topography of the locality has entirely changed. The marshy and impassable region that it once was, is now the foundation of a growing and prosperous city. Bloody Island is the offspring of a period more recent than the first white settlers, for it was born with the present century. It grew into place and importance, and in time has became the theatre of metropolitan activity and commercial power.

Would London ever have attained its present commanding position, as the mistress of the world's commerce, without having made subservient to its wants, both shores of the Thames? Would the proud city upon Manhattan Island now be the great metropolis of this continent, without a corresponding grandeur of its auxilliaries upon the opposite shores of the North and East River? So too, as the grand center of continental commerce, St. Louis cannot expect to reach its destiny without utilizing the entire channel and both shores of the great river, the western half of which alone is included within its political dominion.

The river's natural advantages inherent to the opposite Illinois shore are bound to play a conspicuous part in the development and maturing of St. Louis as the greatest inland city of the globe.

The want at all times, and under all circumstances, of unbroken, certain means of communication with the germ of greatness in St. Louis in the past, prevented the materializing of those inherent advantages into permanent good to either side of the river.

The Eads bridge, with arms of steel, supported by massive piers of granite, themselves resting upon the bed-rock of the Mississippi river, has physically filled the void and practically united the east and west shores of the Mississippi.

It has opened an avenue through which the overflowing prosperity of St. Louis may upon the rich and fertile lands of the American bottom, at the east end of the great bridge, become the nucleus of a new growth, regardless of State lines or political borders, reflecting its own progress upon the parent: St. Louis. These reflections justify us to add as a necessary chapter of our work, a brief history of the young and promising city of

EAST ST. LOUIS.

The municipality of East St. Louis includes a cluster of "towns," separately laid out at different periods. It comprises, territorially, the northwest corner of the extensive common fields of Cahokia, and parts of the commons of that village, also several ancient grants and small parcels of sectionized lands, parts of township 2 north, range 10 west of the 3rd Principal Meridian. The oldest improvement upon the site of the city is shrouded in mystery, or at least uncertain as to its exact location and precise period of existence.

In 1750, one Chevalier Richard McCarty was appointed by the King of France,

Governor of Upper Louisiana, of the Province of New France. This province then included the entire Mississippi Valley, from the Gulf to the source of the river, including its tributaries to an unlimited extent. It was divided into Lower and Upper Louisiana. Fort Chartres, near Kaskaskia, was the seat of authority for the latter, and New Orleans for the former. Chevalier McCarty took up his residence at Kaskaskia, then the seat of the flower of the chivalrous explorers of the Great Valley and of their followers. It appears that during his lifetime, how early history does not tell, he built a grist mill on the bank of Cahokia creek, near and north of the common fields of the village of Cahokia, at a place about opposite the shops of the Ohio and Mississippi railway company, now occupied by the Missouri Car and Foundry company. Every vestige which might identify its situation has long since disappeared. The mill was a thing of the past as early as 1805, when United States Commissioners passing upon claims to ancient titles to land in this vicinity, confirmed four hundred acres (United States survey 627), extending from present St. Clair avenue to the middle of Illinois avenue, and from the southeast side of Tenth street to within three hundred feet of Stock-Yard avenue, to the heirs of the Chevalier, by reason of the building of the mill by their ancestor prior to 1783.

The Cahokia common fields, with a breadth of almost four and a half miles, reaching from the village of Cahokia to the middle of Illinois avenue in East St. Louis, extend from Cahokia creek to the bluffs, a depth of about six miles. These fields are perhaps of even greater antiquity than the McCarty Mill. If their origin is coincident with that of the village of the inhabitants who cultivated them, then they existed even before the year 1700.

Cahokia and Kaskaskia were founded by missionaries between 1670 and 1680, soon after the discovery of the "Father of Waters" by Lasalle.

In 1721, Father Charlevoix, a European priest upon a tour of inspection, reports them as quite respectable settlements, chiefly of Canadian French and half-bloods.

Wild beasts and hostile savages at the time possessed and roamed as lords and masters through the broad and unreclaimed domains of the West. Residing upon isolated farms was in those days totally impractical. Self-protection forced settlers to congregate in villages, and economy and convenience, as well as better security, advised the inclosure under a common fence of the fields necessary for the production of their wants.

A strip of heavily timbered bottom land about half a mile wide all the way from near the present town of Brooklyn to the mouth of Cahokia creek then near the village of that name, extended at the time and to near 1820, along the west bank of Cahokia creek, and between it and the Mississippi river.

There was no "Bloody Island" then. Deep sloughs to the north and south of Dyke avenue and a part of Bloody Island, later and now mark the space of that strip of timber land. This was the condition of the things in April 1763, when, by the treaty of Paris, France ceded to England all its possessions in North America east of the Mississippi, New Orleans excepted. Cahokia was then a flourishing

DD

village, whilst the present city of St. Louis was not even thought of. Not a mark of civilization indicated or permitted an indication of its future existence.

This treaty was kept secret for nearly two years from the country which it affected.

Late in the fall of 1763, Laclede, a French resident of New Orleans, clothed with special authority from the King of France, with considerable of an outfit and with quite a retinue of followers, ascended the river ostensibly for exploring purposes, but undoubtedly upon a secret mission to pave the way to the peaceable transfer of the country east of the Mississippi river to Great Britain. The almost natural antipathy of the French settlers to British rule might reasonably have been anticipated as resulting in little less than open revolt upon the promulgation of the treaty and the change of authority. History, as at our disposition, does not make the real mission very clear.

He landed in Kaskaskia in December 1763, late in the month. His commission placed the conveniences of the neighboring Fort Chartres as a base of operation, at his service.

He visited Cahokia early in 1764, with Pierre and Auguste Chouteau, where the latter established a trading store. In the spring of that year they proceeded up the river and spread their tents at the present site of St. Louis, and established a permanent post, whence Laclede and the Chouteaus soon after transferred the bulk of their stores, which they had left behind them at the Fort.

Within six months after their settlement upon the site of the present great city, the fact of the treaty leaked out. It created alarm as might have been expected. We can well imagine the despondency of the easy-going, jolly French, at the thought of passing under the dominion of their hereditary foe—the English. For twenty-three years they had fought them with their Indian allies, upon the lakes of the North, and as far east as the junction of the Allegheny and Ohio rivers.

Emigration was the parole of the day. They needed but to cross the river—the Mississippi—to escape the dreaded future. There was the new posts of St. Louis convenient to Cahokia, and Ste. Genevieve as handy to Kaskaskia.

Thus it seems that the treaty of Paris of 1763, by which France ceded the vast territory east of the Mississippi to Great Britain, caused the origin of St. Louis. And the loss of Kaskaskia and Cahokia proved the gain and advantage of Ste. Genevieve, and particularly of St. Louis.

The latter proved the more attractive because of the facility it afforded for trading with the many Indian tribes who annually, upon returning and resting from their hunting trips, assembled and camped upon that strip of timber land between Cahokia creek and the Mississippi river, almost opposite the old market place in original St. Louis, and hereinbefore referred to.

It was from this place, too, that in the spring of 1780, during the Revolutionary war, Indians, aided and abetted by British emissaries, assailed St. Louis, and massacred quite a number of its inhabitants, which event ever since was remembered as the year of the "*grand coup.*" Nothing worthy of note in connection with the territory of East St. Louis occurred during the twenty years of British rule.

By another treaty of Paris in September 1783, England in turn ceded its authority over the territory which in 1763 it acquired from the French, as far north as the present Canadian frontier, to the successful United States.

In fact and practice, Virginia, under General Roger Clark, had possession of most of the country ever since 1778, and afterward claimed it by right of conquest as a part of its own dominion.

In 1784, Virginia, upon conditions, amongst which was a reservation to the friendly inhabitants of Cahokia and other villages, of their ancient rights and possessions, surrendered its authority to the United States, which, upon negotiations between that Commonwealth and Congress, and upon modification of the terms of the cession, was made final in 1787.

In 1788, Congress passed resolutions confirming to each of the inhabitants of Cahokia, etc., who professed himself on or before 1783 a citizen of the United States his possessions and titles, and a tract of four hundred acres of land besides. This measure evidently was calculated to befriend the pioneers of the Far West upon the outskirts of the new domain. Meanwhile, the part of New France west of the Mississippi, under a secret treaty with Spain, had passed under authority of Dons and Hidalgos.

It appears that Congress, not satisfied with assisting the emigration of original settlers at Cahokia and elsewhere upon the Mississippi in the Illinois country, but also feeling the necessity of strengthening its adherents upon its western borders, in 1791 passed another act by which it granted to each head of a family who had resided in the country in 1783, and removed therefrom afterward, *and who would return within five years from the passage of the act*, not only his old origina possessions, but also four hundred acres alike with those who had remained and declared themselves citizens of the United States.

Quite a number of emigrants, it is claimed, returned from the Missouri shore, and even from Canada.

Most of General Clark's Virginia Militia returned to the Old Dominion after the treaty of 1783. Of those who remained was one Captain James Piggott. He appears to have been both a scholar as well as a warrior, and a man of considerable enterprise.

His first act recorded in history is the building of Fort Piggott, about 1790, near the present town of Columbia, in Monroe county. It was to protect the early settlers of that vicinage against the Indians.

In 1789, General St. Clair, Governor of the Northwestern Territory (comprising the present States of Ohio, Indiana, Illinois, Wisconsin and Michigan), established three courts of common pleas for the Illinois country—one at Kaskaskia, one at Prairie du Rocher, and one at Cahokia. John Dumoulin, a Swiss, was first judge of the Cahokia Court. He died in 1795, and was succeeded by Captain James Piggott. He held the office till his death, in 1799.

From its first establishment in 1764, Laclede's "Post St. Louis" rapidly developed. Immigration from the country upon the east bank of the river, induced by the change of sovereignty, was a considerable factor in this development. It is not at all unreasonable to presume that Laclede and his associates, at least could foresee, and foresaw, the consequences of the transfer of sovereignty. It is more than likely, considering their standing and authority with which they appeared in the winter of 1763, that upon their departure from New Orleans in November 1763, they were fully informed of the terms of the treaty of Paris, concluded in April of that year, even if they were not specially entrusted with bringing the news to the authorities of Upper Louisiana, then quartered at Fort Chartres and Kaskaskia.

The gain of Post St. Louis correspondingly affected Cahokia as a commercial point. The post was just opposite the great rendezvous of the many Indian tribes of the Northwest, east of the Mississippi.

To 1797 its means of communication with Cahokia was by a road down the west bank of the river to a few huts where a rude ferry was plied, between them and the village of Cahokia on the opposite shore. This settlement was at first known as "Louisbourg," later as Carondelet, nicknamed *Vide-Poche* (empty pocket), and now known as South St. Louis.

There was also a road on the Illinois side of the river, leading from the village of Cahokia along the east bank of Cahokia creek, northwardly, along the west line of the common-fields, quite probably as far up as McCarty's old mill.

Captain—Judge Piggott, endowed with a keen eye to business, observed the growing importance of " Post St. Louis," and considered the establishment of a rival ferry immediately opposite it, and a road connecting the ferry with that common-field road from Cahokia village, an inviting speculation. To this end he located a hundred acre militia claim upon the *quasi* Indian reservation between the creek and the river, just opposite the market place of " Post St. Louis." He then built at his own cost a road across this land, from the banks of the Mississippi to Cahokia creek, about opposite Market street of the town of Illinois, and also a bridge across the creek at that point, to connect with the Cahokia common-fields road on the east bank thereof.

Thus a rival route between St. Louis and Cahokia was complete, all but the ferry between Piggott's road and the west shore of the Mississippi. In 1797, Piggott applied to and obtained from Señor Trudeau, Spanish Commandant at St. Louis, the necessary concession for a ferry at that point, and established it immediately. His first craft in that service was constructed of two long canoes at a suitable distance apart, lashed together, with a floor upon and between them capable of accommodating a one-horse team or cart, as then fashionable and in vogue. Piggott did not live to see the consequences of his venture, or to reap the fruit of his enterprise. He died in 1799, but his ferry survived him to become the wealthiest monopoly of the kind in the country.

At that period the presence of the Indians proved a serious detriment to the neighborhood.

The Piggott hundred-acre tract at the first ferry landing here, was the principal part of the quasi reservation upon which the tribes then remaining in the Illinois country had their annual rendezvous. It extended between Cahokia creek and the Mississippi river, from near Mullikin street on the north to a line about three hundred feet south of the Vaughan Dyke.

These Indians were composed of the Kaskaskia, Mitchigamia, Cahokia, Tamarois and Peoria nations. They claimed all of the territory between the Wabash and the Mississippi, and between the Illinois and Ohio rivers, regardless of the surrender of the country by Great Britain under the treaty of 1783 and nevertheless its cession by Virginia in 1784 and 1787. They claimed it by right of possession by their ancestors of several generations. It seems they persisted in this claim so as to induce Congress, by Wm. Henry Harrison, then Governor of the Territory, as Commissioner Plenipotentiary on the part of the United States, on the 13th of August 1803, at Post Vincennes, to treat with them for the surrender of their claims, which they did by a compact of that date, in consideration of a guaranteed reservation of about two thousand acres near the village of Kaskaskia, and an annuity of $1,000. The Peoria nation of these Indians was not present at these negotiations and succeeded as late as the 25th of September 1818, by another compact, authorized by Congress, to obtain for themselves a special annuity of three hundred dollars for ratifying the release of 1803. Meanwhile great changes had taken place by the immigration of the Caucasian race, especially by pioneers from the States and by the advent of steam navigation. Piggott's ferry, more or less improved upon its original style, continued in existence under lessees of the Piggott family. Its last tenant, Calvin Day, was at the same time the first justice of the peace in the town of Illinois, which at that time was called into existence, as the germ of the present East St. Louis. He was appointed upon a petition of residents of the American Bottom presented to the Territorial Legislature.

Between 1805 and 1809, one Etienne Pinçoneau, a Canadian Frenchman of considerable wealth and enterprise, by purchase acquired a considerable tract of land, part of the Cahokia commonfields, with Cahokia creek separating it from the Piggott ferry tract.

Upon this land, almost on the bank of that creek, facing the road leading to Piggott's ferry, at the corner of Main and Market streets, Pinçoneau built the first house in the city of East St. Louis. It was a two-story brick house, built for a tavern, to afford accommodation to the travel then seeking that point for transit to the "future great city of the world." The exact date of its construction is not known. It had existence in 1811. Quite likely it was erected simultaneously with the Jarrot mansion at Cahokia. Both were then the first, and for a long time after, the only brick houses in the Territory. The Jarrot building still remains, with the rent in its south wall caused in 1811 by the earthquake, which sunk the country around New Madrid in Missouri. The Pinçonneau house decayed and is in ruins since 1868.

The growth of St. Louis, then the distributing center of the pioneer population of the West, unquestionably promised the east shore quite a future. Pinçoneau must have foreseen this. The Piggott land between him and the river was subject to abrasion, and withal not available for division and sale in parcels on account of the minority of several of the Piggott heirs.

The year 1815 opened up auspiciously. Five-sevenths of the Piggott heirs in February conveyed their interest in the ferry and the adjoining hundred-acre tract to the most enterprising firm of merchants and land operators at that day in St. Louis: John McKnight and Thomas Brady, doing business by the name of McKnight & Brady.

They at once reconstructed the bridge across Cahokia creek, first built by Judge Piggott in 1797, and substituted animal power for propelling their ferry boat.

Pinçoneau, in the spring of the same year, ventured to lay out a town on his adjoining land, with his brick tavern on the road to the ferry, then occupied by one Simon Vanorsdal, as a nucleus. He called it "Jacksonville." The plat of the town cannot be found; but there is a deed of record for a lot in it. It bears date 17th March 1815. Etienne Pinçoneau and Elizabeth, his wife, by it convey to Moses Scott, merchant of St. Louis, in the Missouri territory, for $150.00, "all that certain tract, parcel, or lot of land being, lying, and situated in the said county of St. Clair, at a place, or new town called Jacksonville, containing in depth one hundred feet, and in breadth sixty feet, joining northwardly to Carroll street, facing the public square, and southwardly to Coffee street."

Later conveyances by McKnight & Brady, referring to this lot of Moses Scott, locate it as lot 5 in block 8 of the town of Illinois, at the southeast corner of Market and Main streets. Scott at once erected a store upon the lot and at that corner conducted the first mercantile establishment in this city.

This was the only sale made of lots in this "Jacksonville."

On the 20th of January 1816, Pinçoneau sold the entire tract of land he had on Cahokia creek (including Jacksonville), extending in breadth from near Railroad street to Piggott street, to McKnight & Brady.

The year 1817 marks a momentous period in the history both of St. Louis and East St. Louis. The first steamboat, the "General Pike," arrived at the St. Louis levee in the summer of that year, and, at the instance of McKnight & Brady, made several trips between both shores, demonstrating the advent of a new era in navigating the Father of Waters, even for ferry purposes.

The immediate result was the consummation, by McKnight & Brady, of Pinçoneau's project of a new town. They platted the "Town of Illinois" upon the site of Pinçoneau's Jacksonville. They re-located the public square, widened the streets and enlarged the lots, and put the plat of record. Under the excitement and enthusiasm produced and existing by reason of the feat performed by the "General Pike," they advertised and held a great sale of lots in the Town of Illinois. The sale took place at the auction room of Thomas T. Reddick, real estate agent at St. Louis, on November 3, 1817. Thus was made the first record evidence of a town-plat in East St. Louis. Another part of East St. Louis, lately added, bears however as old a date—Illinois City.

It appears that the success of the "General Pike," in stemming the current of the Father of Waters, called forth a like enthusiasm all along the shores of the river, even in Cahokia, which was then about entering upon its Rip Van-Winkle sleep—whether from exhaustion or from chagrin at its successful rival—St. Louis—we know not.

The Cahokians hearing of the attempt of McKnight and Brady to establish a competing settlement upon the Illinois side of the river, determined to head-off the movement. Just above their common fields and adjoining the McCarty tract they had a magnificent piece of commons—United States survey 777. This they selected as the site for *their* new town.

On the 18th of September 1817, a public meeting was held at Cahokia, at which the villagers agreed unanimously to give life to the scheme. From amongst themselves they selected five prominent citizens their agents to plot and name the new town, and to distribute the lots amongst the inhabitants of Cahokia. Nicholas Jarrot, Jesse B. Thomas, John Hay, John Hays and Francis Turcotte were these agents. They performed their task with credit, and with a liberality of spirit foreign to those days. They appropriated nearly four hundred acres for the purpose. Bounding a public square of four acres they made four principal avenues, each ninety-nine feet wide, extending full length through the plot; all other streets were made seventy-four feet five inches wide. All blocks are of uniform size—squares of four hundred and seventeen feet to the side; each square is divided into eight lots of over one hundred feet front by nearly two hundred feet deep.

Every block is divided by a twenty-one feet wide alley. All streets cross at right angles; one set being parallel to the long lines of the Cahokia commonfield, which bear about S. 43° E. from Cahokia creek.

Half a block in opposite corners in the northeast tier of blocks were set aside, one for a "Catholic" graveyard, and the other for an "English" graveyard. "English" in those days was synonymous with "Protestant." A quarter of a block in close proximity to each graveyard was in like manner dedicated for a "Catholic" church and an "English" church respectively.

The public schools were also not forgotten. A very high and eligible lot was in the same way given for the purpose, and so noted upon the plat of record.

In spite of these extraordinary inducements, held out for competition, it appears Illinois City did not prosper as a town, for many years thereafter.

McKnight and Brady's town was better located, upon the highway of travel to the daily growing ferry, leading to the rising metropolis on the other side.

Yet the firm of McKnight & Brady were not to have it all their own way. Just north of their Piggott land there was another hundred-acre tract, like it extending from Cahokia creek to the Mississippi, which must have offered like inducements for another town. Thus in September 1817, Simon Vanorsdal, John Scott, Joseph Clegg and Daniel Sullivan, as owners of part of that land, agreed by an instrument of record, to contribute equally the necessary funds to perfect their title and to lay the land out into a town. They seem to have succeeded to acquire the last of the title they needed in 1819, and immediately laid it out into the town of Washington, and established what was then known as "Upper Ferry." The west shore of the river, originally about on a line with Fourth street of the Third ward, had been rapidly receding by the caving in of the Illinois bank. The land disappeared so fast under the encroaching waves of the Mississippi, that near the close of the year most of Washington was buried beneath its waters, and its proprietors did not deem it necessary to put the plat of it of record in order to enable the Sheriff to sell them out, as he did in the spring of 1820.

Meanwhile, McKnight & Brady had not been slow in developing the town of Illinois. Market street was the center of business. They built the first mill in the town near Cahokia creek, a little south of Railroad street, upon what since then was called and known as the Mill tract, and in later years used as the Belleville coal yard. It was a grist mill, propelled by oxen walking upon an inclined circular platform revolving upon its axle.

In 1818 there appeared upon the scene an adventurous emigrant from Rhode Island—a mariner by calling—Samuel Wiggins. With an unerring eye he took in the situation, and forecast what was bound to come. The gigantic fabric of his building, and the manner and means he used toward accomplishing his end, all point to a well-conceived and thoroughly-matured plan of operations. There was McKnight & Brady's ferry, and half a mile further up, the new or upper ferry at the embryo town of Washington.

Calvin Day, once the lessee of the Piggott heirs, then holding under McKnight & Brady, first sold to him his leasehold interest in the ferry. McKnight & Brady only owned five-sevenths of the old Piggott title to both land and ferry. Wiggins, it seems, on discovering this, promptly contracted for the outstanding two-sevenths of the Piggott title, for himself.

Illinois had now become a State. Its first General Assembly, under a State government, met in 1819. Thither Samuel Wiggins wended his steps. Then and there he procured the most remarkable ferry charter on record.

He was granted the right to establish a ferry on the Mississippi, near the town of Illinois, and "to run the same from lands at that place that may belong to him, and that no other ferries except those then existing should be established within one mile of the ferry established by that act, and that any person who, contrary to the provisions of that act, should run any ferryboat, he, she or they should forfeit any such boat, with the furniture and apparel, to Samuel Wiggins, his heirs and assigns."

Armed with this franchise, he returned, perfected his purchase of the two-sevenths Piggott title, and laying siege to McKnight & Brady's five-sevenths, soon after, in 1821, consolidated the whole title in himself. For a trifle, he next acquired the town site of Washington, with its "Upper Ferry" landing. There was then no other ferries, and none were to be established within a mile, under an extraordinary penalty of forfeiture of all but the life of the daring trespasser.

Bloody Island, in 1810 was a mere speck of a bar north of what is now known as that body of land. It grew southwardly by accretions opposite the receding eastern main shore.

In 1817, the Island received its baptism of human blood—Colonel Thomas H. Benton, there in that year met and slew in mortal combat, under the then prevailing code of honor, Judge Charles Lucas. The year following, Thomas F. Rector, brother of the United States Surveyor General of the Northwestern Territory, fell upon the same spot, pierced by a ball sped by the hand of Joshua Barton, his antagonist. Thenceforth the Island became the favorite rendezvous of the duellist until a late day, and was and remained known as "Bloody Island" until 1865, when it was made the Third ward of the city of East St. Louis.

In 1827, the foot of Bloody Island extended to near the corner of Fourth street and Christy avenue, and was then purchased by Samuel Wiggins, who at that time by other purchases had become the sole proprietor of the Illinois shore from near the Illinois and St. Louis Railroad and Coal Company's spur-dyke, about vis-a-vis Chouteau avenue of St. Louis, to beyond the St. Clair county line, near opposite North Market street of St. Louis, a distance of about three miles.

In 1826, a very high flood inundated the town of Illinois, and malarial fevers in its wake almost depopulated the place. Both McKnight and Brady had then gone to their long home. Their heirs were non-residents, and as it appears took no interest in advancing the settlement or the development of the town.

The ferry was the principal business. Steam had superseded animal power in moving the boats as early as 1826, after the subsiding of the flood of that year. Wiggins and his associates, Andrew and Samuel Christy, became wealthy in the enjoyment of their ferry franchise and monopoly of the business. They and their successors, the Wiggins Ferry Company, incorporated in 1853, until quite a late date pursued a policy which reaped them rich dividends from ferry toll, but at the same time laid like an invincible incubus over the development of their extensive landed estates. To force trade and traffic to the other side of the river for exchange and for storage, even if for re-shipment east again, increased their ferry revenues, but left their exceedingly available real estate a comparative waste. The spanning of the river by the Eads bridge, under the shadow of which, it is true, a part of their fleet of boats yet exists and competes for transit from shore to shore, is turning away from them the bright side of the picture they so long and so persistently worshiped. Howsoever, during their long reign from 1820, the owners of Wiggins' Ferry, as a matter of course, took a lively interest in every-thing tending to make their ferry the prominent point of crossing the Father of Waters for the vast immigration at an early day setting out for the Far West.

In 1829 they procured the passage of a State Act appropriating a quarter of a million of dollars for the construction of the *Great Western Mail Route*, a State road extending from their ferry, at the town of Illinois, to Vincennes, on the Wabash river. In 1837 they succeeded to have a further appropriation of $30,000 of State money applied for the improvement of that part of this route lying between their ferry and the bluffs at French Village, part of the present Belleville turnpike.

In 1836, Vital Jarrot of Illinoistown, ex-Governor John Reynolds and Samuel

B. Chandler of Belleville, Louis Boismenue of Cahokia, and George E. Walker of St. Louis, Missouri, in their individual capacity built the first railway in the State of Illinois. It extended from Pittsburg, about six miles distant, to the Great Western mail route in the town of Illinois, about where now the Illinois and St. Louis Railroad and Coal Company has a station near Railroad street, with the privilege of extending on that street to the creek. A branch of this railroad curved southwestwardly from near Tenth street to Cahokia, near where now the Illinois Patent Coke Company's works are located.

This road was built expressly, if not exclusively, to transport bituminous coal from where it cropped out at the bluffs to the St. Louis market, that is, as near to it as possible. This individual venture of operating the first railroad tapping the Mississippi river, proved an unfortunate one to the owners.

In 1841 they sold out (more or less voluntarily) to the St. Clair Railroad Company, chartered that year. With varying success, and under successively changed corporate names, such as the "St. Clair Railroad and Coal Company," in 1853; the "Pittsburgh Railroad and Coal Company" in 1859, and the "Illinois and St. Louis Railroad and Coal Company" since 1865, the road and its business continued to the present day, with fair prospect of eventually meeting the success which the enterprise of its founders, as pioneers in railroad business in the West, and particularly in the State, and the perseverance of their successors so richly merited and merit.

The establishment of this first railroad stimulated the neigborhood of the first railroad depot in the State—a little above McKnight & Brady's Town of Illinois, to fresh action. In 1837, one John L. St. John (Dr. St. John) of Orange county, New York, appeared upon the scene. He purchased of Vital Jarrot, for twenty-seven dollars per acre, twenty-seven acres of land, nearly all of the Cahokia commonfield surveys 127 and 128 between the railroad termini and Cahokia creek, and laid it out into a town plat called "Town of St. Clair," almost identical with the present "St. Clair Subdivision of East St. Louis."

Narrow fifty feet wide streets, small lots, blocks without alleys, evidently operated against the improvement of St. John's new town. It did not prosper. The crisis which followed soon after, by the demolition of the United States Bank, the State Bank and its numerous branches, assisted in making the speculation a failure—so much so that within a few years thereafter St. John attempted, by some kind of a document of record, to vacate the town plat into a more profitable field or pasture.

It appears that soon after the darkest of the clouds of the financial storm had passed over the country in 1839, 1840, etc., in 1842 and '43, a new set, a fresh relay of venturesome spirits arrived in the town of Illinois, to take advantage of the great facilities it afforded as a commercial point: Aaron and Alfred Crosby, Matthew Woodruff, Stephen Lumrix, John and Jacob Ensminger, Wellington and Alexander Weigley, Nathan Cole, James Reynold, Abner B. Cole, James McLaughlin, John Brundig (Brundy), Green Erskine, Philander Braley, W. W. Singleton and Milton N. McLean, all men of unusual force of character, came to cast their lot here with the older residents, above whom for enterprise and pluck Vital Jarrot towered head and shoulder.

The town of Illinois as it were took a new start. Houses sprang up dotting and reviving old streets; mills, an extensive distillery and pork-packing establishments were erected, and a weekly newspaper, the first in East St. Louis, owned and edited by Jarrot and Lumrix, the *American Bottom Gazette*, was called into life.

A superior locality, evidently long and unpardonably neglected, was about rising to a normal condition, when the most fatal blow it ever received prostrated, if not annihilated its present, and, as it were, completely paralyzed the victim for the next future. With the "June rise" of 1844, the overflowing Mississippi all but swept every mark of the town out of existence. Its parallel had never before been witnessed; not since 1785 had there been such a flood, if then.

The depth of the water upon present Broadway, near its junction with Main street, was fully twelve feet.

Naught but the mounds, until recently in existence, on Collinsville avenue, between Illinois and Ohio avenues, and a few high knolls on Tenth street between Ohio and Pennsylvania avenues were dry, and these dry spots were very much circumscribed.

Ordinary steamboats plied between the bluff and Second and Third streets in St. Louis, over the roofs of some and along the roofs of other remaining houses in our ill-fated town.

East St. Louis—town of Illinois then—never recovered from this terrible affliction until the commencement of general railroad building, about ten years later. The first newspaper succumbed in the flood. Its proprietors left the town—Jarrott went on a farm, Lumrix returned East. Desolation and general prostration and discouragement marked the place. Many left before the encroaching waters and never returned, abandoning houses and lots to be sold for taxes. In this way a dreary existence was maintained by the survivors and remaining inhabitants. This last flood had yet another consequence, materially affecting more the distant than the near future of East St. Louis.

Before its advent, the channel of the Mississippi opposite St. Louis, though uncertain and troubled with shifting bars in its harbors, was never seriously threatened with utter destruction. Thereafter bars formed from the head of Bloody Island, then a little farther north than now, to the Missouri shore, almost closing entirely the channel washing the St. Louis shore. The whole current of the river, and the only available and safe channel between St. Louis and the town of Illinois, was between the Island and the town of Illinois. Through this cause, by the current sweeping to the east of it, the upper part of the Island was entirely washed away, not, however, without causing a corresponding deposit upon its southern end, which at that time was near opposite the present East St. Louis Elevator, and growing still further in that direction. Under the greatest of difficulties only and by circuitous routes could boats at all land at the St. Louis levee. Navigation then being the chief, if not the only means of communication between commercial points and from a commercial center as St. Louis then was growing to be, was the main stay of the importance, present and prospective, of that city. This was realized fully, and to such an extent as to arouse public attention and to excite public alarm to a high degree in the Mound City. Public meetings were held, largely attended, at which the terrible fate of St. Louis was the subject of consideration.

In 1847, ordinances were passed by the City Council of St. Louis, appropriating money, and directing work to be undertaken on the Illinois shore, as the only means of salvation.

Nothing less than a permanent dike across the then principal channel of the Mississippi to the east of Bloody Island promised reliable and sure relief. This of course meant destruction to the harbor of the Town of Illinois and to its ferry landings on the main shore. At that time the city of Alton made strong pretensions of rivalry with St. Louis as the prospective metropolis in the Mississippi Valley. As such it wielded considerable political influence in the State of Illinois. Alton calculated that what was to the disadvantage of St. Louis was *ipso facto* a benefit to Alton.

The feeble complaints of the Town of Illinois were fanned into a state of fearful excitement. The laborers upon the dike about being built by St. Louis across the eastern channel of the river were driven away by force. Cannons were planted upon the banks, the State militia turned out, and thus State sovereignty and Alton policy were victorious, for a while at least.

Not content with this, an injunction was sworn out of the St. Clair Circuit Court against any attempt on the part of the city of St. Louis to re-open like projects. This happened late in the year 1848. Early in 1849, the Legislature of Illinois, for the purpose, waited upon by a large and most respectable delegation from St. Louis, in a spirit of magnanimity worthy and becoming wise legislators, raised themselves above the level of the petty jealousies and short-sightedness of the advocates of a less friendly course, and, by a joint resolution, granted the city of St. Louis the fullest possible relief, all the authority necessary for the construction of cross and wing-dikes upon the Illinois shore opposite, so as to thoroughly protect and secure its harbor.

The only conditions of note attached to this grant was that St. Louis should construct upon some of these dikes, roadways, especially upon the main dike across the to-be-closed eastern channel of the Mississippi from the Illinois main shore to and across Bloody Island. This road was to be made "a safe, commodious public highway, even forever free from toll or tax;" the necessary rights of way were to be obtained by St. Louis.

Under cover of this enactment, St. Louis projected and pushed rapidly to completion costly dikes and embankments, under the succeeding administrations of the Honorable John M. Krum, James B. Barry and Luther McKennett, mayors, and Messrs. Henry Kayser and General Curtis, chief engineers.

The main dike was nearly done in the spring of 1851, all but the road upon it. It was built of rock throughout, and for a large part of the way, in the channel to be closed, in more than forty feet of water ; at its eastern end, where the main shore was almost identical with the west bank of Cahokia creek, at about the foot of Brady street of the Town of Illinois, a bridge had been thrown across the creek, to connect the prospective dike road with the Great Western Mail route, which at that time intersected Main street only about a block southeast of that bridge.

Then came the fearful flood of that year, but four feet less in height than that of 1844. It swept away the bridge across the creek and most of this dike, and cast a new pall over the vision of those yet in ill-fated Illinoistown, who attempted to call back the prosperity and promising future as before 1844, by renewed efforts. Many who had survived the last named flood and had remained now left for good. Amongst them were the Crosby brothers, who in the year following became the founders of Centralia, in Marion county, Illinois ; W. W. Singleton, who became the founder of the prosperous St. Louis mercantile firm, now Moody, Michel & Co.; Thomas Lapsley, M. N. McLean and others. Not only desolate was the then present, but the prospect of a change for the better was all but promising.

All this gloom and darkness, however, was that of the impenetrable, black, yet *passing* clouds. Beyond them soon could be seen a silver lining, a ray of sunshine and a future brighter than ever, aye brilliant indeed, if the minds and hands of enterprising men would but dare to make it. And they dared. They are up and doing.

To properly connect notable events we have to retrace our steps to the year 1847. In that year the Legislature chartered the St. Clair County Turnpike Company, to build and maintain a turnpike road from the Mississippi river at the town of Illinois to High street in Belleville, the county seat, upon the site of the old western mail route, which, as already stated, through the bottom land, for a distance of seven miles, in 1837 and 1838, at an expense to the State of $30,000, had once been made an excellent road by John Waistanley, of St. Clair county, and Philip McDonald of St. Louis, Missouri, as State contractors.

Though in manner this dike and the road upon it was not finished, and as such turned over by the city authorities of St. Louis to those of Illinois until 1858, the road was made use of more or less as early as 1855. In 1857, the St. Clair county Turnpike Company had their charter amended so as to authorize them to re-locate their western terminus to the east end of this dike.

Accordingly, they constructed a turnpike road upon Broadway of St. John's Town of St. Clair, laid out in 1837. This street offered very nearly a straight connecting line between their road and the east end of the St. Louis dike; at least as far as Cahokia creek.

From the commencement of the construction of the first cross-dike by St. Louis in 1848, and the practical closing of the eastern channel of the Mississippi, the harbor of Illinoistown and its ferry landings were changed as often as once a month, to follow the ever shifting current along the shore. From opposite where now the roundhouse of the Cairo Short Line is situated to quite a distance below where the so-called Pittsburgh Railroad dike projects into the river, the boats of the Wiggins' Ferry Company made landings at times and for a while. After the partial completion of the last built main cross-dike, late in 1854, the county of St. Clair reconstructed the bridge across Cahokia creek, near the foot of Brady street and over it, and over the land now occupied by the large car sheds and roundhouse of the Indianapolis and St. Louis Railroad Company ; travel wended its way to the new dike-road, and over it to the first *permanent* ferry landing on the west shore of Bloody Island.

In the spring of 1852, under imposing ceremonies, Luther M. Kennett, Mayor of St. Louis, attended by the City Council of that city, and by a vast assembly, broke ground in the town of Illinois for the construction of the Ohio and Mississippi Railroad. This occurred upon lot 4 of block 28 of the Town of Illinois (Illinoistown), between Main street and the St. Clair County turnpike, near Brady street, the site selected at the time for the temporary western terminus of that road. The embankment then thrown up still exists. A Conradin Hoesli, as purchaser of the lot in 1855, erected a dwelling upon it, which still marks the spot. The road was projected to follow the west side of the Belleville turnpike, to near present Tenth street, following the latter to opposite the Plabbert farm. Near Pennsylvania avenue it was to cross Tenth street, to follow a course almost identical with that of the St. Louis and Southeastern Railway, to and through the bluffs, making Belleville a way-point. This route, however, was soon abandoned, through the influence of Colonel John O'Fallon, of St. Louis, a director and large stockholder of the company. He owned extensive coal fields in and adjacent to Caseyville ; and as a result, the original route was abandoned and the present one, which runs by way of Caseyville about Central through over two thousand acres of coal lands of the O'Fallon estate adopted. This left Belleville high and dry, and distant from this great artery of trade and travel.

Colonel Don Morrison, now of St. Louis, then of Belleville, and in the prime of his power, to recompense the latter city for this disappointment, procured the passage of the charter of the Belleville & Illinoistown railroad Company, with the extraordinary privilege of building a railroad from Belleville to Illinoistown, " and to build extensions so as to connect it with any other railroad in the State, now existing or hereafter constructed."

·It was immediatly buit and extended northwardly beyond Illinoistown to Wood river, near Alton. There it was met by an extension of the Terre Haute & Alton railroad, over which it connected not only with the latter, but also with the Chicago, Alton & St. Louis railroad, both of which used it as a means to reach St. Louis, or rather East St. Louis—Illinoistown then. The shrill whistles of the locomotives and the ringing of their bells announced, as it were, the dawning of a new day upon unfortunate and down-cast Illinoistown.

At first all these railroads: the Ohio & Mississippi, the Belleville & Illinoistown, the Terre Haute & Alton and the Chicago, Alton & St. Louis all landed and had their stations in or adjacent to Illinoistown, in, above or below it, *upon the east side of the Cahokia creek.* Connections thence with St. Louis were, of course, attended with many inconveniences.

The Ohio & Mississippi railroad at that time entered present East St. Louis upon what is now Fourth street of the Second ward, and extended southwardly in a straight line for nearly a mile south of and beyond the present limits of the city of East St. Louis, upon lands of Wiggins' Ferry Company and the commons of Cahokia. In fact all four of the railroads named, from the nature of things could not have permanent stations at Illlinoistown. They had to follow the ferry landings as they moved until a permanent one was established on the west shore of Bloody Island, at the foot of the dike road then being built by St. Louis. As soon as this latter road was permitted to be used by the public, even before entire completion, the business of these companies began to cluster opposite the east end of this road — that is on the east side of Cahokia creek opposite. There the Ohio & Mississippi Railway Company built a temporary depot or station on its line where it crossed Broadway near the site of the Wies building, occupied by the Workingmen's Bank, and the opposite St. John building. Thence it and the other railroads transferred passengers and freight by omnibuses and wagons over the dike and Wiggins ferry to St. Louis.

Henry Brundy, son of one of the older settlers, not anticipating the change of things then soon to come, erected an extensive and costly three-story brick hotel, convenient to these stations, at the corner of Railroad and Main streets. It thrived for quite a while, first as the "Western Hotel," and then as "International Hotel;" but with the transfer of these stations to the west side of Bloody Island, nearer the ferry landing and nearer St. Louis as the objective point of all railroads, business began to languish and to decrease. The location proved a failure. Brundy quit and left, and on the first of January 1862, the hotel burned to the ground and has been in ruins ever since.

The Ohio & Mississippi Railroad Company were first to pull up stakes and to shift their station westward to the new shore of the Mississippi, the place now used as their coal depot. Trains were run to the new terminus in July 1855. The other roads had to follow as a consequence.

The Terre Haute & Alton, and Belleville & Illinoistown railroads became consolidated as the Terre Haute, Alton & St. Louis Railroad Company, and acquired land for a permanent depot, about forty acres, opposite the roundhouse of the Cairo Short Line, extending out to the river's edge, *vis-a-vis* Spruce street ferry landing in St. Louis. For temporary purposes they leased from Wiggins' Ferry Company a piece of land extending along present Front street, from Crook street to and beyond Pratte street. This they occupied until at a later day they exchanged their first purchase for the lands now used by the Indianapolis and St. Louis Railroad Company and the Cairo Short Line, between Bogy and Pratte streets, for East St. Louis stations.

In 1857 the St. Clair County Turnpike Company macadamized Broadway, of St. John's "Town of St. Clair," from the old turnpike to Cahokia creek, where and across which a bridge was built by the county, soon after the same year, to connect the turnpike with the dike road to the new river front.

St. John had died in 1846. His town now promised to become the principal theatre of activity, as a part of the resurrected Illinoistown. In the absence of the heirs, who as proprietors claimed this particular locality, they being in litigation with each other, and non-residents, squatters took possession, and shanties sprung up on sites convenient to the new source of business.

Thus, once more in the years 1855, 1856, 1857 and 1858, Illinoistown took a new start and under auspices more flattering than ever.

Page & Bacon, the bankers of St. Louis, Mo., undoubtedly having much faith in this recuperative power of a situation so favorable, invested heavily in the extensive unimproved lands adjoining Illinoistown. By rapidly successive purchases they became the owners of the McCarty tract, the adjoining tracts of John Jacob Astor, William Hempstead and Vital Jarrot, in all about fourteen hundred acres of land, in and contiguous to the present city of East St. Louis. Forty-two acres of the McCarty tract they sold to the Ohio and Mississippi Railroad Company, upon which the latter at once erected extensive machine shops, both for the construction and repair of cars and locomotives. These shops are now occupied by the Missouri Car and Foundry Company. Upon their erection in 1855 and 1856 there were employed therein at a time and constantly, and for nearly eighteen years afterwards, many hundreds of laborers, mechanics and artisans. The failure of Page & Bacon, in their extensive business as bankers, for a while delayed their plan of dividing their lands into town and city lots. Eventually, in 1857, their landed properties passed into the hands of William N. Aspinwall, Samuel W. Comstock, Henry Chauncey and S. L. M. Barlow, of New York.

In 1858, the latter were about to carry out the original project of making a large and valuable addition to rejuvenated Illinoistown, when the old scourge of every former attempt at progress made its appearance again. A flood exceeding in height and destructive consequences that of 1851, and but about three feet below the level of that of 1844, in 1858 swept over the town, and swept away many of the newer buildings, but not the resolve of the owners to stick and to win. But little of the present city south of Summit avenue was above water.

The loss of property and the interruption in business and the entailment of malarial diseases, as a consequence to the many stagnant pools remaining, was greater than after any previous flood; but a different set of people, at least a different spirit, now inhabited the place. As if by magic, buildings were replaced and multiplied upon the waste left by the receding waters. The opportunities for improvement were too great; the determination of those who were attracted too firm, to yield to obstacles which they clearly saw were within human power to overcome, and to overcome permanently and triumphantly.

In January 1859, Joseph Griffith, J. T. Taylor, Wm. F. Lee, and W. J. Enfield applied to the State Legislature and obtained the first charter of a municipal corporation upon the site of East St. Louis. The corporate name given it was "Town of Illinoistown." The town government consisted of a Police Magistrate and four Trustees, elected annually. Other officers were appointive. The Police Magistrate was ex-officio President of the Board of Trustees. The corporate limits were: on the west, Cahokia creek, and on the north, south and East, about the same, rather indefinitely however, as later and now, Illinois city excluded.

Wiggins Ferry Company for a time successfully resisted the effort to include Bloody Island and the land on the old main shore west of Cahokia creek within the corporate limits. They were the sole owners then of all that land. The first town government was composed of: Wm. Hamilton, Police Magistrate; W. J. Enfield, Samuel W. Toomer, Andrew Wettig, and Henry Jackiesch, Trustees.

J. W. Kemps was appointed Clerk, Daniel Sexton Treasurer, and Gorge W. Johnston Marshal. There was no other police but the Marshal and the precinct county Constables.

The first corporate improvement made was the erection of the brick calaboose at the corner of Second and Railroad streets, which survived until a year ago as the feared "black hole of Calcutta."

The erection of a market building was agitated and contemplated, but not carried out until near ten years later, on account of disagreement as to *where* it should be built.

The same year, 1859, General Lewis B. Parsons of St. Louis, as the authorized agent of the non resident owners of the old Page and Bacon property, caused about nine hundred acres of it to be divided into town lots by the plat name of "Town of East St. Louis." All the land between St. John's Town of St. Clair platted in 1837, and "Illinois City" platted in 1817, he appropriated for the purpose. He made the division line between the McCarty and the Astor tracts identical with the center line of Illinois avenue, and that between the Astor and Hempstead tracts the middle line of Missouri avenue.

The plot is made on a liberal scale. Avenues are broad, streets and alleys are wide, and the lots are roomy.

On 10th November 1859, the first sale of lots of the "Town of East St. Louis" was made at public auction on the land, Leffingwell & Miller of St. Louis acting as auctioneers. The average price at which property was disposed of at that sale did not exceed one dollar and twenty-five cents per foot front. What has proved since to be the most valuable property then brought the least price.

A second sale was held in May 1860, but with no better success.

Lots on Missouri avenue between Collinsville avenue and Cahokia creek, found but few purchasers at one dollar per foot front. A few were sold at that price, and because no more than seventy-five cents per foot was offered for adjoining ones, the sale was abruptly stopped.

It must be remembered that in 1859 and 1860, what is now the Second and Fourth wards of East St. Louis contained but a few straggling houses and no street improvements whatever. Indeed every street north of Broadway, excepting only the Collinsville plank road, had existence solely on the paper plat of the town of record.

Fourth street all the way up from Broadway to Illinois avenue was marked by the original embankment of the Ohio & Mississippi railroad, or rather what was left of it after the flood of 1858, with deep ditches on both sides; and all of the Fourth ward between the Collinsville plank road, Tenth street, Illinois avenue and St. Clair avenue was a broom-corn field, and the adjoining land from Illinois avenue to Division avenue and from the Collinsville plank road to the Belleville turnpike was a pasture, and both were so occupied till the spring of 1862.

Tim Callaghan, James Mullen, both dead, and Christ. Buesse, yet living, were the last tenants of these fields.

On December 5, 1859, E. D. Walker was appointed first Street Inspector. He recommended the marking out of the street lines and the construction of sidewalks upon the more frequented streets; but in this behalf plead to deaf ears. His extravagant ideas were ridiculed.

At the annual election in April 1860, Daniel Sexton was elected Police Magistrate, and Richard Hennesey, Timothy Canty, R. E. Bland and B. B. George, the second Board of Trustees. Samuel W. Toomer succeeded to the office of Town Treasurer. J. W. Kemps remained Town Clerk, and became ex-officio Street Inspector, whilst E. D. Walker accepted the Marshal's office.

In the spring of 1861 a new town charter with enlarged powers and better defining, but not materially enlarging the corporate limits, was procured. Under special clauses in it, its adoption and the question whether or not the corporate name should be changed to "East St. Louis," was to be submitted to a popular vote. The election upon those propositions was held on the 11th of March and the first charter election thereunder on the 1st of April 1861. Excitement ran high. Exaggerated stories as to the provisions of the new charter were set afloat to secure its defeat. The new charter provided that the town might regulate and license or suppress dramshops not only within its limits, but also within half a mile outside of its boundaries.

The childish prejudice in favor of the time-honored (?) name of "Illinoistown," also was a serious obstacle to the proposition to change the name of the corporation to "East St. Louis." "St. Clair City," or "St. Clair" simply, would undoubtedly have been a more appropriate name than East St. Louis. This was well understood at the time, but another fact forced itself as prominent for recognition. The railroads all were terminating upon Bloody Island. Their stations there were known as "East St. Louis."

That Bloody Island could not much longer remain without a municipal government was also evident. From the nature of things a second "East St. Louis" would not likely be chartered or incorporated, and when the opportune time should come for absorbing "Bloody Island," the absorption of it in "East St. Louis" would be less serious an undertaking than the alternative of two adjoining but distinct municipalities. In other words if one had to be the whale and the other Jonah, it was preferable to be the whale. However, both propositions, to adopt the charter and to change the name, carried the day, but by very small majorities.

Thus East St. Louis as a corporate municipality became a fact. It comprised three distinct town plats. That of the Town of Illinois, of McKnight & Brady, that of the Town of St. Clair of St. John, and that of Town of East St. Louis proper, by Wm. H. Aspinwall and others. The new government consisted of a president and board of four Aldermen. Two Aldermen were to be elected each year, and the president biennially. Samuel W. Toomer was the first president, and John Moneghan, Frank Karle, Florence Sullivan and Samuel B. Walker, were the first Aldermen. Appointed were John O'Reilly as Town Clerk, Andrew Wettig as Treasurer, and Ed. D. Walker as Marshal. John B. Bowman was elected Police Magistrate. The same legislature which passed the new charter, also enacted the law under which the St. Clair county Turnpike Company erected, and yet maintain a tollgate on the dike-road, built by the city of St. Louis, across the eastern or Illinois channel, of the Mississippi. Its road surface averaged forty feet in width, and its length is just about half a mile. For keeping this road in repair, the Company were permitted by the Legislature to charge the public for using it : five cents for a one or two horse wagon, and correspondingly more for large vehicles.

Ten cents per mile toll upon a road built from other funds, than those of the corporation collecting the tolls ! This road was to be to the inhabitants of Illinoistown, now East St. Louis, a kind of compensation for surrendering their harbor as a sacrifice to St. Louis, in the days of its needs !

In the spring of 1861, when the Turnpike Company commenced the construction of the toll gate, a cry of indignation over the stupidity or malevolence of the Legislature who had furnished the excuse for it, was raised throughout the county. Large public meetings were held in East St. Louis for the purpose of organizing opposition, to invoke the aid of courts as a relief against the usurpation, which it was considered to be.

The commencement of the civil war, the march of volunteers to the front, the noise and clatter of drums and arms contemporaneous with the toll gate outrage, stifled or rather overwhelmed whatever feeling had arisen in opposition to it. Under the greater burden of the civil conflict, the lesser of the toll-gate exaction was forgotten in a manner—until the opportunity of the 14th September 1873, when the gate accidently burned down, was offered. An attempt was then made by the city authorities of the day, John B. Bowman, as Mayor at the time leading, to prevent its re-construction. A peremptory writ from the United States Circuit Court at Springfield, soon after issued at the instance of Hudson E. Bridge, a non-resident stockholder, of St. Louis, to permit the re-building of the hated structure under the penalty attached to contempt of that court.

This, however, is not the finality of the question involved. A writ of quo-warranto was meanwhile sworn out of the Circuit Court at Belleville, attacking the validity of the law under which the gate was located, and the binding force of it. At the April term 1876 of the St. Clair Circuit Court, on the trial of the cause, a judgment against the Turnpike Company and a writ of ouster against them was ordered by the Honorable William H. Snyder. From this the company appealed to the State Supreme Court, where it was taken under advisement at the last June term. If the judgment in the Circuit Court is sustained, that will be an end to the gate.

Bloody Island, because of its many railroad terminii, was made a central rendezvous of troops for transportation over different routes. The marauding elements, unavoidable excrescences to military bodies in times of war, were not wanting. They created considerable insecurity, not only on Bloody Island but also in adjoining East St. Louis. The town could not at that date afford a police which would efficiently have met the emergency existing. Hence a "Vigilance Committee" was organized to give wanted protection to property, and to secure the maintenance of peace and order.

On the first May 1861, the committee organized.

S. W. Toomer, the president of the Town Council was appointed captain. Police Magistrate J. B. Bowman was its secretary, and J. J. Simons, J. W. Kemps, Frank Karle, J. V. Tefft, S. B. Walker, L. A. Delorme and B. B. George were made sergeants, one for each day in the week. Each sergeant commanded a squad of from four to six privates—all volunteers, patriots, serving without fee or reward.

At the same time there was organized under the general laws of the State "the East St. Louis Independent Hook and Ladder Company;" the first institution of the kind in the town. John V. Tefft was captain, John B. Bowman, secretary, and S. W. Toomer treasurer. J. B. Sikking and Fred Mehring were foremen. There were about forty members in all.

From voluntary contributions an entire outfit was purchased, with which the company, whilst it existed, for about two years rendered valuable services.

On the 17th of March 1862, the corner stone of St. Patrick's Church was laid under imposing ceremonies, conducted by the Right Reverend H. D. Junker (now deceased), Bishop of Alton, assisted by Reverend J. J. Brennan, the parish priest, and founder of the church, and many other clerical dignitaries from abroad.

Louis A. DeLorme, John O'Connell, Florence Sullivan and Henry Jackiesch with S. W. Toomer as president, constituted the town council for the second fiscal year, from April 1862 to April 1863.

On the 20th day of April 1862, the annual spring flood in the Mississippi again overflowed its banks and inundated the larger part of East St. Louis. The area of water surface was very large, but the shallow depth and the want of a destructive current, such as there was in 1858, prevented more serious damages. All from Market street to Illinois avenue, south of Third street, of the second ward, with the exception of the western part of Broadway, were then under water.

As an incident worthy of preservation in connection with that flood, may be noted that but for military interference from St. Louis, the waters could and would have been kept out. The railroad embankments, which then as now surrounded that part of our city, then the "Town" of East St. Louis, were complete barriers on the three exposed sides. The road beds of the Ohio & Mississippi, then on the old curve over the present site of the Saint Louis and Southeastern round house, on the north, the Saint Louis, Alton & Terre Haute railroad (now Indianapolis & St. Louis), on the west, and the Cairo Short Line road on the south, were an effectual protection.

There was, however, a large culvert in the curve of the Ohio & Mississippi embankment about midway between Third and Fourth streets of the Second ward. Through this lurked danger. This opening was promptly closed just as the overflowing Mississippi was about entering through it. H. D. Bacon, then acting president of the Ohio & Mississippi railroad, had it opened again. The people of East St. Louis closed it another time. Volunteer guards protected the closed gap. On the night from 19th to 20th April, a squad of United States soldiers appeared on the scene, sent at the request of President H. D. Bacon, by General John C. Kelton then in command at St. Louis. The citizens were driven away at the point of the bayonet. One John Shea was carried away, as it was feared mortally wounded, though after a long period of suffering he finally recovered. Under the protection of these troops the gap was reopened. Within less than two hours after that, the unfettered element had spread in a torrent over the entire town or so much of it as was submerged that year.

On the 27th October 1862, the first sidewalks in East St. Louis were ordered built by the Town Council. They were located on the north side of Broadway, west of Collinsville Plankroad, on the southeast side of Main street, from Broadway to Market street, and on the southeast side of Collinsville Plankroad street, from Broadway to Illinois avenue. The last named was built first. J. J. Simons was awarded the contract at ten cents per lineal foot. Three grub planks, twelve inches wide each, were laid side by side, lengthwise with the street. Quite an animated discussion preceded the passage of the order. F. Sullivan advocated and Henry Jackiesch opposed the proposed improvements. "Not yet time for it," "Can't afford it," "Too extravagant," "Premature," etc., were the arguments against the innovation. On the passage of the order, Mr. Jackiesch was the only one who voted no and who was in favor of continuing the "good old times."

From the outbreak of the civil war Bloody Island became the gathering place of a multitude and variety of lawless characters. The police courts of St. Louis with perfect impunity made it the Botany Bay of that city. Crime in all its phases not unfrequently held high carnival there; of course not without reflecting its painful effects upon the town separated from it only by Cahokia creek. Thus, early in the spring of 1863, a fresh attempt was made to bring that territory under the municipal regulation of the town of East St. Louis. The Hon. Wm. H. Underwood, of Belleville, representing the city in the State Senate, succeeded to have a bill pass the Upper House to so enlarge the jurisdiction of the existing municipality. A special committee appointed by the opponents of consolidation composed of Messrs. Henry Jackiesch and Henry Schweickhardt, backed by the then almost omnipotent influence of Wiggins' Ferry Company, defeated the measure in the Lower House.

At the April charter election, 1863, Henry Jackiesch, as a conservative, succeeded S. W. Toomer as president, and with Hugo Feigenbutz, John O'Connell, Michael Murphy and Henry Oebike as members, constituted the Town Council until the inauguration of the *city* government in April 1865.

Material changes for the better, and a much promising spirit of enterprise and improvement began to develop, during the period from 1863 to 1865.

Ever since the spring of 1863, Wiggins' Ferry Company attempted to have their dominions set apart as a distinct precinct; undoubtedly as a forerunner to a separate municipality. They nearly succeeded at the June Term of the County Court, 1863.

It was averted by the agreement between the two Justices then elected for Illinoistown precinct, which included Bloody Island, that one should keep his office near the river front on the Island. J. B. Bowman and J. W. Kemps, the two Justices concerned, drew lots. Kemps accordingly removed his office to Bloody Island, and Bowman remained on the east side of the creek.

In the meantime, efforts were made to bring order out of chaos concerning the streets and highways of the town.

The town territory was a conglomeration of three separate and distinct town plats, laid out at different periods, regardless of each other, and, as it seemed, with the end in view to put the greatest possible difficulties in the way of a reasonable and proper adjustment. The original Town of Illinois is to date the best laid out part of the city. All streets cross at right angles; all blocks are of uniform size, three hundred feet square; all streets run in one direction parallel to each other, or at right angles thereto; they are of uniform width, whilst the rear of every lot opens upon a twenty feet wide alley. One set of streets is sixty, the other sixty-six feet wide. The town of St. Clair had but one principal street, Broadway, eighty feet wide, running, however, parallel to one set of streets in the town of Illinois; all the rest were either only thirty or fifty feet wide, and none of the cross-streets corresponded with the streets of the older town of Illinois. Not an alley was there in any block or to any lot.

The town of East St. Louis, adjoining the latter on the north, with Division avenue marking the boundary, in turn paid no regard to the plan of the town of St. Clair, recognizing and adopting only the Collinsville Plank Road and the St. Clair Turnpike, of all existing highways. To shape these vastly different plans into one harmonious whole, was a task accompanied with more than ordinary difficulties. The controlling interest of the intervening town of St. Clair was in the hands of one Louisiana St. John, a maiden sister of its founder, John L. St. John. She was a woman of more than ordinary understanding and information, and withal possessed of a will which seemed to require every thing before it to bend or to break.

All this while, no local public press enlightened the existence of the town, or announced its advantages to the outside world. Early in 1865, another effort was determined upon to unite the territory between the town and the river under one regime, under a city charter. The charter was prepared by Messrs. S. M.

Lount and J. B. Bowman, under the direction of a committee of the Town Council.

It was sent to Springfield, and after encountering and overcoming many difficulties, toward the close of the session, was reported ready for passage in the Lower House. On the Saturday preceding the Wednesday fixed for final adjournment, the charter was called for third reading and passage, when lo! *"it turned up missing!"* "It had been stolen from the room of the committee," was the report. What was now to be done? There was no duplicate of it in existence. Messrs. Lount and Bowman at once went to work and completed another draft of a charter as near alike the first as was possible, and with it hastened on Monday night to Springfield.

The committee which was to introduce and to recommend its passage, as a substitute for the lost one, awaited its arrival. That night yet it passed their scrutiny, and the objections of every one of the corporations, who were property-holders on Bloody Island, and otherwise adversely interested.

Passing this ordeal successfully entailed many changes in the original draft. The railroad companies had to have unrestricted liberty as to the location of their depots upon the newly acquired territory. Wiggins' Ferry Company insisted upon limiting the license on ferry boats to one hundred dollars per annum. The Belleville Turnpike Company, with a bad conscience concerning the dike toll gate, was not satisfied without inserting the clause that nothing in the charter should affect any of its vested rights, etc. Each one demanded some concession in consideration of yielding its opposition, which might have been fatal to the bill at so late a day. On Tuesday morning the substitute for the lost charter was introduced in the House, especially recommended, the rules were suspended, the bill was read three times and passed. It was at once sent to the Senate. That body promptly referred it to a committee, to report on it next morning, when the bill was passed by a vote of 13 to 11.

The limits of the new "City," included all the incorporated "Town" of East St. Louis, and all the territory between it and the middle of the Mississippi river. Besides, by the new charter those limits could be further enlarged by the City Council by including "any tract of land adjoining, laid off into city or town lots, a plat of which being duly recorded in the recorder's office of the county."

Under this provision the town plat of "Illinois City" was added and made a part of the city of East St. Louis in May 1875.

The city was divided into three wards, the first one included the old "Town of Illinois" with the south half of the "Town of St. Clair," the middle of Broadway being the conditional line; the second ward comprehended the other half of that town plat, and all of the platted Town of East St. Louis not south of Tenth street; the third ward included the newly acquired territory from the west bank of Cahokia creek to the limits of the city of St. Louis, in the middle of the Mississippi.

The city government was to be a mayor, and two aldermen from each ward. All were to hold office two years except one alderman for each ward *of the first ones elected*. Their places were to be filled the next year and biennially thereafter. All other officers were appointive.

The first city government consisted of John B. Bowman, Mayor, and of the following aldermen: Michael Murphy and John O'Connell of the First ward; Henry Schall and James S. Hazen of the Second ward, and John Trendley and J. B. Lovingston of the Third ward.

A fruitless effort to induce the *Miner*, a weekly publication at Belleville, soon after discontinued, to locate in East St. Louis, caused the establishment on the 20th of May 1865, of the *Sunday Herald*, of James L. Faucett, proprietor and editor. It was issued weekly on Saturday, though bearing the name of a Sunday paper. As already stated, the flood of 1844 had swept away its first predecessor, the *American Bottom Gazette*, published in the town of Illinois by Sumrix & Jarrot. Thus the *Herald* was the second public journal published upon the site of East St. Louis. It in turn was succeeded by the *East St. Louis Gazette* on the 28th of June 1866. It was founded by John B. Bowman as proprietor and by Macauley, Crabb & Straube, practical printers, as its first publishers.

Up to the spring of 1865, Missouri avenue was only known by its name on the paper plat of the city, and by a few corner stones and stakes indicating its location. Not a house facing it marked its lines. The improved carriage-way and spacious side-walks now composing the avenue, and a necessity for public convenience, were then not known, if at all thought of as in prospect.

John B. Bowman, the new Mayor, following the business of a real estate agent was the first one to locate on the avenue. He removed his two-story frame office building from the south side of Broadway, where it stood, opposite Collinsville avenue, to the south side of Missouri avenue, near Fourth street, whence a few years after it was removed to the rear of the lot, opposite the present Center Market, and converted into the Pittsburg Hotel by John Ziska. William Conway and Matthew Brady, both of St. Louis, Missouri, soon after in May 1865, erected the two next buildings—two story frames—upon the avenue, upon diagonally opposite corners at its intersection with Third street.

The Brady building burnt down a few years ago, and was succeeded by the two-story brick Refrigerator Saloon of F. Heim & Bro. The Conway Building still survives as the Emmet House, kept by John B. Carroll, whose name has since become famous in the suit of Carroll *vs.* East St. Louis, (reported in 67 Illinois Report, page 568,) in which the Supreme Court of the State for the first time passed upon and determined the want of right and authority of foreign corporations (incidentally the Connecticut Land Company), chartered for speculating or land trading purposes, to acquire or hold lands in the State of Illinois.

The Legislature which incorporated the city, also granted charters for the establishment of the "East St. Louis Real Estate and Savings Bank," which name was changed to "East St. Louis Bank," by amendment to its charter in 1869, and also the East St. Louis Gas Light & Coke Company.

On the 20th November, the stockholders of the bank elected their first board of directors, and they appointed Francis Wittram the first president, and Emile Karst of St. Louis the first cashier. The bank was located in the frame building of Louis Wies', at the corner of Broadway and Fourth street, which last year gave way to the high grade stone and brick block of the same proprietor, now occupied by the Workingmen's Banking Company.

In September 1865, the Ohio and Mississippi Railway Company, by condemnation acquired, and removed its passenger business to new depot grounds—those until recently occupied by it, and the St. Louis and Southeastern Railway Company—a strip of land about four hundred and fifty feet wide, reaching from Christy avenue to Wiggins street, extending from Front street to Cahokia creek; the north line of Christy avenue (Bowman's dike) being its south boundary.

The price paid was upward of one hundred and sixty thousand dollars.

On 11th November following, the completion of "Douglas school" house, (recently destroyed by fire) at the corner of Mullikin and Fourth streets in the third Ward, was celebrated by a feast and ball given there under the auspices of the school directors of the district. The building cost six thousand dollars.

On the eighteenth day of the same month a new fire company was organized, whose purpose was to revive and to improve upon the original "East St. Louis Independent Hook and Ladder Company," of 1861, which in a manner had disbanded, by many of its members enlisting during the war. William Conway, Garrett Stack and Fred. Van Haren were made its board of trustees, Matthew Brady was elected Captain, and Daniel Sexton director of hose, etc.

During the following winter the Pittsburg Railroad Company, now the Illinois and St. Louis Railroad Company, commenced the construction of their dike, known as the Pittsburg dike, by which the course of Cahokia creek was diverted to its present mouth, north of that dike. Before then and till then, it wound its sluggish current along the old main shore for nearly three miles further south.

Considerable uneasiness was manifested as to the effects of this dike upon East St. Louis. It caused the creek-bed through the city to be raised by deposit to the extent of several feet. Thus the general level of the ground water under the city was raised accordingly. The dangers resulting, not being directly discernible and slow in demonstrating themselves, the subject was soon dismissed by the public at large.

The dike narrows the bed of the Mississippi river, opposite Chouteau avenue, in St. Louis, to less than fifteen hundred feet in width. Its cost was borne by the Coal Company and the city of St. Louis, in equal shares. It was completed some time in June 1866.

The annual charter election of April 1866, made no change in the representation of the First and Third wards in the City Council; but in the second, Thomas Hickey took the place of James S. Hazen. The Mayor held over.

On the 28th of June 1866, the first number of the *East St. Louis Gazette* made its appearance, and has continued without intermission as a weekly, and as the official paper of the city to this day. Since April 1876, it has appeared also as a daily evening paper.

In the early summer of 1866 the "East St. Louis Turnverein" was organized as a private association. It purchased one hundred and fifty by one hundred and forty feet of ground on the north-east corner of St. Louis avenue and Ninth street, and erected thereon a spacious building, with a commodious and well arranged hall, with galleries on three sides. This building was duly dedicated by a general participation of "Turnvereine"—like associations, throughout the State, on Sunday, August fifth, of that year. Dr. Neubert, of Belleville, delivered the oration of the day.

The subject of a permanent grade for the streets of the city now began to agitate the public mind. A grade reasonably permanent and answering the future prospective importance of the place, became at that early day a pressing want on the part of those, especially, who contemplated the erection of solid and enduring buildings. About the same time the extension of Main street from Broadway to Missouri avenue, was publicly advocated.

The necessity of another avenue besides the tolled dike, a really free road from the east side of Cahokia creek to the river front, became apparent in like manner. The cost of the latter, estimated at about thirty thousand dollars, was the obstacle in the way of its immediate undertaking by the city. Such a sum at that time for a single improvement was out of question.

Reverend F. H. Zabel, pastor of St. Patrick's church, commenced the erection, as a residence, of the splendid edifice upon the church block on Illinois avenue, at the corner of Seventh street. Soon after its completion he converted it into St. Aloysius College. Since then it has been converted into a female academy, conducted by the first colony of the Ursuline sisters in the city.

Hugo Feigenbutz and William Albrecht, in the fall of 1866, established the first foundry and machine shop in the city—on the northwest side of Collinsville avenue, about opposite Pennsylvania avenue, and called it the "East St. Louis Novelty Works." They started out with a large order for railroad dump cars, and prosperity seemed to await the enterprise, when, unfortunately to both owners and the community, the establishment burnt to the ground and thereby bankrupted the owners.

As an initiative step to the cause way, at a later time constructed on line of Christy avenue from Cahokia creek to Front street, Mayor Bowman, in July 1866, as a private enterprise, undertook the construction of a bridge across Cahokia creek at the foot of Missouri avenue, and for the purpose collected individual subscriptions sufficient to contract for its building.

Work upon it commenced on 26th September 1866. It was completed in February 1867.

The first sewer drainage was attempted in September 1866, by means of an eighteen inch iron pipe, laid in the Third Ward, on the line of Mullikin street, from Second street to low water mark in the river. It has been and yet is of immense service, as a drain for quite a large neighborhood, ever since. In October 1866, the City Council ordered a sidewalk to be built on both sides of Dike avenue, from the creek to Front street, but the objections of Wiggins'

Ferry Company, as owners of the adjacent land, succeeded in procuring a delay of action thereon, until the summer of 1867, when, upon a compromise, the order was modified to a sidewalk on the south side of the dike only—the present walk. In the same month of October, the City Council directed the opening of Second street of the First Ward, to Broadway, and the extension of Main street to Missouri avenue, but were immediately restrained by temporary injunction, on complaint of Louisiana St. John. The injunction was afterward dissolved and the streets were opened as they are open now.

Quite a large number of plank sidewalks were ordered and built along the more prominent thoroughfares, as on Collinsville avenue, from Broadway to the city limits, etc. Their usefulness was quickly and thoroughly appreciated, and as a consequence, petitions for more walks on other streets were regularly received and favorably acted upon at every succeeding meeting of the City Council.

East St. Louis was then entering upon the most prosperous of its times. The grading and macadamizing of the carriage-way on Missouri avenue, from the Belleville turnpike to the bridge over Cahokia creek, then in course of construction, was undertaken by the owners of property on the avenue, under the lead of Mayor Bowman, acting, however, not in an official capacity in the matter. A rivalry between Missouri avenue and Broadway for pre-eminence, stimulated more lively action than ever. The improvements upon Missouri avenue, the prospects of its early connection with Front street, by a free road, gave its settlement quite an advantage.

Colonel Vital Jarrot, originally of Cahokia, but at an early day prominently identified with incipient East St. Louis as already noted, once more made the city his home and the theatre of his activity.

The frost of sixty winters had bleached his hair, but not subdued or weakened the vitality of the spirit of enterprise, which in years past had made him the leader in every progressive movement in the ancient "Town of Illinois." As if a matter of course he at once resumed the position in the front ranks of the new leaders in the new city.

On the 17th November 1866, a largely-attended and earnest public meeting was held at Turner's Hall, presided over by Dr. Solon Stark, now of St. Louis, Missouri, to consider and recommend steps necessary to secure as permanently as possible, the American Bottom lands of St. Clair county, *and especially East St. Louis*, against danger from floods, and a system of drainage necessary to secure health to its inhabitants.

A committee composed of Vital Jarrot, John B. Bowman, Thomas Winstanley, Joseph Boismenue and Wm. G. Kase were appointed to report resolutions to that effect to an adjourned meeting.

At that meeting on the first of December 1866, they reported in favor of the American Bottom Board of Improvement, as an existing corporation, to under-take the proposed improvements, and recommended as a suitable plan the diversion of Cahokia creek into the Mississippi above East St. Louis near the town of Brooklyn, the building of a levee on both sides of its new channel to the river and a levee thence to the head of Bloody Island, which was an embankment itself, thence using Front street raised to a proper height to opposite the Cairo Short Line Railroad's embankment, connecting with it near the roundhouse, and thence another levee, following the old main shore of the river through Cahokia to the bluffs.

It suffices here to say that the question of diverting Cahokia creek away from the city remains yet to be done. The levees from Brooklyn to the head of Bloody Island, and from the foot of Front street to the Cairo Short Line roundhouse, have yet to be attempted. The only part of the above programme carried into execution is the elevation of Front street to above high water mark, and the construction of a levee from East St. Louis, along the old river bank, to and through Cahokia. The former was done under the direction of the city of East St. Louis, and the latter under the auspices of the American Bottom Board of Improvement, by the East St. Louis & Carondelet Railway.

The Legislature in session that year amended the city's charter in part, principally in relation to the exercise of the right of eminent domain. This was to block action upon the proposed extension and relocation of streets tending to develop that part of the city of which Missouri avenue was the battle-field, as it were. It also amended it so as to shorten the Mayor's term of office to one year, and prohibited that officer from becoming his own immediate successor.

A charter was granted for the organizing of the Broadway and Dike Horse Railway Company. An attempt at organization under it, a few years later, proved abortive, since the "East St. Louis Railway Company," with like powers, chartered in 1869, then occupied the field.

The Legislature also enacted a Metropolitan Police law, applicable to East St. Louis only. The police force in the city was to be under the sole and independent control of three Commissioners, appointed by the Governor of the State. These Commissioners were to have unlimited power in appointing policemen, officers and other agents and servants. They were to be answerable and accountable for their acts and expenditures *only* to the State Legislature, biennially in session. It directed also that the city should, upon annual requisitions, provide the funds by the Commissioners deemed necessary for their purposes. The Commissioners were to have power to issue evidences of indebtedness, *as of and binding the city*, bearing ten per cent. interest, wherewith to raise such funds as the city should refuse them. These certificates were to be salable at their discretion at public or private sale, and at any price.

The promulgation of the law *raised* an unprecedented storm of indignation. A bitter, and—after a long and tedious struggle—successful opposition, was at once organized.

The city council in power unanimously voted to resist the enforcement of this law, to the bitter end. A resolution was passed and widely published, warning everybody against the purchase of any such certificates, and against accepting employment under the Commissioners, with the idea of receiving compensation from the city.

Within a month after this, the annual charter election took place. The issue was distinctly upon the question of unrelenting hostility to the imposition of this hated system of police.

The "Metropolitans," as the friends of that system were called, met with an inglorious defeat. The opposition candidates were elected with overwhelming majorities.

J. B. Lovingston was elected Mayor. Murphy and O'Connell continued to represent the First ward, Dennis Ryan and Thomas Hickey represented the Second, and John Eddy and Benedict Franz the Third ward.

In every succeeding year, till the final overthrow of the Metropolitan State Police in the summer of 1870, every charter election was conducted upon the same issue, and without a single failure.

In June 1870, the Supreme Court decided that though the Legislature had power to impose such a system of police upon any municipality in the State, it could not burden its cost upon a community which did not desire it, and had so unmistakably repudiated it as had the people of East St. Louis. The Court suggested that the Commissioners' power to exercise their functions was not invalid, but so far as the city of East St. Louis was concerned, they and their employees would have to work without compensation.

The bitterest feud, which for nearly four years had in a measure divided the people of the city, was thus determined, and for good.

Since then, as before 1867, the city government appoints, controls and pays its own police.

The East St. Louis Elevator and Warehouse Company was chartered in 1867, and at once organized and erected the first one of the two elevators now opposite Pratte street, extending out to and beyond low water mark of the Mississippi.

The question of bridging this river had grown in prominence since the development of the extensive system of railways centered in East St. Louis. In the winter, often for a month and even longer, the commerce of St. Louis was prostrated for want of means of communication, when ferry boats could no longer make headway against the moving masses of ice.

The St. Louis & Illinois Wire Suspension Bridge Company had been chartered in 1849. Its bridge was to cross near Carr street, and terminate on the Illinois side near Pappstown, over-spanning almost the entire territory of present East St. Louis.

Nothing became of the scheme.

John How, James H. Lucas, John O'Fallon, Andrew Christy and others of St. Louis, and Colonel Morrison, Vital Jarrot, Joseph Gillespie, and John M. Palmer and others of Illinois, by the Illinois Legislature, had been incorporated in 1855 as the St. Louis & Illinois Bridge Company, to build a bridge at or near the city of St. Louis across the Mississippi for common travel and railroad cars. The lowest part of the bridge was to be eighty-six feet above the greatest height reached by that river in 1844, equal to one hundred and twenty-seven feet above low water mark.

EAST ST. LOUIS.

In 1857 the charter was amended so as to permit the lowest part of the bridge to be one hundred feet above low water mark; yet the project was premature or otherwise impracticable, for this bridge too was not built.

In 1864, another St. Louis and Illinois Bridge Company was organized in St. Louis, under the laws of Missouri. By a special act of the Illinois Legislature of 1865, the Missouri Company was also recognized and organized as an Illinois corporation, but was restricted in locating the east end of the bridge to either one hundred feet north or that distance south of Dike avenue. No more than a survey and the filing of the plat of the center line of the proposed bridge in the recorder's office at Belleville, in St. Clair county, Illinois, was the visible result of this charter until 1867.

In the latter year, Joseph Gillespie, John M. Palmer, Wm. R. Morrison, T. B. Blackstone, L. B. Parsons, R. P. Tansey, Levi Davis, L. B. Boomer and a few others were incorporated by an Illinois charter as "The Illinois & St. Louis Bridge Company," *with the exclusive right for twenty-five years* to construct and maintain a toll bridge from any point on the Mississippi opposite St. Louis to the western line of the State. The Company was to commence construction within two years; was to expend not less than $50,000 the first year, and was to finish the bridge in five years or forfeit its charter. By a later general law the time for its completion was extended.

Chicago enterprise stimulated the new company. L. B. Boomer, the famous American bridge builder, president of the American Bridge Company of Chicago, the founder of Bridgeport, a flourishing suburb of that city, principally inhabited by artisans, mechanics and laborers of that company — was put at the head of the scheme. A corporation of like name was organized under the laws of Missouri, and both were consolidated and work commenced at once. The Boomer Bridge was located at the foot of Missouri avenue on the East St. Louis side, to a point midway between Carr and Wash streets in St. Louis. The substructure was to be of pneumatic piles, and the "post-truss" its superstructure. The St. Louis & Illinois Bridge Company now too began operations at the levee upon the Missouri side, where the west pier of the Eads bridge now is. The Boomer Bridge Company, on the strength of its exclusive privilege, enjoined the St. Louis & Illinois Bridge Company from building in Illinois. This war between both at last ended in their consolidation; in the abandonment of the Boomer project and the adoption of Eads' plan of the magnificent structure which now connects St. Louis with its much promising Illinois suburb, the subject of this sketch, East St. Louis.

The consolidation of the two companies took place on the 5th March 1868. The name of the Illinois corporation was retained.

A failure to procure a special charter for the purpose in 1867, induced the organization in January 1868, under the general laws, of the "East St. Louis Mutual House Building Company." Wm. B. Vermillion was its president, Francis Wittram its treasurer, and Wm. O'Neill its secretary.

However, before active operations were undertaken, the Legislature in 1869 incorporated the "Franklin House Building Company." The "Franklin" succeeded and absorbed the "Mutual," and still exists, doing much good.

In the summer of 1868, the long-projected and expected roadway connecting Christy avenue with Missouri avenue across the slough, in effect extending Missouri avenue in a straight line to Front street, and to the upper ferry landing, was successfully carried out under the direction of J. B. Bowman, who in the spring of that year had succeeded J. B. Lovingston as Mayor.

The cost of this roadway, known as Bowman's dike, like that of the bridge at the foot of Missouri avenue, was totally defrayed by individual contributors.

In the fall of 1868, the East St. Louis Bank removed from its original location on Broadway to its own quarters, at the corner of Collinsville and Missouri avenue, the lot whereon its bank building was erected having been donated for the purpose by Mrs. Rebecca W. Sire, of St. Louis.

Since November 1867, the "East St. Louis Library Association," a private institution, originally endowed by individual contributions, filled a void, which began to be felt, but which never, until the establishment of the City Public Library and Reading Room, in July 1872, was fully satisfied. The latter enjoys an enviable reputation for its selections and the manner in which it is made available to the public. The most prominent of the journals of every State and Territory in the Union, as part of its extensive collection of current literature, are kept on file in the public reading room attached to the Library. It enjoys the fostering care of the municipal authorities, and justly is a pride to every East St. Louisian.

In the fall of 1868, the Center Market building was contracted for, and completed during the following spring and summer. Its splendid hall is now divided between the Library and the Court of Record.

In 1869, the Mississippi rose nearly as high as it had been in 1862. The embankments which would have been a protection in 1862 but for the gap in that of the Ohio & Mississippi railway, on this occasion proved ample protection. The damages were not serious, except such as resulted from siepage, and the washing away of the Bowman dike. The basement of the East St. Louis Bank, and other like localities, were submerged, but no street was under water; it was simply a gentle reminder, as it were, to be about providing against the recurrence of a still higher flood and incalculable damages. It was the premonitor to the "high grade" movement, which on the 14th of February was inaugurated, at the first public meeting held in the Market House Hall. Ex-Mayor Bowman submitted the proposition that the time had arrived, when not only necessity existed, but that the city was now large and rich enough in resources, without further delay, to commence public works tending to secure its inhabitants from further floods, and their calamitous consequences upon health, security and comfort, and no less so the continuity of the community's then prospering condition.

The hall was crowded to its utmost capacity; well it might have been, the subject for discussion was generally felt paramount to every interest any one at all interested in East St. Louis could have.

Mr. Bowman explained his ideas to the effect that the raising of the streets and the building of sewers under them emptying into the Mississippi near the southern end of the city would be all that was necessary, and that this could be accomplished according to estimates of undoubted experts at an expense of about two millions; that the city having comparatively no debt then outstanding, might appropriate the first proceeds of the regular debt to a commencement of the work, and prosecute the same from year to year as the means of the city would allow; that the adoption of such a plan, the commencement of work and the prosecution of it, would be a guarantee as nothing else could be, to the outside world. The vast aggregate of natural and artificial advantages, congregated at East St. Louis should no longer be held captive in the clutches of the demon of floods. He submitted further that to start a movement properly, resolutions addressed to the city council recommending action to the purpose be adopted by this meeting.

Strange to say, the owners of a vast amount of unimproved lands in and near the city, the Connecticut Land Company, just then incorporated under the Connecticut charter, became by purchase the owners of the lands originally belonging to Page & Bacon, bitterly opposed the project by their attorneys, who denounced it as a scheme on the part of contractors and speculators; that to pay for the work would entail taxes, unbearable to the poorer people; that the speculators anticipated the sale of the poor man's little house and home for these taxes as a consequence. Demagoguery defeated for the time being the project for which the meeting had been called, not, however, without convincing quite a number that the road of East St. Louis to its destiny, which sooner or later it will reach, is only on streets elevated above endangering floods.

During the year 1870, large public improvements were set on foot, as the rebuilding of the Bowman and the construction of the Vaughan dikes. Work upon them was not finished until 1876.

In March 1871, an ordinance was passed establishing the Fourth ward. The Second ward being too large, the Fourth was formed of all that territory northeast of Illinois avenue.

On December 7, 1871, the East St. Louis Railway Company first commenced the running of its cars upon our streets. Its line of rail then was from the East St. Louis Bank, facing on Missouri avenue, to the terminus of Christy avenue, over and along that street. Since then, the first road that the company laid has been partly abandoned, its route now being from a point near the St. Louis National Stock Yards, on St. Clair avenue, to Collinsville avenue andd own that thoroughfare to Missouri avenue, down Missouri avenue to Third street, along Third street to Dike avenue, and down Dike avenue to opposite the eastern approach of the Eads bridge.

On the 8th of June 1872, the incumbent Mayor, Dennis Ryan, died, and was buried with imposing ceremonies.

In the same year, McCormick, Adams & Armington erected a second grain elevator, adjacent to Front street and the Chicago & Alton Railroad Company's depot—"The Advance Elevator."

In December 1872, East St. Louis Fire Company No. 1, organized, and is in existence ever since, doing valuable service with limited means at its command. The city furnished the company with one of the largest sized "Babcock's," on wheels. Its first officers were: William O'Neill, president; Charles Hauss, vice-president; Benedict Franz, captain; J. W. Kirk, secretary; J. V. Tefft, treasurer.

In 1872, East St. Louis for the first time had the opportunity of sending one of its citizens to the Legislature, as one of its members—the Honorable L. H. Hite. Principally through his indefatigable exertions, a bill was passed by that body, at its special session in the winter of 1874, authorizing the establishment ot "Courts of Record" in cities of the size of East St. Louis. Such a court was needed ever since the more rapid improvement of the city; without such, parties litigant in the city were forced to await their turn at the Circuit Court in Belleville, at a great loss of time and money. The court was promptly established in the summer of 1874, and the Honorable Daniel McGowan elected first Judge. His term of office is four years. It holds three terms per annum—one in March, June, and November respectively. Its jurisdiction is co-extensive with that of Circuit Courts, excepting cases of murder and treason.

In the same year, under a special ordinance, Front street, opposite the Chicago & Alton Railroad Company's depot, to Dike avenue, was filled to high grade, (higher than the flood of 1844), and macadamized full width.

In 1871, the subject of constructing great national stock yards on this side of the river was projected by some public-spirited and foreseeing men, and the agitation in favor of the project was pursued to a successful termination, which was brought about by a company made of Eastern and Western capitalists, who proceeded at once to purchase the required ground, six hundred and fifty acres, and thereupon make the most ample and substantial improvements, the whole of which were completed and opened to the public in 1873. This marked a new era in the growth of the city, as subsequent improvements fully demonstrate. These yards are well known to be the most extensive establishment of the kind in the country; they are well situated, north of the city, and have an inexhaustive supply of good water.

Extensive slaughtering and packing buildings form a part of the improvements, and are constantly kept in operation, doing an immense business. A banking house and a fine hotel are also connected with the stock yards, which affords ample accommodation for all who go there to transact business. These yards are also well connected with all the railroads belonging to the great system that converges at the great Illinois and St. Louis bridge; and thus connected, no other yards can draw trade so easily from all parts of the country.

On the 21st of November 1873, the last prize-fight which the St. Louis sporting circles attempted to have come off on Illinois soil, that of Hogan against Allen, came to an inglorious end in East St. Louis. The steamer Continental, with a motley and desperate cargo, loaded down to its guards, was chartered to carry the champions of the ring and their admirers to the Illinois shore above East St. Louis, but, owing to a very high wind and the unmanageable condition caused by its overburdened load, was driven to the East St. Louis levee, above the bridge. The greatest efforts of the crew to prevent its touching the shore were unavailing. In the meanwhile, the boat had been watched from the Illinois side by Mayor Bowman, who was ready with a tug, aided by authority from the Governor of Illinois, and the personal presence of Sheriff Cooper of Madison county, Sheriff Hughes of St. Clair county, Michael Walsh, City Marshal, and the entire police force under the lead of J. W. Renshaw, its chief, to follow the boat and to prevent its landing on the Illinois side, or to arrest the principals at least. When it became evident that the steamer could not avoid touching the shore at East St. Louis, quite a number hastened to where it struck. Mayor Bowman and Michael Walsh were the first to board the boat, and there effected the breaking up of the proposed fight by driving the two gladiators singly in skiffs to the Missouri shore. Jack Looney, the stake-holder, had just time to bundle up the piles of money on the cabin table, and to pass it off in the crowd, but not to escape arrest. Quite a number of pugilists, including the captain and mate of the boat, were apprehended, and brought before a Justice in East St. Louis, and bound over to await an indictment before the grand jury.

On the fourth of July 1874, the highway part of the great Eads' bridge was given over to the public for uninterrupted use. It is the opinion of many citizens, that had the vast crowds which from and after that date daily poured over it on the west side, had found the city government of East St. Louis busily at work (if no more than their means allowed) in raising the city streets to above flood height, the advantages of the opening of this highway and of its permanent character, would not have altogether redounded to the benefit of municipal St. Louis alone. The bad effects of it upon the most busy portion of East St. Louis did not become visible as a fact until the Union Railway & Transit Company, as agents of the Illinois & St. Louis Bridge Company, attached its locomotives at East St. Louis to almost every train that came in, to take it to the Union Depot in the other side of the river.

On the third of December 1874, the City Council passed an ordinance fixing the grades of all highways in the city, not now higher than that, upon a grade of eight feet above the city directrix (the plane of the directrix of East St. Louis and that of St. Louis is the same) at street crossings rising to the middle of blocks not exceeding one foot per hundred. By this ordinance, directions were given for the construction of principal and side sewers on the streets, to be built co-temporaneous or in advance of the filling of the street overhead.

All the unexhausted credit of the city (the difference between its existing debt and five per cent. of the aggregate of the assessed value of the city) was to furnish the means for a commencement, and only the growth of the credit of the city was from year to year to authorize the prosecution of the work. The work was to be prosecuted under plans and specifications furnished on request by the most eminent engineers Henry Flad and Thomas Whitman, of St. Louis. So the ordinance provides. Under it a main sewer of brick is to be built from the then northeastern boundary of the city, St. Clair avenue, on Collinsville avenue to Broadway, and on Broadway to Main street, and on Main street and in line of its straight extension to the Mississippi river. Over this sewer the street was to be raised with sidewalks on each side, with convenient crossings at street intersections, at an estimated cost of one hundred and twenty thousand dollars.

The passage of this ordinance was accompanied with much excitement and hot debate on the part of the public attending the Council meeting, and the interest manifested by the Council. Mayor Bowman was in the chair. Upon a final call of the ayes and noes on the ordinance, eight members constituting the Council, and a majority being requisite to pass it, the following voted in favor of its passage: Anson Gustin, John Benner, John Niemes, John Doyle, and John V. Tefft.

As Mayor Bowman very pertinently remarked, in delivering an address at the Centennial celebration at East St. Louis, this year, that in times to come, when East St. Louis shall, as it will be, raised above the dangers of all floods, and teemed with business, and be the healthy and comfortable home of hundreds of thousands, instead of ten or fifteen thousand as now, the records of the city will point out the names of these Councilmen, as those who were to be honored as the drawers of the declaration of independence of East St. Louis from the water foe and his accompanying evils, as much as we to-day (fourth of July 1876,) revere the memory of the signers of that other declaration signed to-day one hundred years ago in Philadelphia, which secured to this country the freest government on the globe. Though the road seemed now to be clear to the commencement of this all-important improvement—for bids had been invited through the principal St. Louis daily papers, and had been received in response, for the entire work, at a price *within* the estimate—yet the short-sighted friends (?) of East St. Louis, low-graders, so called, once more proved triumphant. They obtained an injunction out of the Circuit Court at Belleville, inhibiting the Council from letting the work. During the fight for the dissolution of this injunction, the once available, unused city's credit, became less from time to time, until now it is but $30,000 to reach the constitutional limit of five per cent. on the aggregate of taxable property, by drafts against it to pay for other and minor, but seemingly necessary, public improvements.

But the day will be, when injunctions will no longer avail to arrest the growth of the city, upon that basis upon which alone it can stand and grow.

On the 12th of November 1874, the city was first lighted with illuminating coal gas of "The East St. Louis Gas Light and Coke Company," that Company's first product. The city now has 303 public lamps, well distributed upon its streets.

In April 1875, an attempt was made to incorporate, under the general laws, the territory, about two miles deep, bordering the city upon the north-east and south. Under the law it was to be submitted to a vote of the inhabitants of that territory. Uncertain of its result, the City Council of East St. Louis, before the day of the election, under its charter powers once before mentioned, annexed the most populated portion of the embryo city—Illinois City—to and thereof, and made it a part of East St. Louis, which action has since been ratified by a decision of the Supreme Court of this State.

In September 1875, the Missouri Car and Foundry Company leased the abandoned extensive machine shops of the Ohio and Mississippi Railway Company in the Fourth ward, and removed their entire establishment from St. Louis, on account of the cheapness of coal, which they contract for at East St. Louis at their furnace doors, from six to seven cents per bushel: an item of advantage which will adhere to East St. Louis as long as the Mississippi divides both shores.

Other establishments, as the St. Louis Bolt and Iron Company, for the same reason located in East St. Louis.

In September 1875, the corner stone of the magnificent brick block belonging to Louis Wies, at the southeast corner of Broadway and Fourth street, now occupied by the Workingmen's Banking Company, was laid, amid a large concourse of people, attracted by a fact, that the owner had determined to make it conform to the high grade established in December 1874. And it was the first structure so to be built, and built.

Thus the city, in the absence of means to commence the high-grade movement with sufficient momentum to insure its completion, is quietly awaiting the adjudication of pending injunctions. The basis of the new future (they well understand), lies within the hands of the people and their municipal representatives.

In the ratio in which the city will be raised out of the water-danger, and health secured by sewerage, so East St. Louis will bound up to that normal condition which is its evident destiny if its affairs are led by intelligent and progressive ideas.

Who will say that when St. Louis shall count its inhabitants a million or more, one-fourth of that number, then will not populate the city on the east shore as an integral part of it?

Can the future great city itself attain its apex, without making tributary to its manufacturing and commercial interests, both shores of the Mississippi river? Such a use of the shore and development of this side of the river guarantees a brighter future to East St. Louis than its most sanguine friends dare imagine.

THE RAILROADS

Terminating, by their charters, in East St. Louis, are as follows:

I.—THE CHICAGO AND ALTON RAILROAD COMPANY.—The main line extends by way of Alton, Carlinville, Springfield and Bloomington to Joliet, with branches from Dwight to Macon, and from Roodhouse to opposite Louisiana, Mo. Total, three hundred and sixty miles.

The parent road was the "Alton & Sangamon Railroad Company," chartered in 1847, from Alton to Springfield.

In 1852 the name was changed to the "Chicago & Mississippi Railroad Company," with authority to extend to Bloomington and through Joliet to Chicago, provided that it make no connection with any eastern road through Indiana, except *in or through* Chicago, and to arrange for connection between Alton and St. Louis.

In 1855, as the "Chicago, Alton & St. Louis Railroad Company," it was authorized, jointly with the "Terre Haute & Alton Railroad Company," from Alton to run upon the latter's extension to Wood river, and thence jointly with it over the Alton extension of the "Belleville & Illinoistown Railroad Company," run to East St. Louis.

Under foreclosure of mortgages in 1857, and a special Act of that year, the company's property passed to the "Alton, Chicago & St. Louis Railroad Company," a new corporation.

In 1861, "The Chicago & Alton Railroad Company" was chartered to acquire and use the property and franchises of the "Alton & Sangamon Railroad Company," "Chicago & Mississippi Railroad Company," "Chicago, Alton & St. Louis Railroad Company," and to renew arrangements for the use of the "Chicago & Joliet Railroad Company," etc.

In 1859 the "Alton & St. Louis Railroad Company" was organized, with power to purchase of the "Sangamon & Northwestern Railroad Company," its branch then constructing between Alton and East St. Louis. A remnant of an abandoned embankment of the latter road is still visible on the north side of the slough, north of Bloody Island. This last organized company constructed a new track from Alton to Front street, in East St Louis, and in 1861 became consolidated with the "Chicago & Alton Railroad." The latter company also operates under leases and over the same track, from Alton south to East St. Louis, the trains of: 1st, the St. Louis, Jacksonville & Chicago Railroad," 150 miles in length.

This road was first chartered as the "Jacksonville & Carrollton Railroad Company," in 1851; to run from Jacksonville by way of Manchester, Whitehall, Carrollton, and Jerseyville to Alton.

In 1857 its name was changed to "Jacksonville, Alton & St. Louis Railroad Company," and authorized to consolidate with any railroad running from Alton to East St. Louis.

In 1863, it was consolidated with the "Ionica and Petersburgh Railroad Company," and given power to extend through Ottawa to Chicago, under the name of the "St. Louis, Jacksonville & Chicago Railroad Company." It was however only extended to Bloomington.

Second. The "Quincy, Alton & St. Louis Railroad Company," chartered in 1867, to extend from Quincy via Alton to East St. Louis.

It was built from Quincy down the east bank of the Mississippi to opposite Louisiana, Missouri, a distance of forty-two miles, and there connects with the branch of the main line of the Chicago & Alton Railroad Company to Roodhouse.

The Chicago & Alton Railroad Company also holds under a perpetual lease the thirty-eight miles of road from Joliet to Chicago, of the Chicago and Joliet Railroad Company.

This makes a total of main track tributary to East St. Louis over this one line equal to five hundred and ninety miles.

II.—THE INDIANAPOLIS & ST. LOUIS RAILROAD COMPANY.—This is an Indiana corporation owning only seventy-two miles of road in Indiana, from Indianapolis to Terre Haute. It holds under a perpetual lease the old main line of the St. Louis, Alton & Terre Haute Railroad Company, from Terre Haute to East St. Louis, one hundred and eighty-nine miles in length. Total length of its line, two hundred and sixty-one miles.

III.—THE TOLEDO, WABASH & WESTERN RAILWAY COMPANY.—This company was chartered in Ohio and Indiana, and by consolidation and purchase acquired the property and franchises of the "Great Western Railway Company," the "Quincy & Toledo Railway Company," the "Illinois & Southern Iowa Railroad Company," and the "Decatur & East St. Louis Railroad Company."

Under the charter of the latter granted in 1867, it enters East St. Louis; all together they constitute the principal company's main lines:

Thereof are in Ohio	75	miles.
In Indiana	166	"
In Illinois	365	"
Total	606	"

Under leases it also operates lines to the following points:

To Pekin, Illinois	67	miles.
To Pittsfield, Illinois, and Hannibal, Missouri	52	"
From Hannibal to Moberly, Missouri	70	"
To Lafayette, Indiana, two branches	117	"
From Camp Point to Quincy, Illinois	22	"
Total of leased lines	328	"

The aggregate of main tracks of this road owned and leased tributary to East St. Louis, is nine hundred and thirty-four miles.

IV.—THE ROCKFORD, ROCK ISLAND & ST. LOUIS RAILROAD COMPANY.— Chartered in 1865, to build and operate a railroad from Rockford in Winnebago county, by way of Sterling in Whiteside county, to Rock Island, and thence to East St. Louis. Accordingly it is two hundred and ninety-nine miles in length from Rock Island to Alton Junction. There it connects with the "Indianapolis & St. Louis Railroad," and over its track for a distance of twenty and a half miles enters East St. Louis. Thus this road brings two hundred and ninety-nine miles of additional track to East St. Louis.

V.—The St. Louis, Vandalia & Terre Haute Railroad Company.—The "Vandalia Line," though of recent construction, is one of the first lines *projected* across the State of Illinois.

Terre Haute was the focus, on the Indiana line, of Eastern railroads for a long time. Alton was to have a corresponding position upon the western borders of Illinois.

Repeated efforts from 1849 to 1854, to obtain a charter for a railroad direct from Terre Haute to St. Louis, avoiding the long circuit by Alton, fell under the ban of the "Alton Policy," which then had a strong hold upon the Legislature.

In 1852, John Brough, later—during the civil war—Governor of Ohio, took hold of the scheme, and, despite failure in attempts for a special charter, organized the "Mississippi & Atlantic Railroad Company," for a line of road as near an air line as possible between Terre Haute and the Town of Illinois.

In 1854, Brough's indomitable determination wrenched from the Legislature a special act of recognition and approval of his enterprise.

A charter was granted him that year. The route was at once surveyed, passsing almost foot for foot over the route now occupied by the Vandalia line. The right of way for a large part of the route, was purchased and the work of grading and bridging let—and progressing. Solid rock abutments for a proposed bridge over Cantine creek at Caseyville, still attest the enterprise of that day and the progress made.

The forecasting shadows of the money crisis of 1857 stopped the undertaking, and the combined intrigues of several rival roads for the time defeated the project altogether. Its means failed and work was stopped. In 1859, an Act was passed authorizing the Company to wind up business and to sell its property.

After the close of the war, J. F. Alexander, of Greenville, Illinois, on the line of the road, subsequently president of the new Company, and recently deceased whilst acting receiver for the St. Louis & Southeastern Railway Company, applied for a new charter, for the most feasible and most promising railroad in the State. He succeeded.

Thus in 1865, the St. Louis, Vandalia & Terre Haute Railroad Company was called into existence. In 1867 this charter was amended and construction commenced. It was completed in July 1870; and was at once leased to the Terre Haute & Indianapolis Railroad Company, of Indiana. This company operates its own road from Indianapolis to Terre Haute, with a few branches into the block coal region of Indiana, over a distance of ninety-seven miles altogether. The leased track of the St. Louis, Vandalia & Terre Haute Company is one hundred and fifty-eight miles in length. This gives to the Vandalia Line a continuous stretch of main track from East St. Louis of two hundred and fifty-five miles.

The "Vandalia Line" combination has furthermore, a standing arrangement by which the "Illinois Central Company" runs daily two passenger trains between Chicago and East St. Louis, over the track of the "Vandalia Line" from Effingham; hence the distance over the "Illinois Central," between the last named city and Chicago, 199 miles, might well be added to the aggregate of miles of track branching out or centering at East St. Louis.

VI.—THE OHIO & MISSISSIPPI RAILWAY COMPANY.—In 1851 a charter was granted for the organization of the Ohio & Mississippi Railroad Company, with power to build a railroad from Illinoistown to the State line, near Vincennes. Similar charters, for like companies, were granted the same year by the Legislatures of Indiana and Ohio, to connect Cincinnati with St. Louis by way of Vincennes.

Without much delay, the road was constructed during the years 1852, 1853 and 1854. In contradistinction to all other roads, it adopted the broad gauge of six feet—same as the Atlantic & Great Western and New York & Erie railways, with which together it was intended to make up, and did so constitute, a uniform and continuous line from New York to East St. Louis.

In 1854, the company was authorized to change its terminus from Illinoistown to Deep Water, on the west shore of Bloody Island, and accordingly removed thither the following year, where its coal depot still is.

In 1861, the present corporation, the OHIO & MISSISSIPPI RAILWAY COMPANY, were chartered with power to purchase and use the properties and franchises of the Ohio & Mississippi Railroad Company, upon a sale thereof under a decree of court — then imminent.

The company also organized a branch road from North Vernon to Jeffersonville, in Indiana, giving it direct connection with Louisville, Kentucky. In 1875, it purchased the road of the Springfield & Illinois Southeastern Railway Company, which extends from Shawneetown, on the Ohio, via Flora, on the main line, through Springfield, the capital of Illinois, to Beardstown on the Illinois river. The total length of main track operated by the company therefore is:

From St. Louis to Cincinnati..340 miles.
Louisville Branch... 53   "
From Shawneetown to Beardstown.......................................226   "
                                                                        ———
                   Total.............................619 miles.

VI.—THE ST. LOUIS AND SOUTH EASTERN RAILWAY COMPANY (Consolidated).

It was chartered in 1869, to run from East St. Louis, by way of Ashley on the "Illinois Central Railroad," by Mount Vernon, the seat of the Southern Grand Division of the State Supreme Court, through McLeansboro, to Shawneetown, with a branch from McLeansboro to Evansville, Indiana. It is the latest of all *specially* chartered railroads in the State.

The main line is 142 miles long; the Evansville branch adds 62 miles, making a total of 204 miles of main track out of East St. Louis.

At Mt. Vernon it is to connect with the "New Albany & St. Louis Air Line Railroad Company." The latter's road is partially constructed. The panic in 1873 delayed and stopped it. When the latter shall be finished, both together offer the shortest route by many miles between Louisville, Kentucky, and East St. Louis.

By a consolidation with Kentucky and Tennessee lines, the St. Louis & Southeastern, by way of Evansville and Madisonville, Kentucky, is also a through route to Nashville, the capital of Tennessee. Its East St. Louis terminus is adjacent to the east end of the great bridge, hence more advantageously located than any other.

VII.—THE ST. LOUIS, ALTON & TERRE HAUTE RAILROAD COMPANY dates back to 1851. Then it was chartered as the "Terre Haute & Alton Railroad Company," for a road from Terre Haute, by way of Paris, in Edgar county, Charleston, in Coles county, Shelbyville, in Shelby county, Hillsboro, in Montgomery county, Bunker Hill, in Macoupin county, to Alton, with power to extend from Terre Haute eastward, through Indiana. Whatever its eastern connections, Alton was *to be* its western terminus.

When it was discovered that the routes of trade and commerce were about as ungovernable by human hands as the elements, and when trade and commerce *would not* concentrate at Alton, but gravitated further down the river, to the more natural and more adapted center at St. Louis, Alton gracefully yielded, and in 1853, the "Terre Haute & Alton Railroad Company" procured an amendment to its charter, authorizing it to extend its tracks from Alton south to Wood river, there to meet the "Alton Extension" of the "Belleville & Illinoistown Railroad Company," projecting north from Illinoistown. The Company was also authorized to contract for the use of that "Alton Extension," over which to reach East St. Louis. It availed itself of this without delay—aye, found this southern extension so valuable that soon after it purchased the entire road and franchises of the "Belleville & Illinoistown Railroad Company," and thereafter was known as the "Terre Haute, Alton & St. Louis Railroad Company." Alton thereby became simply a way station.

In 1861, the old company being bankrupt and about to be sold out under a decree of foreclosure, the present "St. Louis, Alton & Terre Haute Railroad Company" was chartered and organized, and in 1862 became the purchaser, owner and operator of its roads and appendages. The road from East St. Louis to Terre Haute was recognized as main line, and that from East St. Louis to Belleville as "Belleville Branch."

Under a perpetual lease from the "Belleville & Southern Illinois Railroad Company," made in 1866, it also operates the road of the latter company from Belleville to Du Quoin, on the Illinois Central, and thus using the latter's road, thence to Cairo between that city and East St. Louis, is known as the "Cairo Short Line."

Its main line was and is leased to the Indianapolis & St. Louis Railroad Company, as already stated.

Its "Belleville Branch" is fourteen miles long; from Belleville to Du Quoin, there are fifty-seven miles of track, and from Du Quoin to Cairo the distance is seventy-six miles, hence the aggregate of track entering East St. Louis over the Cairo Short Line, is one hundred and forty-seven miles.

The "Belleville & Illinoistown Railroad Company," absorbed by the St. Louis & Terre Haute Railroad Company, was chartered in 1852, under circumstances referred to in the sketches of the Ohio & Mississippi Railway Company, and the Chicago & Alton Railroad Company.

Colonel Don Morrison was the special champion of the road, and to his energy mostly is due its speedy completion.

It was he that perceived the folly of the Alton people, and tendered relief by extending the Belleville Railroad along up the Mississippi to Wood river, where it was met by both the Terre Haute & Alton, and the Chicago & Alton Railroad Companies, in 1856.

The Belleville & Southern Illinois Railroad Company was chartered in 1857, to build from Belleville by way of Pinckneyville to the Illinois Central Railroad. Nothing was done.

In 1865 it was authorized to extend its road from Belleville to the Mississippi. Now it threatened rivalry and competition to the old Belleville Railroad, hence its lease to the St. Louis, Alton & Terre Haute Railroad Company the following year. The road, however, was not completed till about 1870.

A very *special provision* in this company's charter is worthy of reproduction. It undoubtedly has quite an interesting, but to the writer, unknown history. It reads as follows:

Every conductor, baggagemaster, engineer, brakesman or other servant of said corporation, employed in a passenger train, or at a station for passengers, shall wear upon his hat or cap a badge, which shall indicate his office, the initial or style of the corporation. No conductor or collector, without such badge, shall demand, or be entitled to receive from any passenger any fare, toll or ticket, or exercise any of the powers of his office: and no other of said officers or servants, without such badge, shall have any authority to meddle or interfere with any passenger, his baggage or property, in forming passenger trains. Baggage or freight, or merchandise, or lumber cars, shall not be placed in the rear of passenger cars; and if they, or any of them, shall be so placed, and any accident shall happen to life or limb, the officer or agent who so directed or knowingly suffered such arrangement, and the conductor or engineer of the train, shall each and all be held guilty of a misdemeanor, and shall be punished accordingly. The certificate of the secretary of said company, under the corporate seal thereof, shall be received in all courts of justice, and elsewhere, as evidence of the regular organization of said company under its charter, and of any act or order of the board of directors of said company.

VIII.—THE CAIRO AND ST. LOUIS RAILROAD COMPANY was chartered in 1865. Inadvertently it stimulated the earlier completion of the "Cairo Short Line," by DuQuoin and Belleville, and it, in turn, having opened direct communication between Cairo and East St. Louis, retardingly reflected upon the promoters of this company. The Hon. William R. Morrison, of Monroe county and S. Staats Taylor, of Cairo, were the leading and pushing members of the organization.

At last, in 1872, the road was built as a "narrow gauge road"—three feet wide track—by way of Columbia and Waterloo, in Monroe county, and by Murphysboro in Jackson county, to Cairo. From near East Carondelet it runs upon the right of way of the "East St. Louis & Carondelet Railway" to East St. Louis.

The valuable qualities of the Big Muddy coal fields, only found in the State upon the line of this road, secures to it an incontestable, certain patronage. Considering the many embarrassments and difficulties it has until recently encountered, its management has been an exceeding able one.

It will not be fully developed until it either connects with more lines of the same gauge, or widens its own to the regular standard of other roads—four feet, eight and a half inches. The entire length of its main track is one hundred and fifty miles.

IX.—THE EAST ST. LOUIS & CARONDELET RAILWAY was chartered in 1857, by the name of "American Bottom Lime, Marble & Coal Company," as a local railroad company, not to extend out of the county of St. Clair. It was intended chiefly to be instrumental in bringing to market the vast deposit of lime and other building stone as well as coal, with which the bluffs of the county abound.

In 1870 the Company, having been organized some years before, at last began active operations. It had the extensive levee constructed, now extending along the old main shore from the Cairo Short Line round-house in East St. Louis to East Carondelet, and thereupon located its railroad to a distance of about two miles below Cahokia, then deflecting to the famous *Falling Spring*, where valuable quarries were at once opened, and have been worked ever since. In the spring of 1873, the name was changed to the present title. The establishment of the railroad ferry by the "Atlantic & Pacific Railroad" upon the Mississippi, at the east terminus of their cut-off road from Kirkwood to Carondelet, near the "Vulcan Iron Works," induced the Company to extend a branch road upon the extended levee to opposite that ferry on the Illinois shore, at a point which since then became the flourishing village of East Carondelet.

By means of this cut-off road, this ferry and the East St. Louis & Carondelet Railway, an independent and competing connection is established between the Pacific Railroad, on the Missouri side of the river, and all railroads at East St. Louis. The Eads' bridge monopoly is thereby practically not dangerous. The East St. Louis & Carondelet Railway connects at East St. Louis, with every railroad there, and with the National Stock Yards, hence offers unusual facilities for intercommunication of other roads, at that point not directly connecting, or having no access to those yards. It is so made use of to a considerable extent. This road has also been the means of lowering the price of building stone in East St. Louis. Before its advent, such had to be brought either from Alton by cars, a distance of twenty-four miles, or by the more tedious method of boating from Carondelet.

Now, building rock is brought from the quarries at the Falling Spring, at a great reduction—which as East St. Louis improves and is being built up with permanent houses, will be more and more appreciated as a material advantage. In fact, large quantities of stone from these quarries are beginning to be distributed from East St. Louis, over roads running south and east, whose lines are bare of this commodity.

The entire length of main line and branch of the East St. Louis & Carondelet Railway, is nearly eleven and a half miles.

X.—THE ILLINOIS & ST. LOUIS RAILROAD AND COAL COMPANY.—We feel free to lay the origin of this corporation, as the oldest in the State as far back as 1831. In that year, Samuel C. Christy, John Messenger and Joseph Green, of St. Clair county, were by the Legislature appointed a commission to examine and to report upon the feasibility of a railroad from the bluffs, across the American bottom, to the Mississippi. Whether they ever reported is unknown, but the fact that in 1836, Vital Jarrot, of Illinoistown, the brother-in-law of this S. C. Christy, associated with ex-Governor John Reynolds and others, as already stated, actually built such a railroad—the railroad now operated by the company whose name heads this sketch, and that John Messenger acted as their surveyors, in locating the route, seems to justify a connection of the building of the road with that appointment in 1831.

As said, the individual enterprise failed in 1839 and 1840. In 1841, the Legislature chartered the St. Clair Railroad Company, which absorbed by purchase the road of Jarrot and others, and operated it for a while under that name. After several fruitless other attempts to make the road pay, and after having been abandoned again for about five years, in 1863, John How and associates resurrected it. In 1865 it was given its present name, and the right to run a ferry to St. Louis. In 1870 it extended its road from the bluffs to near Belleville. Its entire length of main track is near sixteen miles.

XI.—UNION RAILWAY & TRANSIT COMPANY, was organized in East St. Louis in April 1874. A corporation of like name was organized in St. Louis, under the laws of Missouri. Both united act as the agents of the Illinois & St. Louis Bridge Company, in transferring, under its charter rights, railroad cars from the Illinois shore to the Union depot in St. Louis, and *vice versa*. The tracks on the bridge and approaches belong to the Bridge Company. Where these intersect in East St. Louis the tracks of other railroads, the Union Railway & Transportation Company has running arrangements, under which they are enabled to perform the duties required of them.

96

MUNICIPAL COUNCIL OF EAST ST. LOUIS SINCE ITS ORGANIZATION.

YEAR.	MAYOR.	COUNCILMEN.			
		First Ward.	Second Ward.	Third Ward.	Fourth Ward.
1865	John B. Bowman	Michael Murphy, John O'Connell	Henry Schall, James Hazen	John Trendley, John B. Lovingston	John Scullon, John V. Tefft
1866	John B. Bowman	John O'Connell, Michael Murphy	Thomas Hickey, Henry Schall	John B. Lovingston, John Trendley	John V. Tefft, John Scullon
1867	John B. Lovingston	Michael Murphy, John O'Connell	Dennis Ryan, Thomas Hickey	John Eddy, John B. Lovingston,†	John Scullon, John V. Tefft
1868	John B. Bowman	John O'Connell, Patrick Vaughan	Garrett Stack, Dennis Ryan	Patrick McCormack, John Eddy	John V. Tefft, John Scullon
1869	Vital Jarrot	Michael Murphy, Patrick Vaughan	Garrett Stack, Dennis Ryan	Patrick McCormack, John Doyle	John V. Tefft, John Scullon
1870	Vital Jarrot	Patrick Vaughan, Michael Murphy	George W. Davis, Garrett Stack	John Doyle, Patrick McCormack	John V. Tefft, Christian Rohn
1871	Dennis Ryan	Patrick Vaughan, John B. Bowman	John McMullen, George W. Davis	Richard Gilchrist, John Doyle	Christian Rohn, John V. Tefft
1872	Dennis Ryan *	Cornelius Buckley, John B. Bowman	John Benner, John McMullen	John Doyle, Richard Gilchrist	
1873	John B. Bowman	Anson Gustin, Cornelius Buckley	John Niemes, John Benner	Joseph Ryan, John Doyle	
1874	John B. Bowman	Patrick Vaughan, Anson Gustin	John Niemes, John Benner	John Doyle, Joseph Ryau	
1875	Samuel S. Hake	Patrick Vaughan, Maurice Joyce	John Niemes, John Benner	John Doyle, Nicholas Colgan	
1876	Samuel S. Hake	Maurice Joyce, Ernest W. Wider	John Niemes, John Benner	Nicholas Colgan, John Doyle	

* He died in June, and was succeeded by John B. Bowman.

† He was elected Mayor in 1867; his place was filled at a special election, by Benedict Franz.

HISTORICAL LECTURE

DELIVERED BEFORE THE LITERARY AND HISTORICAL SOCIETY OF EAST ST. LOUIS, ILLINOIS, BY DR. ISAAC N. PIGGOTT, AUGUST 4, 1871.

LADIES AND GENTLEMEN: By request of the Literary and Historical Society of the city of East St. Louis, I will give you a synoptical description of the natural scenery of the landscape whereon this flourishing city now stands, as it appeared in A. D. 1799, and note some of the wonderful changes that have transpired therein since that date, etc., especially in the channels of the rivers Mississippi and Abbe, the latter most commonly called Cahokia creek, which runs through your city, and which formerly did not run into the Mississippi, where it now does, but formed its junction south of Piggott's addition to Illinoistown with the slough which then run at the head of an island, described in the "Western Annals" as being opposite South St. Louis, and with said slough run past the village of Cahokia, below which the only ferry from Illinois to St. Louis could then be kept.

By reference to the seventy-second page of Mr. Butler's History of Kentucky, it will be seen that Cahokia creek was knee-deep in front of Colonel Clark's camp at Cahokia when he treated with the Indians in September 1778.

But so great has been the change there that neither slough, creek, nor island can now be properly recognized at that place. As some persons may have been misinformed, and may be incredulous of the facts I am stating, and to enable those who have not known this place over sixty years to comprehend the subject in all its bearings, I will refer you to some ancient documents; and although historians have not mentioned some of the facts of which I am speaking, because unknown to them, or having transpired since their writing, yet I will read to you from the 122d page of the "Western Annals" the description derived from the late Auguste Chouteau. When speaking of the first settlement of St. Louis, he said:

"At that time a skirt of tall timber lined the bank of the river, free from undergrowth, which extended back to a line about the range of Eighth street; in the rear was an extensive prairie the first cabins were erected near the river and market; no 'Bloody Island' or 'Duncanss Island' then existed. Directly opposite the old market square the river was narrow and deep, and until about the commencement of the present century persons would be distinctly heard from the opposite shore. Opposite Duncan's Island and South St. Louis was an island covered with heavy timber and separated from the Illinois shore by a slough. Many persons are now living (1850) who recollect the only ferry from Illinois to St. Louis was from Cahokia, below the island, and landed on the Missouri shore near the site of the United States Arsenal."

Although that description is correct as far as it goes, it does not attempt to describe the landscape at this place; nor when and how Duncan's Island and Bloody Island were formed, and why so named; nor why the only ferry from Illinois to St. Louis had to be from Cahokia, below the island, opposite south St. Louis, and landed on the Missouri shore, near the site of the United States arsenal; nor when, and by whom, the Wiggins ferry at this point was first established. But when you are correctly informed, you will perceive that a ferry at this point, at that date, would have been worse than useless, because it could not have been reached by the inhabitants of Illinois until a road was made, and the river l'Abbe was bridged above its junction with the slough, which then run at the head of said island, and which is now known as Cahokia commons, south of East St. Louis. And all the space above the slough, between the rivers Mississippi and l'Abbe, including the ferry division of East St. Louis, and what is now known as Bloody island, and the dyke and ponds of water in that vicinity was then bottom land, covered with majestic forest timber, interspersed with pea-vine, rushes, and winter grass, on which stock kept fat all the seasons of the year. The distance between the two rivers then was about half a mile in width. This was also used as the common camping ground for all the friendly Illinois Indians that traded at St. Louis, and sometimes by hostile Indians. Therefore, to make the first bridge, and build the first road, was not only costly and laborious, but an extremely dangerous undertaking; for, although Colonel Clark, in 1778, had taken all the territory northwest of the river Ohio from the British lion, yet that country's allies, the Indians, like tigers, thirsting for blood, still claimed and occupied, and, like lords of the forest, roamed through this vast region of wild country.

Just look at the surroundings of the few white people at that time in this country, for, excepting a few French villages in this bottom, the whole country, northwest of the Ohio river, was the abode of ferocious beasts and savage men. Those first heroes of the West were without roads, bridges, newspapers or mail carriers. Many of them had assisted in the erection and defense of Fort Jefferson in 1780-1781; and had come with their captain and formed the first purely American settlement at the Great Run. But I will now have to read to you their own statement, as printed on the fifteenth page of the first volume of American State Papers on Public Lands; and also from the fifty-ninth and sixtieth pages of Governor Reynolds' History of his own times:

"GREAT RUN, May 23, 1790.

"*To his Excellency Arthur St. Clair, Esq., Governor and Commander-in-Chief of the territory of the United States northwest of the river Ohio:*

"We, your petitioners, beg leave to represent to your excellency the state and circumstances of a number of distressed but faithful subjects of the United States of America, wherein we wish to continue, and that under your immediate government; but unless our principal grievance can be removed by your excellency's encouragement, we shall despair of holding a residence in the State we love.

"The Indians, who have not failed one year in four past to kill our people and steal our horses, and at times have killed and drove off numbers of our horned cattle, renders it impossible for us to live in the country any way but in forts or villages, which we find very sickly in the Mississippi bottom; neither can we cultivate our land but with a guard of our own inhabitants, equipped with arms; nor have we more tillable land, for the support of seventeen families, than what might easily be tilled by four of us; and as those lands whereon we live are the property of two individuals, it is uncertain how long we may enjoy the scanty privileges we have here; nor do we find by your excellency's proclamation that those of us which are the major part, who came to the country since the year 1783, are entitled to the land improved, at the risk of our lives, with the design to live on these, with many other difficulties which your excellency may be better informed of by our reverend friend, James Smith, hath very much gloomed the aspect of a number of the free and loyal subjects of the United States. In consideration of which, your petitioners humbly request that, by your excellency's command, there may be a village, with in-lots and out-lots, sufficient for families to subsist on, laid out and established in or near the Prairie-de-Morivay. We know the other American settlers, near the Mississippi, to be in equally deplorable circumstances with ourselves, and, consequently, would be equally benefited by the privileges we ask. And that those of us who came to the country and improved land, since 1783, may be confirmed in a right of pre-emption to their improvements, is the humble request of your petitioners. And we, as in duty bound, shall ever pray.

"JAMES PIGGOT, and forty-five others."

"When the citizen soldiers abandoned Fort Jefferson, Capt. Piggott, with many of his brave companions arrived at Kaskaskia, and remained there some time. These energetic immigrants, so early as the year 1781, were the first considerable acquisition of American population Illinois received. Many of the most worthy and respectable families of Illinois can trace back their lineage to this illustrious noble ancestry. About the year 1783, Capt. Piggott established a fort not far from the bluffs, in the American bottom, west of the present town of Columbia, in Monroe country, which was called Piggott's fort, or the fort of the Grand Ruisseau, *alias* Great Run. This was the largest fortification erected by the Americans in Illinois at that day, and was well defended with cannon and small arms. Capt. Piggott and forty-five inhabitants at this fort (called in English Big Run) petitioned for grant of lands, etc." (See the petition above.)

" I presume it was on this petition that the act of Congress was passed, granting to every one on the public land in Illinois, four hundred acres to each man enrolled in the militia service of that year.

"Governor St. Clair, well knowing the character of Captain Piggott, in the army of the Revolution, appointed him the presiding judge of the court of St. Clair county." (The then county seat was at Cahokia.)

"I will now speak of the establishment of the first road-bridge and ferry, viz: When Governor St. Clair in 1790, first organized civil government in Illinois, he held council with the people; and in view of the prospective importance of this place, he advised his newly-made judge (Piggott) to establish himself at this place. To look at the surroundings of the country, it had very much the appearance of a forlorn hope, but the Governor knew his man. The inhabitants of both sides of the Mississippi felt the great need of such a ferry, and co-operated heartily in it. At that time there was no other man willing to take the risk. In the summer time, men could not work here. In the winters of 1792–93, while the river l'Abbe was frozen, Judge Piggott erected two log cabins at this point; and continued every winter to carry on his improvements until 1795. After General Wayne had conquered and treated with the hostile Indians, he then removed the family from his fort at the Great Run, to this point, among the friendly Indians.

"As soon as the Judge had completed his road and bridge, and established his ferry from the Illinois to the Missouri shore, he petitioned (15th day of August, 1797) for, an obtained the exclusive right to collect ferriage in St. Louis (at that time a Spanish province). As a relic I give the petition in full :

> "St. Clair County, Territory of the United States,
> Northwest of the River Ohio.

To Mr. Zenon Trudeau Commander at St. Louis:

"Sir:—Though unacquainted, † through a certain confidence of your love of justice and equity, I venture to lay before you the following petition, which, from reasons following, I am confident you will find just to allow :

" The petition is, that your honor will grant me the whole benefit of this ferry, to and from the town of St. Louis. I do not desire to infringe upon the ferry privilege below the town, which has been long established. But that no person in the town may be allowed to set people across the river for pay (at this place), so long as you shall allow that the benefits of this ferry hath made compensation for my private expenses, in opening a new road and making it good from this ferry to Cahokia town, and making and maintaining a bridge over the river Abbe, of 150 feet in length.—Your consideration and answer to this is the request of your humble petitioner; and as an acknowledgment of the favor petitioned for, if granted, I will be under the same regulations with my ferry respecting crossing passengers or property from your shore as your ferry-men are below the town : and should your people choose to cross the river in their own crafts, my landing and road shall be free to them.

" And should you wish me to procure you anything that comes to market from the country on this side, I shall always be ready to serve you.

"And should you have need of timber or anything that is the product of my land, it may be had at the lowest rates.

"I am, sir, with due respect, your humble servant,

"August 15, 1797.   JAMES PIGGOTT."

Although the Spanish commandant at St. Louis was anxious to have the ferry regularly carried on by Piggott, because of its great use to St. Louis, yet he devised a plan by which it was done without having it said that he granted the ferry right to a foreigner, viz.: he granted Piggott the ferry landing below Market street, on which Piggott then erected a small ferry-house, which was occupied mostly, however, by one of his ferry hands, who, at any time could cross foot passengers in a canoe; but when horses, etc., were crossed, the platform had to be used, which required three of his men to manage.

Neither skiffs, scows, nor yawls, were then used; but the well-made Indian canoe and pirogue were the water-craft used at the ferry at that early day.

The ferry tract of land which then lay between the creek and river, and belonged to Piggott, has been regularly conveyed by several deeds to the Wiggins ferry company; and allow me to say that the ferry company has ever been composed of honorable, energetic and liberal men, who, a great expense, have successfully contended against many cross-currents, and greatly improved the place for the public convenience as well as their own profit.

From the commencement of this ferry it was carried on under the immediate supervision of Piggott until the 20th of February, 1799, when he died, leaving his wife the executrix of his will. She first rented the ferry to Dr. Wallis for the year 1801-2; then to —— Adams for the year 1803-4. This Adams was then the husband of the distinguished Sarah Adams of Duncan's Island notoriety.

About this time the widow of Piggott married Jacob Collard, and removed from Illinois to St. Louis, Missouri. Before leaving she leased the ferry to John Campbell for ten years, from the 5th day of May, 1805. This Campbell proved treacherous, and procured a license for a ferry in his own name during the time of the lease; and hence for a short time, it was called "Campbell's Ferry." But after a law-suit, Campbell and confederates were beaten, and the ferry re-established to Piggott's heirs—one of whom, assisted by men named Solomon, Blundy and Porter, operated the ferry until part of the heirs sold out to McKnight & Brady.

The other heirs of Piggott conveyed to Samuel Wiggins their share of the ferry. He very soon succeeded in buying out his competitors, and thus obtained the whole ferry. He superintended it in person.

You must bear in mind that I am only giving a synoptical description of the subject matter under consideration, and therefore it would not only be beyond my strength of body but also beyond the proposed plan, if I should make a detailed statement of everything that transpired, and the names of the several tenants who occupied said ferry under Campbell and McKnight and Brady—such as Lockhart, Day, Vandostal, and others.

But you wish to be informed when and how the half-mile width of land, in 1799, lay between the rivers l'Abbe and Mississippi—which was covered with majestic timber, and used as the camping ground of all the Illinois Indians trading at St. Louis, Missouri—because transformed into what has been called Bloody Island, with its slough, dike, etc., from which it is now so rapidly being reclaimed. You will recollect the description given by Auguste Chouteau; and I will add thereto, that the main channel of the Mississippi, in 1800, ran nearly straight from the chain of rocks—supposed to be about nine miles above St. Louis—toward and close to the old western boundary of the Cabanne Island; and from thence striking the rocky shore of Missouri above St. Louis, near where the Sturgeon market now is; thence running deepest against said rocky shore to Market street, below which a sand-bar formed, which grew into what is now called Duncan's Island, causing the current to deflect to Cahokia Island, (before mentioned in the "Western Annals," and carried off a great part thereof. Meanwhile, accretions accumulated on the west side of the Cabanne island. This caused the current to carry off a great deal of the Missouri shore, and formed what was called the Sawyer bend above what is called Bissell's Point. In the fall of 1798, a sand-bar was formed in the Mississippi similar to the one now opposite this place, and near the same locality. It increased rapidly, and soon became an island covered with willow and cottonwood. In time this island received the prefix "Bloody"—from the many bloody duels it was the theatre of. Among the prominent duelists who made the island the place whereon to settle (according to the code *duello*) their differences, were the following parties : Charles Lucas fell by Colonel Benton, Joshua Barton fell by —— Rector, Major Biddle and —— Pettes fell together, —— Waddell fell by —— Mitchell, and others.

In process of time the main channel for steamboat navigation run east of Bloody Island; and the current thus deflected against the Illinois shore, it was worn away rapidly. I believe the whole Mississippi river, would, ere now, have been running east of this place had it not been prevented by diking. But before dikes proved a success, the Mississippi had washed away all the land heretofore described as the Indian camping-ground lying between the rivers, and filled up the old mirey bed of the creek at the southwest corner of Illinoistown — about the northwest end of Main and Market streets, and a mile below it.

Various and expensive efforts were made to force the Mississippi back to its old channel west of this island. After several dikes or rock piers had been made along the Illinois shore, so far as to deflect the current toward the Missouri shore, and also Dike avenue having stopped the current from running on the east of this place, the slough which had run there has been rapidly filling up.

That you may judge how great the change of the natural scenery has been since 1795, examine the old plat of Illinoistown, and you will see at the northwest end of Main and Market streets, marked the place where the bridge and road, made in 1795, crossed the river l'Abbe, which is now the bed of the slough. To disabuse the public mind, I will inform you that, however many have been the several tenants that occupied the ferry tract of land, yet none of them had a fee title therein, excepting James Piggott, his heirs and their assigns.

On the 4th of January 1815, five-sevenths of Piggott's heirs conveyed their interest in the ferry to McKnight & Brady, who had, under special contract, been running it on trial one year previous. And on the 4th of March 1820, the other two-sevenths of Piggott's heirs conveyed their interest in the land and ferry to Samuel Wiggins, who under special contract with them, had been running a ferry in competition with McKnight & Brady during 1819; and the 19th of May 1821, McKnight & Brady conveyed their right of ferry to Samuel Wiggins. Since that time, Wiggins, and those claiming under him, have held the whole concern.

You will understand from what I have endeavored to explain to you what mighty obstacles have been overcome; the slough at the head of this island is already filled up; it is again attached to the mainland, and the other part of it is diked in several places, and rapidly filling up. Properly speaking, this place is no longer Bloody Island, but the law-abiding ferry division of the city of East St. Louis.

Surrounded with the best prospects of increasing wealth and prosperity, I ask you to consider the following facts: viz., the two greatest rivers in the United States form their junction just above us, giving us here a fine navigable channel of about sixty feet in depth by —— in width, and connecting us, by means of ferryboats, with the metropolis of the West — St. Louis. Consider how vast and fertile are the regions of country, east, west and north drained by those rivers; how rich and various are the productions thereof, and one of the best outlets for their transportation is this place; and see how the rapidly far-seeing capitalists are constructing their various railroad routes both at West and East St. Louis, from which they diverge to and converge from all parts of the country. And wisely have the streets in this part of the country been laid out, with the future view of allowing railroad tracks to be put down, for the purpose of moving goods in a more expeditious manner to and from the various railroad depots. And this city is the portal through which all travel from the East must enter to reach the great emporium on the southwest bank of the Mississippi.

Having mentioned a few of the facts in regard to the past and present condition of this place, let us take a look at its future prospects. East St. Louis enjoys the same facilities for navigation as the greater city on the other side of the river does. And why not the acorn become an oak in time? The material is here, if properly handled. The coal-fields surrounding this city are hourly pouring in their treasures. The iron mountains of Missouri are at a convenient distance to us; and how naturally will the coal and iron meet at this place. Is not East St. Louis the real terminus of all the railroads east of the Mississippi?

Hitherto the lack of elevators prevented the shipping of grain at this point, and the " sluggard said there was a lion in the way." But enterprising farmers, merchants and capitalists obtained, on the 6th of March 1867, a liberal charter from the Illinois Legislature, and are astonishing the natives by the erection of an elevator and warehouse 140 by 300 feet, with a railroad track in the center, so that cars loaded with grain will run into the warehouse to be unloaded; and there is 300 feet of river front so arranged that boats loaded with grain can safely land alongside and be unloaded with great dispatch. Everything is arranged for speed and safety.

The result will be to add to the value of all the grain productions of Illinois sent to this place for shipment to St. Louis. The unnecessary ferriage will be avoided, which caused loss to the grain and damage to the cooperage. To show how much saving can be effected, I call attention to an article in the St. Louis *Democrat*— 6th day of May last—in which it is stated that the cost of transfer of grain and flour, for the past year, exceeds $220,000, being a tax on flour of twelve cents per barrel and three and a half cents per bushel on wheat and corn. The greater part of this enormous freightage can be saved by storing at the warehouse of the elevator. It will be ready for the reception of the growing crop of this year. The farmers of Illinois should bear this fact in mind. Egbert Dodge, Esq., is the indefatigable and energetic superintendent, who can be found at his office adjoining the elevator at all seasonable hours.

Pardon this incidental digression. Perhaps I should have spoken of the mortal combat, as given by the Indians who killed Jacob Grotz, grandfather of the late Captain Carr; of the former appearance of the landscape on the east side of the river l'Abbe; of the surveys and resurveys of the Cahokia common-fields; of the laying out of old Illinoistown, in 1817, etc., and other exciting incidents prior to that time, but I will stop here for the present. At some future time I may elaborate more fully.

While speaking of the early history of East St. Louis, we perhaps cannot do better than to refer to some of the brave pioneers who were conspicuous in that early day. Among the most prominent who took an active part in advancing the interests of this once savage wild, was Captain James Piggott, of whom Ex-Governor Reynolds makes the following mention in his " Life and Times." It conveys a graphic picture of who Captain Piggott was, and the ordeal the early settlers passed through, in this severe contest with savages and wild beasts :

Although Fort Jefferson was established before MY OWN TIMES, says Governor Reynolds, yet so many incidents arising out of the establishment of this fort, extending into MY OWN TIMES, and so many of the pioneers of Illinois being connected with it, I deem it proper, in the scope of my work, to give some sketches of the history of the Fort.

In 1781, the Government of Virginia, the great statesman, Thomas Jefferson, being Governor, knew that the Spanish Crown pretended to have some claim on the country east of the Mississippi, below the mouth of the Ohio; and to counteract this claim, ordered George Rogers Clark to erect a fort on the east side of the Mississippi, on the first eligible point below the mouth of the Ohio.

General Clark, with his accustomed foresight and extraordinary energy, levied a considerable number of citizen soldiers, and proceeded from Kaskaskia to the high land, known at this day as Mayfield's creek, five miles below the mouth of the Ohio. Here, on the east side of the Mississippi, he erected a fort, and called it Jefferson, in honor of the then Governor of Virginia. It was neglected to obtain the consent of the Indians for the erection of the fort, as the Governor of Virginia had requested. This neglect proved to be a great calamity. Clark encouraged immigration to the fort, and promised the settlers lands. Captain Piggott, and many others followed his standard.

The fort being established, General Clark was called away to the frontiers of Kentucky, and left the fort for its protection in the hands of Captain James Piggott, and the soldiers and citizens under him.

Captain Piggott was a native of Connecticut, and was engaged in the privateering service in the Revolutionary war. He was in danger of assassination by the enemy in his native State, and emigrated to Westmoreland county, Pennsylvania. He was appointed Captain of a company in the Revolution by the Legislature of his adopted State, and served under Generals St. Clair and Washington. He was in the battles of Brandywine, Saratoga, and marched to Canada. By severe marches, and hard service, his health was impaired so that he was forced to resign his captaincy, and with his family, he left his residence in Westmoreland county, and came West with General Clark.

Several families settled in the vicinity of Fort Jefferson, and some in it; but all attempted to cultivate the soil to some extent for a living.

The Chickasaw and Choctaw Indians became angry for the encroachments of the whites, and in August 1781, commenced an attack on the settlements around the fort. The whole number of warriors must have been ten or twelve hundred, headed by the celebrated Scotchman Calbert, whose posterity figured as half-breed. These tribes commenced hostilities on the settlements around Fort Jefferson. The Indians came first in small parties, which saved many of the inhabitants. If they had reached the settlement in a body, the whole white population outside of the fort would have been destroyed.

As soon as the preparation for the attack of the Indians on the fort was certainly known, a trusty messenger was dispatched to the falls of the Ohio, as it was called at that day and for years afterward, for more provisions and ammunition. If support did not arrive in time, the small settlements and garrison would be destroyed, and it was extremely uncertain if succor would reach the fort in time.

The settlement and fort were in the greatest distress; almost starving, no ammunition, and such great distance from the settlements at Kaskaskia and the Falls.

The first parties of Indians killed many of the inhabitants before they could be moved to the fort, and there was great danger and distress in marching them into the fort. Also the sickness prevailed to such extent, that more than half were down sick at the time. The famine was so distressing, that it was said that they had to eat the pumpkins as soon as the blossoms fell off the vines. This Indian marauding and murdering private persons, and families, lasted about two weeks before the main army of Indian warriors reached the fort. The soldiers aided and received in the fort, all the white population that could be moved.

The whole family of Mr. Music, except himself, was killed, and inhumanly butchered by the enemy. Many other persons were also killed.

In the skirmishes a white man was taken prisoner, who was compelled, to save his life, to report *true state of the garrison*. This information added fury to the already heated passions of the savages.

After the arrival of the warriors, with Calbert at their head, they besieged the fort for six days and nights. During this time no one can describe the misery and distress the garrison was doomed to suffer. The water had almost given out. The river was falling fast, and the water in the wells sunk with the river. Scarcely any provisions remained, and the sickness raged so in the fort that many could not be stirred from their beds. The wife of Captain Piggott, and some others, died in the fort, and were buried inside of the walls, while the Indians besieged the outside. If no relief came, the garrison would inevitably fall into the hands of the Indians and be murdered.

It was argued by the Indians with the white prisoner, that if he told the truth, they would spare his life. He told them truly, that more than half in the fort were sick—that each man had not more than three rounds of ammunition, and that scarcely any provisions were in the garrison. On receiving this information, the whole Indian army retired about two miles to hold a council. They sent back Calbert and three Chiefs with a flag of truce to the fort.

When the whites discovered the white flag, they sent out Captain Piggott, Mr. Owens, and one other man, to meet the Indian delegation. This was done for fear the enemy would know the desperate condition of the fort. The parley was conducted under the range of the guns of the garrison.

Calbert informed them that they were sent to demand a surrender of the fort at discretion; that they knew the defenseless condition of the fort, and to surrender it might save much bloodshed. He further said: that they had sent a great force of warriors up the river to intercept the succor for which the whites had sent a messenger. This the prisoner had told them. Calbert promised he would do his best to save the lives of the prisoners, all if they would surrender, except a few, whom the Indians had determined to kill. He said, the Indians are pressing for the spoils, and would not wait long. He gave the garrison one hour for a decision.

On receiving this information, the garrison had an awful and gloomy scene presented to them. One person exclaimed, " *Great God direct us what to do in this awful crisis!* "

After mature deliberation, Piggott and the other delegates were instructed to say, that nothing would be said as to the information received from the prisoner. If we deny his statements you may kill him—we cannot confide in your promises to protect us; but we will promise, if the Indians will leave the country, the garrison will abandon the fort and country as soon as possible. Calbert agreed to submit this proposition in council to the warriors. But on retiring, Mr. Music, whose family was murdered, and another man, shot at Calbert, and a ball wounded him. This outrage was greatly condemned by the garrison, and the two transgressors were taken into custody. The wound of Calbert was dressed, and he guarded safely to the Indians.

The warriors remained long in council, and by a kind of providential act the long wished-for succors did arrive in safety from the " Falls."

The Indians had struck the river too high up, and thereby the boat with the supplies escaped. The provisions and men were hurried into the fort, and preparations were made to resist a night attack by the warriors.

Every preparation that could be made for the defense of the fort was accomplished. The sick and small children were placed out of the way of the combatants, and all the women and children of any size were instructed in the art of defense. The warriors, shortly after dark, thought they could steal on the fort and capture it; but when they were frustrated, they with hideous yells and loud savage demonstrations, assaulted the garrison and attempted to storm it. The cannon had been placed in proper position to rake the walls, and when the warriors mounted the ramparts the cannon swept them off in heaps. The enemy kept up a stream of fire from their rifles on the garrison, which did not much execution. In this manner the battle raged for hours; but at last the enemy were forced to recoil, and withdrew from the deadly cannon of the fort. Calbert and other chiefs again urged the warriors to the charge; but the same result to retire was forced on them. Men and women at that day were soldiers by instinct. It seemed they could not be otherwise.

The greatest danger was for fear the fort would be set on fire. A large, dauntless Indian, painted for the occasion, by some means got on top of one of the block houses and was applying fire to the roof. A white soldier, of equal courage, went out of the block house and shot the Indian as he was blowing the fire to the building. The Indian fell dead on the outside of the fort, and was packed off by his comrades.

After a long and arduous battle, the Indians withdrew from the fort. They were satisfied the relief had arrived in the garrison, and they could not storm it. They packed off all the dead and wounded. Many were killed and wounded of the Indians, as much blood was discovered in the morning around the fort. Several of the whites were also wounded, but none mortally. This was one of the most desperate assaults made by the Indians in the West, on a garrison so weak and distressed and defenseless.

The whites were rejoiced at their success, and made preparations to abandon the premises with all convenient speed.

The citizen soldiers of Fort Jefferson all abandoned the fort; and some wended their way to Kaskaskia, and others to the Falls. Captain Piggott, with many of his brave companions, arrived at Kaskaskia and remained there some years.

This flood of brave and energetic immigrants, so early as the year 1781, was the first considerable acquisition of American population Illinois received. Many of the most worthy and respectable families of Illinois can trace back their lineage to this illustrious and noble ancestry, and can say with pride and honor, that their forefathers fought in the Revolution to conquer the Valley of the Mississippi.

About the year 1783, Captain Piggott established a fort not far from the bluff in the American Bottom, west of the present town of Columbia in Monroe county, which was called Piggott's Fort, or the fort of the *Grand Ruisseau*. This was the largest fortification erected by the Americans in Illinois, and at that day was well defended with cannon and small arms. In 1790 sometime Captain Piggott and forty-five other inhabitants at this fort, called the BIG RUN in English, signed a petition to Governor St. Clair, praying for grants of land to the settlers. It is stated in that petition that there were seventeen families in the fort.

I presume it was on this petition that the act of Congress was passed granting to every settler on the public land in Illinois, four hundred acres, and a militia donation of a hundred acres to each man enrolled in the militia service of that year.

Governor St. Clair knew the character of Captain Piggott in the Army of the Revolution, and appointed him the Presiding Judge of the Court of St. Clair county.

Captain Piggott, in the year 1795, established the first ferry across the Mississippi, opposite St. Louis, Missouri, known now as Wiggin's ferry; and Governor Trudeau, of Louisiana, gave him license for a ferry and to land on the west bank of the river in St. Louis, with the privilege to collect the ferriage. He died at the ferry, opposite St. Louis, in the year 1799, after having spent an active an eventful life in the Revolution, and in the conquest and early settlement of the West.

[Chicago Legal News, August 2, 1873.]

CIRCUIT COURT, TWENTY-SECOND JUDICIAL CIRCUIT.

BELLEVILLE, ST. CLAIR COUNTY, ILLINOIS.

LAVELLE, Supervisor, vs. STROBEL.

1. EJECTMENT—TITLE.—In actions of ejectment the rule is that the plaintiff can only recover upon the strength of his own title, and not upon the weakness of that of his adversary. It is sufficient for the defendant to show title out of the plaintiff. He need not show title in himself.

2. PUBLIC LANDS—FRENCH SOVEREIGNTY.—The letters patent issued by the French Government to LaSalle on May 12, 1678, and the possession taken by that officer of the country traversed by the Mississippi river, may be considered as vesting the sovereignty of the country in France, notwithstanding the adverse pretensions of Spain and England.

3. TREATY OF PARIS—TREATY OF PEACE WITH GREAT BRITAIN.—By the treaty of Paris in 1763 the sovereignty of the country claimed by France was vested in the Government of Great Britain; and the cession by the State of Virginia, in 1784, of that portion of the country conquered by her in 1778, together with a treaty of peace with Great Britain at the close of the Revolutionary war, vested in our Government the absolute sovereignty and proprietorship of the soil not disposed of at the time.

4. Under the act of March 3, 1791, the Congress of the Confederation instructed the Governor of the Northwestern Territory to proceed to the French settlements on the Mississippi river, and examine the titles and possessions of those settlers and make confirmations.

5. The United States Government granted the commons of Cahokia to be used by the inhabitants as commons until otherwise disposed of by law.

6. In 1812, Congress confirmed a grant of about 4,500 acres as a common of Cahokia village.

7. A right of common is a right to use and enjoy property. It is not a right of ownership.

8. Under a suit to recover land in fee simple the plaintiff cannot recover a right in common.

9. Adverse possession for twenty years will deprive the original claimant of title.

The opinion of the Court was delivered by GILLESPIE, Judge.

This is an action of ejectment brought for the recovery of lots in what was formerly known and called "Illinois City." In this action, the plaintiff, as supervisor of Cahokia commons, under the authority of the act of 1865 (private laws of that session, 4th vol., page 25), brings suit and claims that the lands belong in fee simple to the inhabitants of the village of Cahokia, as having been granted to them by the Government of France, while that nation claimed and exercised dominion over this country. In actions of ejectment, the rule is, that the plaintiff can only recover upon the strength of his own title and not upon the weakness of that of his adversary. It is sufficient for the defendant to show title out of the plaintiff. He need not show title in himself. The hypothesis of the plaintiff is, that the inhabitants of the village of Cahokia, whom he represents, derived their title to the premises in question from the French authorities and not from the Government of the United States; that all that the latter Government did was to confirm, ratify and give its consent to the concession made by the French Government, and that under the treaties of 1763, whereby the country was ceded by France to England, and of 1783, whereby it was ceded to the United States, and by the deed of cession of Virginia to the United States, the titles and possession of the French inhabitants were to be confirmed. In order to determine the correctness of this position, it will become necessary to traverse the action of the French authorities upon this question, and in so doing, we find from the facts recited in the case of Hebert et al. vs. Lavalle, reported in the 27 Illinois, 450, etc., and other sources, that in 1673, Father Marquette entered the Mississippi river, proceeding by way of Green Bay and the Wisconsin river, and passed down to the mouth of the Arkansas, and returned home by way of the Illinois river in September of the same year. The French Government determined after that upon an exploration on a grander scale; and on the 12th of May 1678, Robert Cavalier De LaSalle obtained letters-patent from Louis XIV., authorizing him to explore the western part of New France, as this country was then called, and to construct forts wherever necessary, and hold them on the same terms as he did Fort Frontenac under his patent of March 13, 1675. Under this authority LaSalle, on the 9th day of April, 1682, reached the mouth of the Mississippi and took formal possession of the country through which he passed, in the name of Louis XIV., king of France, and in his honor called it "Louisiana."

This may be considered (so far as this case is concerned) as vesting the sovereignty of the country in France notwithstanding the adverse pretensions of Spain and England. LaSalle erected Fort St. Louis at the Starved Rock on the Illinois river, and others on the lakes and Mississippi river, and had, or seemed to have, entire control of the country until 1690.

In the meantime, the Jesuit missionaries advanced into the country from the seminary of the Quebec, one of whom, James Gravier, in 1695, established the village of "our Lady of Kaskaskias."

In July 1698, the bishop of Quebec granted letters-patent to the directors and superiors of the seminary of foreign missions there, for the establishment of a mission for the "Tamarois and Cahokias," living between the Illinois and Arancies. By virtue of this authority, the mission of St. Sulpice was established among the Tamarois and Cahokia Indians, and a village grew up called the village of the "Holy Family of Cooquias," populated by Indians, fur-traders and tillers of the soil, within the shadow of the church of the mission, which church was the nucleus of the village—the land for the use of the church and villagers being. readily obtained from the native owners.

Up to this time, the Government of France had not exercised the right of disposing of the soil, as the titles or land was obtained from the *natives*, we are told, and the Jesuit missionaries exercised all necessary control over the people; but on the 14th of September 1712, letters-patent were granted to Anthony Crozat, giving him control over the whole commerce of the country. In 1717, he surrendered his patent to Louis XV, when the Company of the West, or of the Indies, was formed, having power in conjunction with an officer of the crown, to grant away the royal domain. This is the first appearance of any attempt on the part of the Government of France, or any other authority that I have been able to discover, to claim and exercise the right of proprietorship of the soil. The early records of this State, preserved in the French language, are said to be full of grants made by this company between 1717 and 1732, when the company was dissolved, and its powers reverted to the crown. Among these records is to be found a grant, substantially as follows:

"We, Pierre Duquet de Boisbriant, knight of the military order of St. Louis, and first lieutenant of the king in the province of Louisiana, commandant in the Illinois; and Marc Antonio de la Loire des Ursins, principal commissary of the royal company of the Indies:

"On demand of the missionaries of the Cahokias and Tamarois to grant to them a tract of four leagues square, in fee simple, with a neighboring island, to be taken a quarter of a league above the small river of Cahokias, situated above the Indian village, and in going up, following the course of the Mississippi, and in returning, towards the Fort Chartres, running in depth to the north, east and south for quantity;

"We, in consequence of our powers, have granted the said land to the missionaries of Cahokias and Tamarois, in fee simple, over which they can from the present work, clear and plant the land, awaiting a formal concession which will be sent from France by the directors-general of the royal company of the Indies.

"At the Fort of Chartres, this 22d June, A.D., 1722.   " BOISBRIANT,
            [Signed]   " DES URSINS."

This concession was made by the representatives of both the crown and the company to the *missionaries*, and is to be regarded as merely *preliminary* and not final. It is inferable from documents exhibited on the trial of the case of Herbert *et al. vs.* Lavalle, that a village grew up at Cahokia, but whether upon this land or not, I am unable to determine, as the description is so vague and indefinite (as will appear hereafter).

On the 10th April 1732, the Company of the West was dissolved, and its powers reverted to the crown, from which all future grants emanated. It is said that in August 1743, the above grant was recognized by the French Government through Mons. Vaudreuil, then Governor, and Jolmon, commissary of the province of Louisiana. We find no further connection on the part of the French Government with this grant. The Supreme Court intimates that the title derived under this grant was in fee simple, and that, upon the land granted, the missionaries established their church and village. I am, however, unable to perceive how a grant made to a religious association or corporation could inure in or pass title to the lay inhabitants of the village of Cahokia. I should much rather incline to the opinion that the title, vested in the missionaries by this grant, descended to the proper, ecclesiastical dignitary of the Roman Catholic Church authorized to hold the title to its lands. Whether this right of the Church to this specific land has been lost by its *laches* or not, or whether, if the Government has granted lands (of right and according to treaty stipulations belonging to the Church) to other parties, it is bound in *fora conscientia* to make requittal, I am not now prepared, if it were necessary to do so, to decide. It is enough (if such is the fact) to determine that the title is not in the plaintiff, or, in other words, in the inhabitants of the village of Cahokia.

England may be considered (for the present purpose) as having acquired by conquest and the treaty of Paris in 1763 this country, and she never interfered with the French grants.

In 1778, the country was conquered by Virginia, in the expedition under George Rogers Clark, and ceded by that State to our Government, March the 1st, 1784. This, together with the treaty of peace with Great Britain at the close of our Revolutionary war, vested in our Government the absolute sovereignty and proprietorship of the soil not disposed of at that time. The sovereign power gave the Government the right to determine the extent and character of the titles of those claiming under grants from France, England and Virginia under the treaty stipulations and the international law. The deed of cession of Virginia provided (with a high sense of justice and a particular regard to the condition of the old settlers) that the French and Canadian inhabitants and other settlers of the Kaskaskias, Saint Vincents, and the neighboring villagers, who have professed themselves citizens of Virginia, shall have their possessions and titles confirmed to them, and be protected in the enjoyment of their rights and liberties.

Under the act of March 3, 1791, the Congress of the Confederation instructed the Governor of the Northwestern Territory to proceed without delay to the French settlements on the river Mississippi, and to examine the titles and possessions of those settlers—"In which they are to be confirmed." The Governor of the Territory, under this authority, was empowered to make absolute confirmations and issue patents for the lands confirmed by him. Hence, originated a class of titles known as "Governor's confirmations," one of which is found in the case of Doe *ex rem*, etc., *vs.* Hill, Breese, 236. Governor St. Clair proceeded, according to directions of Congress, and it appears from the report of Backhouse and Jones, commissioners appointed by Congress under the act of March 6, 1804, that the commons before that time occupied by the inhabitants of Cahokia, were incapable of ascertainment on account of the obscurity of the boundaries, and that Governor St. Clair recommended to them to have a tract of about five thousand acres surveyed, the grant of which he would recommend to the United States Government. He then returned East, and was no further concerned in the examination or confirmation of land claims in the Territory.

The very act, while it provided for granting lands to the inhabitants and settlers at Vincennes and the Illinois country, in the Northwest Territory, and for confirming them in their possessions, by its 5th section provides (amongst other things) "that a tract of land, including the villages of Cohos and Prairie-Du-Pont, heretofore used by the inhabitants of said village as a common, be and the same are hereby appropriated to the use of the inhabitants of said village, *to be used* by them *as a common until otherwise disposed of by law*.

The National Government (Illinois not then being a State) had, by virtue of its sovereignty, the right of determining the character of the titles by which its citizens held their property, and they determined that this property was to be *used*, not *owned* by the inhabitants of the village of Cahokia (which was intended for *Cohos*, as misspelled in the act). It was not to be theirs, even as a common, forever, but only *until otherwise disposed of by law*. Here, then, in my judgment, is the origin of the title of the inhabitants of the village of Cahokia to these commons (not their village lot, nor common field, which are treated as distinct from the commons,) with its character as commons distinctly stamped upon it; and it may be regarded as a gratuity to them by the Government of the United States, which was properly disposed to be extremely liberal to the French inhabitants of the country, with a view of making the change of government to which they were subjected acceptable.

In 1804 Congress created three land offices—one at Vincennes, one at Detroit, and another at Kaskaskia, and provided that the registers and receivers of each should constitute a board for examining into the rights of claimants to ancient grants, military, and headrights. These commissioners had not the power that was vested in the Governor under the act of the 30th of March 1791; they could only inquire into and report to Congress the result of their inquiries. The inhabitants of the village of Cahokia presented before these commissioners the survey which was made by or for them under the arrangement with Governor St. Clair; but instead of containing about 5,000 acres, as agreed upon, it appeared to comprehend about 20,000 acres. The commissioners could not look with any favor upon this extraordinary claim, and as the tract was not located to the best advantage for the use of the inhabitants of the village, it was agreed upon between them and the commissioners that another survey of a common should be made of about 5,500 acres, more convenient for the village, which the commissioners agreed to recommend for approval by the Government. This arrangement was carried out; and in 1810 and 1812 Congress distinctly confirmed the report of the commissioners in favor of the inhabitants of Cahokia village *as a common*. Here, then, is the consummation of the title of the inhabitants of the village to this land *as a common;* and is so held by the Supreme Court in the case of Herbert *vs.* Lavalle, 27 Illinois, 454.

A right of common is a right to use or enjoy property, the title or ownership of which is in another, a right of common is inconsistent with ownership. One could not, with legal accuracy, say that he had a right-of-way over his own land, for then he would be both the debtor and creditor. If the inhabitants of the village of Cahokia had never parted with their right of *common*, the ownership in fee simple must be in the Government of the United States, and if it is the allegation in the declaration in this case which states the title in fee simple to be in the plaintiff or the inhabitants, it is untrue. It is well established that a party suing for lands and claiming in fee simple cannot recover upon proof of a different character. He may recover, if he claims in fee simple upon proof of title in *fee simple* to a party, but he cannot claim in fee simple and recover upon proof of an interest for life, or years, or in common. He cannot where he sues for the whole, recover an undivided part. This then would dispose of the case against the plaintiff upon technical grounds; but I think the merits of the case are overwhelmingly against the plaintiff. In 1817, the inhabitants of the village of Cahokia appointed five persons, as their agents, to lay off a portion of this common into a city, known as Illinois City, and had the lots distributed among themselves fairly and to their entire satisfaction. Application was made to Congress to ratify this proceeding, and to grant the lots to the inhabitants *in fee simple* (they not regarding themselves as owners of the fee before). Congress on the first of May, 1820, complied with their request, and ratified their title to the lots as they had procured them to be laid off and distributed, and thus parted with the residuary interest it had held up to this time in this part of the common.

It is contended that Congress had no right to intermeddle in this matter after Illinois became a State. The reply to this is that Congress has the exclusive right of regulating the manner of its disposal of the public lands, even within a State, and this proceeding was nothing more than the primary disposal of its lands. I admit that after the United States has finally disposed of its lands within a State, its power over them (except in cases where it is authorized by the Constitution to act) ceases, and the land becomes subject to the jurisdiction of the State. But in this case, the United States merely ceded to these inhabitants a residuary interest it had in the lands. But a further answer to the objection that these lands must always remain in *statu quo* is the fact that this change from commons to a fee simple interest, and their division and distribution is expressly sanctioned by the State Constitution of 1818, which in the eighth section of the eighth Article, Illinois, after ordering that all lands held in common by any town, village, etc., " shall not be sold, leased or divided, under any pretense whatever; provided, that nothing in this section shall be so construed as to affect the commons of Cahokia," thus excluding the Cahokia commons from the operation of the general principle, and making them an exception. It would be strange if the rule governing the general principle and the exceptions were the same. The *exception* would no longer belong to that category when it corresponded with the *rule*. The rule of division is applicable, by virtue of this constitutional provision, to the commons of Cahokia, and its opposite, or the rule of *no division* is applicable to other commons in the State. But this is not all.

On the fifth of March 1819, the Legislature of this State passed an act, which, after reciting in the first section the language of the clause in the Constitution and proviso, etc., concludes that "nothing contained in this act should deprive the inhabitants of Cahokia from leasing, selling or dividing all the land that was surveyed and laid off into a town on the commons of Cahokia,

EAST ST. LOUIS.

nearly opposite east of St. Louis." I have stated that the merits of this case were against the plaintiff. The i nhabitants obtained from the United States a free gift of the right of common (for they had no ancient right to this land) afterward ; they laid out a town or city, and divided most of the lots amongst themselves satisfactorily, and which, in general, descended or were sold to the present claimants. It would be unjust, even if it were not illegal, for the plaintiff to recover in this action. The inhabitants of the village of Cahokia have once received an equivalent for these lots.

In regard to th e change of this property from being held in common to individual ownership, we have the sanction of the donor—the United States—and donée—the inhabitants of Cahokia—as well as of the State go vernment—both in the Constitution of the State and the acts of the Legislature—and if this is not sufficient to authorize a change in the manner in which property is held, there is no earthly power by which the change can be accomplished—not even by the courts— the action of which would have been futile in this case, as the United States could not be made a party in a State court, and compelled to surrender its interest in the premises. This, it will be obvious, could only be done by its voluntary act.

The map in this case is evidence of the conveyance of the lots in Illinois City as against the plaintiff, or any one claiming through or under an inhabitant of the village of Cahokia. It appears that lot No. 17 was not sold, but the title remained in the inhabitants of the village, who were liable to the same r equirements, in respect to the payment of taxes, as other persons, and were subject to the operations of the law of limitations the same as individuals; and it having been clearly proven that lot seventeen has been in the actual adverse possession of either the defendant, or the persons through whom he claims, for more than twenty years, the title of the inhabitants to that lot is lost by their neglect to assert their rights in time. The plaintiff having laid his right in fee simple cannot recover a right of common, but must declare for such. If this ever was a fee simple right in the inhabitants of the village of Cahokia, it was made so for the moment by operation of the act of Congress of the first May 1820, and that act ratifies the passing the title out of them to the distributees of the lots under the division.

From the views I take of this case, it is entirely unnecessary to consider the question arising upon the defense, and to determine as to the sufficiency of the claims of title set up thereunder.

Judgment is rendered for defendant for costs.

1686

HISTORY

OF

ST. CLAIR COUNTY,

ILLINOIS.

With Illustrations

DESCRIPTIVE OF ITS SCENERY,

AND

Biographical Sketches of some of its Prominent Men and Pioneers.

BY

BRINK, McDONOUGH & CO.,

PHILADELPHIA.

CORRESPONDING OFFICE, EDWARDSVILLE, ILL.

1881

PREFACE.

IT gives us great pleasure to return our sincere thanks to those who have so generously assisted us, in various ways, in making this work thorough and complete. For some of the incidents relative to the early settlement of the county we are indebted to a few of the older inhabitants. In localizing events, and correcting dates, we acknowledge our obligations to the writings of ex-Governor Reynolds, Rev. John M. Peck, Captain Pittman of the English army, the American State Papers, and the writings of the Jesuit Fathers. Many old and valuable manuscripts, both in the FRENCH and ENGLISH languages, have been examined These rare papers have made plain and intelligable some of the earliest incidents and anecdotes pertaining to this region of the state.

For other facts we are indebted to a class of intelligent men and women, who amid the ordinary pursuits of life have taken pains to inform themselves as to the past of the county.

Among those who have specially contributed to the completeness of this history are William McClintock, Ira Manville, Felix Scott, Mrs. Ortance Brackett, Judge William H. Snyder, Col. John Thomas, James Affleck, Capt. John Trendly, Hon. H. H. Horner, Prof. Samuel H. Deneen, Hon. Gustavus Koerner, Rev. Father Hinssen, William R. Padfield, Benj. Hypes, Joseph B. Lemen, Hon. Jefferson Rainey, Dr. Julius Kohl, Hon. Philip Postel, the Eisenmayer Bros., Risdon A. Moore, Simeon Badgley, James W. Hughes, Russell Hinckley, Stephan Vahlkamp, J. C. Hamilton, William Costello, and J. H. Reichert. We also desire to return our thanks to the county officials for the many courtesies extended. The editors of the several newspapers have also rendered assistance in that prompt and cheerful manner so characteristic of the journalistic profession.

To the clergymen of the various denominations whose articles appear in this work, we express our thanks for information furnished relative to the history of their churches. Among the chapters most fruitful in interest to a great number of our readers, will be found those which treat of the early history of the churches.

We have endeavored, with all diligence and carefulness, to make the best use of the material at our command. We have confined ourselves, as nearly as possible, to the original data furnished. The subject matter has been carefully classified, and will be a great help to the public as a book of reference concerning the past of the county. We expect criticism. All we ask is that it be made in the spirit of charity. We hope our patrons will take into account all the difficulties to be overcome, the care necessary in harmonizing various memories, and of reconciling diverse dates, and localizing events. The facts are gathered from a hundred different sources, and depend largely, not on exact written records, but on the recollections of individuals. We have tried to preserve the incidents of pioneer history, to accurately present the natural features and material resources of the county, and to gather the facts likely to be of most interest to our present readers, and of greatest importance to coming generations. If our readers will take into consideration the difficulties of the task, we feel sure of a favorable verdict on our undertaking.

We present the work to the public, trusting that they will approve our labors, and give the volume a generous reception.

THE PUBLISHERS.

TABLE OF CONTENTS.

branches only are being taught. Thus the parochial schools of St. Peter's Congregation are divided into four different classes for boys; four for girls; English school, and Kindergarten, in which altogether nine Sisters and one male teacher are engaged in teaching about 650 children. Besides all the branches taught in the public schools of the country, Bible History of the Old and New Testament and Catechism alternately are being taught in all classes for half an hour every day. The girls are also instructed twice a week in needle work. Singing classes are given twice a week, half an hour in the afternoon, in which singing is taught systematically, so that for the last five years the children of the parochial school have been able to sing every first Sunday of the month at High mass and the psalms at Vespers in the afternoon in St. Peter's church, to the great pleasure of the juvenile singers, and the edification of the whole congregation.

Examinations take place in all schools twice a year—in the beginning of December, and at the end of April, after the latter part of which, in the month of May, a public exhibition, consisting of singing, declamations, and tableaux, is given in the grand hall of the Sisters' Convent, at which all children of the parochial schools and their parents are present. It is the great gala day of the children, because they know their fathers and mothers are among the audience, listening to their songs and plays. Though the world generally ignores the labors of the good sisters, St. Peter's Congregation offers them a tribute of gratitude by declaring that the day of their coming to Belleville was one of great blessing. Thousands of its members thank them for their education, secular as well as religious. In the records of Heaven alone will we find all they have done for the furtherance of the holy work, and there, too, in that abode of bliss, is their reward awaiting them.

A day or select school, divided into three departments, is also in charge of these Sisters, and open to the children of Belleville in general. All the branches required for a finished education are taught in these classes. Charges are: Primary department $6.00, Intermediate department $8.00 and Senior department $10.00 per session of five months. Vocal music in class, three times a week, no extra charge. Private vocal lessons $20.00 per session. Instrumental music, lessons given daily, also $20.00 per session.

Many ladies of Belleville and vicinity have received their musical education from the Sisters de Notre Dame, and it is a source of gratification to these Sisters to know that many of their former pupils now conduct church choirs, and play the organ during divine service in different parts of the country.

The boarding-school for young ladies, known as "Institute of the Immaculate Conception," offers every advantage of similar institutions. The Sisters, feeling bound to respond to the confidence placed in them by parents and guardians, give their pupils a Christian and thorough education. Pupils of all religious denominations are received. The course of study, pursued in this institution, embraces the English, German and French languages, with all useful and ornamental branches taught to young ladies.

Private examinations are held every two months and written reports sent to parents and guardians. Premiums are distributed to the most deserving, at the commencement, held annually in the Exhibition Hall, towards the end of June.

The building is very spacious, measuring one hundred and eighty feet front, and one hundred feet deep, thoroughly ventilated, heated by furnaces, lighted by gas, and furnished with all modern improvements.

A beautiful chapel, built in the Byzantine style, occupies a part of the western wing. Over the main altar is a life-size figure of our "Lady" carved in wood. A silver lamp, in the shape of a dove,

16

gives forth its light, by night and day, before the sanctuary of the Holy of Holies. Young lady boarders have access to the chapel for general and private devotions.

The moderate prices, together with the healthy location and many advantages of this institution should be an inducement to parents and guardians to place their children or wards in care of these excellent teachers.

Board and tuition per annum only $150.00; music, painting, etc., form extra charges.

Prospectuses will be furnished with pleasure, on application.

HOWE LITERARY INSTITUTE.

EAST ST. LOUIS, ILLINOIS. BY REV. S. F. HOLT.

This institution takes its name from the late Mr. Lyman Howe, by whose liberality it was founded. Mr. Howe was an intelligent merchant, who had been for several years engaged in business on what is known as Bloody Island, just opposite the city of St. Louis. Wishing to leave some memorial of himself that would, at the same time, be a substantial benefit to the community then just beginning to gather at that point, he embodied in his will a bequest of ten thousand dollars "for the building of a church, or school-house, or both, on Bloody Island."

The custody and expenditure of this bequest was especially committed to the Hon. Jno. B. Lovingston, the executor of the will, without other instructions than those contained in the single sentence above quoted. But Mr. Lovingston had been a business partner of Mr. Howe, and was in hearty sympathy with his liberal impulses and enlightened public spirit, and believing that the wishes of the testator would be best attained by the establishment of an educational institution, he decided to appropriate the fund to that purpose.

It was desirable that such an institution should have the fostering care of some organized body, interested in education, that would be perpetual in its own existence, and would give the institute a constant and permanent support. With this object in view, Mr. Lovingston proffered the control of the enterprise to the South District Baptist Association, and this body, after due consideration, decided to accept the trust.

In October, 1871, an educational association was formed for this purpose, composed chiefly of prominent citizens of St. Clair and Madison counties. An incorporation under the general law of the State was effected, and a Board of Trustees chosen.

Of this association Hon. J. B. Lovingston was made President, Hon. Jas. P. Slade, Secretary, and Rev. J. M. Cochran, who had been most active in promoting the enterprise thus far, was chosen Corresponding Secretary and Financial Agent. The Board of Trustees then chosen has continued substantially to the present time. Including some changes caused chiefly by death, the list comprises, in addition to the officers above-named, the following gentlemen, who have also been the principal supporters of the institute: Jno. T. Lemen, M. W. Weir, G. W. Darrow, David Ogle, L. M. St. John, W. R. Begole, Chas. Gooding, W. A. Darrow, Warren Beedle, M. T. Stookey, Fred. Merrill and W. M. Anderson.

This association decided to establish at East St. Louis an educational institution, bearing the name, *Howe Literary Institute.*

At the early date of Mr. Howe's death, he did not anticipate, nor did any one else then foresee, how completely Bloody Island would be occupied by the numerous railroads since built, which converge to a common focus upon it, rendering it a quite unsuitable

C. B. Clarke, Architect.   Chesnut st. St. Louis.

HOWE LITERARY INSTITUTE, EAST ST. LOUIS, ILLINOIS.

location for the building he had provided for. With the concurrence of the executors and the heirs of the estate, a decree in Chancery was obtained, authorizing a change of location ; and the present site, donated in part by Mr. Lovingston, was fixed upon. The campus contains about one acre, healthily and pleasantly situated on the highest ground in East St. Louis, just outside the present limits of the city, and about one and a half miles directly east of the Great Bridge.

In the summer of 1873 the trustees began the erection of the institute building. At that time the whole country was in the full tide of commercial and business prosperity, and the work of building was entered upon in the confidence which that prosperity inspired, without apprehension of, or provision for, the disastrous changes which were soon to follow. Overtaken by the sudden financial panic in the autumn, the trustees were obliged to suspend the work, and the walls were left standing unfinished several months. In the spring of 1874, as money could not be otherwise

raised, the needed funds were borrowed, the building completed, and the school opened in October, under the supervision of Rev. S. F. Holt, A. M., who had been elected President of the institute in the spring, and had been actively engaged during the summer in finishing and furnishing the edifice. The cost of the edifice, exclusive of the site, was about $20,000.

During the several years of "hard times" which followed the opening of the institute, its history was a continuous struggle, not so much for success as for existence. Returning commercial prosperity brought a better patronage to the institute, and greatly brightened its prospects. It now promises to become a permanent and successful institution of great benefit to the city in which it is located, and to the people of the surrounding country.

The annual attendance has varied from sixty to one hundred and seventy. It has a carefully-arranged course of study, upon the completion of which a diploma is given. The number of graduates thus far is fourteen. Its first President still continues at its head.

Besides the above, there is a boarding house and seven saloons. The village was incorporated in 1876, and the following are the first officers elected:—*President*—Walter Murray; *Trustees*—J. C. Sinclair, S. H. Parker, E. D. Ankeny, J. J. Schumaker, and John Ortgier. Thomas Jamison was appointed clerk. The present officers are—L. G. Cross, pres.; Fred Luce, John Simons, A. Murphy, S. H. Parker, and John Schumaker, trustees. J. W. McCormic, clerk and police magistrate, and Samuel McGregor, marshal.

The present population of the village is about 400, and bids fair some day to be one among the busy towns that shall dot the banks of the Mississippi.

FALLING SPRING.

This is one of the romantic spots in Illinois. It is situated at the bluff, one mile south-east of Prairie du Pont village. It derives its name from a spring that gushes out of a perpendicular rock of the bluff, with a fall of sixty or seventy feet. The bluff at this point is a solid wall of limestone, about one hundred and thirty feet in height. The spring flows from an orifice situated midway between the top of the bluff and the rocky bottom beneath. Many years ago a grist mill was constructed at this point, and the water utilized for a power, but no trace of it remains at this time to be seen. Several years ago a hotel was built near the spring, and the place was made a summer resort by the people of East St. Louis and other towns. The hotel is yet standing, and is now converted into a saloon. There are three stone quarries in full blast not far from the spring, and owned by the following companies:—Otto & Parent, William Richards, and Henry Deering. They employ in all about seventy-five men, and load on an average twenty cars per day. A branch of the Conlogue railway runs to the quarries. A stone-crusher dump is in process of erection here by the Vandalia railroad company. We were informed by the foreman that it would take about 200,000 feet of lumber to construct it, and will cost, including machinery, upwards of $50,000. When in running order it will employ about fifty hands, and will have the capacity to crush fifty car-loads of stone per day. Although there is no town here—nothing but boarding houses for the men—yet it presents the appearance of life and business.

PRECINCT AND CITY OF EAST ST. LOUIS.

AST ST. LOUIS, precinct, formerly called Illinoistown, occupies the extreme north-western corner of St. Clair county, and was organized as a township the 6th day of June, 1820, the boundaries being as follows: Beginning at the bluff on the Madison county line; thence west on said line to the Mississippi river: thence with the Mississippi to the Cahokia line on the same; thence with said line eastward to the bluff; thence along the bluff northward to the place of beginning. By order of the county commissioners' court, September 14th, 1821, Illinoistown and Cahokia were made one election precinct, with the voting place at Augustus Pensoneau's residence in Cahokia. In 1851, Illinoistown became a separate voting precinct, and French Village was named as the place of holding the election. Again, in 1857, it was divided into two separate parts, respectively called Illinoistown and French Village precincts, the division line running due west from south-west corner of section 15, in township No. 2, north range, No. 9 west, to the north-west corner of section 21, same township, thence south on the west line of section 21, to the south-west corner thereof, thence west on the section line to the Mississippi through Cahokia precinct, from which a strip of about one-half a mile in breadth is taken from the northern part and annexed to Illinoistown precinct. The foregoing are the boundaries that the precinct embraces at this time. In 1866, the precinct appears under the name of East St. Louis, and that of Illinoistown

dropped. This change of name is not made a matter of record, and the presumption is that by common consent, or usage, it assumed the name of its leading town, East St. Louis, which by a vote of the people of the corporation in 1861, gave it its present title At the time of its organization, a strip of heavy timber about half a mile wide, extended south from the present town of Brooklyn to the village of Cahokia. What is now the city of East St. Louis was mainly covered with heavy timbers of oak, walnut, elm, etc., and was a favorite stamping ground for the hunter and the trapper.

The first blow struck toward civilization in this vast solitude, was in the year 1770, by one Richard McCarty, familiar known in those days as English McCarty. He obtained an improvement right or title, to four hundred acres of land, extending on both sides of Cahokia creek, and now included within the present limits of East St. Louis. Here he erected a grist mill on the bank of the creek, and for a time it did quite a flourishing business, but on account of the banks being so easily washed away, a permanent dam could not be constructed. He left the country for Canada in 1787, where he died, leaving heirs to this property. The United States Commissioners appointed by Congress in 1805, to pass upon claims to ancient titles in Cahokia and other French villages, confirmed this tract to the heirs of McCarty. No vestige of the old mill site exists at this time. Another mill was constructed in 1805, by Nicholas Jarrot on the creek not far from where McCarty's mill was located. It has long since disappeared As late as

1855, the machinery was utilized in a mill at Brooklyn by Morris & Son.

The oldest house, now standing in the precinct, was built by Nicholas Boismenue in 1817, and is situated about one mile south of the city limits, on the road leading from what was formerly called Papstown, to the village of Cahokia. It is built after the old French style, with upright hewed walnut logs, and weather-boarded, with porch extending around the entire building. It is occupied by Joseph Boismenue, and is the oldest house in St. Clair county, outside the village of Cahokia and Prairie du Pont.

The founding of the present city of East St. Louis, is due to the foresight of the pioneer, Capt. James Piggott. He was an officer under General Clark, who had command of the Virginia militia stationed on the frontier. Capt. Piggott was one of those who remained after the treaty was made in 1783, and cast his lot with the hardy pioneers of the west. At this time St. Louis was but a small trading port, and Cahokia the metropolis.

No doubt Capt. Piggott's keen business perceptions led him to believe, from the natural surroundings, and other advantages, that in future time the little village of St. Louis would some day take the lead among the few towns then settled along the Mississippi. Accordingly he located a militia claim of a hundred acres on the east side of the river opposite the village of St. Louis, and by his own exertions succeeded in constructing a bridge across Cahokia creek, near the road leading to that village. This was in 1795. In 1797, he had erected two small log cabins near the shore, where he had established a rude ferry system across the river, by the consent of the Spanish Commandant at St. Louis. Thus the first ferry was established, out of which grew one of the wealthiest monopolies of the west. Capt. Piggott died in 1799, scarcely dreaming of the magnitude his enterprise in after years would assume.

The first house of any pretensions built on the present site of East St. Louis, was erected by Etienne Pensoneau, in the year 1810. It was a two-story brick building, and situated on what is now the corner of Main and Menard streets, in the first ward. It was constructed for a dwelling, but was afterwards utilized for a hotel, to afford accommodations to the immigrants, who were then rapidly pushing to the frontier. It has long since passed away with the things that were.

The oldest house now standing within the city limits is situated in the First ward, near the corner of Second and Market streets, and was built about 1818, by the "Old Man" Rail, for a dwelling, and is still used as such. Its structure is of the primitive style, with hewed logs placed *upright* a few inches apart, and filled between with cement or mortar. The outside is weather-boarded for the better protection from the winter blasts.

The following, relating to the first laid-out town in East St. Louis, we glean from Reavis' history of " *The Future Great City:*"

"In 1815, Etienne Pinconeau (now spelled Pensoneau), ventured to lay out a town on his adjoining land, with his brick tavern on the road to the ferry, thence occupied by one Simon Vanorsdal, as a nucleus. He called it 'Jacksonville.' The plat of the town cannot be found; but there is a deed of record for a lot in it. It bears the date 17th of March, 1815. Etienne Pinconeau and Elizabeth, his wife, by it convey to Moses Scott, merchant of St. Louis, in the Missouri territory, for $150, 'all that certain tract, parcel, or lot of land, being, lying, and situated in the said county of St. Clair, at a place, or new town called Jacksonville, containing in depth one hundred feet, and in breadth sixty feet, joining north-wardly to Carroll street, facing the public square, and southwardly to Coffee street.'

"Later conveyances by McKnight & Brady, merchants and land

operators at that time in St. Louis, referring to this lot of Moses Scott, locate it as lot 5, in block 8, of the town of Illinois, at the south-east corner of Market and Main streets. Scott at once erected a store upon the lot, and at that corner conducted the first mercantile establishment in this city. This was the only sale made of lots in this 'Jacksonville.' On the 20th of January, 1816, Pinconeau sold the entire tract of land he had on Cahokia creek (including Jacksonville), extending in breadth from near Railroad street to Piggott street, to McKnight & Brady.

"The immediate result was the consummation, by McKnight & Brady, of Pinconeau's project of a new town. They platted the 'Town of Illinois' upon the site of Pinconeau's Jacksonville. They re-located the public square, widened the streets and enlarged the lots, and put the plat on record. They advertised and held a great sale of lots in the town of Illinois. The sale took place at the auction-room of Thomas T. Reddick, in St. Louis, November 3d, 1817. Thus was made the first record evidence of a town-plat in East St. Louis."

The first railroad constructed in the state was built from Illinois-town to the bluff, a distance of about six miles. It was constructed in 1836, under the personal supervision and efforts of Governor Reynolds, Vital Jarrot and a few others. It was expressly built for the purpose of transporting coal from where it cropped out at the bluff (now Pittsburg) to the St. Louis market. This was an enterprise of no small dimensions at that day. They were obliged to bridge over two thousand feet across Big Lake, which was performed by driving down piles spliced together to the length of eighty feet, upon which the track rested. At times they employed one hundred hands, and so vigorously was the undertaking prosecuted that it was completed in one year. Thomas Winstanley was the first engineer and conductor of the road; that is, he drove the mules that hauled the cars over the route. It proved a non-paying investment, and in 1841 they sold out the concern to the St. Clair Railroad Company.

Captain Trendley built the first school-house in 1840, and the cost was $240. It was a small frame building, 14x16, and was situated on the public square. William Singleton established the first church in 1845. It was of the Methodist denomination, and located on Brundy street, between Second and Third. It is yet standing, and is owned by the colored Baptists. The first blacksmith-shop was built by Francis Delorem in 1826, and was situated on what is now known as the Rock road. It was a very meagre and unpretentious affair, but answered the wants of the people at that time.

BLOODY ISLAND.

This island was made in about 1800. Its first appearance was a small sand-bar, below Bissel's Point, near the Illinois shore. At this angle in the course of the Mississippi, the force of the current gradually wore into the mainland, and left a corresponding deposit upon the bar extending southward. In course of time this bar developed into a considerable island, with half the river flowing between it and the Illinois shore. The first to inhabit it was a man by the name of Duncan, who built a small log house within its solitude, and lived there for some time afterwards. The exact date of his location is not known. The next to settle here was a Mr. Lindsey, in 1842, who built two or three little shanties, and kept a small dairy and garden. He named his place "Hoboken Garden." The island now constitutes the Third ward of the city. The early history of the island is stained with human blood; hence the name, Bloody Island. For several years it was not definitely established to which shore the island belonged. It was therefore considered neutral ground, and was the favorite resort for settling differences by mortal combat, according to the then prevailing code of honor. The first duel fought here was in 1817, between Col. Thomas H. Benton and Judge Charles Lucas. Col. Benton was the challenging party. Their differences grew out of harsh invectives employed by them in the trial of a case in which they were opposing attorneys. This challenge Judge Lucas declined, on the plea that he would not respond in deadly combat for words uttered in a professional capacity. They, however, met afterwards, in the same year, when the duel was fought, and Lucas was the unfortunate victim.

In 1823, another duel occurred, between Thomas C. Rector and Joshua Barton, United States District Attorney. The trouble grew out of a newspaper attack made by Barton against Gen. Wm. Rector, brother of Thomas C. Rector. They met June 30th, in the above-named year, when Barton fell and died shortly afterward. The most disastrous meeting was between Maj. Thomas Biddle and Hon. Spencer Pettis, both of St. Louis, and occurred the 27th of Aug., 1830. The trouble was engendered in the heated political canvass of that year. Maj. Biddle was the challenged party, and having the choice of distance, named five paces, on account of his being shortsighted. At the giving of the word, they wheeled and fired simultaneously. They both fell mortally wounded. Capt. Trendley was an eye-witness to this sad affair, and helped to convey the body of Pettis to St. Charles county, Mo., where it was buried. The name, Bloody Island, having many unpleasant recollections connected with its memory, has long since been dropped, and is now simply known as "The Island."

THE FLOODS.

No place in the United States has had more to contend with to prevent its growth and prosperity than the city of East St. Louis. Nothing but the natural advantages of being situated opposite the great city of St. Louis, and the indomitable perseverance of its inhabitants, have kept it from perishing from the earth long ago. What with numerous floods and the encroachment of the river upon the banks, it has nearly yielded up its existence several times to the fates that be. The first flood that did damage to the little hamlet of Illinoistown occurred in 1826. The town was inundated to the depth of several feet, and the malarial fevers that followed nearly depopulated the village. It, however, struggled for existence, and up to 1844 had gradually increased to a town of considerable thrift and importance, when the most vital stroke it ever received almost blotted it from existence. The flood which occurred in June of that year inundated the American Bottoms so that large steamers plied from bluff to bluff. But few of the houses of Illinoistown were to be seen above the water, while no dry land was observable for miles toward the eastern bluff, except a few mounds and high knolls to the east and south of the village. So complete was the destruction that the town never recovered from it until the general centralizing of the railroads at this point about fifteen years ago. It is said at the time of this flood that the steamer called "Little Bee," plied between the city of St. Louis and the coal mines on the bluffs at Pittsburg, the captain of which, if living at this time, would be presented with a medal from the "Humane Society," for being the most tender-hearted man on the continent. When the rush of waters came, a sow and her brood took refuge on the top of a mound, situated not far from the farm now owned by Abraham Jones, south-east of the city. The captain of the Little Bee stopped his steamer at this point every day, and gave the refugees a bountiful supply of food for their wants. Thus were the lives of the porkers preserved until the flood receded. Mr Abraham Jones tells us of keeping a dairy at this time of eighty cows on Gov. Reynolds' farm, near the bluff, and marketing the milk in the city of

St. Louis. The flood came and he was cut off from his customers. He remedied this, however, by loading his cows on a flat boat, and conveying them to St. Louis, where he remained until the river was again within its banks. The floods of 1851-8, and 1862, did much demage to the town, and for a time nearly disheartened the people, the details of which would fill a volume. The erection of the dikes, which will be noticed in the proper place, have been auxiliary in protecting the city from subsequent overflows.

The outline of the city of East St. Louis is in the form of an irregular pentagon, and acquired its present limits in time and manner as follows: Illinoistown was laid out by McKnight and Brady, May 14, 1818. Reavis, in his history of "The Future Great City," places the date as 1817; but the records at Belleville show that the former is the correct date. Illinois City was formerly a part of the Cahokia Commons, and was laid out by the Cahokians in the fall of 1818. John Hays, John Hay, and Francois Turcott were appointed commissioners to plat and name the new town by the inhabitants of Cahokia, which proceedings were legalized and confirmed by a special act of Congress in 1820. It became a part of the city in May, 1875. The towns of St. Clair and East St. Louis, the Ferry divisions, the Oebike and Kase addition, are also included within the city limits. The city obtained its charter by a special act of the Legislature in the spring of 1865. The charter was prepared by J. B. Bowman and S. M. Lount, under the direction of a committee of the town council. At the first election Hon. J. B. Bowman was elected Mayor. The following named officers were elected aldermen: First ward, Michael Murphy and John O'Connell; Second ward, James S. Hazen and Henry Schall; Third ward, Capt. John Trendley and J. B. Lovingston. Wm. G. Kase was elected City judge.

As will be seen from the above, the city was divided into three wards. It is now divided into four wards, bounded as follows: The first ward includes all the territory extending east from Cahokia creek to the city limits, and south of Broadway. The Second ward lies between Broadway and Illinois avenue, and extends from Cahokia creek east to Tenth street. The Third ward includes all the territory lying between Cahokia creek and the middle of the Mississippi, and the city limits north and south. The Fourth ward embraces all the territory lying north of Illinois avenue and east of Cahokia creek to the city limits including Illinois City.

At this writing, March 21, 1881, the following are the city officers:

Maurice Joyce, mayor; James Shanon, clerk; John W. Renshaw, marshal. Aldermen: First Ward—John C. Prottsman and Earnest W. Wider. Second Ward—Thomas Hanifan and John J. McLean. Third Ward—Patrick H. O'Brien and Henry Sackmann. Fourth Ward—Levi Baugh, Jr., and James J. Rafter. These constitute the officers and members of the sixteenth Board of Aldermen of the city since its incorporation.

There is no city of its size in the United States that has the railroad facilities of East St. Louis. No less than eleven roads, by the conditions of their charters, terminate here, which are as follows: The Chicago and Alton; Indianapolis and St. Louis; Wabash, St. Louis and Pacific; Rockford, Rock Island and St. Louis, now known as the Chicago, Burlington and Quincy road; St. Louis, Vandalia and Terre Haute (Vandalia Line); Ohio and Mississippi; St. Louis, Alton and Terre Haute; (Cairo Short Line); Louisville and Nashville, formerly St. Louis and South Eastern railway; Cairo and St. Louis; East St. Louis and Carondelet; Illinois and St. Louis; Union Railway and Transit Company. The latter was organized in East St. Louis in 1874, and a like organization was also effected in St. Louis under the laws of Missouri. These, united, act as agents for the Illinois and St. Louis Bridge Company in transferring cars and merchandise from city to city. All of the above roads centre at the Relay depot, except the Cairo and St. Louis railway.

The city contains several miles of excellent paved streets; the following are macadamized entire: Dyke avenue, Front street, Broadway and Main streets, Collinsville, Missouri and Illinois avenues, and Market street. Fourth and Summit streets and St. Clair avenue are partly graded and macadamized. There has been some agitation upon the question of adopting a high-grade system of building and paving the city. The cost would necessarily place a heavy indebtedness upon the people, but the reward would undoubtedly more than recompense them for the outlay. The health and future prosperity of the city hang upon this improvement. We predict that it is only a question of time when the people will with one accord act upon this line of policy.

WIGGINS' FERRY AND THE BRIDGE.

Believing that no more complete history of the above could be given than that rendered by Dr. Isaac N. Piggott before the Literary and Historical Society of East St. Louis, in August, 1871, we take the liberty to give our readers an extract:

" From the commencement of the ferry, it was carried on under the immediate supervision of Piggott, until the 20th of February, 1799, when he died, leaving his wife the executrix of his will. She first rented the ferry to Dr. Wallis for the year 1801–2; then to ——— Adams for the year 1803–4. This Adams was the husband of the distinguished Sarah Adams, of Duncan's Island notoriety. About this time the widow of Piggott married Jacob Collard, and removed from Illinois to St. Louis. Before leaving she leased the ferry to John Campbell, for ten years. This Campbell proved treacherous, and procured a license for a ferry in his own name during the time of the lease; and hence, for a short time, it was called "Campbell's Ferry." But after a lawsuit, Campbell and confederates were beaten, and the ferry re-established to the Piggott heirs, one of whom, assisted by men named Solomon, Blundy and Porter, operated the ferry until part of the heirs sold out to McKnight & Brady. The other heirs of Piggott conveyed to Samuel Wiggins their share of the ferry. He soon succeeded in buying out his competitors, and thus obtained the whole ferry, which he afterwards superintended in person."

This was in 1818. The following spring Mr. Wiggins was authorized by an act of the legislature to establish a ferry on the Mississippi adjacent to his lands, near the town of Illinois. This act also provided that Samuel Wiggins should have the right to one mile of the shore extending along the river bank at this point.

Capt. Piggott's means of transportation was a rude affair, composed of canoes or "dug-outs," lashed together, over which was constructed a platform convenient for storage. The propelling power was by means of paddles or sweeps. Wiggins, however, soon improved upon this mode of conveyance, by building a fair-sized ferry-boat, and propelling it by horse-power, until 1828, when the first steam ferry-boat was launched upon the river, and called the "St. Clair." In 1832 another boat, the "Ibex," was put on the line," and on account of the increase of business, and therefore a demand for capital, Mr. Wiggins sold an interest in the ferry to several parties, thus forming a joint-stock company. In 1853 they obtained further privileges by an act of the legislature, and the business grew and prospered beyond the most sanguine expectation. To this enterprise is largely due the growth and prosperity of East St. Louis. Since the completion of the St. Louis and Illinois bridges the business of the ferry has necessarily diminished to some extent, but at this time the possession of ferry stock is by no means a poor investment.

The construction of the bridge was commenced in the spring of 1869, and was completed in June, 1874. It was formally dedicated to the public on the 4th of July following. Its total length, including arches and abutments, is 2,046 feet, and is connected with the Union depot in St. Louis by means of a tunnel, 4,866 feet in length. The cost of the bridge and tunnel was nearly $13,000,000. The sum total of the weight of metal in its construction is upwards of 5,000 tons. On the top of the arches is a roadway for the convenience of vehicles and foot-passengers, while underneath rolls the merchandise and human freight from the Atlantic and Pacific coasts. For a more complete history of the bridge and the railroads see chapter on Internal improvements.

We glean the following history relating to the construction of

THE DIKES

from Reavis' History of East St. Louis: Before the advent of the great flood of 1844, the channel of the Mississippi opposite the city of St. Louis, though uncertain and troubled with shifting bars, was never seriously threatened with destruction. Thereafter bars formed from the head of Bloody Island, then a little further north than now, to the Missouri shore, almost entirely closing the channel washing the St. Louis shore. The whole current of the river, and the only available and safe channel between St. Louis and the town of Illinois, was between the Island and the town of Illinois, Under the greatest of difficulties only, and by circuitous routes, could boats at all land at the St. Louis levee. Navigation then being the chief, if not the only means of communication between commercial points and from a common centre, as St. Louis then was growing to be, was the mainstay of the importance, present and prospective, of that city. Realizing this fact, public meetings were held, at which the terrible fate of St. Louis was the subject of consideration.

In 1847 ordinances were passed by the city council of St. Louis, appropriating money, and directing work to be undertaken on the Illinois shore, as the only means of salvation. Nothing less than a permanent dike across the then principal channel of the Mississippi to the east of Bloody Island, promised sure relief. This, of course, meant destruction to the harbor of the town of Illinois, and its ferry landings on the main shore. Alton, then a rival of St. Louis, calculated that what was to the disadvantage of St. Louis was *ipso facto* a benefit to Alton. The feeble complaints of the Town of Illinois were fanned into a flame of fearful excitement. The laborers upon the dike about being built by St. Louis across the eastern channel of the river, were driven away by force. Cannons were planted upon the banks, the state militia turned out, and thus state sovereignty and Alton policy were victorious, for a time, at least.

In 1848, an injunction was sworn out in the St. Clair Circuit Court, enjoining the authorities of St. Louis against any attempt to re-open like projects. Early in 1849, the legislature of Illinois was waited upon by a large delegation from St. Louis, and after due consideration, becoming a question of such magnitude and importance, by a joint resolution, it granted to the city of St. Louis for the fullest possible relief, all the authority necessary for the construction of cross and wing-dikes upon the Illinois shore opposite, so as to thoroughly protect and secure its harbor, with this proviso, that St. Louis should construct upon some of these dikes, roadways, especially upon the main dike across to the to-be-closed channel of the Mississippi from the Illinois main shore to and across Bloody Island.

Under this enactment, the work pushed rapidly to completion, so that in the spring of 1851, the main dike was finished except the road upon the embankment. It was built of rock throughout, and for a large part of the way, in the channel to be closed, in more than forty feet of water; but strong as it was, the fearful flood of that year swept the most of it away. In the fall, however, another dike was projected which was situated a fourth of a mile north and nearly parallel with the former dike. This was finished in 1856, and cost $175,000. It is still standing as a monument to the perseverance and genius of its builders. Thus the channel on the east side of the river was diverted from it course, and the pier of St. Louis re-established. Other dikes have since been constructed, and the city is now comparatively safe from future inundations.

FIRE DEPARTMENT.

The East St. Louis Fire Company, No. 1, was organized in December 1872. Its first officers were as follows: William O'Neill, president; Charles Hauss, vice-president; James W. Kirk, secretary; John V. Tefft, treasurer; Benedict Franz, captain; Adolphe Donard, first engineer; John Easton, second engineer. The company was furnished with the largest kind of Babcock engine, on trucks, and was supplied with 500 feet of hose.

Island Fire Company, No. 1, was organized November 25th, 1874. The officers elected in 1875 were: Nicolas Colgan, president; Wm. L. Johnson, vice-president; Maurice F. Tissier, secretary; Geo. W. Shields, assistant-secretary; Adolphus Lovingston, treasurer; Henry Sackmann, captain; John Keiflin, lieutenant. We are informed that since 1878, these companies have partially disbanded.

PRIZE-FIGHTING.

This was quelled in 1873, through the united efforts of the city and county authorities. Much is due to the prompt efforts of Captain Renshaw, chief of police, Ex-Mayor Bowman, Michael Walsh, and the then sheriff of the county. The warrants were sworn out by Captain Renshaw, the ringleaders were arrested, and the whole gang bound over to await the action of the Grand Jury. This wholesale onslaught and determined action on the part of the authorities, had the effect of breaking up the clan, since which time there have been no attempts to revive the prize-ring once so formidable in this part of the West.

STREET RAILWAY.

The permit for the construction of this railway was obtained by city ordinance in 1872. The company was duly organized with Harry Elliott as president, and Thomas Winstanley, manager. By the conditions of the charter the company was authorized to build the road with single or double tracks, and all necessary switches for the convenience of the road. The first line of rail extended from Bowman's Dike, near the levee, to the corner of Missouri and Collinsville Avenues. Its terminus is now at the approach of the National Stock Yards on St. Clair Avenue. It contains upwards of two miles of track, and cost, including rolling stock, etc., about $20,000. It is at this writing under the special management of Mr. Winstanley, who, by giving the enterprise his main attention, is labouring to make it a convenience to the public and a profit to the company.

EAST ST. LOUIS PUBLIC LIBRARY.

This noble enterprise was created under a city ordinance. July 16, 1872. It was organized August 13, 1872, and opened to the public February 5, 1874.

The following is gleaned from the published report, made by R. Lee Barrowman in 1876: The total number of persons enrolled and furnished with cards is 495, which are in constant daily use. The total number of volumes on hands are 4,437; of this number 433 are in the German language, 3 in the French, 9 in the Spanish, and 1 in the Hebrew. The number purchased was 1,409. The number of books donated was 67, pamphlets, 37. The percentage of the circulation is as follows: Novels, 69; historical and miscellaneous, 20; juveniles, 11.

The library also contains eighty-nine American newspapers and periodicals, among which are (dailies) Philadelphia, Times, Baltimore Sun, Boston Post, Chicago Times, St. Louis Globe-Democrat, New York Herald, Cincinnati Enquirer, etc.; (weeklies) Appleton's Journal, Irish World, Danbury News, and many others; (monthlies) Aldine, Atlantic Monthly, Harper's and Scribner's Magazines, and twenty-seven other first-class journals.

There are fourteen British publications, and nine German, among which we find the following: London Times (daily), Dublin Nation, Blackwood's Magazine, London Quarterly Review, Edinburgh Review, St. Louis Westliche Daily Post, Berliner Kladderadatsch, and the Ueber Land und Meer.

The whole number of visitors attending the rooms were 30,954, making an average daily attendance of 86. The attendance on Sunday was upon an average twenty-five per cent. more than upon other days of the week, although open only from 2 P.M. to 10 P.M. The number of books loaned out in the time was 12.924 volumes, making a daily average of 36 volumes.

Mr. Barrowman in the closing of his report gives the following gratifying information: "An extra and successful effort has been made to bring within the influence of the Library, the many boys and youth who stroll about our streets during evening hours. Let me here state the result. They were first kindly invited to come to the Library, and by supplying them with such books and papers as they took an interest in, they were thus induced to continue and renew their visits. There were some unruly ones among them, but by reproof, and expelling some of the worst, the others have remained, and at present are as well behaved as any that attend the library and give promise of becoming useful and bright members of society." And we will add, may the Reading Rooms of East St. Louis ever exist and grow in importance and influence to the last generation.

CEMETERIES.

The first interment made within what is now the city limits, was on survey No. 116, in the First ward, where the Pittsburg railway crosses said survey. This was abandoned after the flood of 1844, on account of the liability to overflow. Many a ghastly skeleton, by that flood, was washed from its resting place, to meet the gaze, perhaps, of the friends that had but a short time ago followed it to its lonely abode. To make secure from further disasters of the kind the inhabitants selected for their burial place the old Indian mound, then situated between what is now Collinsville avenue and Fourth street, and at the foot of Ohio avenue. It is said that the Indians had used it for centuries, so far as any one knew to the contrary, for a place of burying their dead. The mound was about four hundred feet in diameter at the base, and forty feet in altitude from summit to base. At that time (1844) and for years afterward it was covered mostly with heavy oak timber. In 1871–2, it was removed and the earth utilized to fill up a slough in the Second ward, and to make the ground at the south-east round-house. Nothing but a vacant lot now marks the spot. When the earth was removed, human bones and many kinds of shells were found to the depth of thirty feet. These were no doubt the remains and trinkets of a pre-historic race, called mound builders. The most of the remains of those who had been buried in our own times, were cared for by their friends and conveyed to the new cemetery. For months, however, a grinning skull might have been seen peering from the fresh cut bank of the mound at the passer-by, and so close to the street that the hand of the pedestrian could touch it as he passed.

The city at this time contains two cemeteries, both situated in Fourth ward, not far from the National Stock Yards. These were laid off for grave-yards, when the Cahokians first established Illinois city; but were not used as such until about fifteen years ago.

THE NATIONAL STOCK YARDS.

Prior to 1845, the live stock trade of St. Louis was carried on at what was formerly known as Papstown or New Brighton, and situated in the south-eastern portion of the present city of East St. Louis. About this time yards were established on the west side of the river at St. Louis. Here the business was conducted until the opening of the National Stock Yards on the east side of the river in 1873. The subject of constructing these yards was mooted as early as 1871. The agitation of the question culminated by the united efforts of several prominent Eastern and Western capitalists, who proceeded at once to purchase six hundred and fifty acres of land on the east side of the river near the city limits of East St. Louis. In July, 1872, mutual covenants were entered into between the company and the city authorities. The former were to construct a hotel to cost not less than $100,000, and to contain commission offices, brokers' offices, telegraph and post-offices, with all modern conveniences for transacting business. The stock yards were to exceed in completeness and magnitude any institution of the kind in the United States.

The city on its part covenanted to refrain from infringing, by constructing streets, or any city improvements whatsoever upon the survey, No. 627, and owned by said company. To all of which was attached the city seal and signature of A. M. Allerton, manager and attorney of the company. The yards were opened for business in the fall of 1873. One hundred out of six hundred and fifty acres purchased, are enclosed and laid out with all the convenient appurtenances of a first-class live stock market. The form of the enclosure is a rectangle and describes nearly a square. It is laid by avenues which intersect each other at right angles. Four of these avenues extend entirely through the enclosure from east to west. The floors of the yard are paved with stone, and the sheds are comfortable and well arranged for the convenience of stock. The arrangements for receiving and shipping the same are complete. No less than seventy cars can be loaded and unloaded at the same time. It contains one mile of cattle pens, which can accommodate upwards of 10,000 head of cattle. The hog and sheep houses are models of convenience and cleanliness. Over the entrance to the hog-house is inscribed the words, "Hotel de Hog," and of the sheep house, "Hotel de Sheep." The hog-house is eleven hundred and twenty-two feet in length, and capable of accommodating upwards of 20,000 head. The sheep-house is upwards of five hundred feet in length, by a hundred in width, and has the capacity of holding, if necessary, 10,000 head. The stable is a fine building, two hundred and eighty-five feet long, by eighty wide, and fitted with stalls for the accommodation of three hundred head of horses. The racks and mangers are constructed of iron; the former are supplied with hay by wooden cylinders, and the stalls are well arranged for drainage. There are two hog barns, and each has a capacity to hold eleven hundred tons of hay and fifteen thousand bushels of corn. At the approach of the yards from the south-east, on St. Clair avenue, is situated the "Allerton House,"

a magnificent building of brick with free-stone facings, and all the belongings of first-class material. It is two hundred and fifty feet in length, by one hundred and forty in breadth, and has one hundred rooms for the accommodation of guests. There is a telegraph communication with the exchange building, and every other convenience to the drovers or traders. Its cost, including furniture, was upwards of $150,000.

The Exchange Building is centrally situated, and conveniently arranged for the transaction of all business connected with the yards. It is a large brick building, plain in architecture, and three stories in height, including basement. In the north wing of the latter are the offices of the railroad stock agents, and in the center and south wing are a bar, billiard hall and refreshment room. The first floor is occupied by the officers of the yard company, bank and commission firms. On the second floor is situated the telegraph office, printing office, etc.

The Stock Yards Bank, situated in this building, is one of the important features of the concern. It materially facilitates the business of all who have transactions at the yards, its daily business aggregating upwards of $300,000.

The water-works of the yards are situated on the east bank of Cahokia creek, near the packing houses. Along the avenues are placed watch-boxes, each containing a hydrant and fire-hose, and so arranged as to cover any fire with one or two hydrants. The tank-house is a substantial building seventy feet in height, and contains three tubs, each thirty-two feet in diameter by thirty feet deep, and capable of holding 600,000 gallons of water. The total expenditure in establishing the yards, including lands, buildings, etc., is upwards of a million and a half dollars. They are complete in every arrangement, and the rapidity with which stock can be transferred from the Missouri side to the yards, or from point to point, is a matter that every shipper is interested in, as "time is money" to the live business men. Hon. Isaac H. Knox, vice-president and manager for the company, is the right man in the right place. He is a clear-headed business man, combined with affableness and rare executive ability. Under his management the business has materially increased, and become one of the most important stock markets in the country. The following is a table showing the receipts of the yards since their opening:

	Cars.	Cattle.	Hogs.	Sheep.	Horses.
1874—	17,264	234,002	498,840	41,407	2,235
1875—	13,938	232,183	181,708	46,316	2,385
1876—	18,052	234,671	333,560	84,034	2,616
1877—	24,342	322,571	425,389	119,165	2,366
1878—	31,003	317,830	833,446	82,549	2,534
1879—	35,641	333,155	1,163,748	99,951	4,338
1880—	38,294	346,533	1,262,234	129,611	5,963

OTHER BUSINESS AT THE YARDS.

St. Louis Beef Canning Company.—This company was organized in the fall of 1876, with a capital of $200,000, and promises to be in time the largest establishment of the kind on either continent. It is situated on St. Clair avenue, and occupies eight acres of ground. The main building is 324x100 feet, and four stories high. The slaughter house is 240x76 feet, two stories high, and is adjoined to the main building. The warehouse is also two stories in height, and 176x100 feet on the ground. In addition to these there is an engine room 60x61, tank-house 76x30, and smoke-house 24x60. The establishment furnishes employment to nearly one thousand persons, two-fifths of whom are boys and girls. One thousand head of cattle are slaughtered daily, and the annual value of manufactured products is between four and five millions of dollars. Hon. Isaac H. Knox is president of the company, but the establishment is under the immediate supervision of Mr. Patterson, secretary and treasurer.

East St. Louis Packing and Provision Company.—This enterprise was established in 1873, under the firm name of W. E. Richardson & Co., and merged into a stock company in 1875. The grounds, on which this packing house stands, contain ten acres, seven of which are covered with the buildings. They are mainly three stories in height, and all of them are constructed of brick. It is one of the most extensive packing houses in the West, and when worked to its full capacity, gives employment to seven hundred men. The nominal capacity of the works is 8,000 hogs per day, and the value of its annual shipments is from three to five millions of dollars. It is under the efficient management of D. L. Quirk, president, and W. E. Richardson, vice-president.

Francis Whitaker & Sons.—This packing house was erected in 1877, at the expense of upwards of $100,000. The main building is 185x185 feet, and is three and a half stories high, with a cellar under the entire building. A tank-house 80x90 feet joins the main building, and adjacent to the former is the slaughter-house, 30x60 feet. Besides these there are eight pen-houses, all under one roof, 120x120 feet, and a platform packing apartment 40x185 feet. The average capacity of the house is 3,000 hogs per day, and employs about three hundred hands.

North-Western Fertilizing Company.—This is a branch establishment of a well-known Chicago firm. The works commenced operations here in the fall of 1877. The building is a frame structure, and covers one acre of ground. The machinery of the factory is run by a one hundred-horse power engine. Fifty hands are employed daily to conduct the works. It has the capacity of manufacturing, annually, 15,000 tons of fertilizer, which, when thrown upon the market, will bring upwards of $400,000. Within the last year the company has added machinery for the purpose of manufacturing "Plant-Food," specially adapted for house plants and lawn use, on account of its being entirely odorless. Large quantities of both the Fertilizer and Plant-Food find a demand in the eastern markets.

McCarthy Live Stock and Packing Company, situated on the corner of Provision street and the plank road. The building was erected in 1877-8, by Arch. Allen, but is now owned by F. G. Rowe, and the business is conducted by John McCarthy. The building is a snug two-story brick, and with the attachments, covers nearly an acre of ground. It has the capacity of slaughtering and packing daily 1000 head of hogs and fifty head of cattle. It gives employment to twenty men.

St. Louis Carbon Works.—These works were established in 1875 at a cost of $10,000, and are situated on the National Stock Yards railroad. They were first known as the "Western Fertilizing and Chemical Works," and in 1878 again changed the name to "Keeler's Carbon Works." They afterwards assumed the former title, and are so-called at this time. The company owns three acres of ground, upon which the factory is situated. The building is a frame, 150 by 300 feet, the main portion of which is two stories high. The machinery consists of a fifty horse power engine, a bone mill and bone kiln. It manufactures from five to six thousand tons of bone yearly, and employs from thirty to forty hands. The annual manufactured product is upwards of $600,000. Max Dietrich is the superintendent of the works.

Carey's Beef and Pork Packing House is situated on Provision street, and north of McCarthy's packing house. It was established by Richard Carey, sole owner and proprietor, in the year 1880, at a cost of $10,000. The building is a snug two-story house, with stone basement, the upper portion being built of brick, and in size is 48 by 55 feet. There is also a boiler and tank-house, 30 by 40 feet, which is detached from the main building. This is also built of brick, and is two stories in height. When worked to its full capacity, it can pack 600 hogs and 100 beeves daily, and gives employment to forty persons.

St. Louis Rendering Works. Levi Baugh, jr., proprietor. These were established in 1872, and located on the east side of Provision street and the Stock Yards railway. The building is a frame two-story structure, 68 by 80 feet on the ground floor, with a side room for cooling purposes 16 by 30 feet. The engine-room, attached to the main building on the north, is 30 by 30 feet. The cost of the works was $2,500, and they give employment to about twelve men. The establishment, under the efficient management of Mr. Baugh, is capable of rendering 150 hogs and 50 beeves per day.

George Mulrow & Company, Pork Packers.—This institution is situated between the East St. Louis Packing House and the National Stock Yards enclosure, and was established in 1880. The building is a frame, two stories, and 50 by 150 feet in size, and cost, including machinery, etc., $3,000. It has the capacity of slaughtering and packing 300 hogs per day, and employs on an average fourteen hands. James Lillay, foreman.

Baugh's Catch Basin is situated just across Cahokia creek, outside of the limits of the Stock Yards. It was constructed in 1880, at an expense of about $600, and is utilized to catch the superfluous grease that escapes through the sewer from the packing houses. Formerly the sewer opened into Cahokia creek, but the city authorities made complaint; hence at this point a flume was built across the creek, and Mr. Baugh erected this basin. It is 30 by 40 feet in size, and contains eight vats, four on each side. Here the water is retained and cooled, when the grease floats, it is skimmed from the surface and deposited in barrels arranged for that purpose. When the packing houses are all in full blast, from fifteen to twenty barrels of grease are caught daily.

St. Clair Rendering Company.—This institution is owned and operated by M. E. Richardson and Capt. Clubb, and is situated on St. Clair avenue, between the National Stock Yards and the town of Brooklyn. It was established in the spring of 1880 by Rogers & Mullholl, and passed into the hands of the present proprietors the fall following. The main building is two stories high, frame, and in size 76 by 76 feet, and cost, including necessary machinery, $5,000. It has the capacity of pressing ten tons of tank stuff, and drying one ton of blood daily, besides rendering three hundred and fifty hogs per week. It employs on an average fifteen hands, and manufactures $100,000 worth of products annually. Foreman, Wm. H. Courtney.

CITY MANUFACTURES.

St. Louis Bolt and Iron Company.—This is the largest manufacturing establishment in the city, and is situated near the Cairo Short Line railroad. The officers of the company are T. A. Meysenburg, president; O. W. Meysenburg, superintendent; Geo. S. Edgell, treasurer. The works contain six puddling furnaces, three heating, six spike, and two bolt furnaces, besides all the necessary machinery peculiar to the works, such as planers, lathes, etc. Street rails, T rails, bolts and spikes are made a specialty of manufacture by the company. The works are in operation day and night, the laborers being divided into two sets or watches. These works employ about one hundred and fifty men, and have the capacity of manufacturing daily forty tons of finished iron, ten tons of railroad spikes, and several thousand strap or trace bolts. From three to four thousand dollars are paid to the employees every two weeks. The company own two-and-a-half acres of ground and two railroad switches where the works are situated. The products are shipped to points both east and west.

Grape, Sugar, and Glucose Works, O. W. Heyer & Co., proprietors. These works are situated in the Third ward, on the river front, and were erected in 1869 by Brotherton & Morse for milling purposes. The present company purchased the property and remodelled the building suitable to their wants. They commenced operations of manufacture in the spring of 1875. The present factory, as remodelled, is made up of three departments or buildings. The main building, or manufactory proper, is four stories high, and 45 feet square. The engine house is 20 by 36 feet, besides a starch room, used exclusively for the manufacture of starch. The whole structure on the ground covers 50,000 square feet. The cost of the building and appurtenances thereto was $150,000. It has the capacity of grinding 3,000 bushels of corn daily, and can manufacture in the same time one hundred and fifty barrels of syrup. From seventy-five to one hundred persons are constantly employed in the works. The approximate value of manufactured product is $100,000 annually. The business is under the immediate supervision of Louis Strehl.

Railroad Frog Works.—This establishment dates from 1874, then under the sole supervision and management of George and Henry Elliot. In 1875 Mr. George Elliot died, and the institution passed into the hands of the present owners, H. & H. Elliot. The works were established for the purpose of manufacturing railway crossings, frogs, switches, and track tools, and are located on Main and Broad streets, near the East St. Louis and Carondelet railway. The main building, or machine shop, is 39 by 90 feet, with other convenient attachments. The works were constructed at a cost of $10,000, and give employment to about sixty men, who receive for their labor from $1.75 to $3 per day. The capacity of manufacture is about 4,500 frogs and 100 crossings per annum. Value of products, $150,000.

Heim's Brewing Company.—This is the only Brewing Company in East St. Louis. It was established by Nick Spannagel in 1856, and was afterwards purchased by the present company. It is situated on the corner of Tenth street and Belleville Turnpike. The buildings occupy the identical site of the old hotel, built and kept in an early day by Mr. Condit, and the place known as Papstown. The main building is a splendid three story brick structure, and with the attachments covers nearly an acre of ground. The cost of the building and machinery aggregates $150,000. Its capacity is from fifty to sixty thousand barrels annually, and gives employment to about forty persons. The annual value of manufactured goods is over $500,000. The company is attaching an ice machine for the purpose of cooling the cellars, which is an entirely new departure in the brewing business.

East St. Louis Gaslight Company was established in 1874, and situated at the junction of the Illinois and St. Louis railroad, near Cahokia creek. The size of the tank is sixty feet in diameter and twenty feet in depth. It has the capacity of supplying 58,000 feet of gas, and is supplied with seven-and-a-half miles of pipe. The capital invested is about $125,000, and at present receives an income of upwards of $7,000 from the annual manufactured material. Wm. H. Watts is the efficient superintendent of the works, and has under his supervision the employment of eleven men.

East St. Louis Flouring Mills.—St. Louis has been one of the most unfortunate cities in the country with regard to the destruction by fire of her flouring mills. Many have been built, and but one is now standing. This was first constructed in 1855, by F. H. Krite

39

and A. De Clansel for a saw-mill near the old Belleville depot. In 1861 it was sold to a company who transformed it into a grist-mill; this was torn down in 1865, and a large four-story brick erected in its place. The latter was a first-class mill in every respect, and was built and operated by Notley, Krite & Co. In the fall of 1866, it was destroyed by fire, involving a heavy loss to the owners. The present building was erected in 1868–69, on the old site, and is the only flouring mill in the city. It is a four-story brick building with basement, and in size 40x80 feet. The cost of construction exceeded $80,000, having all the modern machinery and improvements for manufacturing flour. The mill has the capacity of making four hundred barrels of flour per day, containing seven run of stones, three for meal and four for flour. It employs about twenty-five hands, and handles annually nearly $500,000 of manufactured material. Mr. F. H. Krite is the secretary of the firm, and has the general supervision of the mill.

City Planing Mill.—This factory was originally located at Litchfield, Ill., and was removed to this city in 1877. It is now owned by Theodore Wiegreffe, and situated on Fourth street, between Missouri and St. Louis avenues. It is a frame building, mainly two stories high, and 86x112 feet, on the ground. The cost of the factory, including all the appurtenances, was upwards of $6,000. From twelve to fifteen hands are constantly employed, and manufacture over 8,000 pork-packing boxes annually, beside making a large quantity of doors, sash, blinds, etc. The amount of manufactured goods is $15,000.

East St. Louis Elevator Company.—This institution is one of the leading industries of the city, and was established in 1867, by an act of the legislature, approved March 6th of that year. It is situated on the river front below the bridge, and occupies the ground on the line of the dike, which was built to improve the harbor in 1842, by Capt. Robert E. Lee, then Chief Engineer of the United States army. The company owns five hundred feet front on the river, by four hundred feet deep, and by the conditions of the charter it may extend these boundaries to one thousand feet front by the same in depth, and occupy by purchase any other lands within three miles of Bloody Island. The capacity for storing grain is upwards of one million bushels. The cost of the grounds, building, machinery, etc., was nearly $1,000,000.

The Advance Elevator and Warehouse is situated on the island, near Front street, between the Chicago and Alton, and Ohio and Mississippi railways. It was established in 1872, by Messrs. McCormic, Adams and Armington, at a cost of $125,000. In 1880 it passed into the hands of the present company. The elevator and warerooms covered 20,400 square feet of ground. The elevator proper is 50x60 feet, 130 feet high, and has convenient connections with the river and all the roads leading into East St. Louis. It has an engine of eighty horse-power, and all necessary machinery for handling grain. From twelve to fifteen men are employed daily, and seventy car-loads of grain can be elevated in one day. Three tracks pass through the entire building. It has the capacity of storing 400,000 bushels of grain. The present company are R. S. McCormic, C. W. Isaacs, D. P. Slatery, Jno. Jackson, and H. Rogers.

Pioneer Warehouse.—This was established by Benj. F. Horn in the spring of 1880, and is situated east of the East St. Louis Flouring Mills, and south of the Illinois and St. Louis railway track. The building is a frame, one-story, and 20x60 feet. It has the capacity of manufacturing 270 flour barrels per day, and gives employment to twenty men. Richard Zimmerman, foreman.

HALL'S PATENT DRY PRECIOUS METAL SEPARATOR, EAST ST. LOUIS, ILL.

Hall & Co's. Manufactory was established in the spring of 1880, with the following officers representing the company: Giles Hall, President; J. M. Macdonald, Vice-President; Ferdinand Heim, Treasurer; Wm. P. Launtz, Secretary. The machines manufactured by this company are for the purpose of separating or extracting gold and other precious metal from auriferous deposits. This process is ingeniously effected by means of compressed air in connection with chemicals (see cut above). It is entirely a new invention, and if it succeeds in performing what the inventor claims for it, the company has certainly struck a bonanza. The capital stock is $12,000. The factory is situated on Collinsville avenue, between Broadway and Missouri avenues.

C. B. & Q. Elevator Company.—This is a new enterprise, and the elevator is now in process of construction. It is owned by, and will be conducted in the interest of the Chicago, Burlington and Quincy Railway Company. It is situated at the terminus of the road, and a little north of the company's freight-house. The foundation is composed of seventeen piers besides the outer walls, and the size of the main building is to be 87x177 feet, and 148 feet in height. The cost of its construction, machinery, etc., will exceed half a million dollars, and it will have the capacity of storing 750,000 bushels of grain. Four tracks are to be laid through the building.

Turning Factory, Henry Sternkopf, proprietor. This factory was established in 1876, and is located on Brady street, between Main street and Cairo Short Line railway track. The building is a frame structure 24x30 feet, and cost, including machinery, $1,500. Mr. Sternkopf has in his employ from four to six men, and manufactures all articles in wood work. Wooden faucets are made a specialty, turning out from fifteen to twenty gross per week. The annual sales of manufactured goods are from two to three thousand dollars.

Soda Factory.—This enterprise was established in 1870, by C. Lutt & Co. The business is carried on in a fine two-story brick building, 40x80 feet in dimensions, and it is located on Main street, between Broadway and Railroad street. The cost of construction, with the necessary appliances, was $4,500. The factory is capable of manufacturing three hundred boxes of soda-water per day. It gives employment to four persons, and handles a manufactured product of $25,000 per annum. Seltzer-water is also manufactured to some extent by this firm.

Lumber Mill is situated south of the Cairo Short Line Roundhouse, and was built in 1878, by J. H. Modrell, owner and proprietor. It is driven by an engine of thirty horse-power, and is capable of sawing $75,000 worth of lumber annually. Its construction cost the proprietor $3,000. Six hands are kept in employment the greater portion of the year. There are two circular saws, one arranged above the other, for the purpose of handling, properly, the largest sized logs. The timber for sawing is mostly shipped from Tennessee, and is manufactured into lumber suitable for bridge building.

Schroeder's Soda Factory.—These works were established by John Kerns in 1862, and became the property of Edward Schroeder in 1864. It was the first establishment of the kind built in East St. Louis, and is located on Illinois avenue, between Ninth and Tenth streets, and west of Heim's Brewery. Both soda and Seltzer are manufactured, having the capacity of making daily upwards of four hundred boxes of the former. The building is a substantial brick structure, and is supplied with all the necessary machinery and apparatus peculiar to the business.

Ice Houses.—Smith & Sons own three of the largest houses in the city. They are situated just south of the river bridge. They each have room to stow upwards of 7,000 tons of ice.

C. Lutt & Co., have four ice houses near the Relay Depot. They have the capacity of 4,000 tons each.

BANKS.

There are two banking institutions in the city, besides the one in the Exchange building at the Stock Yards, which has already been mentioned.

Working Men's Banking Company.—This Bank was organized August 15th, 1870, by John McMullin, George W. Davis, Henry Schell, E. W. Wider and others, and has a capital stock of $50,000. It is located on the corner of Broadway and Fourth street, and is one of the finest buildings in the city, and is the only house in East St. Louis built above high-water mark. President, R. J. Whitney; Cashier, Geo. W. Dausch.

East St. Louis Bank was established in 1865, and has a capital stock of $100,000; surplus, $26,000. The bank is situated on the corner of Missouri and Collinsville avenues. Thomas Witstanley, President; Henry Jackiesch, Vice-President; Theodore Meumann, Cashier.

Besides the foregoing, the city contains nine round-houses, some of which are equal to any institutions of the kind in the state; five large warehouses, with several others of smaller dimensions. The following is a condensed showing of other industries represented in the city: Bakeries, 6; cigar manufactories, 5; harness, 2; wagons, 1; blacksmiths, 5; tinners, 4; tailors, 2; jewelers, 2; carpenters, 44; printing offices, 2; shoemakers, 15; butchers, 9; undertakers, 1; dentists, 1; painters and glazers, 2. There are upwards of thirty hotels, and over seventy-five places where liquors are sold. There are three wholesale grocery houses, two dry-goods, two hardware establishments, and one wholesale liquor house. The retail business of every kind is well represented. The various churches are also numerous, there being two Catholic (Irish, and German), one Methodist, one Presbyterian, one Lutheran, and two Colored churches. There are eight distinct schools in the city as follows: First ward, two; Second ward, three; Third ward, one; Fourth ward, two. For further information on schools, churches, and printing offices, see special chapters relating to the same.

The following is a tabular showing of the number of inhabitants, families, and buildings that the city contained (with a slight discrepancy) in 1880:

	Inhabitants.	Families.	Buildings.
1st Ward	2,047	451	380.
2d Ward	2,330	—	—
3d Ward	1,959	380	350.
4th Ward	2,263	457	383.

SECRET SOCIETIES.

East St. Louis Lodge, No. 504, A. F. & A. M., was organized in October, 1866, with 28 charter members. Its place of meeting is in Masonic Hall, over Schaub's hardware store, and meets the first and third Thursday evenings in each month. The Lodge has a fine hall and is in a prosperous condition.

East St. Louis Chapter No. 156, R. A. M., was chartered in October, 1873, with a membership of 31, since which time it has materially increased. Meets in Masonic Hall every second Thursday night in each month.

Golden Rule Lodge, No. 374 I. O. O. F.—This Lodge was instituted June 16th, 1868, and chartered October 13th, 1868. The number of charter members were 8, and the present membership is 55. Meets in Odd Fellows' Hall every Thursday evening in each week. The Lodge is in a prosperous condition and good working order.

Pride of the Valley Lodge, No. 435, I. O. O. F., was chartered the 11th of October, 1870. Number of charter members, 10, present membership, 51. Meets every Monday night.

Harmony Encampment, No. 102.—This institution was chartered the 12th of October, 1869, with a membership of 12. It meets in Odd Fellows' Hall the second and fourth Thursday nights in each month.

Helvetia Lodge (German), No. 480, I. O. O. F., was instituted February 22d, 1872, and chartered October 8th, 1872. Charter membership, 11; present number of members, 55. Meets every Friday night.

Naomi Rebecca Degree Lodge, No. 5.—Chartered October 11th, 1870, with a membership of 27, since which time it has largely increased. Meets in Odd Fellows' Hall the first and third Thursday evenings in each month.

Eureka Lodge, No. 81, K. of P., was organized December 26, 1878, and chartered October 23d, 1879. Number of charter members, 24; present membership, 55. The Lodge is in a flourishing condition. Meets in Schaub's Hall every Monday evening.

Illinois Lodge, No. 268, K. of H.—This Lodge received its charter Dec. 5th, 1876, with the names of nineteen members. It has had an unprecedented growth, having a present membership of 160. Convenes in Odd Fellows' Hall every Wednesday evening.

Catholic Knights of America.—This institution was organized March 19th, 1880, with a membership of 8 Knights; present membership, 53. They meet the first and third Sundays of each month in St. Patrick's Church Hall. This is a wide-awake and prosperous organization.

Olive Branch Lodge, No. 335, K. & L. of H., is under dispensation, granted May 28th, 1880. Charter membership, 46; present membership, 54. The Lodge meets at Fink's Hall the first and third Mondays in each month.

F. W. Arnold, No. 44, B. of L. & F., was chartered May 2d, 1880. Number of charter members, 18; present membership, 23. Meets the first and third Tuesday nights of each month in Fink's Hall.

East St. Louis Sængerbund was instituted March 23d, 1872, with 25 members; present membership, 50. The organization meets at Jackiesh Hall every Wednesday night.

DIRECTORY

OF THE

CITY OF EAST ST. LOUIS

ST. CLAIR COUNTY, ILLINOIS,

FOR

1893.

GIVING AN ALPHABETICAL LIST OF ALL THE INHABITANTS, WITH THEIR
RESIDENCE AND OCCUPATION. ALSO AN INDEX TO THE AD-
VERTISERS AND BUSINESS HOUSES REPRESENTED IN
THIS BOOK, TOGETHER WITH A LIST OF THE OFFI-
CERS OF THE GOVERNMENT SINCE ITS IN-
CORPORATION IN 1859, BESIDES
OTHER HISTORICAL DATA.

PUBLISHED ANNUALLY BY

C. B. CARROLL.

VOLUME IV.

PRICE, $2.00 EACH.

1893.
JOURNAL BOOK AND JOB PRINT,
EAST ST. LOUIS, ILL.

INTRODUCTION.

The East St. Louis Directory has become an absolute necessity, not only on account of its worth to the local merchants and business men by furnishing them with an alphabetical list of all the inhabitants, but to the outside world who have learned to patronize it as well, and every merchant in St. Louis now desires to transact business with the people here, and as a means of becoming acquainted finds no easier method than a liberal use of the directory affords.

The whole country now treats East St. Louis as a great city, which must be dealt out in a business way. The old town methods will no longer suffice, as the change of conditions have also caused a wonderful change in business, and the manner of procuring it. A few years ago none of the great firms of St. Louis cared about working the field on this side, but now on account of an abundance of first-class houses at home, nothing but constant attention on the part of oursiders will give a footing in the commercial line here. All classes of business have progressed wonderfully and according to the opinions of men who have fortunes invested in East St. Louis, the city will continue to advance in all lines, until it reaches that position in the commercial and manufacturing world, which nature and the great work of financiers, railroad men and its staunch friends desire it to fill. Although it has progressed greatly in many branches, it seems to be specially favored as a manufacturing center, and long before the end of the next year, it will no doubt far surpass any city in the west of its size as a mart in this line. Elliot's Frog and Switch Works, Wuerpels, the Tudor Works, the Malleable Iron Works, the Western Forge Works, the Freeman Wire Works, the Todd Pulley Works, the Steel Post and in fact every other class of iron factory has almost doubled its capacity in the past year, and it is said all contemplate making more extensions to their plants. The great stock yards on the north end handled more stock last season than in any two former seasons. The cattle, hogs and sheep have not been sent to this place as a main watering station either. Vast herds, flocks and droves of the animals have arrived at the pens on foot, but in a short space of time were killed and cured in one or the other of the great packing and storage houses at the yards. In former years, many loads were merely transferred from one road to another after a day's feeding but now with the increased facilities for killing and packing, the owners of all consignments find a ready market at the place, and as a consequence the stock market here has become one of the leading industries of

Fourth cemetery, the city one, in Illinois City.

Fifth cemetery, St. Henry's, on the St. Clair county turnpike.

Sixth cemetery, St. Peter's, on the St. Clair county turnpike.

Seventh cemetery, Mount Carmel, on the Bluff.

First stock yards at Papstown, present New Brighton portion of city.

National Stock Yards established in 1873.

City court of record, established in August, 1874.

East St. Louis Gas Light and Coke Co., established in 1874.

East St. Louis Bank established in 1865.

Workingmen's Banking Company established in 1870.

First railroad—ground broken for the Ohio and Mississippi, near Broadway and Main streets, in 1852; the road in operation in 1857.

Earthquake in 1811.

Tornado, March 8, 1871.

First Masonic lodge, February 22, 1866.

First flood, in 1826; second, in 1844; third, 1851; fourth, in 1858; fifth, in 1862.

Lowest stage of water in 1832.

First brick house built here in 1810, by Etienne Pensoneau, corner Main and Menard streets.

The first railroad built in Illinois, from East St. Louis to the bluffs, in 1836, as a coal road.

The first school house built here was by Capt. John Trendley, in 1840.

The first church established here was of the Methodist persuasion, in 1845.

The Methodist Episcopal church of Illinois Town was organized in 1849; reorganized in 1868 as St. John's M. E. church; reorganized in 1887 as the Summit Avenue M. E. church.

St. Patrick's Catholic church organized in 1861, by Rev. John J. Brennan; church built in 1862.

St. Henry's Catholic church organized in 1866, by Rev. Father Rinkes.

Evangelical Lutheran church organized in 1863, by Rev. P. Buenger

The Presbyterian church organized in 1868.

Episcopalian church organized in 1870; reorganized by W. H. Tomlins, in 1886.

Howe Literary Institute, Baptist, organized in 1873-4.

The first duel on "Bloody Island" was on August 12, 1817, between Col. Thos. H. Benton and Charles Lucas; Lucas wounded.

Second duel, same place, between same parties, on September 27, 1817; Lucas killed.

Third duel, same place, between Thos. C. Rector and Joshua Barton, U. S. Dist. Attorney, on June 30, 1823; Barton killed.

Fourth duel, same place, between Maj. Thomas Biddle and Congress man Spencer Pettis, on August 27, 1830; both died from wounds received.

Dual government and municipal difficulties, 1877 and 1878.

City hall building and public library destroyed by fire in 1881; police station burned in 1883.

First city charter in 1865; amended in 1867; a new one in 1869; incorporated under General Law of State, August 28, 1888.

Ex-Mayor John B. Bowman assassinated on November 20, 1885.

Railroad employes' difficulties, 1886.

New registration and election law adopted by East St. Louis in November, 1886.

M. M. Stephens elected Mayor, April, 1887.

The new, progressive and prosperous era for East St. Louis, inaugurated in April, 1887.

East St. Louis Indebtedness Funded in 1888-9.

First granite pavement, Front street, 1887-8.

Streets commenced to be raised to new grade, 1889, starting with Broadway.

Population of East St. Louis, in 1870, 5,000; in 1880, 9,000; in 1888, 16,000.

FIRST OFFICERS.

First mayor, John B. Bowman, 1865; first city clerk, John O'Rielly, 1865; first city treasurer, Francis Wittram, 1865; first city marshal, Timothy Canty, 1865; first city auditor James W. Kirk, 1872; first chief of police, Ben Godin, 1871; first city engineer, Daniel McGowan; first police court judge, Wm. G. Kase; first city court of record judge, Daniel McGowan; first clerk of court, Thomas Hanifan; first city comptroller, James W. Kirk, 1888.

EAST ST. LOUIS JOURNALISM.

First newspaper, American Bottom *Gazette*, in 1842; Sunday *Herald*, in 1865; East St. Louis *Gazette*, 1866; People's *Gazette*, in 1871; *The Press*, in 1873; *National Stock Yards' Reporter*, in 1873; *Daily Press*, in 1874; *Tri-Weekly Press*, in 1875; *Daily Gazette*, in 1876; St. Clair *Tribune*, in 1875; East St. Louis *Herald*, in 1878; East St. Louis *Signal*, 1882; East St. Louis *Star*, in 1888; East St. Louis *Journal*, in 1889; East St. Louis *Daily Journal*, in 1890; East St. Louis *Truth*, 1892.

HISTORICAL

ENCYCLOPEDIA

OF

ILLINOIS

EDITED BY

Newton Bateman, LL. D.   Paul Selby, A. M.

AND HISTORY OF

St. CLAIR COUNTY

EDITED BY

A. S. Wilderman   A. A. Wilderman

VOLUME II.

ILLUSTRATED

CHICAGO:
MUNSELL PUBLISHING COMPANY,
PUBLISHERS.
1907.

PREFATORY STATEMENT.

To the Citizens of St. Clair County:

Having been repeatedly requested to prepare a history of St. Clair County, to be published in connection with the "Historical Encyclopedia of Illinois," as a special St. Clair County edition, I have, after mature consideration and consultation with friends, consented to do so to the best of my ability. I am prompted to assume the task because I believe it a duty that every citizen owes to old St. Clair—the Mother of counties—to assist in presenting to the world her story which, reaching backward into the latter half of the seventeenth century, is rich in all that goes to make up the aggregate of the history of our American Nation. Indeed, I do not believe there is any county in the whole country comprised within the original boundaries of "Territory Northwest of the River Ohio" that surpasses St. Clair in the richness of the material which gives interest to its early, as well as its later, history.

Within its limits were established the first permanent white settlements in the Mississippi Valley, and by these settlers were planted those village communities which still exist, with their peculiar land systems so vividly described by Sir Henry Maine, so unique and so little understood by the present generation, but so dear to the Indo-Germanic stock of both the West and Far East. The earliest of these white settlers were those daring Frenchmen who sought to establish a French Empire in the New World, and those devoted French Catholic fathers who came to teach the great lesson of humanity to the Indian aborigines. A century later came a stream of hardy American pioneers, whose descendants are, to-day, pushing onward and upward in the march of progress, making this country, once a wilderness and the home of wild beasts and wilder men, one of the foremost in all that conduces to the welfare and prosperity of the human race. A little later there came the frugal and thrifty Germans, the mercurial, good-humored Irishmen, as well as the sturdy Englishmen, to enjoy the advantages of our country's fertile soil, its exhaustless mines, its proximity to the early markets and its choice climate, and to assume their share of the burdens and responsibilities incident to the development of a new country, the making of it the home of comfort and culture. It is the story of these people—especially of the pioneer men and women—their struggles and sufferings, their patriotism and their triumphs, which it is the purpose of the proposed publication to tell.

It is to be regretted that this enterprise could not have been undertaken when the stories of those who were the chief actors in our earlier history could have been learned from their own lips, but the task, important as it is, should be deferred no longer. Many of you, like myself, have spent your lives in this county; have grown up with it and been a part of its history. Believing that you will feel a just pride in the story of St. Clair County, I feel justified in appealing to you for assistance in this undertaking. Many of you are, no doubt, in possession of facts pertaining to our local history and representative families, and these you are earnestly requested to communicate to me in brief outline, by mail at Belleville. It may not be possible to use all material in full as furnished, but all important facts, thus communicated, will find their proper place in the work.

A. S. Wilderman

Editor.

PREFACE.

The foregoing letter, written by my father when he first undertook the preparation of this History of St. Clair County, is self-explanatory. Before assuming the duties and responsibilities of the same as historian and editor, he obtained my co-operation as assistant in this capacity, and we labored in conjunction with each other for months, gathering from many and varied sources the material necessary for the completion of the work. While a large proportion of the data was in hand at the time of his decease, some of it had not been placed in manuscript form for printing. With redoubled energy and intensified interest, I have, therefore, sought, in the completion of this history—which may well be regarded as my father's last great life-work—to bring it, with well rounded proportions, to a reasonable degree of completeness and, as nearly as practicable, up to date. In the performance of this task I have been ably assisted by some of my father's life-long and intimate friends, a number of whom have furnished contributions, which appear in the body of the work under their respective names.

My intimate association, from the outset, with my father in the task which he had undertaken, allied me very closely to the motives which inspired him to the assumption of his duties in connection therewith. It was his belief that a debt due not only to the past and present, but also to future generations, could be best discharged by a competent and lasting record, which might serve, in the future, as a mile-stone in history. This history has been undertaken and has been written in the belief that it is needed; that man's immortal instincts revolt at the thought of past virtues and achievements being buried in oblivion—that the fruitage of lives which have accomplished results, epitomized in the word "History," should be forgotten—that lessons of faithful doing, of self-sacrifice, zealous faith and daring courage should fail of their high accomplishment by way of example and inspiration to others, because no one has recorded them—or that present and future generations should be deprived of these teachings, examples and educational forces, simply for the want of a proper and available published record of many facts, now having an existence only in the memory of a few individuals who cannot long remain, and whose passing away will place them beyond the reach of those who come after.

Hence this history, with the deficiencies, imperfections and shortcomings always incident to human authorship, is submitted in the belief that it will have a value, not only to the citizens of St. Clair County, but to many others interested in State history.

I desire to express the sincere thanks not only of myself but of our family, to my father's many friends for their helpful assistance rendered in

CHAPTER XVIII.

CITY OF EAST ST. LOUIS.

GENERAL HISTORY—RICHARD M'CARTY FIRST SET-
TLER—CAPTAIN PIGGOTT AND OTHER EARLY ARRI-
VALS—WIGGINS FERRY ESTABLISHED IN 1816—
LAFAYETTE'S VISIT—"BLOODY ISLAND" AND SOME
NOTABLE DUELS—FLOODS AND TORNADOES—JACK-
SONVILLE AND ILLINOISTOWN EARLY VILLAGES—
COMMERCIAL AND INDUSTRIAL DEVELOPMENT—
RAILROADS, MANUFACTURES AND LIVE-STOCK
TRADE—CITY INCORPORATED — MUNICIPAL OFFI-
CIALS — POSTMASTERS — PROSPECTIVE FEDERAL
BUILDING — BUSINESS MEN'S ORGANIZATIONS—
THE EADS BRIDGE—OTHER LOCAL IMPROVEMENTS
—NATIONAL STOCK YARDS — CHURCHES AND
SCHOOLS — PRESS AND PUBLIC LIBRARY — LAW-
YERS AND PHYSICIANS—TO WHOM HONOR IS DUE.

EAST ST. LOUIS HISTORY IN OUTLINE. (Contributed by Thomas L. Fekete.)—To write a
history of East St. Louis that would, in any
sense, be complete, would require more space
than should be expected of us, but we here
reproduce the main features of the city's history. In so doing we must refer to its location opposite the great metropolis of the Mississippi Valley and in the heart of the "Great
American Bottoms"—probably the richest strip
of land in the United States; while the "Father of Waters," the mighty Mississippi River,
one of the greatest arteries of commerce, flows
beside her, and is spanned by that vast engineering triumph, the Eads Bridge, which unites
the largest city of Southern Illinois with St.
Louis.

For more than one hundred years there has
been something of a community where East
St. Louis stands. In 1765 Richard McCarty
(known as "English McCarty") settled here,
owning 400 acres of land on both sides of Cahokia Creek. Twenty years later the whole section was devastated by a flood, pronounced by
the Indians as the greatest whose memory was
preserved in their traditions. White settlers,
however, soon repaired the damage wrought
by the flood, and a little group of houses,
mainly inns and houses of entertainment, appeared in the south part of what is now the
city of East St. Louis. At that time farmers

from the country who wished to transport
their produce to the growing settlement of St.
Louis left their teams where East St. Louis
now is and crossed on canoes and on flat boats
bringing back goods in the same way. In
1797 a ferry to accommodate these people was
instituted by Captain Piggott. In 1810 the
first brick house was built by Etienne Pensoneau at what is now the corner of Main
and Menard Streets. The first steamboat to
ascend the Mississippi, having been launched at
Pittsburg, came to East St. Louis in 1811.

Just after the battle of New Orleans in 1815
the residents planned "Jacksonville," which
name was changed two years later to Illinois
Town, though the plat was not recorded until
1825. Fifty years afterward this was made a
part of East St. Louis. In 1810 "Bloody
Island," now called "The Island," and embracing the territory between Cahokia Creek and
the Mississippi, received its first public notice.
It was here, in 1817, that the first noted duel
between St. Louisans was fought. On August 12 of that year Colonel Thomas H. Benton
and Charles Lucas met here, according to the
code then prevailing, and Mr. Lucas was seriously wounded. Six weeks later they met
again at the same place and this time Mr. Lucas was killed.

In 1818, the Wiggins Ferry was established
and has ever since been one of the commercial
institutions of East St. Louis. In 1902 the stock
in this company was bought up by the association that controls the Eads Bridge.

Another duel was fought, June 30, 1823, on
Bloody Island, between Thomas C. Rector and
Joshua Barton, in which Barton was killed.
By this time the code had fallen into disre-
pute, but it was not until 1830, when, on August 27, in a duel between Thomas Biddle and
Spencer Pettis, both principals were killed,
that the frown of society was formidable
enough to prevent further encounters of this
kind.

In 1825, on the 29th of April, the Marquis
de Lafayette visited East St. Louis. In 1826
occurred another overflow of the Mississippi
River, which spread to a great depth over the
lowlands. In 1828 the Wiggins Ferry began
to operate with steam as a motive power. It
was in 1836 that the first railroad in the State
of Illinois was built from East St. Louis to
the Bluffs. It was owned by the Illinois &

St. Louis Coal Company and its cars were drawn by horses. Four years later, the first schoolhouse within the present limits of the city of East St. Louis was built by Captain John Trendley and, in 1841, the firm of Sunrix and Jarrot began the publication of the first newspaper, "The American Bottom Gazette," near the corner of Main and Market Streets.

In 1844 occurred the greatest Mississippi flood in the memory of white men. The overflow extended from the Missouri Bluffs to those in Illinois, covering the entire bottoms on both sides of the main channel so that a steamboat is said to have crossed over to the Illinois bluffs over the bottom lands. After the subsidence of the waters a settlement called "Papstown" was started near where the Heim's Brewery was afterward built.

The first church within the corporate limits of East St. Louis was built by the Methodists in 1845. The Methodist Episcopal Church of Illinois Town was erected in 1849. This, in 1868, became St. John's Methodist Episcopal Church and, again in 1887, was reorganized as the Summit Avenue Methodist Episcopal Church. In 1905 this congregation moved to an elegant stone church at Thirteenth Street and Summit Avenue.

On February 13, 1847, the St. Clair County Turnpike Company was incorporated. This was the first turnpike in the State of Illinois and is still in existence under the name of The Rock Road. The same year the first dyke was built on the site of Vaughn's dyke, but the flood of 1851 destroyed it.

The ground was broken for the first steam railroad, the Ohio & Mississippi, in 1852, though the road was not formally opened until 1857.

In 1854 the St. Louis, Alton & Terre Haute Railroad Company opened a branch line from East St. Louis to Belleville under the name of the Belleville & Illinoistown Road, which later (1873) was extended, under the name of the Belleville & Southern Illinois, to Duquoin, there forming a connection with the Illinois Central Railroad and giving a direct line to Cairo. These two sections now constitute a part of the Illinois Central System known as the "Cairo Short Line."

The construction of the first division of this line marked the real beginning of East St. Louis, though it was still some years before the town received its now famous name. This growth is to be attributed primarily to the Ohio & Mississippi Railroad, which bore to the East the market staples of St. Louis and the Western country. Buffalo meat and robes, bear carcasses, venison, fine furs and abundant supplies of wheat, corn and other farm products began to roll to the Atlantic ports from St. Louis, the new city of the West, which had hitherto been connected with them only by wagon conveyance, canals, or the slow early-date steamboats which dubiously plowed their way up the Ohio River, when disaster did not prevent. Soon curious, adventurous spirits came to the Western city to test the mood of Dame Fortune in commercial ventures. Gradually this infusion of Yankee blood stirred the old French metropolis west of the river into a growth some part of which was shared by the village on the eastern shore. Railroad after railroad now entered their competitive forces for the wealth of the West. The Chicago & Alton, the Toledo & Western, the Terre Haute & Indianapolis, and other routes long since absorbed by the gigantic trunk lines of Gould, Vanderbilt, Harriman and Hill, slowly and laboriously built their several tracks into East St. Louis, where they were compelled to locate their termini and establish their western bases. These great institutions, the Wiggins Ferry Company and the St. Louis Transfer Company, originated and gained power from this fact, and have grown stronger and more prosperous as the years went by. Thus it has been that East St. Louis became a railroad center, and its population of engineers and firemen, of conductors, brakemen, switchmen, machinists and other railroad employes became a marked factor in building up the new town.

The rolling mills—one of which was built where the Republic Steel Works now stand, the other on the site of the present Relay Depot—gave a new element to the rapidly growing population. The Heims Brewery supplied its foaming beverage to the thirsty residents, and a flour-mill and elevators arose along the river bank. All this time residences, stores, saloons and shops were being built in all directions. In 1859 the town of East St. Louis was platted and entered of record. This did not include the part of the city then known as Illinois City, which came in 1887. In 1865 the town was incorporated under a special charter as a city, and though this charter was once amended, it was abandoned in 1888, and East St. Louis was organized under the general law.

In 1854 the first hotel, the Western, or Bundy House, was opened at what is now 120 South Main Street. Four years later came another of the great floods that have so often spread over the bottom lands of the Mississippi River.

The first President of the First Board of Trustees of Illinois City was Daniel Sexton, elected in 1859.

The first flour-mill in East St. Louis was organized in 1861 by F. H. Krite, now with the Hezel Milling Company.

In 1861, Rev. J. J. Brenman organized St. Patrick's Catholic Church. Its house of worship was built in 1862 and an addition to it was made in 1871 by Rev. F. H. Zabell, now at Bunker Hill, Ill., who also built St. Aloysius' College at the corner of Seventh Street and Illinois Avenue.

The first plank sidewalk was built on Collinsville Avenue in 1862, the year of the "fifth flood."

In 1863 the first Lutheran Church was organized and its building was erected by Rev. P. Pflueger.

The first Mayor of East St. Louis was John B. Bowman, who was one of the most persistent and distinguished of those exponents of the spirit of the present day who, in a determined struggle for good government, raised the city to a comparatively high grade. These principles he championed consistently until his tragic death in 1885.

In 1865 the first fire company was organized and, in 1866, the first Masonic lodge was instituted. In 1866 St. Henry's German Catholic Church was organized and the edifice at St. Louis and Collinsville Avenues was built by Rev. Father Rinks. The first Board of Health was organized in 1867, and the first Board of Trade in 1868.

In the local politics of those days there were many warm arguments and many heated elections. Railroad men, rolling-mill men, English, Welsh and Irish, some descendants of the early French pioneers, a few Americans, a sprinkling of Germans, detachments of the negro exodus from the South that followed the soldiers home from the Civil War—all these made up an incongruous mass, factious and cosmopolitan, ready and eager for political strife, who, di-

vided into warring factions as their self-interest dictated, managed for years to keep up so great a turmoil that the name of East St. Louis became synonymous throughout the country with misgovernment. Party leaders of these banditti of politics quarreled like the Colonna and Orsini families of Old Rome and bid their "donatives" for the support of the fickle henchmen. The more quiet and respectable citizens finally tired of all this and, combining, succeeded in overthrowing the oligarchy, and since that time comparative decency has marked East St. Louis politics. Money instead of nearly worthless scrip was paid out to city employes; streets arose from the mud, and everything assumed an air of progress. Manufacturers, noting the improvement in methods of government and recognizing the splendid location of the city, began the erection of mammoth plants here, which caused the population to increase by leaps and bounds.

In 1869 the first work was done on the Eads Bridge, which was opened for business July 4, 1874. The first City Hall in East St. Louis was dedicated in 1869, and Bowman's Dyke, on the Island, was constructed the same year. In 1870 the Workingmen's Bank, now the Southern Illinois National Bank, was established, as was the first Episcopal Church during the same year.

On March 8, 1871, a tornado swept over the western portion of the city, killing one man and severely injuring twenty-one. The loss to property was about $60,000. June 1, 1871, the National Stock Yards was begun and was formally opened for business November 20, 1873.

An ordinance, passed January 14, 1872, conveyed the necessary permission for a street-car line, which operated by horse-power on Missouri, Collinsville, Broadway and Front Streets. The first cars ran on this line July 18, 1872.

During 1873 the Howe Literary Institute (Baptist) was opened. It was established by prominent citizens, carrying out the will of the late Lyman Howe. Its career was one of non-success, and the building erected for it was destroyed by the tornado of 1896. In 1874, Elliott's Frog and Switch Works was established and no other institution in East St. Louis has tended more to help build up the south end of the city.

The cornerstone of the First Presbyterian Church of East St. Louis was laid by Rev. William Gans, of St. Louis, July 12, 1877. In 1881 fire destroyed the City Hall and Public Library building.

Ex-Mayor John B. Bowman, who had been a leading spirit in the improvement of East St. Louis, was murdered by some unknown person as he was about to enter his residence in the old Howe Institute building on the night of November 20, 1885. The citizens of East St. Louis promptly offered a reward of $5,000 for the arrest of the assassin, but so far no one has been convicted of the crime.

The village of New Brighton was annexed to East St. Louis, February 14, 1887, and in that year was laid the first granite pavement in the city.

M. M. Stephens came into power as Mayor in 1887, and was destined to serve in that capacity fourteen years. After his induction into office, East St. Louis began to grow so rapidly that it is very difficult to keep pace with its many changes. The streets were first lighted by electricity February 8, 1890. The first daily paper, "The Daily Journal," was established March 12, 1890. The new St. Peter's Lutheran Church, Rev. H. Meyer, pastor, was dedicated the same year, and the East St. Louis Electric Street Railway received a franchise and began the construction of a road. In 1890 the city refunded its municipal indebtedness amounting to three-quarters of a million dollars, compromising the same for $628,143.10. It was also in 1890 that the East St. Louis Bank became the First National Bank. St. Mary's Hospital was dedicated that year, and the cornerstone of St. Mary's Church was laid; the Merchants' Bridge was also opened in that eventful year.

It was not until 1893 that the First Baptist Church, at the corner of Rock Road and Brighton Place, was dedicated. The consolidation of the Eads and Merchants' Bridges took place July 1, 1893.

In 1894 a resident citizen of East St. Louis, in the person of E. J. Murphy, was elected to Congress.

The Henrietta Hospital building, on the corner of Sixteenth Street and Illinois Avenue, was begun in 1897. The new City Hall was dedicated in 1898.

It was on May 27, 1896, at 5:22 P. M., that the "Great Cyclone" struck St. Louis and East St. Louis and, in a few seconds, did damage to the extent of hundreds of human lives and hundreds of thousands of dollars' worth of property. The relief fund from charitable sister communities reached the sum of $98,000. No fewer than 105 people were killed in East St. Louis.

The Suburban Railway line, connecting East St. Louis with Belleville by trolley line, was opened May 28, 1898, and a year later the Day Line, a close rival of the former, was opened. In 1902, Clark Brothers, then the owners of these two roads, bought the Eads Bridge line. August 31, 1902, the cornerstone of Sacred Heart Church and school was laid, and St. Joseph's Catholic Parish was established in May of that year. Both of these churches now have thriving congregations. The United Presbyterian Church, at Twelfth Street and Summit Avenue, and the English Lutheran Church at Thirteenth Street and Summit Avenue were built in 1902.

The year 1903 marked the inauguration of the first wholesale grocery store in East St. Louis.

In the spring of 1903, after having been Mayor of the city seven terms, M. M. Stephens was defeated for that office by Judge Silas Cook, who had presided over the City Court for several years.

Many miles of streets have been paved and sewered, and two new modern fire engines have been purchased and the damage wrought by the disastrous flood of 1903 has been, in a large measure, repaired since Mayor Cook assumed office. The public confidence in him was so great that he was re-elected in 1905.

East St. Louis is at present in a very flourishing condition and there are in contemplation two movements, equally intended to benefit the city. One is a levee system, contracted for, to protect the city from future overflows of the Mississippi River. The other is a gigantic outlet sewer, with the most powerful centrifugal pumps, to dispose of the city's waste and sewage and any surface water that might otherwise prove a damage to property or a menace to health. These will be followed by still other improvements, and the future development of the city will inevitably be great as a consequence of these progressive steps by the city government.

All history is concerned not only with the past of nations, but with their present, and an intelligent comparison may be made and needful lessons be drawn from the comparison. Accordingly, a few facts concerning the East St. Louis of today are appropriate here as showing what has developed from the little village that once nestled here.

Twenty-seven lines of railroads make East St. Louis their center or terminal point; the city is encircled by two belt lines connecting all these main lines. Factories situated on these belt lines can ship on any of these roads and, by reason of competition, manufacturers secure lowest freight rates. Many have taken advantage of these conditions to secure factory sites along the belts, though there is still abundance of valuable ground to be had along them. All kinds of raw material from any part of the Union can be landed cheaply in East St. Louis. Coal is mined almost at the very door of the city, and ranges in price from sixty cents to $1.20 a ton. .

East St. Louis has, moreover, one of the finest water systems in the Western States. Some $2,000,000 has been spent on the waterworks, filters and mains, that supply a clear water fit for household or factory purposes. Taxes are low and manufacturers are exempted from municipal taxation for periods of years, according to the magnitude and importance of their manufacturing plants.

The East St. Louis death rate is phenomenally low. Were it not for railroad accidents it could not be excelled in this regard by any city in the country.

Over $700,000 has been expended in stone and brick buildings for educational purposes, there being, at present, sixteen brick school-buildings devoted to elementary education and a beautiful high school building. For ten months in the year school is conducted under approved principals of high attainments and wide experience. High school graduates from East St. Louis are admitted to the State Universities of Illinois and Missouri and to colleges in other eminent centers of higher education. Many parochial schools are maintained by Catholic and Protestant congregations.

Twenty-two churches serve to keep alive the religious sentiment in East St. Louis. Over these preside ministers wholly devoted to their calling, who are as earnest and eloquent men as can be found in any similar community. Sociability and fraternity are fostered by a great number and variety of lodges and clubs.

Two large and comfortable hospitals, supplied with trained nurses, physicians, and surgeons, minister to the injured and infirm, while six undertaking establishments bury the dead.

During the decade between 1890 and 1900 East St. Louis increased in population from 15,-000 to 30,000. Ever since, she has been adding to her population until now she is estimated to have a population of over 55,000 within her corporate limits. So rapid is the influx of population that builders can hardly keep pace with it. What is best of all, these new comers are all intelligent, progressive and estimable citizens.

There are in East St. Louis today concerns engaged in the following lines of manufacture: Iron Works making malleable iron products of all kinds, such as car trucks, car springs, whole steel cars, stoves, spikes, railroad locomotives, forgings for machinery, forgings for gold stamp mills, enameled iron-ware, tools, nails, steel work, frogs and switches and sheet iron; Glass Works; Aluminum Works; Glucose Works; Cotton-Oil Works; Barrel Works; staves and heading factories; four of the largest packing plants in the world; five large bakeries; car-roofing manufacturers; a fancy fire-works factory; factories making pneumatic tools; Car-works; Ice and Cold Storage Plants; a Fertilizer Plant; Shot Works; Frame Works; manufactories of bridge-building materials; two large breweries; Concrete-block Works; Structural Iron Works; Structural Wood Works, etc. One of the largest Stock Yards in the country is located here; also the largest horse and mule market in the world, the largest baking powder plants in the United States, two large chemical plants, railroad machine shops, and walnut and other lumber mills are among the important local enterprises.

The third city in size in Illinois, East St. Louis is easily second in importance. Its real estate is valued at $24,000,000. Railroads, ferry-boats and the Eads Bridge connect it with St. Louis, Mo. It has a commodious Union Depot, several first-class hotels, an elegant city hall, a city court, a Federal court, two theaters, the longest driving pavilion in the world, 150 miles of water main, four banks, three trust companies, five building and loan associations, forty miles of brick and granite paving, seventy-five miles of granitoid side-walk, electric-lighted streets, extensive silica works, Bell and

Kinloch telephone systems, a gas plant, two daily and four weekly newspapers and one monthly publication, forty miles of well equipped street railway, six lines of fine suburban electric railway, two large cotton warehouses and six large grain elevators. In one month its bank deposits amounted to $5,825,000. It has expended $4,000,000 in street improvements and $16,000,000 in corporate business and residence improvements in ten years. In the same time its property values have increased from fifty to five hundred per cent. It pays out $1,250,000 to wage earners every month, and its finished products and raw materials are shipped away and received at less average cost than those of any other city in the Union.

"In the Beginning."—(General History.)— In 1770, the first move toward civilization in this locality was made by Richard McCarty, who obtained an improvement right to 400 acres of land on both sides of Cahokia Creek, now included in East St. Louis, and built a grist-mill on the bank of the creek. In 1787, he left for Canada, leaving heirs to his property. In 1805, United States Commissioners, appointed by Congress to pass upon claims to ancient titles in Cahokia and its neighborhood, confirmed this tract to Mr. McCarty's heirs. The old mill has long ago disappeared, also one built in 1805 by Nicholas Jarrot. As late as 1855, the machinery of the latter was used by Morris & Son in a mill at Brooklyn, a suburb of East St. Louis.

The founding of East St. Louis was due to the foresight of Captain James Piggott, an officer under General Clark, who commanded the Virginia militia on the frontier. After the treaty of 1783, Captain Piggott settled down to frontier life here, while St. Louis was only a small trading post. In 1795, he located a militia claim of 100 acres on the west side of the river opposite St. Louis, and constructed a bridge across Cahokia Creek. In 1797, he had built two small log cabins near the shore and established a rude ferry across the river, by consent of the Spanish Commandant at St. Louis. From this humble beginning grew in after years one of the wealthiest monopolies of the West.

The first house of any pretension on the site of East St. Louis was built by Etienne Pensoneau in 1810. It was a two-story brick building, on the corner of Main and Menard Streets, first occupied as a dwelling but later used as a hotel. It long ago passed out of existence.

Joseph Pepin entered the southeast quarter of Section 4 (160 acres), September 16, 1814. Joseph Jonville entered 320 acres of the west half of the same section, September 28, 1814. William Russell entered 131.92 acres on Section 6 on December 15, of the same year. These were the first local land entries.

In 1811 the first steamboat came up from North Cairo to this point. During this year the poeple hereabout were alarmed by the seismic disturbance which has passed into history as the New Madrid earthquake. In 1815 the steamboat Pike came to the landing here.

In 1826, Francis Delorm opened the first blacksmith shop on the Rock road.

The first railroad in the State was built in 1836, from Illinoistown to the bluff, six miles away, under the personal supervision of Governor Reynolds, Vital Jarrot and others. Its purpose was to transport coal from the bluffs to St. Louis. Thomas Winstanley drove the mules that hauled the first cars over this road. The investment did not pay, and in 1841 it was sold to the St. Clair Railroad Company.

The first school-house, a small fourteen by sixteen-foot frame structure, costing $240, was built by Captain Trindley in 1840. In 1845, the Methodist Church, the first church edifice, was built by William Singleton on Brundy Street, between Second and Third.

Illinoistown Township was created June 6, 1820, with the following boundaries: "Beginning at the bluff on the Madison County line; thence on said line to the Mississippi River; thence with the Mississippi to the Cahokia line on the same; thence with said line eastward to the bluff; thence along the bluff northward to the place of beginning." In 1821, Illinoistown and Cahokia were made one election precinct, with the voting place at Augustus Pensoneau's residence at Cahokia. In 1851, Illinoistown became a separate voting precinct and elections were ordered to be held at French Village. In 1851, Illinoistown was separated from the French Village part of the precinct, and ten years later it became known as East St. Louis Precinct in honor of the embryo city that had come into being within its borders. The boundaries of the precinct, as established in 1851, were as follows: "A line running due west from the southwest corner of Section fifteen, in township No. two north, range nine west, to the northwest corner of section twenty-one, same township; thence south on the west line of section twenty-one, to the southwest corner thereof, thence west on the section line to the Mississippi through Cahokia precinct, from which a strip about one-half a mile in breadth is taken from the northern part and annexed to Illinoistown precinct."

The following, relating to the laying out of the first town within the present borders of East St. Louis, is quoted from Reavis's history of "The Future Great City:"

"In 1815 Etienne Pinconeau (now spelled Pensoneau) ventured to lay out a town on his adjoining land, with his brick tavern on the road to the ferry, then occupied by one Simon Vanorsdal, as a nucleus. He called it 'Jacksonville.' The plat of the town cannot be found, but there is a deed of record for a lot in it. It bears the date '17th of March, 1815.' Etienne Pinconeau and Elizabeth, his wife, by it, convey to Moses Scott, merchant of St. Louis, in Missouri Territory, for $150, 'all that certain tract, parcel, or lot of land, being, lying and situated in the said county of St. Clair, at a place or new town called Jacksonville, containing in depth 100 feet and in breadth sixty feet, joining northwardly to Carroll Street, facing the public square, and southwardly to Coffee Street.

"Later conveyances by McKnight and Brady, merchants and land operators at that time in St. Louis, referring to this lot of Moses Scott, locate it as lot five in block eight of the Town of Illinois, at the southeast corner of Market and Main streets. Scott at once erected a store on the lot and at that corner conducted the first mercantile establishment in this city. This was the only sale made of lots in this 'Jacksonville.' On the 20th of January, 1816, Pinconeau sold the entire tract of land he had on Cahokia Creek (including Jacksonville), extending in breadth from near Railroad Street to Piggott Street, to McKnight and Brady.

"The immediate result was the consummation, by McKnight and Brady, of Pinconeau's project of a new town. They platted the 'Town of Illinois' upon the site of Pinconeau's 'Jacksonville.' They relocated the public square, widened the streets and enlarged the lots and put the plat on record. They advertised and held a great sale of lots in the Town of Illi-

nois. The sale took place at the auction room of Thomas T. Reddick, in St. Louis, November 3, 1817. Thus was made the first record evidence of a town plat in East St. Louis."

McKnight and Brady's Town of Illinois embraced land extending south of the present Broadway, including the present Second and Third Wards and, of course, the east side ferry landing. Before the locality was christened Jacksonville by Pinconeau, it is said to have been known for a short time as Washington.

Illinois City was formerly a part of the Cahokia commons, and was laid out by the Cahokians in the fall of 1818. John Hays, John Hay and Francois Turcott were appointed commissioners to plat and name the new town by the inhabitants of Cahokia, which proceedings were legalized and confirmed by an act of Congress. Illinois City included the northeastern part of the city's present territory, north of St. Clair Avenue.

St. Clair was laid out in 1837.

In 1859, lands belonging to Samuel C. Barclow, Henry Chauncey, William H. Aspinwall and Samuel W. Comstock were platted and their plat was recorded under the name of the Town of East St. Louis. This tract, which included some land once owned by John Jacob Astor, lay within United States survey No. 626 in the name of Richard McCarty, United States survey No. 625, in the name of Francois Perry, the United States surveys Nos. 131 and 132 in the name of A. Chouteau, United States survey No. 129, in the name of Gregorie Sarpy and United States survey No. 130 in the name of Jean St. Germain. This Town of East St. Louis extended from Broadway to St. Clair Avenue and from Cahokia Creek to Tenth Street. It was incorporated in 1861.

Between 1865 and 1872, the Wiggins Ferry Company, at three different times, platted the "Island" part of the city under the name of "ferry divisions." The Third Ferry Division was platted in the former, the Second Ferry Division in the latter year. The First Ferry Division is said to have been surveyed between the above dates.

The Town of Illinois, Illinois City, Town of East St. Louis, St. Clair, New Brighton, Alta Sita, Winstanley Park, the Ferry Divisions, the Obeike and Kase addition and other additions are included in the East St. Louis of today.

CITY INCORPORATED—OFFICIALS.—The City of

Nicholas Faust

East St. Louis obtained its charter by special legislative enactment in 1865. The charter was prepared by John B. Bowman and S. M. Lount, under the direction of a committee of the Town Council, consisting of Mr. Bowman, Henry Obeike and M. Millard. John B. Bowman was elected the first Mayor, and the first Aldermen were the following: Michael Murphy and John O'Connell, First Ward; James Hazen and Henry Schall, Second Ward; Captain John Trendley and J. B. Lovingston, Third Ward. William G. Kase was elected City Judge. In 1880, the city was divided into four wards. In 1881, the Aldermen were the following: First Ward—John C. Prottsman and Ernest A. Wider; Second Ward—Thomas Hanifan and John J. McLean; Third Ward—Patrick H. O'Brien and Henry Sackmann; Fourth Ward—Levi Baugh, Jr., and James J. Rafter. The succession of mayors has been as follows: John J. Bowman, seven terms; John B. Lovingston, one term; Vital Jarrot, two terms; Dennis Ryan, one term; Samuel S. Hake, two terms; Maurice Joyce, four terms; J. J. McLean, two terms; O. R. Winton, two terms; M. M. Stephens, seven terms; Henry F. Bader, one term. Mayor Silas Cook is now serving his second term. These pushing and public-spirited chief executives have contributed in no small degree to the proud record established by East St. Louis.

The municipal election in East St. Louis for 1906 was a victory for the Citizens' party. Out of fourteen candidates elected the Citizens' party won ten, as follows:

Assessor—John Niemes, Citizens' party, 3,885; Frank O'Neil, Independent Municipal party, 3,714; Niemes' majority, 474.

Chief Supervisor—H. LeRoy Browning, Citizens', 3,714; Joseph Vonnahme, Independent Municipal, 3,552; Browning's majority, 162.

For Assistant Supervisors, Charles Scherer, Robert Lowery, Max Oppenheim, D. M. Sullivan and Adam Howell, Citizens' party candidates, defeated F. Seppi, Jr., J. B. Montgomery, J. H. Hoover, P. Schrautemeir and James Foster of the Independent Municipal party, by a majority of 162.

Aldermen—First Ward, John Dissett, Citizens' 89; W. O'Malley, Independent Municipal, 151. Second Ward—John Jackson, Citizens', 634; Jerre Leehan, Independent Municipal, 440. Third Ward—John Harrigan, Citizens', 352;

James Whalen, Independent Municipal, 356. Fourth Ward—J. H. Liebig, Citizens', 549; O. C. Davis, Independent Municipal, 477. Fifth ward—A. Gallenbeck, Citizens', 476; Richard Gither, Independent Municipal, 572. Sixth Ward—Christ Anderson, Citizens', 827; Frank Maule, Independent Municipal, 757. Seventh Ward—M. J. Buckley, Citizens', 860; M. O'Day, Independent Municipal, 876.

The Independent Municipal party elected Aldermen in the First, Third, Fifth and Seventh Wards. The City Council, with seven hold-over Aldermen, will now stand nine members for the Citizens' party and five for Mayor Cook and the Independent Municipal party.

POLICE DEPARTMENT.—George O. Purdy, Chief; Michael Doyle, Lieutenant. Office 111 North Main Street.

BOARD OF HEALTH.—Mayor Silas Cook, Dr. H. J. de Haan, Dr. C. W. Lillie, Dr. A. E. Linder; Dr. A. A. McBrien, Health and Milk Inspector; George O. Purdy, Chief of Police; Thomas J. Williams, Secretary.

City Court is held in the City Hall. Regular terms begin on the first Monday of June, the fourth Monday in August and the first Monday in December. The Hon. William J. N. Moyers is Judge and Thomas J. Healy, Clerk.

POSTMASTERS.—Wiggins Ferry was the name of the first postoffice within the present limits of East St. Louis. The following were appointed Postmasters at the dates indicated: Samuel Wiggins, August 7, 1826; William Orr, January 19, 1830; Samuel C. Christy, December 7, 1831; J. B. Pentecost, December 3, 1834; A. H. Cook, October 28, 1839; Michael Walsh, February 18, 1842; Alexander H. Cook, June 9, 1842; George Bisson, November 4, 1844; A. P. Crosby, October 20, 1850.

In 1851 the name of the postoffice was changed to Illinois Town. The following named Postmasters served from dates given: Harrison Voden, October 7, 1851; Henry Brundy, March 29, 1852; Andrew Wettig, February 14, 1854; Ernest E. Wilder, February 16, 1858; Daniel Sexton, February 19, 1857; Ernest W. Wilder, April 2, 1861.

The postoffice took its present name April 22, 1864, and the following named persons have served successively as Postmasters from the dates mentioned: E. W. Wilder, April 22, 1864; J. B. Sikking, April 7, 1869; Joseph Vonnahme, July 8, 1865; Alexander Fekete, December 21, 1889; F. G. Cockrell, April 23, 1894; D. C. Marsh, March 5, 1895; M. M. Stephens, July 29, 1896; Thomas L. Fekete, May 12, 1897; Henry F. Bader, January 16, 1902.

The East St. Louis postoffice force ten years ago comprised a Postmaster, four carriers and two clerks, and the postoffice received in revenue $10,000 a year. In 1905 there were a Postmaster, an Assistant Postmaster, sixteen clerks, twenty-six carriers, three sub-carriers and one rural carrier. There were nine sub-stations. The revenue was $70,000.

PROSPECTIVE FEDERAL BUILDING.—The Hon. William A. Rodenburg, Representative in Congress from the Twenty-second District, has placed the citizens of his home town under lasting obligations to him by his efficient co-operation with others in securing to East St. Louis a new Federal building which, it is believed, will be ready for occupancy within two years after the contract for its erection has been awarded. The limit upon cost of building and site, fixed by act of Congress, is $300,000, and of area a lot 165 by 170 feet. The lot has not yet been selected, but proposals submitted are as follows:

John P. Metzen, lot bounded by Broadway, Sixth Street, Division Avenue and Seventh Street, 300x270 feet; $35,000.

M. P. Peugnet and others, property at the corner of Sixth Street, St. Louis Avenue and Seventh Street, 300x120 feet, $27,000; same parties, interior lot on Sixth Street, 154 feet 7 inches by 140 feet, $7,750; same parties, interior lot on Seventh Street, 125x140 feet, $6,500.

P. J. Soucy, Illinois Avenue, Ninth and State Streets, about 26,260 square feet, $59,237.50.

Marie Schroeder, Ninth Street and Illinois Avenue, 180x165 feet; $400 per front foot.

S. D. Sexton, corner Seventh Street, Missouri Avenue and Eighth Street, 170x300 feet, $52,500; same parties, southeast corner Eighth Street and Missouri Avenue, 170x165 feet, $31,500; same parties, southeast corner Seventh Street and Missouri Avenue, 170x165 feet, $31,500.

C. M. Foreman, corner Sixth Street and Illinois Avenue, 147x150 feet, $36,000; same party, corner St. Louis Avenue and Fifth Street, 165x170 feet, $55,750; same party, corner Sixth Street and St. Louis Avenue, 170x165 feet, $41,750; same party, corner Eighth Street and Illinois Avenue, 180x150 feet, $36,000; same party,

corner Main Street and Division Avenue, about 102x200 feet, $55,000; same party, corner Collinsville and Summit Avenues, 150x175 feet, $40,000; same party, corner Sixth Street and Ohio Avenue, 175x150 feet, $25,000.

The probabilities are, it is said by men who ought to know, that a location will be selected between Broadway on the south, Illinois Avenue on the north, Sixth Street on the west and Eighth Street on the East. The prices for the sites offered range from $125 to $500 a front foot. The site must be not less than 165x170 feet and bounded by two streets and an alley.

The building will be of colonial architecture, and will be practically a duplicate of the Federal building at Macon, Ga. It will be 120x100 feet, three stories high, with basement and attic, of steel construction and fireproof throughout. It is to be of Bedford stone, with marble and terra cotta trimmings, tile roof, tile floors, marble wainscotings and marble stairways. The basement will contain a carriers' gymnasium, engineers' and janitors' rooms, machinery, fuel and store rooms. The first floor will be devoted to the postoffice department, with a center space sixty-four by seventy feet, containing a lobby fifteen by one hundred and seventeen feet, money order and registry departments, Postmaster and Assistant Postmaster's rooms, fireproof vaults and mailing vestibule. The most approved type of postoffice furniture will be installed. The second floor will be devoted to the use of the Federal Circuit and District Courts, and will be divided into the following rooms: Courtroom, suite for the Judges, witness room, grand jury room, petit jury room and rooms for the Clerks of the courts. The third floor will be divided into rooms for the District Attorney, Internal Revenue officers, United States Marshal, Civil Service Board and Pension Examiner. The attic will be used for a time for storerooms. Entrance will be made to the building by massive marble steps.

After the site has been accepted by the Government, the District Attorney will pass upon the title to the property and his report will be submitted to the Attorney General of the United States for his approval. The plans and specifications will then be drawn by the Supervising Architect of the department, and advertisements will be published calling for bids for the construction of the building.

BUSINESS MEN'S ORGANIZATIONS.—The Retail

Merchants' Association of East St. Louis has its headquarters in room 20A North Main Street. Its officers are: H. C. Thoene, President; B. Haumener, Vice-President; C. F. Merker, Second Vice-President; L. F. Tusler, Secretary; G. W. Brichler, Treasurer.

The East St. Louis Builders' Exchange has its office in room 1, Elks Building, 206 Collinsville Avenue. Its officers are as follows: C. H. Way, President; C. Guenther, First Vice-President; Frank Keating, Second Vice-President; A. Anderson, Treasurer; Charles Broderick, Secretary; William Flannery, Sergeant-at-Arms.

The East St. Louis Real Estate Exchange has its office in room 7, Boul Block, 20A North Main Street. Its officers are: J. M. Chamberlin, Jr., President; H. T. Renshaw, Vice-President; M. L. Harris, Secretary; P. J. Soucy, Treasurer.

WIGGINS FERRY AND THE BRIDGES.—About 1794, Captain James Piggott obtained, upon promise of payment of a yearly stipend in fowls and wild game, privilege from the St. Louis authorities to establish a ferry landing on the west side of the Mississippi River opposite Market Street. On the Illinois side there was no one who claimed rights superior to his. The river then extended beyond Cahokia Creek, the "Island" territory having been then inconsiderable. He established his eastern landing at a point opposite the site of what is now the Elliott Frog and Switch Works, between Main Street and Cahokia Creek, and threw a rude bridge over the creek. It was not until 1797 that he got his ferry in operation. His first boat was simply a railed-in platform supported on log canoes and propelled by creoles by means of poles and long sweeps. Captain Piggott died on February 20, 1799.

To this date the enterprise was under Captain Piggott's immediate personal supervision. Great as had been his foresight, he passed away having builded, perhaps, more wisely than he knew. His wife was the executrix of his will. She first rented the ferry to Doctor Wallis for a year embraced in 1801-02; then to one Adams for a year embraced in 1803-04. About this time Mrs. Piggott married Jacob Collard and moved over the river to St. Louis. Before leaving, however, she leased the ferry to John Campbell for ten years. Campbell selfishly and treacherously procured a license for a ferry

8

in his own name, during the term of the lease, and for a short time the Piggott ferry was known as Campbell's ferry. Mrs. Collard took her claim into the courts and after some litigation, which ended in the defeat of Campbell and his abettors, re-established the enterprise in the proprietorship of the Piggott heirs. One of the latter, with men named Solomon, Porter and Blundy, operated the ferry until part of the heirs sold their interest in it to McKnight and Brady. The other heirs conveyed to Samuel Wiggins their rights in the ferry and its franchise. He bought out all other shareholders, thus obtaining all rights to the ferry, which he operated under his personal supervision.

This was in 1818. In the spring of 1819 Wiggins was authorized by act of the Legislature to establish a ferry on the Mississippi adjacent to his lands, near the Town of Illinois. The act also provided that he should have the right to one mile of the shore extending along the river at this point. Before East St. Louis had been born, Wiggins had fenced it in. The astute and far-seeing Wiggins soon proved that he was enterprising and inventive in more directions than one. He went on preparing for the future by improving upon Piggott's mode of conveyance. He built a fair-sized ferry-boat and propelled it by water power. That was a promising beginning. In 1828, he launched the first steam ferry-boat on the river and named it the "St. Clair." In 1832 another steam boat, the "Ibex," was put on the line. The business grew so rapidly that it demanded the investment of more capital than Wiggins had provided for, and now he sold an interest in the ferry to several men, thus bringing into existence a joint-stock company. In 1852, the company was incorporated and soon obtained further privileges by legislative enactment. It secured valuable concessions on both sides of the river and grew and prospered even beyond the prophecies of its promoters. After the completion of the Eads Bridge, and the later completion of the Merchants' Bridge, the business of the ferry necessarily diminished, but ferry stock was still considered a good investment. In 1902, it was all bought up by the Eads Bridge Company.

The construction of the Eads Bridge was begun in 1869 and the bridge was completed and opened July 4, 1874, with imposing civic and military ceremonies, President Grant being present with his staff. This bridge, extending from the foot of Washington Avenue, St. Louis, to East St. Louis, cost more than $10,000,000. Its entire length is 6,220 feet, its width fifty-four feet, and it stands fifty-five feet above high water. It consists of three steel arches, supported on either side by massive stone abutments, and adjoining these are stone piers 500 feet from either abutment. It is fully described in the chapter devoted to railroads. The Merchants' Bridge, extending from the foot of Ferry Street, St. Louis, to a point in Illinois north of St. Clair County, is a steel bridge, designed only for railway traffic. It was completed in May, 1890.

This is the era of the bridge, but the ferry had its day and there are those who prophesy that the river will again be a factor in the commerce of the Mississippi Valley. The origin of East St. Louis is based on traffic between the east side of the river and St. Louis, and the Wiggins ferry was long the only medium for that traffic, and as such was a paramount agency in the creation and development of the goodly, growing city that we are now considering.

Captain James Piggott, the originator and founder of this great public utility, was an officer of Virginia militia under General Clark, and was one of those who remained after the treaty of 1783 and cast his lot with the pioneers in and about what is now St. Clair County. He located a militia claim of 100 acres "opposite St. Louis."

BUILDING OF THE DIKES.—Before the great flood of 1844, the Mississippi Channel opposite St. Louis, though it had shifting bars, was never seriously menaced. After that flood, the only available channel was between Bloody Island and the Town of Illinois and it was not without great difficulty and danger that any boat landed on the Missouri side of the river. This condition threatened the future of St. Louis, and public meetings were called to consider it.

As the only means to its salvation, St. Louis, in 1847, tried to construct a dike across the then principal channel of the river to the east of Bloody Island. This meant destruction to the harbor and ferry landings of the Town of Illinois. The Town of Illinois objected. Alton, a rival then of St. Louis, came to its assistance. The controversy produced great public excitement. Workmen on the menacing dikes were driven off by force. Illinois State militia planted cannon on the Illinois shore. For a time State sovereignty and Alton policy were triumphant. In 1848 a Belleville court enjoined the city of St. Louis from ever attempting to construct such a dike.

Early in 1849 the Illinois Legislature, by a joint resolution, granted to St. Louis full authority to construct cross and wing dikes on the Illinois shore before the Town of Illinois, so as to secure and protect its own harbor, across the river, with the proviso that St. Louis should, for the benefit of the Town of Illinois, construct roadways on some of its dikes, especially on the main dike across the channel of the Mississippi to be closed, from the Illinois main shore to and across Bloody Island. The main dike was finished with the exception of the roadway on the embankment in the spring of 1851, and the great flood of that year swept most of it away. In 1856 a dike a quarter of a mile north of this was finished at a cost of $175,000. Thus the channel on the east side of the river was diverted from its course and the St. Louis pier was re-established. Other dikes have since been constructed. Though East St. Louis is comparatively free from danger from future inundations, its citizens have planned a system of protection that will make assurance doubly sure.

THE NATIONAL STOCK YARDS.—Before 1845, the live-stock trade of St. Louis was conducted at Papstown (New Brighton), in the southeastern part of the territory of the present city of East St. Louis. Then yards were established on the St. Louis side of the river. The construction of the National Stock Yards at East St. Louis was discussed as early as 1871. The talk about the project resulted in the united efforts of several prominent Eastern and Western capitalists, who bought 650 acres of land in East St. Louis, with a view to the establishment of stock yards greater and more complete than any others in the country at that time. The stock yards promoters engaged to erect a suitable hotel and office building, fitted up with all modern facilities for the transaction of business, and the city covenanted to construct no streets or other improvements that would interfere with the operation and development of the enterprise. The yards were opened for business in the fall of 1873. The stock yards water works are on the east side of Cahokia Creek, near the packing houses. The total expense of establishing the yards was more than $1,500,000 and large sums have been spent since in their operation and improvement. The promptness with which stock can be sent from St. Louis to the yards and unloaded from the trains has been long recognized as one of the wonders of the live-stock trade.

The daily capacity of the National Stock Yards is 15,000 cattle, 17,000 hogs, 12,000 sheep and 3,500 horses and mules. It has unexcelled facilities for marketing all kinds of live stock. It is the fastest growing market in the country, being continually enlarged and improved to meet the requirements of the trade. Buyers for four different large packing houses and many small packing houses and city butchers induce lively competition. There is a good demand for stockers and feeders from an enlarging territory. There is a yearly increase of about ten per cent. in the total volume of business, and the packing capacity has increased about fifty per cent. in the past three years. Receipts for three series of five years each, ending in 1904, having been:

YEAR.	CATTLE.	HOGS.	SHEEP.	H. & M.
1904	4,927,457	8,577,951	2,675,545	688,052
1899	3,681,223	7,862,696	2,496,639	496,143
1894	3,214,590	4,538,468	1,670,575	76,343

The above figures are an index of the growth and vastness of the St. Louis market. The geographical location of St. Louis, situated as it is in the central part of the United States, makes it the natural market for both the shipper and buyer of live stock. All roads lead to St. Louis, and no market has the superior advantages for concentrating and distributing live-stock products which abound here.

Here is, perhaps, the greatest horse and mule market in the world. The National Stock Yards constitute the natural gateway to the South and East for the great product of the Western States. Here, it is claimed, is to be found the largest and most varied supply of mules on earth, and here a trainload can be bought as easily as a pair, provided the buyer has the necessary funds. The yards are provided with a new auction pavilion, new and commodious stables, and unlimited accommodations. There are auction sales almost every day, while private sales are carried on during all business hours. Many commission firms do business at the yards.

The following are the names of present officials of the St. Louis National Stock Yards Company: Edward Morris, President; C. G. Knox, Vice-President; C. T. Jones, General Manager; L. W. Krake, Assistant General Manager. William E. Jameson is manager of the horse and mule market.

The Horse and Mule Commission Association, with its offices at the Stock Yards, has as its Secretary James A. Searcy. The Stock Yards Veterinary Hospital is a useful auxiliary. Convenient to the stock yards are the packing houses that are its principal customers. These concerns supply St. Louis and much of its tributary territory with meat and by-products of cattle, sheep and hogs. Attention was early concentrated on the by-products and now the entire animal is utilized. The flesh is sold as meat, the blood is dried and sold for clarifying processes, the entrails are cleaned and made into sausage casings, the hoofs are turned into neat's-foot oil, the parings of the hoofs, hides and bones are converted into glue, the finest of the fats are turned into butterine, lard oils and the finest tallow, the cruder fats are made into soap grease, the hides are transformed into leather, from the horns are manufactured combs, buttons, etc., the larger bones are used for making knife handles and for other purposes, the switches and tail ends are sold to hair mattress makers, and the short hair, which cannot be dried and curled for sale, is sold to felt works.

A SEPULCHRAL MOUND.—An ancient mound in East St. Louis stood until 1871-72 on a spot now between Collinsville Avenue and Fourth Street and intersected by Ohio Avenue. It was said that the Indians had buried their dead there for centuries, and according to Indian tradition it had been heaped up by the hands of men of a prehistoric age. The mound was about forty feet high and, at the base, four hundred feet in diameter. Down to about the time of our Civil War it was covered with timber, mostly oak. In 1871-72, it was dug away to fill up a slough and to make ground for a railway round-house. When the earth was removed, human bones and many kinds of shells were found at a depth of twenty to thirty-five feet. These were believed to be remains and trinkets of mound builders. The flood of 1844 having caused the abandonment of an old cemetery on survey No. 116, the people in the vicinity made many interments on the mound in the period 1845-70. The bodies thus deposited there were most of them reburied.

CEMETERIES.—A new cemetery within the boundaries of the Second Ward of today was destroyed by the flood of 1844. Two cemeteries in the old Fourth Ward were laid off when the Cahokians established Illinois City, but they were not used as such until about 1865. A cemetery was opened on Lynch Avenue in 1871. Another public burying ground was opened in 1872. St. Henry's Cemetery, on the Rock Road, was established in 1875-76. St. Peter's Cemetery, on the same thoroughfare, east of Winstanley Park, was opened in 1876. Mount Carmel Cemetery, on the bluffs, was established by St. Patrick's and St. Mary's Churches in 1894.

EARLY FIRE COMPANIES.—The East St. Louis Fire Company No. 1, the first fire company in the town, was organized December, 1872, with William O'Neill as President, Charles Hauss, Vice-President; James W. Kirk, Secretary; John V. Tefft, Treasurer, and Benedict Franz as Captain, Adolph Donald as First Engineer, John Easton as Second Engineer. This company had a big Babcock engine on trucks and 500 feet of hose. Island Fire Company No. 1 was organized November, 1874. In 1875, Nicholas Colgan was President; William L. Johnson, Vice-President; Maurice F. Tissier, Secretary; George W. Shields, Assistant Secretary; Adolphus Livingston, Treasurer; Henry Sackman, Captain; and John Keiflin, Lieutenant. These companies had partially disbanded as long ago as 1878.

The headquarters of the Fire Department is at 113 North Main Street. Edward F. Dowling is Fire Marshal. The number and location of companies is as follows: Engine Co. No. 1—113 N. Main Street; Engine Co. No. 2—714 Collinsville Avenue; Engine Co. No. 4—1500 Missouri Avenue; Engine Co. No. 4—Twenty-third Street and Ridge Avenue; Engine Co. No. 5—524 S. Tenth Street.

FINANCIAL INSTITUTIONS. — The following named financial institutions are duly treated in a chapter entitled "Financial Institutions": The Citizens' Savings and Trust Company, the First National Bank, the Illinois State Trust Company, the Southern Illinois National Bank, the Union Trust and Savings Bank, and the National Stock Yards Bank.

FLOODS.—In 1786 occurred the greatest flood of which Indians have had knowledge. The first flood that did damage to the property of white men in the territory now embraced in East St. Louis occurred in 1826. The town was several feet under water and, after the flood subsided, malaria nearly made way with the population. The flood of June, 1844, inundated the American Bottom so that steamers plied from bluff to bluff. Few houses across the river from St. Louis were to be seen above the water. No dry land was visible for miles toward the eastern bluff, except a few mounds and high knolls east and south of the village. This flood destroyed a cemetery within the boundaries of the Second Ward of today. The floods of 1851, 1858 and 1862 did much damage to the town and were discouraging in their after effects. The erection of dikes has measurably protected the people from subsequent overflows. Later floods came in 1876, 1878, 1883, 1892 and 1903. The two last mentioned surpassed the others in the amount of damage which they inflicted.

TORNADO OF 1871.—A tornado, destructive to life and property in East St. Louis, occurred on the afternoon of March 8, 1871. It was a terrific whirlwind. The Eads Bridge was then in an unfinished state, and apparatus used in the construction of the east pier was destroyed. Large buildings were demolished, trains of cars were derailed and ditched and freight depots were destroyed. Steamers and barges were torn from their moorings in the harbor and sent adrift, badly damaged by the ravages of the storm. At noon, clouds were gathering. At two o'clock, rain began to fall and the wind to blow. At eight minutes of four, St. Louis time, the storm was at its height and destruction was at hand. While the wind wrought its fearful work, rain fell in torrents. It was all over in an incredibly shore space of time—from twenty to thirty seconds—and about twenty men had been killed and many persons had been more or less severely injured. The "great cyclone" of 1896 is referred to elsewhere in this chapter. There was a memorable but not destructive tornado in 1865.

PUGILISM.—In the late 'sixties and early 'seventies, St. Louis followers of the fighting game made East St. Louis their "stamping ground," greatly to the disgust of the better class of its citizens. From time to time, prizefights were pulled off on the east side of the river under the auspices of the outside sporting men. As it became evident that protest would be unavailing, in 1873 Mayor Bowman and his friends resolved to adopt drastic measures to rid the town of an evil that was giving it an unenviable reputation throughout the country. He was certain of the support of the then Chief of Police, Captain Renshaw, and had a stanch henchman in Michael Walsh. He enlisted the aid of James W. Hughes, Sheriff of St. Clair County. Choosing his time when the "sports" were gathered for a prize-fight, he had the whole gang arrested on warrants sworn out by Captain Renshaw and many of them were bound over to await the action of the grand jury. This summary and surprising onslaught had the effect of breaking up the pugilistic "contests" and ridding East St. Louis of an unwelcome class of visitors.

THE EAST ST. LOUIS PUBLIC LIBRARY had its inception in quite a different institution—a circulating library—whose members paid a certain monthly or annual fee for the privilege of borrowing such books as it contained. This library was the child of William O'Neill, a city official, who was responsible in his day for more than one enterprise utilitarian in character.

When the law had been passed granting cities free library rights, O'Neill and Mayor John B. Bowman used this library as the nucleus for a public library, and proceeded to enlarge and strengthen the latter. In 1872, W. S. Larrimer was Librarian, and Miss Laura Painter Assistant.

Among the various citizens who served as Directors of the Library in those early days may be named: J. B. Bowman, Luke Hite, Dr. H. C. Fairbrother, William O'Neill, Edward L. McDonough, J. M. Sullivan (of the Island), and P. M. Sullivan. Among the Librarians and Assistant Librarians were L. D. Caulk, John P. Hite, E. L. McDonough, J. W. Kirk, C. B. Carroll and R. E. Barrowman.

This library had accumulated some 4,000 volumes, some of which would be almost priceless today—such as "Audubon's Birds," and several rare and now unpurchasable European works, when, in 1881, it was totally destroyed by fire. It might be appropriate to state that

it had not been used from the time of the municipal troubles of 1878, because of the unfortunate strife that marked the intervening years. No step was taken during the succeeding decade toward supplying the needs of the city in this direction.

When M. M. Stephens was elected Mayor, he advocated the creation of a new library, and the City Council passed an ordinance May 22, 1891, ordaining its re-establishment. Owing, however, to a shortage of funds, no Library Board was appointed until January 22, 1892, when a full board of nine members was appointed by the Mayor and confirmed by the Council. This board at once organized, and rented the third story of the Adele building at the corner of Main Street and Broadway. It procured such equipment and books as the funds at its disposal would allow, and in August, that year, opened the doors of a free public library once more to the city. Thomas Nelson was elected Librarian, and Misses Myra Gray and Minnie Turner, Assistants.

From the beginning, the library became one of the most popular institutions of the city; and it was but a short time until it was evident to all that quarters much larger and especially adapted to library purposes were imperatively demanded. Accordingly, the Board took steps for the erection of a library building extensive enough to meet all demands for a long time to come, and notified the City Council that, under the law of 1891, they had determined to accumulate a fund for that purpose. They certified a tax of $40,000 for the erection of a building—its collection to extend over a period of five years. Later this amount was increased to $50,000. Through the instrumentality of Mr. J. T. McCasland and others, a lot for a site was donated to the Board, and the building was at once begun. After a Belleville bank had decided not to take a loan of $34,000, to be secured by mortgage on the lot and contemplated structure, which loan was to bear date October 1, 1894, and be paid in three equal annual installments, the money was finally obtained from H. D. Sexton & Bro., of East St. Louis.

There was in the hands of the Board before this loan was made about $16,000. June 14, 1894, the contracts for the building were awarded to Mackie & Rose—the building to be completed by January 1, 1895. The architects and even the members of the Board personally superintended the construction of the building and compelled the contractors to comply with all the terms of the contract, which they at times seemed disposed to evade. Finally, the Board took the contract from the contractors and completed it themselves. The total cost of the building complete, with all its appointments, was $55,863.

This building is an ornament to East St. Louis and would grace any city. It is of classic outline, yet modern in all the conveniences of a library. Its architecture is in the style of the Italian Renaissance. It has a frontage on Broadway of seventy-five feet and a depth of 110 feet on Eighth Street. In height it is three stories, with a twelve-foot basement. When this building had been completed the citizens felt sure that the book fund would increase and prepared to install the library in its new quarters with appropriate ceremonies.

Accordingly, elaborate preparations were made, and the inhabitants of the city turned out en masse to attend the dedication in the new building. The entire Library Board, the officials and employes of the Public and Mercantile Libraries of St. Louis, the Library Board of Belleville and library officials from other localities were guests on this occasion. Addresses were delivered by President D. C. Marsh, of the Library Board, Hon. W. S. Forman, and Hon. W. A. Rodenberg. After this event, the library was well patronized and has continued to grow at a rapid rate, both in contents and patronage. There are now about 25,000 volumes and a museum of curiosities; and the reading rooms are patronized daily by hundreds of persons who use magazines, newspapers and works of reference which, in comprehensive variety, are kept ready for their conveniences.

One librarian and three lady assistants are constantly at work serving the public with unvarying courtesy and energy. The building contains a teachers' room, a children's room and an assembly room, besides immense stack rooms, offices, and unoccupied rooms on the second and third floors. The first floor and basement are leased to a wholesale grocery firm. The building served to house the city government of East St. Louis from the time of the destructive tornado of May 27, 1896, until the completion of the present city hall.

The roster of citizens who have served on the Library Board contains the names of many whose memory must be forever associated with the building of the city. They have given freely of their time to this laudable enterprise. It is but just in this connection to mention them and the officials they have employed to manage the institution.

Nine thousand dollars a year is spent at the present time in maintaining and operating the library. Of this, $3,900 pays the Librarian, his three assistants and the janitor. An additional $1,800 rent will be available; and still the necessities of the library call for more and more liberal appropriations. This is not to be wondered at when we consider the marvelous growth of East St. Louis and the progressive character of its inhabitants.

Following are the names and dates of service of officers and directors of the Library Board and of Librarians and Assistant Librarians since the re-establishment of the library:

Presidents: D. C. Marsh, 1892-96; H. C. Fairbrother, 1896-'98; H. F. Parry, 1898-'99; C. F. Wilhelmj, 1899-1903; H. C. Fairbrother, 1903-'05; George Caughlan, 1905 (now in office).

Vice-Presidents: James P. Slade, 1892-'96; Thomas Knoebel, 1896-'98; G. W. Thompson, 1898-1900; T. J. McDonough, 1900-'03; John J. Townsend, 1903-'05 (now in office).

Secretaries: H. F. Parry, 1892-'96, and 1899-1903; H. M. Hill, 1896-'98; A. L. Keechler, 1898-'99; T. J. McDonough, 1903-'05; J. B. House, 1905 (now in office).

Librarians: Miss Laura B. Painter, 1892 (March to September); Thomas Nelson, 1892-'96; Miss Minnie G. Turner, 1896-'97, 1899-1900; Samuel Buchanan, 1897-1899; H. F. Woods, 1901-'02; John E. Miller, 1902-'04; J. Lyon Woodruff, 1904-'06.

Assistant Librarians: Miss Laura Painter, 1892-'93, 1896-'97; Mrs. S. G. Delerno, 1892-93; Miss Minnie G. Turner, 1893-'95, 1897-1900; Miss Myra B. Gray, 1894-1900; Miss Mary G. Keane, 1899-1906; Miss Bessie Barrows, 1900-'04; Mrs. F. Turpin, 1903-'06; Miss Minnie Rodenberger, 1903-'06.

Directors: D. C. Marsh, 1892-'96; A. L. Keechler, 1892-1904; M. B. Sheridan, 1892-'96; J. W. Kirk, 1892-1903; Samuel Buchanan, 1892-'97; H. F. Parry, 1892-1903; J. P. Slade, 1892-'96; George Worstenholm, 1892-'96; O. C. Bates, 1892-93; G. H. Kemper, 1892-'96; H. M.

Hill, 1896-'98; John Kickham, 1896-'98; Joseph A. Kurrus, 1896-'98; Thomas Knoebel, 1896-'99; Michael Buckley, 1896-'99; H. C. Fairbrother, 1896-1905; C. F. Wilhelmj, 1897-1903; James M. Sheer, 1898-1904; G. W. Thompson, 1898-1904; G. W. Brichler, 1899-1905; T. J. McDonough, 1899-1905; J. J. Townsend, 1903-'06; W. K. Moody, 1903-'06; Andrew Zittel, 1904-'07; Joseph Meamber, 1904-'07; W. H. Horner, 1904-'07; George Caughlan, 1904-'07; J. B. House, 1905-'08; J. W. Holl, 1905-'08; Eugene Thompson, 1905-'08.

THE PRESS—DAILY, WEEKLY AND MONTHLY.—The "East St. Louis Gazette," a weekly newspaper, was founded in 1865 by former Mayor John B. Bowman. A daily issue was begun in 1877, but was soon discontinued. The paper is now owned by Frank B. Bowman, the son of Mayor Bowman, with John H. Suess as publisher and Alonzo B. Suess as business manager. It is Democratic in politics. (For a fuller sketch of the "Gazette," see chapter XVIII. on "Journalism.")

The "East St. Louis Evening Journal" was first issued in 1889. James W. Kirk is its editor. It is published by Frank P. Fox & Co. In politics it is independent.

The "Western Workman" first appeared in 1897. It is a Democratic paper published by Lawrence G. Merrill and edited by John W. Merrill.

The "Republican News," now in its twelfth volume, is published weekly by the East St. Louis Publishing Company. E. C. Singers is Manager, S. W. Baxter, editor.

The "Weekly Message," established in 1902 by William E. Rutledge and still published and edited by him, stands for reforms and makes a specialty of advocating law enforcement.

The "East St. Louis Zeitung," an evening newspaper, was established in 1903. It is published by the German Publishing Company and edited by Dr. William Fargo.

The "East St. Louis Daily Commercial," a Democratic newspaper, is published by J. W. Merrill & Son.

The "Daily National Live-Stock Reporter," the agricultural daily of St. Louis, is published at the National Stock Yards, by the Reporter Publishing Company, W. S. Hannah, Secretary and Treasurer. It is in its seventeenth volume.

The "East St. Louis Advance Citizen," which dates from 1894, is a Republican paper published weekly for colored patrons by H. T. Bowman, who also edits it.

"Poultry Culture," a monthly, established in 1901, is edited by Edwin C. Singers. It is published by the Poultry Culture Publishing Company.

STREET AND SUBURBAN RAILROADS.—The East St. Louis and Suburban Company was incorporated in New Jersey in 1902 and holds the stock and bonds of the East St. Louis Railway Company, the St. Louis & East St. Louis Electric Railway Company, the East St. Louis & Suburban Railway Company and the Citizens' Electric Light and Power Company of East St. Louis, and the bonds of the East St. Louis & Belleville Electric Railroad Company. The East St. Louis and Suburban Company owns all the stock and the bonds of these operating companies, but the companies themselves are operated by the East St. Louis and Suburban Railway. The franchises extend from forty-six to fifty years, with the exception of the Belleville franchise, which expires in 1920. The company also has exclusive right for operating electric cars over the Eads bridge for a period of fifty years. The total trackage operated is 115 miles.

LAWYERS OF THE PRESENT TIME.—Alexander Flannigen, John L. Flannigen, Forman and Whitnel, Jesse M. Freels, Anderson B. Garrett, Robert V. Gustin, Frank B. Hanna, Raymond B. Hendricks, Luke H. Hite, James L. Hopkins, Anthony A. Hunt, Arnold C. Johnson, Samuel S. Jones, Maurice V. Joyce, Keefe and Sullivan, William B. Knowles, Martin D. Baker, William H. Bennett, William Bott, Daniel P. Boyle, Leroy H. Browning, Daniel Burroughs, Bruce H. Campbell, B. H. Canby, Charles B. Carroll, Michael J. Carroll, Eustace W. Chism, William L. Coley, Alfred B. Davis, Dempcy and Baxter, Alfred A. Eicks, Thomas L. Fekete, Robert Flannigan, Victor K. Koerner, Kramer and Kramer, William P. Launtz, Richard J. Long, Louden and Crow, N. C. Lyria, Franklin A. McConaughy, Daniel McGlynn, McHale and Sumner, Joseph H. McMurdo, Joseph B. Messick, Mortimer Millard, Henry W. Moore, William C. Mulkey, John P. Mullane, Charles Neustadt, George F. O'Melveny, Clarence E. Pope, James J. Rafter, Ramsey and Hamlin, Charles E. Ritcher, William A. Rodenberg, William R. Rodenberger, Frank C. Smith, Stein,

Wulff and Ring, D. J. Sullivan, William T. Sumner, William E. Trautmann, Silas W. Trush, Wilton M. Vandeventer, Oswald L. Voigt, Philip H. Wagner, William Warner, Webb and Webb, Wise and McNulty, Daniel G. Wuersch.

MEDICAL PRACTITIONERS OF TODAY.—George C. Adams, Lee D. Applewhite, A. L. Barnard, Hubert B. Beedle, Lyman B. Bluitt, Emmett H. Bottom, Mrs. Cerilda Bromley, Jacob Butler, Henry A. Cables, John C. Caldwell, Richard L. Campbell, Edward W. Cannady, Matthew S. Carr, Richard W. Carter, B. Conrad, James A. Crow, Ora J. Culbertson, Henry J. de Haan, Martin R. Doyle, John W. Dwyer, Charles E. Eisele, Miss Florence L. Evans, Henry C. Fairbrother, Alexander Fekete, John F. Ford, Foulon and Foulon, M. M. Glass, Henry S. Goe, Charles W. Gowan, James A. Grimes, George Gundlach, Thomas Hagarty, Miss Anna M. A. Hahn, Adolph E. Hansing, Henry Hanson, Henry G. Hertel, John I. Higgs, A . C. Housh, Caroline Howes, George O. Hulick, Francis Hirsch, Otto W. Knewitz, Gordon Lederman, Daniel W. LeGrand, Edward J. Leonard, Charles W. Lillie, Adolph E. Linder, Louis J. Linder, John Lippert, E. H. Little, H. M. Little, Robert M. Little, Harlan W. Long, James W. McDonald, Alfred A. McBrien, James G. McBrien, Robert X. McCracken, Andrew J. McGaffigan, Albert B. McQuillan, Albert Miller, Charles L. Moeller, Joseph T. Pace, Joel J. Parker, James W. Rendleman, William H. Renois, Henry Ressel, A. E. Rives, Ulysses S. Short, Charles S. Skaggs, Carroll Smith, Charles A. Smith, Harvey S. Smith, Henry D. Smith, William C. Spannagel, Roy T. Stanton, Joseph E. State, George A. Stewart, Eugene Thompson, F. M. Triggs, Robert A. Twitchell, William E. Wiatt, William S. Wiatt, Leaming J. Wiggins, Charles F. Wilhelmj, Walter Wilhelmj, Augustus B. Wood, Alexander Woods, Ira C. Young, Carl A. W. Zimmermann.

To WHOM HONOR IS DUE.—To bring about the wonderful growth of East St. Louis there have been agencies at work over and above the natural advantages of the city. The people fought for and won the advantage of good government. They considered that essential to the building of a city, and that is what they wanted to do. In all important public movements, leaders are necessary. The East St. Louisans had leaders—born leaders. Thomas L. Fekete, Sr., and Henry D. Sexton were

among these leaders—there were several, along different ways to the same high place. Interested in banking, insurance and real estate operations, they unfalteringly believed in a future city where East St. Louis now stands, and they imbued all with whom they came in contact with some measure of the hopeful and helpful spirit. These men, with Paul W. Abt, should have credit for very much of the growth and prosperity that have given East St. Louis its present proud position. Besides these, certain men who, fortunately, have occupied the Mayor's chair since East St. Louis became a city, have efficiently and patriotically promoted her development.

Readers who look for historic mention of several interests not here mentioned, or at the most only casually attended to, are referred to other chapters in this volume. The plan of this work calls for the consideration of certain interesting topics in a manner broad enough to identify them with general county, rather than local history.

CHAPTER XIX.

TOWNS, VILLAGES AND HAMLETS.

MASCOUTAH — LEBANON — O'FALLON — CASEYVILLE — MILLSTADT — MARISSA — NEW ATHENS — SUMMERFIELD — FAYETTEVILLE — LENZBURG — FREEBURG — DARMSTADT — EAST CARONDELET—CAHOKIA AND ITS EARLY HISTORY—PRAIRIE DU PONT—FRENCH VILLAGE—SMITHTON—OTHER VILLAGES, HAMLETS AND RAILWAY STATIONS—PLACES OF COMMERCIAL OR HISTORIC INTEREST—RURAL NEWSPAPERS OF TODAY—FREEBURG TRIBUNE—LEBANON JOURNAL AND LEBANON LEADER — MARISSA MESSENGER — DER MASCOUTAH ANZEIGER, MASCOUTAH HERALD AND MASCOUTAH TIMES — MILLSTADT ENTERPRISE — O'FALLON PROGRESS—NEW ATHENS JOURNAL.

MASCOUTAH, in Mascoutah Township, on the Louisville & Nashville Railroad, was laid out by T. J. Krafft and John Flanagan April 6, 1837, and named Mechanicsburg. It had then two blocks of six lots each, three blocks of twelve lots each, and one block not divided into lots, called "the mill lot." Samuel Dixon, a hunter, who lived directly south of Postel's mills, built there the first hut within the present limits of Mascoutah. After the town was platted Samuel Mitchell built the first house (a log cabin), and also erected a saw-mill. In March, 1839, Fritz Hilgard, T. J. Krafft and Benjamin J. West laid out an addition containing seventy-two lots, and then was first recorded the name "Mascoutah," by which the town has since been known. Many other additions have since been made, West Mascoutah being laid out in thirty-six lots by H. F. Teichmann, in January, 1857.

Dr. Brewington was the first merchant at Mascoutah, but stayed there only a few months. Lewis Hauck was the first child born in the village. His father, once connected with the "Belleville Zeitung," published a work on chancery, which he dedicated to Judge Sidney Breese. Dr. Smith, a son-in-law of Major Brown, was the first practicing physician. The first church and first school-house were erected north of Postel's mills. Nathaniel Fike was the first local Postmaster. Fike & Crownover bought Brewington's store, which later passed to the ownership of E. Bagby, the second Postmaster, who was appointed by President William H. Harrison.

Hilgard, Conrad & Heimberger bought the old Mitchell Mill in 1835, added a flour-bolt run by hand-power, and ground wheat and corn-meal on the same stone. These men later built the second store building in the settlement, at the corner of Jefferson and Main Streets. Conrad and Philip Eisenmayer bought the mill property in 1839, took in as a partner Philip H. Postel, enlarged the mill and manufactured and exported flour. This old mill, which stood about fifty feet south-east of the present Postel Mill, was moved in 1850 to Clinton County. The second mill—now the Postel Mill—was built by Andrew Eisenmayer and Philip Postel in 1848. This is now owned by the Postels, and is one of the largest mills in this part of the country. There were, a quarter of a century ago, two other large mills in Mascoutah, one owned by Sehlinger & Schubkegel, and the other by Kleekamp & Hussman. Flour was then shipped in considerable quantities from Mascoutah to England, France and Germany.

For a time Mascoutah grew slowly; but from 1840, when German immigration to this region began, up to 1860, it advanced rapidly. It is now a substantial town, with nearly all its principal business houses on one moderately-built-up street. Mascoutah, with 2,500 population, ranks third among the towns of St. Clair County.

In order to afford an idea of the business enterprise of Mascoutah, we present a list of its chief industries, interests and business and professional men:

Lawyers—George F. Wombacher, Peter W. Lill.

Doctors—H. Herold, W. P. Heinrich, E. F. Scheve, George Leibrock.

Banks—Private bank of Gust J. Scheve, founded November, 1892; capital, $30,000. The Cashier is Louis Scheve, son of Gust J. Scheve.

Coal Mines—The Beatty Coal Company has two mines, one north of Mascoutah, the other two miles west. They were sunk about 1874, and are owned by Mrs. Beatty and her sons, who constitute a stock company. Officers—President, James Beatty; Secretary, Nephi Beatty. The Kolb Coal Company's mines are located three miles southwest of Mascoutah. The officers are: President, Philip Kolb; Secretary, E. R. Hagist; Treasurer, Philip Hucke; Vice-President, Jacob G. Mann.

Brick Manufacturers—The Mascoutah Brick Company has a pressed brick plant, which was established in 1902 and employs thirty men. It is southwest of Mascoutah on the Louisville & Nashville track. Officers—President, George W. Lischer; Secretary and Treasurer, John Facht.

Brewers—The Mascoutah Brewing Company was established in 1860 and has changed hands several times. It has been under the present management fifteen years. Officers—President, E. R. Hagist; Secretary, H. F. Teichman; Treasurer, Gust. J. Scheve; Superintendent, Oscar Klinke.

Dairy—The Mutual Creamery Company was established in Southern Mascoutah in 1903. Its products took a silver medal at the World's Fair in St. Louis. Officers—President, George F. Wombacher; Secretary, John Scharth; Treasurer, George Draser; Superintendent, Christ Christensen, who is a man of note in this business.

Millers—The early history of the Philip H. Postel Milling Company has been mentioned in connection with the early history of Mascoutah. Philip H. Postel became identified with the mill in November, 1849. In 1851, a new mill

Endnotes:

(1) For an overview of the Cahokian history of East St. Louis see Joseph M. Galloy, "A Once and Future City: The Splendor of Prehistoric East St. Louis," *The Making of an All-America City: East St. Louis at 150*, ed. by Mark Abbott (St. Louis, MO: Virginia Publishing, 2011), 5-14.

(2) Robert A. Tyson, *History of East St. Louis, for Resources, Statistics, Railroads, Physical Features: Business and Advantages* (East St. Louis, IL: John Haps, 1875); L.U. Reavis, *Saint Louis, the Future Great City of the World: With Biographical Sketches of the Representative Men and Women of St. Louis and Missouri* centennial ed. (St. Louis, MO: C.R. Barns, 1876); *History of St. Clair County, Illinois, with Illustrations: Descriptive of Its Scenery, and Biographical Sketches of Some of Its Prominent Men and Pioneers* (Philadelphia, PA: Brink, McDonough & Co., 1881); A. S. Wilderman and A. A. Wilderman, eds., *Historical Encyclopedia of Illinois and History of St. Clair County* (Chicago: Munnell Publishing Co., 1907).

(3) Tyson cited information from the following works. James H. Perkins and John Mason Peck, *Annals of the West: Embracing a Concise Account of Principal Events . . .* 2nd ed., rev. and enl. (St. Louis, MO: J.R. Albach, 1851); John W. Monette, *History of the Discovery and Settlement of the Valley of the Mississippi, by the Three Great European Powers, Spain, France, and Great Britain . . .* (New York: Harper & Brothers, 1846); John Gilmary Shea, *Discovery and Exploration of the Mississippi Valley with the Original Narratives of Marquette, Allouez, Membre, Hennepin, and Anastase Douay* (New York: Redfield, 1852); W.P. Smith, *The Book of the Great Railway Celebrations of 1857 . . .* 1st ed. (New York, D. Appleton & Co., 1858); Thomas Ford, James Shields, *A History of Illinois, from Its Commencement as a State in 1818 to 1847 . . .* (Chicago: S.C. Griggs & Co.; New York: Ivison & Phinney, 1854); Elihu H. Shepard, *The Early History of St. Louis and Missouri, from Its First Exploration by White Men in 1673 to 1843* (St Louis, MO: Southwestern Book and Publishing Company, 1870).

Chapter 2: Maps of a Growing City

Late-nineteenth and early-twentieth-century maps of East St. Louis supported the keen interest East St. Louisans had in touting the advantages and promises that resulted from the rapid physical expansion and transformations of their city. The maps displayed more than topological features; they illustrated the impact of human activities in reshaping nature and ordering social relationships. The maps reinforced the views of city leaders that East St. Louis greatly benefited from its location on the Mississippi River and the American Bottom floodplain and from its close proximity to St Louis, Missouri, and the geographical center of the nation.

Although not readily apparent to the untrained eye, the maps show that East St. Louisans did not fully accommodate their city to the Mississippi River, which formed the Illinois-Missouri boundary, and the floodplain. Residents did not conquer their problems with annual flooding until the first third of the twentieth century, after decades of expanding and maintaining levees and drainage canals and implementing massive projects to raise the grading of streets and principal buildings above the highest known flood level. In time, city leaders diverted Cahokia Creek north of the city to the Mississippi and filled the city's portion of the creek for further urban development. They recognized the commercial uses of the Mississippi with its north-south traffic that made East St. Louis an inland port. Nevertheless, despite the bridges, city boosters often perceived the river as a barrier to east-west commerce and aggressively used that perception to encourage railroads and industries to site their facilities in the city, especially along the waterfront. On the other hand, the relative flatness of the American Bottom made East St. Louis ripe for physical and economic development, and the maps reflected such changes. The maps show streets and railroad lines running straight as an arrow for miles, generally in an east-

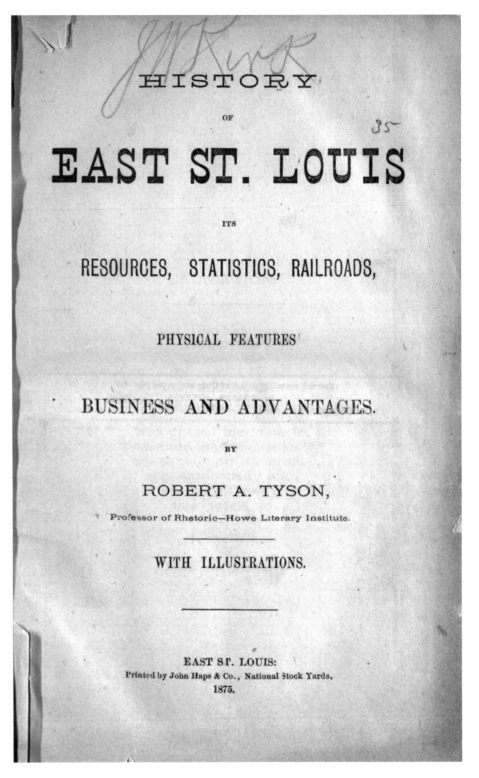

HISTORY

OF

EAST ST. LOUIS

ITS

RESOURCES, STATISTICS, RAILROADS,

PHYSICAL FEATURES

BUSINESS AND ADVANTAGES.

BY

ROBERT A. TYSON,

Professor of Rhetoric—Howe Literary Institute.

WITH ILLUSTRATIONS.

EAST ST. LOUIS:
Printed by John Haps & Co., National Stock Yards.
1875.

west direction. Railroads and industries had ample space to site their facilities. Neighborhoods seemingly interspersed among rail lines and factory complexes.

The maps from Robert Tyson, *A History of East St. Louis* (1875), and the *Standard Atlas of St Clair County, Illinois* (1901) are a study in contrasts in East St. Louis's physical expansion

and land use development. *(1)* Basic, almost hand-drawn in appearance, the Tyson map shows East St. Louis on the eve of its industrialization. East St. Louis' territory did not change between 1861 and 1875. The city was definitely oriented to St. Louis and the Mississippi River, and Tenth Street was its eastern boundary. The Standard

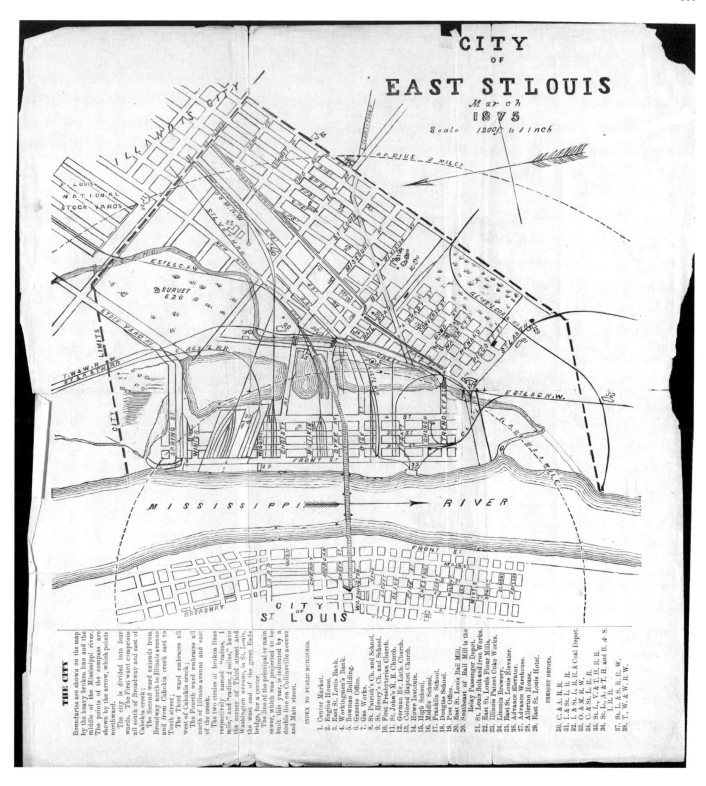

The following is an index appearing on the map.

Atlas multicolored maps, however, dramatized a territorial expanding, industrializing East St. Louis with its railroads, factories, and grid of streets. The plats included names of some of the major landowners of various parcels of land as well as the names of the original villages that incorporated themselves as East St. Louis or that the city had annexed. (The city continued to annex territory until the 1910s.) Overall, these and other maps of East St. Louis, published between the 1870s and the 1910s, gave readers a sense of the city's history of rapid and massive population growth, industrial development, and geographical expansion.

STANDARD ATLAS

OF

St. Clair County

ILLINOIS

INCLUDING

A PLAT BOOK

OF THE

VILLAGES, CITIES AND TOWNSHIPS OF THE COUNTY.

MAP OF THE STATE, UNITED STATES AND WORLD.

Patrons Directory, Reference Business Directory and Departments devoted to General Information.

ANALYSIS OF THE SYSTEM OF U.S. LAND SURVEYS, DIGEST OF THE SYSTEM OF CIVIL GOVERNMENT, ETC. ETC.

Compiled and Published

BY

GEO. A. OGLE & CO.

PUBLISHERS & ENGRAVERS.

134 VAN BUREN ST.
CHICAGO.

1901

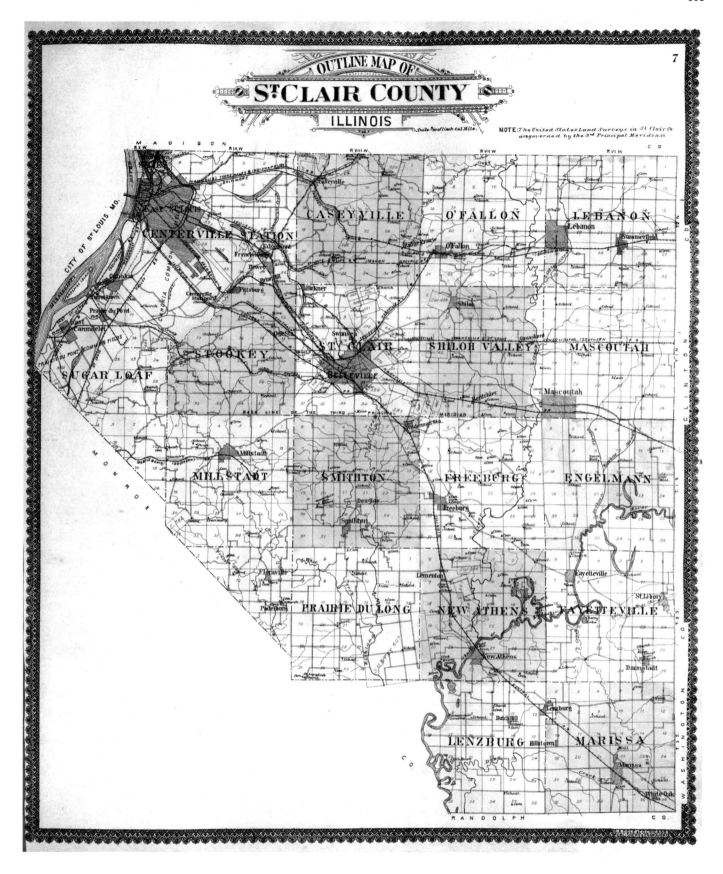

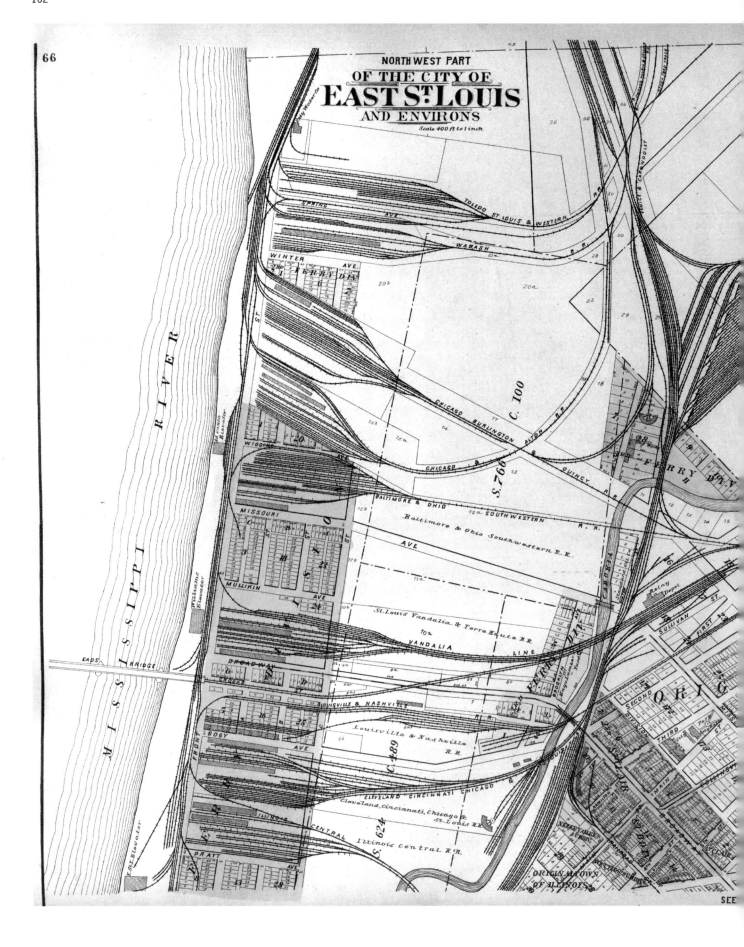

SEE PAGES 82-83

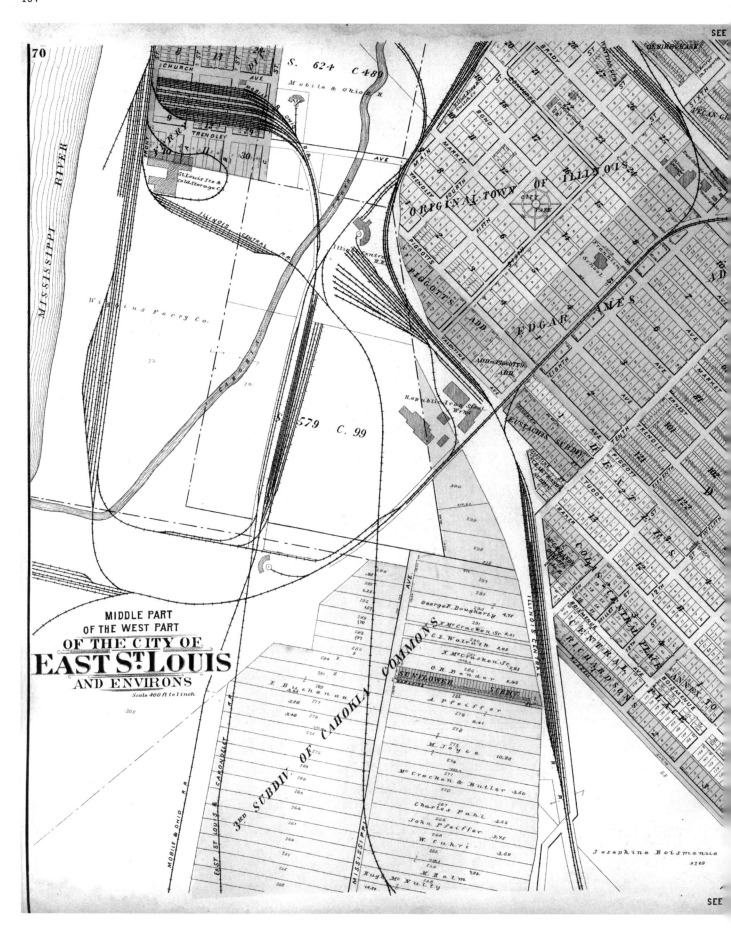

MIDDLE PART
OF THE WEST PART
OF THE CITY OF
EAST St LOUIS
AND ENVIRONS
Scale 400 ft to 1 inch

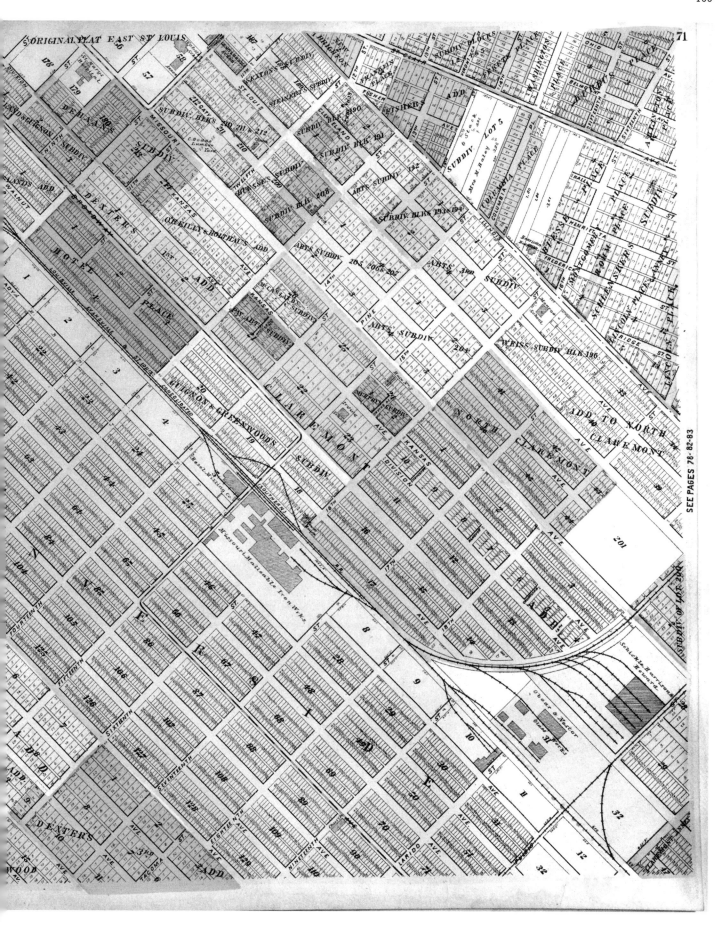

SEE PAGES 78-82-83

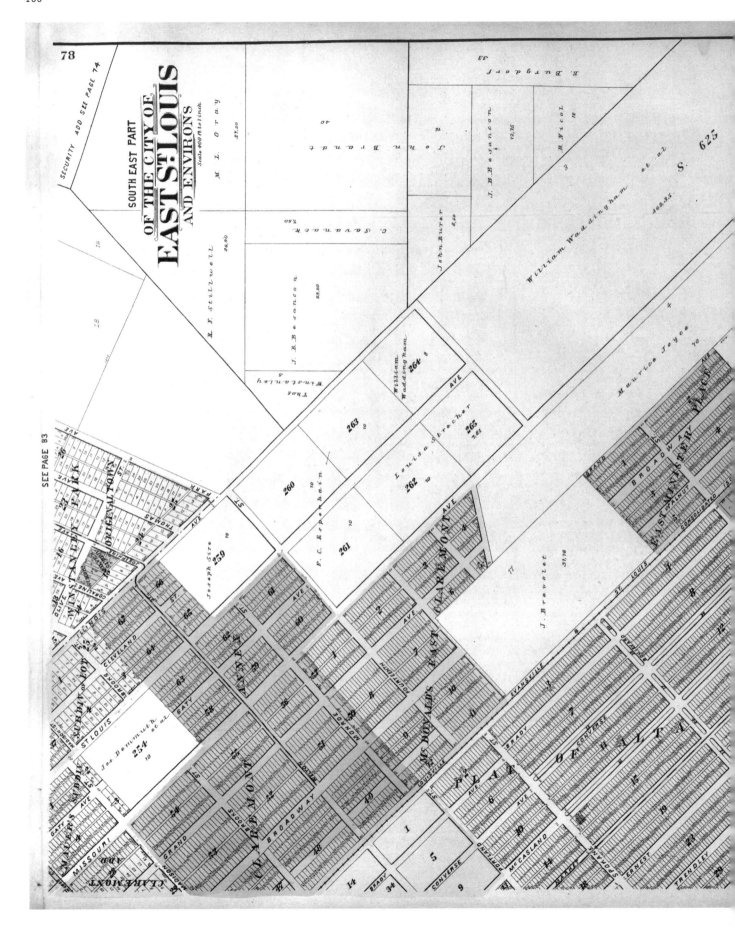

SEE PAGE 83

78

SOUTH EAST PART
OF THE CITY OF
EAST ST. LOUIS
AND ENVIRONS
Scale 400 ft. to 1 inch.

79

SEE PA

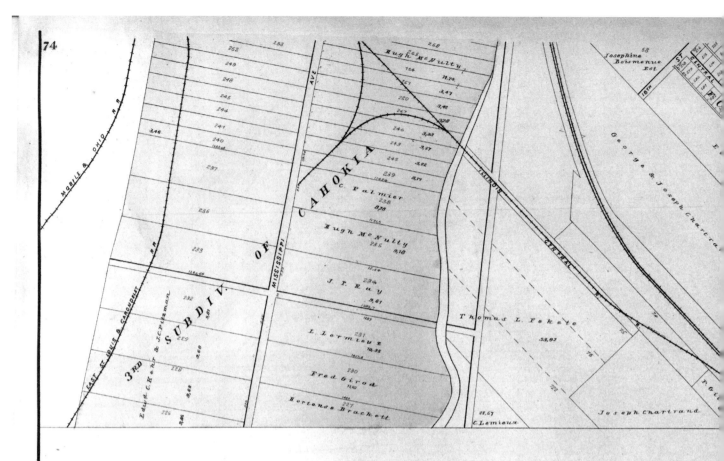

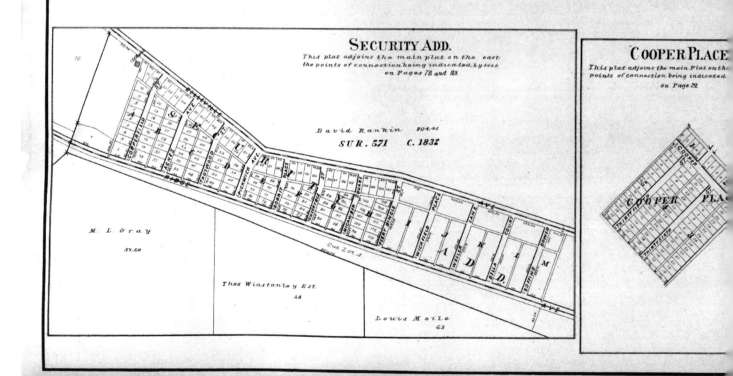

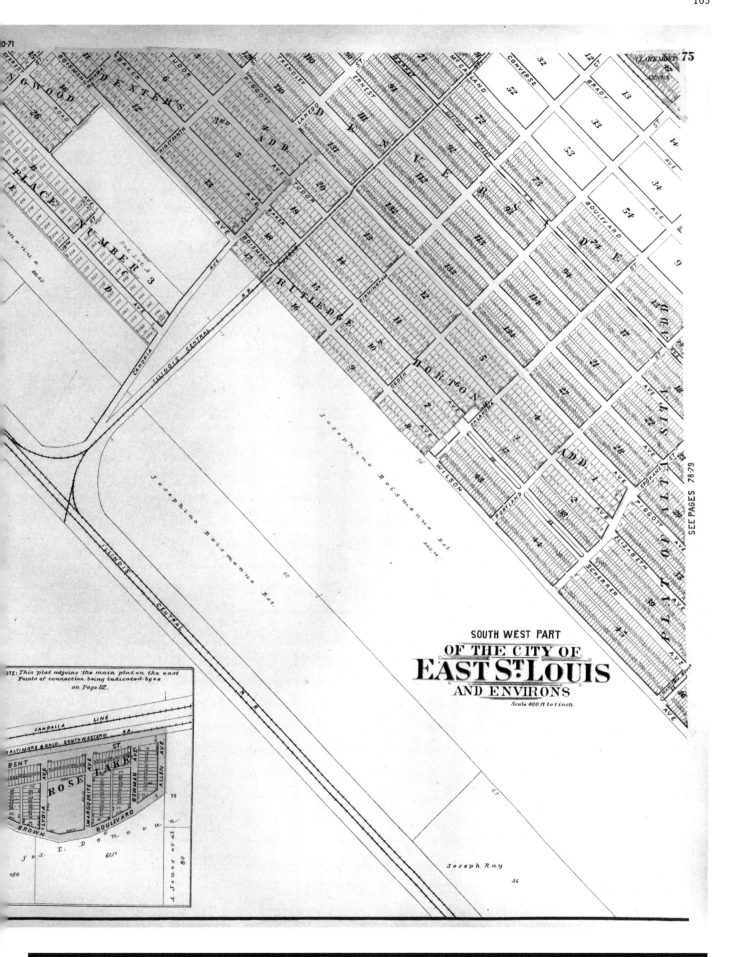

SOUTH WEST PART
OF THE CITY OF
EAST S⸳ LOUIS
AND ENVIRONS
Scale 400 ft to 1 inch

NOTE: This plat adjoins the main plat on the east. Points of connection being indicated by ✸ on Page 82.

SEE PAGES 78-79

The Great National Stock Yards, at East St. Louis, Illinois, contain **656**

hich **100** Acres are enclosed, and **60** Acres are under Sheds.

Endnote:

(1) Robert A. Tyson, *History of East St. Louis, for Resources, Statistics, Railroads, Physical Features: Business and Advantages* (East St. Louis, IL: John Haps, 1875); *Standard Atlas of St. Clair County, Illinois: Including a Plat Book of the Villages, Cities, and Townships of the County* (Chicago: George A. Ogle & Company, 1901).

Chapter 3: Biographical Sketches of Prominent Citizens

Biographical vignettes of prominent individuals compose the bulk of the historical narratives published between the 1870s and 1920s. Most of the vignettes appeared in county and local histories, as well as city directories. Indeed, the sketches form a significant, if not a major, portion of the *History of St. Clair County, Illinois,* and the *Historical Encyclopedia of Illinois and History of St. Clair County,* the two sources excerpted for this chapter. *(1)* This anthology does not include any of the valuable biographical sketches found in the East St. Louis city directory of 1912, probably the greatest source for such material, because it is not part of the archival holdings of SIUE. Nonetheless, those researching the biographies of prominent citizens should consult the 1912 directory for the wealth of information in the vignettes.*(2)*

The biographical sketches in the cited sources have a few features in common. They are about individuals who were pioneer settlers or leading figures in business, civic affairs, and/or municipal, county, state, or national politics and government. Some vignettes in *History of St. Clair County, Illinois,* have a hand-drawn portrait of the subject. Some in the *Historical Encyclopedia of Illinois and History of St. Clair County* have an engraved portrait from a photograph. The vast majority of entries are biographies of white men. A few women appear, but mainly as spouses. (The first biographical sketch of a nonwhite East St. Louisan, African American realtor Pearl Abernathy, appeared in the 1912 city directory. Unfortunately, no drawing or photograph accompanied Abernathy's short biography.) The stories are part "Who's Who" in the city or county, and part genealogy. The typical sketch states the subject's birthplace, ethnicity; his parents' names, birthplaces,

occupations, and influence as a source of the subject's values and ideas; his school and college, past and current residency, membership in churches and fraternal societies, and/or military service, and if married, names of spouse and children and sometimes the spouse's parents and birthplace. Although the sources claimed to be truthful to the facts, the reader needs to be reminded that fact checking was not as rigorous as it should have been. Many biographies of the day conflicted over details, and many were reproduced in multiple volumes.

Of course, *An East St. Louis Anthology* has biographies of only selected East St. Louisans. The selection criteria for the biographies in this chapter rested upon two major factors. First, limitations of space dictated the number of images for this chapter in relation to the other chapters. The other factor derives from the research conducted by the author and his colleagues who determined which names among the most influential are entered herein. Although only ten names are selected for the anthology from the fourteen vignettes of East St. Louisans which appear in the *History of St. Clair County,* the following is a sample from the fourteen. John J. McLean was Mayor of East St. Louis from 1881 to 1882. John Trendley was city councilman during the 1860s. Maurice E. Tissier was city clerk in the 1870s and owner and publisher of the *East St. Louis Herald* newspaper, which he started in 1878. Brothers Ferdinand and Michael Heim founded the Heim Brewery in the late 1860s. Levi Baugh, proprietor of a rendering works, served as city alderman in the 1880s. J.W. Renshaw joined with a few others to organize the East St. Louis Real Estate Exchange in the late 1880s.

Published years after the *History*

of St. Clair County, the *Historical Encyclopedia of Illinois and History of St. Clair County* has a larger number of entries of East St. Louisans as well as St. Clair Countians. Of the 125 East St. Louisans whose vignettes appear in the *Historical Encyclopedia of Illinois and History of St. Clair County,* this volume uses only about two dozen of the most influential figures. The following names are a sample from the 125 sketches. Paul W. Abt was bank officer of the Illinois State Trust Company, founded in 1902, and was a son-in-law of the city's founder. John M. Chamberlin, Jr., was President of the East St. Louis Real Estate Exchange in the early 1900s, but also served in the Illinois legislature and on the East St. Louis School Board; he served as Mayor of East St. Louis from 1913 to 1915. Charles B. Goedde was city treasurer in the early 1900s. Joseph B. Messick was a well-known attorney who practiced law in late-nineteenth-century East St. Louis. William Emil Trautmann was a lawyer and Republican political boss, and was appointed District Attorney for the Eastern District of Illinois by President Theodore Roosevelt.

Overall, the stories are somewhat hagiographical in tone. They project the high ideals the men exemplified in their respective careers, occupations, or professions. The lengthier the biography, the more the source placed much value or significance in the subject. The vignettes hold their subjects in high esteem for their hard work, devotion to livelihood and family, cultural refinement, and/or engagement in civic life. The sketches praise their subjects as virtuous men of middle-class means or status. More importantly, the entries make note if the subjects were poised to or already taking great strides to advance the interests or prosperity of East St. Louis.

1686

→ HISTORY ←

OF

ST. CLAIR COUNTY,

ILLINOIS.

 With Illustrations

DESCRIPTIVE OF ITS SCENERY,

AND

Biographical Sketches of some of its Prominent Men and Pioneers.

BY

BRINK, McDONOUGH & CO.,

PHILADELPHIA.

CORRESPONDING OFFICE, EDWARDSVILLE, ILL.

1881

BIOGRAPHICAL SKETCHES.

THE present mayor of the city of East St. Louis, was born in Cincinnati, Ohio, January 4th, 1841. His father, Milton M. McLean, a lawyer by profession, had acquired considerable property interests in the west, especially in and around East St. Louis, among others, a distillery in 1840. After ten years' management of this property he concluded on changing his residence from his Cincinnati home, to enable him to personally care for his rapidly growing interests here. Hence, in 1850 he took up his abode in East St. Louis. In 1851 he disposed of the distillery and moved to St. Louis, where he continued the practice of his profession until the time of his death, July 4th, 1855. He was one of the largest land owners on this side of the river. For a time he was a partner of Church Blackburn, one of the most eminent criminal lawyers of his day. He had received his education in the Miami University. He ranked with the first young men of the west in point of talent, integrity, and

309

all the virtues that tend to constitute the highest degree of moral worth. At the time of his death the members of the St. Louis bar paid the highest honors to his memory, and he was followed to his grave by hundreds of true and sincere friends as mourners. He was a nephew of Justice McLean, whose worth is known to all.

The mother of John J. McLean was Mary W. Johnson, a daughter of the first Indian Agent ever appointed in Ohio.

A brief and interesting sketch of his life is retained by the family, from which we glean the following:—He was born near Ballyshannon, Ireland, March 3d, 1775. At an early age, soon after the termination of the revolutionary war, he was brought to the United States, locating in Cumberland county, Pennsylvania. He was with Gen. Wayne on the Ohio, in 1793-4; was a captain in Philadelphia in 1798; clerk in the War Department and Indian Bureau, in all thirty-one years. In the war of 1812 he was a pay-master and quartermaster by turns. In 1841-2 he was U. S. Commissioner for treating with the Indians. In all these positions he acquitted himself honorably. In a letter yet extant written by him in his old age, he said "he had suffered political martyrdom thrice for adherence to Whig principles; once by the tyrant Jackson once by the nondescript Tyler, and once by the democratic legislature of Ohio."

Of these families came John J. McLean, the subject of this sketch, a man who has inherited many of their good qualities; a man of energy, of generous impulses, and who is held in high esteem. He received a common school education in the public schools of St. Louis, Missouri, and subsequently attended the Methodist College at St. Charles, in the same state about a year. As a youth in school he exhibited those traits of character,—that same restlessness of disposition that has prompted him to dare and to do whatever he conceived to be right.

He was married to Eliza Griffith, a most estimable lady, in June, 18—. By this marriage there have been born the following children: John Joseph, Clara Belle, Nathaniel Charles, Eliza Laurence, Ralph Edwin, Gertrude Bertha, and Estelle May; all living, and constituting a happy family.

His mother died in Shiloh, this county, Feb. 9th, 1877, in the sixty-third year of her life. To resume his personal history: at the age of seventeen telegraphy possessed for him its charms. He rapidly acquired a knowledge of its mysteries, and for a year remained at this work as operator in the employ of the Ohio and Mississippi railroad. He next learned the trade of machinist, at which he worked for a period of nine years, in the locomotive shops of the same railway company for which he had served as telegraph operator. In 1870 he took charge of one of the boats of the Wiggins Ferry Company, as captain, which position he held for about ten years. From 1867 to 1870 he served as chief of the Metropolitan Police force of East St. Louis. His quickness of perception and promptness of action served him well here, and doubtless at different times saved bloodshed and riot. Possessed of a clear insight into the motives of men, coupled with the nerve to do what he deemed to be right, he never halted until proposed mischief was effected, but before it got under full headway he was on hand to check its tide. This promptitude together with his generous treatment of associates, gave him a strong hold upon the affections of his fellows, and rendered him personally popular with all. He served his constituency in the ward for two terms, of two years each, as member of the City Council, with credit to himself and honor to his supporters. In April, 1881, as a just recognition of his worth, he was elected mayor without opposition; this too, in the face of the fact that he is an ardent republican, whilst his city is strongly democratic. His first presidential vote was cast for Abraham Lincoln. Possessed of sound judgment, of excellent social qualities, of fine executive ability, he is filling his position to the satisfaction of all citizens.

JOHN O. BUTLER

Was born in St. Louis, Missouri, March 10th, 1827. His father was Armstead O. Butler, a physician of large reputation and extensive practice, was born in Mecklenburg county, Virginia, studied medicine in Philadelphia, Pa., and located in Cahokia. His circle of practice embraced a radius of forty miles, throughout which he was recognized as a skilled and erudite physician. The memory of few men is treasured up by the old pioneers of this part of the county more sacredly than that of their old family physician, Dr.

Butler. The mother of the subject of this sketch was Jane Tournot, of the old family of that name known to Cahokia records for perhaps a century. When he reached the age of fifteen years his father died. His widowed mother subsequently became the wife of Dr. A. H. Illinski. He received a fair business education, attending the schools of the day in Cahokia and St. Louis, and afterwards St. Vincent's College at St. Mary's. This institution of learning was moved, whilst he was a student, to Cape Girardeau; thither he went, but did not complete the prescribed course of study. For a time he pursued farming near Cahokia. He was united in marriage to Miss Julia C. Brackett, daughter of Dr. James Brackett, April 25th, 1853. He commenced mercantile pursuits as a clerk in a dry goods establishment in St. Louis. In 1849 he went to California, making it a trans-continental trip, as he was visiting friends on the Atlantic seaboard immediately before starting for the land of gold. In California he was engaged in a variety of pursuits; as mining, keeping a hotel and livery. Returned in 1853, farmed for a time, and then commenced merchandizing in 1856 in Warren, Hancock county, where he was made post-master. In 1863 he went to Montana, where for about eight months he sold goods. He bought out the lumber yards of General Jarrot, in May, 1876, in which business he is yet engaged, in connection with Nicholas McCracken. Last year their sales amounted to over 4,000,000 feet of lumber.

GEORGE W. DAUSCH.

The hope of the country is vested in her young men. If they be possessed of energy, good practical business ideas, and are directed by strong common sense then all is well. Belonging to this class no better representative can be found in East St. Louis than the subject of this sketch. He was born here Oct. 2d, 1855, hence is but twenty-six years of age, although occupying various positions of profit and trust. His parents, George and Julia Ann Dausch, came from Germany to this county during the revolution of 1848. His father was by trade a broker. He died here in 1846, leaving a widow, a son and daughter. His wife, who is yet living, subsequently married Louis Weris, by whom she has a large family of children. George W. Dausch attended the East St. Louis public schools, and afterwards, desirous of perfecting himself in a business education, attended Jones' Commercial College, St. Louis, Mo., where he graduated in 1869, at the early age of fourteen years, among, if not, the youngest graduate ever sent forth from that institution. He also attended a German institution, acquiring there a fair education. In 1846 he engaged in the service of the Workingmen's Banking company as a messenger. Step by step he has worked his way up, filling the various positions of book-keeper, teller and cashier, to which position he was chosen in 1878, and which he fills with great credit to himself. In 1880 he was appointed by the City Council of East St. Louis as City Treasurer, a just recognition of his genuine business worth and compliment to his attainments and integrity. He is a member of the order of Knights of Pythias, in whose working and advancement he takes deep interest. Politically, he is an avowed Republican, having cast his first vote for Rutherford B. Hayes, and last for James A. Garfield. He allies himself with the stalwarts, finding in their leader his beau ideal of manhood. Generous almost to a fault; of an eminently social turn of mind, he is recognized as a hale fellow, well met by all who know him. Guided by strict business principles in all his transactions, his future is full of promise. Few men have battled more successfully for position than he, and few are more esteemed by their fellows.

T. C. Jennings. M.D.

AMONG physicians and surgeons of this part of the state, who have attained distinction in their profession, Dr. T. C. Jennings takes rank with the foremost. He was born in Bloomfield, Chatauqua county, New York, May 8th, 1836. His father, Rev. Thomas J. Jennings, was a Methodist preacher. His mother's maiden name was Catharine Ditmars. When he was about six years of age, his father removed to Ohio, and because of failing health changed his vocation to that of farming. After living about four years in the Buckeye state, he removed to Wisconsin. Here, availing himself of the facilities afforded by the state, the subject of this sketch attended West Bend Academy, a school in charge of Dr. A. H. Hayes, a physician and teacher of rare abilities and high attainments. To him, more than any one else, is the doctor indebted for his aspirations in life, and for his determination to become a physician. Taking him as his model, he commenced the study of medicine under his instruction after he had acquired considerable proficiency in the classics, mathematics and natural sciences, preparatory to admission into Rush Medical College at Chicago. In 1856, he entered this institution, from which he graduated February 17, 1858. Returning to Wisconsin, he located in Mayville, where he prosecuted the practice of his profession a year, and in 1860 determined on finding a southern home, he came as far as St. Louis; at the time mutterings were heard all over the south which grew into threats of rebellion. He concluded to wait until the state of affairs had become more settled, and not desiring to resume the practice of medicine until he had found a congenial home, he enlisted himself among the pedagogues of St. Clair county by

40

taking charge of the school at French Village, where for two years he successfully engaged in this work. The threatenings of secession had become a dread reality; red battle had stamped her thundering feet all along Mason and Dixon's line; his country had become involved in the mighty throes of fratricidal strife: his patriotic heart beat responsive to his country's call for aid, and forsaking the school-room, he promptly offered his services and was accepted as assistant surgeon of the 117th regiment, Illinois Volunteers, November 15th, 1862. With this command he remained until August 5th, 1865, when with the regiment he was discharged with honors. He took part in the Meridian, (Mississippi) the Red River, the Tupelo and Oxford campaigns, (Mississippi) the Price campaign in Missouri, the campaign after General Hood in Middle Tennessee, and in the years 1864 and 1865, in the Mobile campaign. He was engaged in the battles of Fort De Russey and Pleasant Hill, Louisiana, Tupelo, Mississippi, Nashville, Tennessee, and Fort Blakely, Alabama. It is related of him, by his comrades, that his impatience was often such as to impel him to the very front of battle with patriotic cheer to urge on his fellows, when officers in his position were expected to take position in the rear, ready to receive any wounded that might have to be borne from the field of battle. Immediately after the war he located in East St. Louis, where he has ever since prosecuted his life work of practicing his profession. He was united in marriage to Miss Clementine Illinski, daughter of Dr. A. X. Illinski, June 24th, 1867. By this union there have been born four children, three of whom are living, Anna Belle, Clementine and Dio Illinski. Thomas Francis, the third in order of birth, died in childhood. The doctor's pre-eminent fitness for the position caused his friends to single him out as the republican candidate for the legislature from the 49th district in 1878, and most gallantly did he lead on to victory. As a representative, he was active, fearless in his advocacy of the right, gave close and constant attention to the business before the legislature and made an efficient member. In manners and deportment Dr. Jennings is a sociable and agreeable gentleman; as a physician prompt and methodical: and as a man his reputation for integrity of character, and for earnestness of purpose is as wide as the circle of his acquaintance.

D. D. ANTHONY.

AMONG the promising young men of East St. Louis few are more deserving of honorable mention than D. D. Anthony, who was born in Ripley county, Indiana, November 18, 1843. His father, Philip Anthony, was of the good old Puritan stock of New England, a farmer by occupation, and for fifteen years a justice of the peace in his adopted state. His mother, Mary Ann Anthony, was an Ohioan by birth. The subject of this sketch followed farming until the year 1859, when he came to Illinois, locating in Kankakee county. He received a common school education. At the time of the breaking out of the war he returned to Indiana, and on June 16, 1861, volunteered in Co. I, 13th Regiment Indiana Volunteers. Served in the campaign in West Virginia, under General McClellan; then under his successor, General Rosecrans. Was in the various battles and skirmishes throughout West Virginia, among them that at Rich Mountain, Cheat Mountain, Summit and Green Briar. With his command he went to the valley of Virginia and took part in the fight at Winchester, under General Shields. In 1862 his regiment was transferred to the army of the Potomac, with quarters at Suffolk, whose siege—at the hands of Longstreet—they gallantly withstood; left Suffolk for Charleston, with General Gillmore, where they took part in the siege of Sumter; thence to Florida; they were then ordered north, to join Butler's fleet at Yorktown, preparatory to ascending James river; took part in the Petersburg fight, where, on the 10th of May, 1863, he was taken prisoner. His prison life, extended as it was over a space of nine months and eighteen days, and divided between various Southern prison pens, is of great interest. First he was taken to Libby prison, at Richmond, where he was kept about a month; thence taken to Andersonville, where he was subjected to the gross neglect and hard usage for which that prison is so noted. He was an eyewitness to the bursting forth of the spring of water in the beaten path within the pen, spoken of by many prisoners, who—famishing with thirst—looked upon it as God's deliverance. After three months he was taken to Savannah, thence to Charleston, under guns he had himself helped to set months before; thence to Florence, where he suffered terribly. During his four months' imprisonment here he had not to exceed four ounces of salt with his ration of one pint of corn meal per *diem*, perhaps a half-dozen rations of meat, and a spoonful of molasses per week, during the time. At Goldsborough, North Carolina, he was exchanged for a well-fed Southern soldier, February 28, 1864. Being sick—scarcely able, in fact, to walk at all—he was taken to the hospital on David's Island, New York harbor, where for months he was treated with all the skill of army surgeons. His eyesight was almost gone—so far that its recovery was long thought doubtful. He was discharged from the U. S. service June 14, 1865; re-

turned to Indiana, where he was married to Sarah Belle Payton, April, 1866, by whom he has one child. After marriage he went South to Choctaw county, Alabama, where his wife was engaged in teaching a Freedmen's school for one year. During this time he was appointed by General Pope, commanding the Southern division, as re-constructing officer for registration of voters, administering the so-called "iron-clad oath," &c. Was taken sick, and returned to Indiana, where he remained only six months, returning to Alabama to engage in general merchandizing. In 1870 he was appointed assistant U. S. marshal in the Alabama district, during which service he enumerated the census of Choctaw county. When Alabama became democratic, and it was no longer safe for Northern men to express their sentiments in the South, he returned to Indiana, where he was employed by the Ohio and Mississippi railroad company. After remaining a year in their employ he went to Kansas, where he invested in a stock ranche, which he still owns. After a few months "roughing it," he returned to East St. Louis, where he was engaged in the erection of water works at the National Stock Yards. Here he remained several years as an engineer and water supply superintendent. In December, 1880, he was appointed deputy sheriff of St. Clair county by Frederick Ropiequet, a just recognition of his public services in behalf of the success of the republican party and of his worth as a man. Mr. Anthony is a member of the I. O. O. F., being a P. G., Golden Rule Lodge of E. St. Louis. Politically he is a stalwart, out-spoken, fearless republican. During the last campaign he made some very effective speeches in behalf of republican principles, reciting—as his experience enabled him to do—many instances of cruelty in the South. His republicanism was learned in very early years when his father kept an underground railway station on the Polar Star route from Slavery to Freedom. Efficient as an officer, true to all trusts reposed in him, genuine by nature—Mr. Anthony deserves well of his fellowmen.

JOHN B. SIKKING,

THE present efficient post-master of the city of East St. Louis, was born in Wenterswyke, Holland, August 16th, 1836. His father, John B. Sikking, was a carpenter, and emigrated from the land beyond the sea to America in 1844, locating in the city of St. Louis, Missouri. There were in all seven children in the family, of whom John B. Sikking was the fourth in order of birth. He received a common school education, and became a machinist. For thirteen years he engaged his services to the Ohio and Mississippi railway company. He was appointed post-master under Gen. Grant's administration, in 1869. Had officiated in this capacity for about two years prior, during Johnson's administration, as he served out the term of his predecessor and brother-in-law, E. W. Wider. As post-master he has proved faithful and capable, and has won universal esteem. He was married to Sarah E. Cunningham, a most estimable lady from Ohio, on the 24th of December, 1863. By this union there are six children. In politics Mr. Sikking is an ardent, outspoken republican, who has the honor of having always been true to his party, and party friends. Takes an active part in both local and national affairs. He and his wife are members of the M. E. church. He is also a member of the Masonic order. As a citizen he is quiet, unassuming, straightforward, and one that cannot be swerved from the path of duty.

Commerce at Chicago in 1875, as Notary Public, by Governor Richard J. Oglesby, and as member of the State Central Republican Committee in 1876. It was his nature to be active, and whatever he took hold of he did it with his might. True to his friends, a man of broad culture, of goodness of heart; his demise was mourned by many. A friend of the poor; he never turned them from his door, but attended to their wants with cheerfulness. Many prescriptions were filled by him, free of charge, when brought to him by those who were needy. He was married to Dora Sikking, March 21st, 1859, by whom he has had four children, only one of whom is living, Miss Emma, a beautiful and accomplished young lady of fifteen. His death, which occurred July 7th, 1881, was a shock to his family and fellow-citizens. In the full vigor of health but a few short hours before, doing business with his accustomed energy, its suddenness created excitement and surprise. He had returned, the night before, from his farm near Pevely, Missouri, quite exhausted. The morning found him asleep in death. The coroner was summoned, and pronounced the cause to have been congestion of the brain. Thus passed from earth one of East St. Louis' most active citizens, when apparently in the full vigor of manhood.

THOMAS GRANEY

Was born in the county of Kerry, Ireland, September 29, 1839. His father, Edward Graney, a farmer, died when he was but six months of age. He was taken care of by an uncle, Patrick McElligott, also a farmer. During the prevalence of the famine of 1848 throughout Ireland, his uncle and mother, Ellen McElligott, determined on leaving the ill-fated island, and moved to Canada, locating in Guelph, Wellington county, Canada West. Here they remained until 1858, when Thomas Graney enlisted in the 100th, or, as it was popularly known, the Prince of Wales Royal Canadian Regiment, organized for the purpose of going to the East Indies to suppress the war being waged by Nena Sahib. The regiment remained under instruction and drill in England nearly a year, when they were ordered out, and went as far as the heights of Gibraltar, whence they returned to England. As a soldier he stood high in favor, having been one of the thirty chosen from his regiment as a member of the Guard of Honor to the Queen, when she reviewed the troops in Aldershot Camp; was also lance corporal nine months, and lance sergeant eighteen months. He received a good-conduct badge which entitled him to a small pittance extra pay, and a badge for superior sharp-shooting. After three and a-half years' service, he bought his discharge, and in 1865 returned to Canada. In May of the same year he took up his abode in the United States, locating first in Chicago, where he helped in the erection of the Soldiers' Home, thence to Oil City, Pennsylvania, and thence to East St. Louis, where he entered the employ of the O. & M. railway company as blacksmith helper. In this employ he remained until 1874, when he was elected Constable. In 1877 he was elected Justice of the Peace, an office for which he is well fitted, and which he has since held. But one decision made by him among the many cases carried to higher courts has been reversed, and that was on technical grounds. Politically he is a pronounced democrat. He was married to Miss Elizabeth Sheridan, July 4, 1866, by whom he has two children living, Edward John and Ellen. In 1866 a company of Fenians was organized in East St. Louis for the invasion of Canada, in which he was a sergeant. They went as far as Chicago, remained two weeks, and were ordered home. He is at present Assistant Coroner for St. Clair county.

A. M. MEINTS.

When we trace the history of our successful men, and search for the secret of that success, we find as a rule that they were men who were early thrown upon their own resources. A. M. Meints furnishes an apt illustration of this rule. He was born in Hanover, Germany, March 8th, 1844. His father, J. R. Meints, came to America in 1847, leaving his family behind. They followed in 1848, and the same year Mrs. Meints died of cholera in St. Louis, Missouri, so that Mr. Meints was left with two motherless children. Sickness overtook him, and distress to self and family with it. A. M. Meints, the subject of this sketch, when but eight years of age, together with his sister, gathered drift wood from the river to sell, and thus aid in the family support. At the age of nine he obtained employment as a boy in the grocery of H. Houschold, known as the three mile house on Broadway. Here he remained a year and a half; then was engaged by Edward Beckmann & Bro. two years; next by Rabenbury, with whom he remained a year and a half. During all this time Albert gave his earnings to his father. For two seasons he attended the public night school where he received all the education he ever acquired. In the mean time his father, who was a man of great energy, had saved sufficient means with which to purchase a stock of groceries, which he did by opening a store on Market, between 9th and 10th streets, in the year 1861, taking Albert with him. For five years he remained with his father, during which time he formed habits of industry, economy and honesty, that have ever characterized him, and which have crowned his labors with success. His father taught him the value of money, and counseled him to save the quarters which he now and then gave him. With the first twenty dollars he succeeded in saving he purchased a gun. Hunting and fishing were his means of recreation.

At the age of twenty-two he left St. Louis, for the first time since his advent there, for a journey any distance from home. Went as far as Fayette, Missouri, where he passed two pleasant weeks in the society of S. Baumann, a former playmate, and returned home, but not to re-engage his services to his father, who although kind, he thought too rigorous in his dealings with him. Seeing an advertisement, Grocery clerk wanted by H. Jackeisch, East St. Louis; he responded and his services were accepted. He entered this service June 30th, 1866; remained in this employ until April 1st, 1868, when having accumulated about sixteen hundred dollars, he commenced business for himself, first in a building owned by Daniel McGowen, a place quite out of the way of trade, yet the only available place he could secure. In 1869 he purchased the lot he now occupies, and built a store-room 22 x 50, which he opened to the trade in September, 1869. His business has constantly increased, compelling him to erect additional buildings, until now he occupies a building with a frontage of seventy-five feet, and even that does not accommodate his trade. Since commencing business for himself he has been fortunate in every step. His real estate speculations have added largely to his wealth, and now he is the possessor of over twenty tenement houses, and three fine farms in St. Louis county, Missouri. August 30th, 1870, he married a most estimable lady, Miss Sophia E. Hauss, of Louisville, Kentucky. Mr. Meints owes his success to strict attention to business. For eight years, whilst he was laboring earnestly to gain a footing in the world, he availed himself of no species of enjoyment. Once comparatively independent he re-engaged with genuine boyish zest in his old sport of hunting, and is known to-day as one of the Nimrods of East St. Louis. In his career we have exemplified, in the truest sense, a self-made man.

third in order of birth, died in childhood. The doctor's pre-eminent fitness for the position caused his friends to single him out as the republican candidate for the legislature from the 49th district in 1878, and most gallantly did he lead on to victory. As a representative, he was active, fearless in his advocacy of the right, gave close and constant attention to the business before the legislature and made an efficient member. In manners and deportment Dr. Jennings is a sociable and agreeable gentleman; as a physician prompt and methodical: and as a man his reputation for integrity of character, and for earnestness of purpose is as wide as the circle of his acquaintance.

D. D. ANTHONY.

AMONG the promising young men of East St. Louis few are more deserving of honorable mention than D. D. Anthony, who was born in Ripley county, Indiana, November 18, 1843. His father, Philip Anthony, was of the good old Puritan stock of New England, a farmer by occupation, and for fifteen years a justice of the peace in his adopted state. His mother, Mary Ann Anthony, was an Ohioan by birth. The subject of this sketch followed farming until the year 1859, when he came to Illinois, locating in Kankakee county. He received a common school education. At the time of the breaking out of the war he returned to Indiana, and on June 16, 1861, volunteered in Co. I, 13th Regiment Indiana Volunteers. Served in the campaign in West Virginia, under General McClellan; then under his successor, General Rosecrans. Was in the various battles and skirmishes throughout West Virginia, among them that at Rich Mountain, Cheat Mountain, Summit and Green Briar. With his command he went to the valley of Virginia and took part in the fight at Winchester, under General Shields In 1862 his regiment was transferred to the army of the Potomac, with quarters at Suffolk, whose siege—at the hands of Longstreet—they gallantly withstood; left Suffolk for Charleston, with General Gillmore, where they took part in the siege of Sumter; thence to Florida; they were then ordered north, to join Butler's fleet at Yorktown, preparatory to ascending James river; took part in the Petersburg fight, where, on the 10th of May, 1863, he was taken prisoner. His prison life, extended as it was over a space of nine months and eighteen days, and divided between various Southern prison pens, is of great interest. First he was taken to Libby prison, at Richmond, where he was kept about a month; thence taken to Andersonville, where he was subjected to the gross neglect and hard usage for which that prison is so noted. He was an eyewitness to the bursting forth of the spring of water in the beaten path within the pen, spoken of by many prisoners, who—famishing with thirst—looked upon it as God's deliverance. After three months he was taken to Savannah, thence to Charleston, under guns he had himself helped to set months before; thence to Florence, where he suffered terribly. During his four months' imprisonment here he had not to exceed four ounces of salt with his ration of one pint of corn meal per *diem*, perhaps a half-dozen rations of meat, and a spoonful of molasses per week, during the time. At Goldsborough, North Carolina, he was exchanged for a well-fed Southern soldier, February 28, 1864. Being sick—scarcely able, in fact, to walk at all—he was taken to the hospital on David's Island, New York harbor, where for months he was treated with all the skill of army surgeons. His eyesight was almost gone—so far that its recovery was long thought doubtful. He was discharged from the U. S. service June 14, 1865; re-

turned to Indiana, where he was married to Sarah Belle Payton, April, 1866, by whom he has one child. After marriage he went South to Choctaw county, Alabama, where his wife was engaged in teaching a Freedmen's school for one year. During this time he was appointed by General Pope, commanding the Southern division, as re-constructing officer for registration of voters, administering the so-called "iron-clad oath," &c. Was taken sick, and returned to Indiana, where he remained only six months, returning to Alabama to engage in general merchandizing. In 1870 he was appointed assistant U. S. marshal in the Alabama district, during which service he enumerated the census of Choctaw county. When Alabama became democratic, and it was no longer safe for Northern men to express their sentiments in the South, he returned to Indiana, where he was employed by the Ohio and Mississippi railroad company. After remaining a year in their employ he went to Kansas, where he invested in a stock ranche, which he still owns. After a few months "roughing it," he returned to East St. Louis, where he was engaged in the erection of water works at the National Stock Yards. Here he remained several years as an engineer and water supply superintendent. In December, 1880, he was appointed deputy sheriff of St. Clair county by Frederick Ropiequet, a just recognition of his public services in behalf of the success of the republican party and of his worth as a man. Mr. Anthony is a member of the I. O. O. F., being a P. G, Golden Rule Lodge of E. St. Louis. Politically he is a stalwart, out-spoken, fearless republican. During the last campaign he made some very effective speeches in behalf of republican principles, reciting—as his experience enabled him to do—many instances of cruelty in the South. His republicanism was learned in very early years when his father kept an underground railway station on the Polar Star route from Slavery to Freedom. Efficient as an officer, true to all trusts reposed in him, genuine by nature—Mr. Anthony deserves well of his fellowmen.

JOHN B. SIKKING,

THE present efficient post-master of the city of East St. Louis, was born in Wenterswyke, Holland, August 16th, 1836. His father, John B. Sikking, was a carpenter, and emigrated from the land beyond the sea to America in 1844, locating in the city of St. Louis, Missouri. There were in all seven children in the family, of whom John B. Sikking was the fourth in order of birth. He received a common school education, and became a machinist. For thirteen years he engaged his services to the Ohio and Mississippi railway company. He was appointed post-master under Gen. Grant's administration, in 1869. Had officiated in this capacity for about two years prior, during Johnson's administration, as he served out the term of his predecessor and brother-in-law, E. W. Wider. As post-master he has proved faithful and capable, and has won universal esteem. He was married to Sarah E. Cunningham, a most estimable lady from Ohio, on the 24th of December, 1863. By this union there are six children. In politics Mr. Sikking is an ardent, outspoken republican, who has the honor of having always been true to his party, and party friends. Takes an active part in both local and national affairs. He and his wife are members of the M. E. church. He is also a member of the Masonic order. As a citizen he is quiet, unassuming, straightforward, and one that cannot be swerved from the path of duty.

182

John Trendley

IDENTIFIED with the interests of East St. Louis for the last fifty-five years, during which time nothing of public moment has been started but that has had a share of his attention, Capt. John Trendley is looked upon as one of the fathers of the city. To adopt his language, "he wore out in the service as ferryman five horse-boats," and the company are now using the twenty-fifth steam ferry boat, whilst he yet lives to take an active interest in the work. He was born in the Black Forest, Germany, June 20, 1804. Came to America in 1817, landing first at Alexandria, Virginia. Two years after he came up the Mississippi from New Orleans, and located here. He was married to Harriett Aberle, a Swiss lady, March 28, 1828, who died March 21, 1869. Capt. Trendley preserves his faculties in a remarkable degree, and delights in living in the past, recounting the incidents of an active and well-spent life. His contributions to the upbuilding of his adopted city have perhaps been more notable than those of any other one man. He is prepared to spend the evening of life in the enjoyment of comforts, the fruitage of a life of economy and industry. As one of the pioneers, a sketch of his life's work will be found in its appropriate place in this work.

Michael Heim.

So closely interwoven is the history of Michael Heim with that of his elder brother, Ferdinand—whose biography appears on the opposite page—that it is difficult to write of them separately. He was born in Wolfert, Austria, February 12th, 1839, and came to America in 1854 to join his brother, which he did in St. Louis, Missouri, embarking in different enterprises with him. He was married to Anna Beil in October, 1862, by whom he has two children, Ferdinand and John George by name. His wife is a niece of the wife of his brother, so that the relationship between their children is a pleasant conundrum of his joking brother. He is a member of the order of I. O. O. F., also of the Knights of Honor. The firm of which he is a member have been successful in the prosecution of their business, and far-sighted in its management. It is one of the most popular in East St. Louis, as it deserves to be. Never discouraged, ever hopeful, they press on with energy to accomplish their ends. The destruction of their brewery by fire, a few years ago, daunted them not, but phœnix-like, it was caused to spring from the flames better and larger than before.

A MEMBER of the City Council of East St. Louis, was born in Staffordshire, England, October 22d, 1846. His father, who bore the same name, was a worker in iron. He made the first wrought iron twine for blasting purposes ever invented. He came to America in 1858, and at once made his way to East St. Louis *via* Springfield and Alton, Illinois. It was during the prevalence of high waters of that year. Several bridges had been washed away, so that passengers on the C. and A. railroad had to be transferred to waiting cars across streams which the subject of this sketch swam in making his way here. As a result the family lost all their baggage and found themselves on the dyke at East St. Louis quite destitute. They next went to Urbana or Freeburg, as it is now called, where they pursued the work of blacksmithing. Returning to East St. Louis they engaged their services to the rolling mills. At present Levi Baugh, Jr., is Superintendent of the East St. Louis Rendering Works, in which he is a stockholder, and which position he has held since 1873. Politically he is a conservative democrat. Is not active in politics, caring more for business. He is a member of the Knights of Pythias, of which order he is a charter member, and at present Master of Exchequer; also of the Knights of Honor. He was married to Margaret M. Mayerhofer, July 26, 1866, by whom he has had four children, three of whom are living. He is a man of excellent social qualities, fine business tact, and sound judgment.

185

322   *HISTORY OF ST. CLAIR COUNTY, ILLINOIS.*

Captain is a democrat. Has held the position of school treasurer for a term of three years, during which service he had to give a bond for $100,000. So faithfully has he discharged his duties as Chief of Police; so unrelenting has been his warfare against crooks and evil-doers; so earnest his endeavors to maintain the peace, that he is continued in the position for which nature seems especially to have fitted him.

P. H. STACK.

East St. Louis is eminently a cosmopolitan city. Here are gathered representatives of all nationalities. Unlike many cities of like size, no one nation is represented among her people in numerical strength sufficient to control her politics or local government. Among those hailing from the Emerald Isle no one deserves more prominent mention, or is held in higher esteem for his talents and worth as a citizen and man, than he whose name heads this article. A recognized leader among not only his people, but among the people generally, P. H. Stack is an honored name. He was born in Tullihinell, Barrylongford parish, Kerry county, Ireland, May 11, 1828. His father was a farmer of the better class, being a landed proprietor; but reverses came, as come they will, in this instance, growing out of the famine which visited his native island in 1849, by which he lost much property. Gathering together the fragments of his wealth, he determined on seeking a new home across the ocean, and accordingly landed in New York in February, 1849. He brought with him a large family,—eleven in all, to which one was added here, and one was left behind in Ireland, a daughter who had married there. Of this family, six were boys, and eight were girls. Garrett Stack, for that was his name, bought a farm of two hundred and forty acres in Canada. A few years after, he returned to the United States, and died in New York in 1857. P. H. Stack did not remain with his father, but struck out for himself, locating first in Cleveland, Ohio, where he laid the foundation for a liberal education with which he is blessed. From here he went to Nashville, Tennessee, where he became the student of Bishop Miles, then to Carondelet, where he studied with Bishop Kendrick. His wanderings were those of a student; his ambition was to prepare himself for the priesthood. During intermissions from study he engaged his services in several capacities to railroad companies, at times, as foreman on works or as sub-contractor. He built three miles of the Chicago and Alton railroad. This business carried him from place to place; thus we find him at Chicago, Natchez, Memphis and at other places. At Chicago he was married to Margaret Sellis, on the 4th of November, 1855. By this marriage he has four children—Johanna, now the wife of Frank Healey, bridge collector; Garrett J., assistant cashier O. & M. R. R.; John J. student in Jones' commercial college, St. Louis, and Margaret F. The breaking out of the war found him located in Natchez, Mississippi, where he was foreman and paymaster on leveeing. From thence he came north, and was employed by the Missouri & Pacific railroad company, but bushwhackers along the route determined him on finding a safer place; hence he came to East St. Louis,

where he has since resided. Here he has kept a boarding-house, and attended to his growing real estate interests. He owns ten or twelve residences here and a fine farm of one hundred and forty acres near Carlyle, Clinton county, Illinois, together with much other property, the accumulation of a life of energy and pluck. He has held various positions to which his fellow citizens have chosen him, as justice of the peace, for a period of eight years; school director, one term; member of the board of health, one term. He was at one time a defeated candidate for the mayoralty; he is politically a democrat, opposed to monopolies and all grabbing schemes, and refuses to become the tool of corporations. He and his family are members of the Roman Catholic church.

HENRY D. O'BRIEN.

The subject of this sketch was born in Calais, Maine, on the 21st day of January, 1843, and is the son of Wetmore O'Brien and Sarah M., *nee* Smith.

When seven years of age his parents moved to Detroit, Michigan, where he attended school. In 1855 they moved to Minneapolis, Minnesota. After remaining here a short time, he returned to Detroit, where he learned the watch-making and jeweler's trade. Thence he went to Cedar Rapids, Iowa, to attend school, then to his home in Minneapolis.

At the breaking out of the war he enlisted in the 1st regiment, Minnesota Volunteer Infantry. Was wounded at the battle of Gettysburg in the head, hand and side, and while carrying the regimental flag, the staff was shot from his hands. At the battle of Deep Bottom, or Strawberry plains, which was fought on Sunday, August 14th, 1864, he was, whilst making a charge, shot through the right shoulder and lung. After being absent a short time he returned to the regiment, and was present on the field when Lee surrendered. He passed through nearly all the battles in which the army of the Potomac was engaged, and served in every position from that of private to Lieut. Colonel. At the close of the war he was Major of the regiment, and Adjutant General of Morrow's Division, Army of the Tennessee.

Returning to Minnesota, he received the appointment as postmaster of East Minneapolis from President Johnson, and at the expiration of his commission was re-appointed by President Grant, and held the position for nearly seven years. Through the advice of physicians he came to St. Louis in 1873, for treatment of the wound in his shoulder, but notwithstanding the efforts of the best surgeons in the city, is still troubled with it. Mr. O'Brien has been editor and publisher of the *Gazette* for the past four years, and previous to that served in a similar capacity on the *Press*. He is a republican in politics, a liberal in his religious views, a member of the Masonic order, and the Knights of Pythias, having been Past Chancellor in the latter order, and for several years has been a member of the G. A. R. He was married in 1867 to Miss Emma S. Sinclair. She died in February, 1873. He is still a widower.

HISTORICAL
ENCYCLOPEDIA

OF

ILLINOIS

EDITED BY

NEWTON BATEMAN, LL. D.   PAUL SELBY, A. M.

AND HISTORY OF

St. CLAIR COUNTY

EDITED BY

A. S. WILDERMAN   A. A. WILDERMAN

VOLUME II.

ILLUSTRATED

CHICAGO:
MUNSELL PUBLISHING COMPANY,
PUBLISHERS.
1907.

the two sons above mentioned, the survivors in his immediate family are two daughters— Mrs. Lina E. Day, widow of John A. Day, and Mrs. Samuel Brunaugh, of Chicago; and four grandchildren—Helene J. Day, Alice Day, Hallett E. Abend and Adele Brunaugh.

Mr. Abend was virtually a resident of Belleville for seventy-one years. On every public utility of the city, and many of the important industries, he left the impress of his vigorous mind and sound judgment. He was known to all. To many struggling under heavy burdens, he was opportunely helpful. Of kindly countenance and gentle in demeanor, he was nevertheless firm and prompt in action. A man of broad capacity, diligent, faithful, upright, generous, he everywhere inspired profound respect and cordial regard By scores of his neighbors and friends, who were wont to seek his advice and counsel, his death is lamented as would be the loss of one of their own kindred, and the entire community will honor his memory while civic virtue endures.

ABT, Paul William, one of the financial and social pillars of society in East St. Louis, St. Clair County, who has attained his present conspicuous standing through the force of his own innate qualities, was born in Esslingen, Germany, April 25, 1845. He is a son of Wilhelm and Caroline (Class) Abt, who were natives of Germany. Wilhelm Abt, who was born in Ulm, in that country, where he passed the most of his active life, was a merchant by occupation. He was a man of good business qualities and excellent traits of character.

Paul W. Abt attended the public schools of his native place for the customary legal period, utilizing the opportunities for mental development therein afforded with diligence and close application. After the conclusion of his youthful studies, he determined to follow a business career, and became an apprentice in merchandising. In 1864, intent on seeking a broader and more promising field for the exercise of his abilities, he left the fatherland and came to the United States, where, until 1873, he was successively employed in Cincinnati, Chicago, Omaha and St. Louis. In the year named he established himself in the wholesale liquor business in East St. Louis, which he conducted with substantial results for about fourteen years, when he disposed of

21

his interests in this line. On June 1, 1887, Mr. Abt was appointed Cashier of the East St. Louis Bank, acting in that capacity until June 1, 1890. On that date he founded the First National Bank of East St. Louis, of which, for a period of fourteen years, he served as President, discharging its responsible duties with signal efficiency and fidelity. Mr. Abt is now President of the Provident Association in East St. Louis, and has been a member of the Board of Education since 1897.

On December 3, 1874, Paul W. Abt was united in marriage, in East St. Louis, Illinois, with Ottilie Ida Buettner, a daughter of Dr. Ferdinand Buettner, of St. Louis, Missouri, and they have become the parents of four children, namely: Ernst, born in 1876; Martha, in 1878; Paul, in 1880, and Ferdinand, in 1890. In politics, the attitude of Mr. Abt is independent, and in exercising the elective franchise, he uses his best judgment as to measures and candidates. Religiously, he is connected with the German Evangelical Church. In fraternal circles, he is affiliated with the A. F. & A. M.; K. of P.; I. O. O. F.; B. P. O. E. and M. W. A. His relationship with the First National Bank of East St. Louis still continues, his services to that institution being rendered in the capacity of Vice-President. He is regarded as one of the soundest and most conservative financiers in Southern Illinois, and is a very public spirited and useful member of the community in which he lives.

"ADAMS, Capt. Lyman (deceased), formerly a resident of Lebanon, was born at Hartford, Conn., in February, 1779. He was connected with the celebrated Adams family of New England. His father was a Presbyterian minister. At the age of eleven Captain Adams left home and went on board a ship and became a sailor. He followed a sea-faring life for many years, and became captain of a vessel. He was employed in the merchant trade. After quitting the sea he settled in Baltimore, and, for a number of years, was Recorder in the police court of that city. During the war of 1812-14, he commanded a company of militia, raised for the defense of Baltimore, and was present at the battle of Bladensburg. From Baltimore he went to Louisville, Ky., and was there employed in the merchandising and rectifying business. He left Louisville in the year 1829,

dren resulted from this union, namely: Benjamin A. and Magdalena. The mother of these children died on April 6, 1882, and is buried at French Village. After remaining a widower for thirteen years, Mr. Boul was married the second time, on August 21, 1895, to Josephine Fuchs, a widow and a daughter of Captain John Trendley, of East St. Louis.

In general politics, Mr. Boul has long been a steadfast supporter of the Democratic party— in local matters, independent—and has filled with notable ability and fidelity many positions of public trust. He was first elected School Trustee of his township, in which capacity he served from 1873 to March, 1877. He was then appointed to the office of School Treasurer, which he held until 1900. In 1874 he was elected Justice of the Peace and officiated as such until 1882. He was elected Township Supervisor in 1885, and discharged the duties of that position until 1894. In the fall of 1890 he became a Representative in the General Assembly of the State of Illinois, and served as such during the session of 1891, in which Gen. John M. Palmer was elected United States Senator. During the long memorable contest which resulted in his election, when 101 Democrats remained firm in his support from January 7 to March 12, Mr. Boul was one of the unswerving members of that faithful band. For their loyalty in this prolonged and exciting struggle, all received gold medals inscribed with the number "101" and the name of each Representative composing it. In religion Mr. Boul is a consistent member of the Catholic Church of French Village. Fraternally, he is identified with the Knights of Columbus. For more than three-score years his career has been interwoven with the welfare and progress of St. Clair County, and for the morality and stability of his past meridian period of life, none of its citizens is held in more profound regard than he.

BREUSS, Oswald, a real estate dealer of East St. Louis, this county, who is engaged in the liquor trade also, was born in 1866, in Austria, and there was educated. In 1884 he came to the United States and secured employment with the brewing interests. For ten years he traveled for the Heim Brewing Company, establishing branch agencies, and during the last ten years has been engaged in the retail liquor

business, besides dealing in real estate. In 1904 he built a block 140x50 feet in dimensions, at Eighteenth and State Streets, in which he maintains his residence and conducts his saloon and family garden.

In 1886 Mr. Breuss was married to Mary Yeuger, a native of East St. Louis, and they have one child, Ida. Mr. Breuss is a member of the following fraternal organizations and societies: Independent Order of Odd Fellows, Knights of Pythias, Improved Order of Red Men, Eagles, Knights and Ladies of Honor, and Liederkranz and Mozart Societies.

BRICHLER, George W., of the Benner & Brichler Livery and Undertaking Company, 126-128 Collinsville Avenue, East St. Louis, was born near Smithton, St. Clair County, March 16, 1863, a son of John L. and Magdalena (Munier) Brichler. His father, who was a farmer, came from Lorraine, France, in 1832, his mother in 1842, and they were married in French Village in 1855. George W. Brichler completed his education, which was begun in the Belleville Catholic school, in the Franciscan College at Teutopolis, Ill., and for a time assisted his father on the latter's farm. He was a teacher in the Mound City Commercial College, 1888-91; was connected with a publishing house in Chicago, 1891-92; and in the latter year entered the undertaking business in East St. Louis. Since that time he has been a member of the Benner-Brichler Livery and Undertaking Company, incorporated. He is a member of St. Henry's Catholic Church and of numerous fraternal orders. He was married in Belleville Cathedral, May 4, 1897, to Agnes Gundlach, who died February 24, 1902.

BROCKWAY, Richard, who is engaged in the liquor business in East St. Louis, St. Clair County, was born in Coloma, Cal., in 1871, and received his scholastic training in the public schools. His father, S. Henry Brockway, and mother, Ella E. (Carner) Brockway, were natives, respectively, of New York State and San Francisco, Cal. In 1849 the former sailed from New York to California, where he was for some time engaged in prospecting, after which he embarked in the mercantile business. In 1891 he came to East St. Louis, where he and his son Richard were associated for a while in merchandising. At a later period the lat-

ship, and of this union the following four children were born: Esta, Ona, Susan and Ethel Carr. Mr. Carr's parents were Augustus and Catherine (Schook) Carr, the former of whom is a native of St. Clair County.

CARROLL, Charles B., who is accounted as one of the most thoroughly equipped, resourceful and reliable lawyers of East St. Louis, St. Clair County, and whose professional career has been highly creditable both to himself and the community in which he has for many years taken an active and useful part, is a native of Illinois, being born in Bethalto, Madison County, September 19, 1858. Mr. Carroll is a son of John B. and Mary (McDonald) Carroll, both of whom were of Irish nativity. John B. Carroll, who was a contractor by occupation, and a man of sound judgment, diligent habits, honorable character and irreproachable business methods, came to the United States in the year 1854, locating in Madison County, where he followed his accustomed pursuit with successful results. He rendered a gallant soldier's service during the Crimean War, and participated in the famous charge of the "Light Brigade" at Balaklava.

In early youth Charles B. Carroll received his primary education in the public schools in the vicinity of his home, and later became a student in the Christian Brothers' College, at St. Louis, Mo., where he remained three years. After finishing his studies in that institution, he applied himself to the task of learning the printing trade, the details of which he fully mastered. Not feeling inclined to follow that occupation as a means of livelihood, he devoted his attention to teaching school for a while, in the meantime studying law. He was admitted to the bar in 1889, and at once opened an office in East St. Louis, where he has since continued in the successful practice of his profession. Mr. Carroll has attained an enviable standing both as a practitioner and counselor, and is held in high regard by the legal fraternity, as well as by a numerous clientele, whose confidence and respect he has won through able, efficient and faithful service.

On October 11, 1880, Charles B. Carroll was united in marriage with Mary Barron, of St. Louis, Mo., a daughter of Capt. James Barron and Jeannette Barron, also natives of that city. Six children have resulted from this union,

namely: Charles, Mary, Audrey, Percy, Barron and Frank. In politics, Mr. Carroll is a steadfast supporter of the Republican party, in the local councils of which he wields no small influence. From 1891 to 1895, he held the office of City Attorney of East St. Louis, discharging the duties of that position with signal ability and fidelity. In religious belief, he is an adherent of the Roman Catholic Church.

CHAMBERLIN, (Hon.) John M., Jr., President of the East St. Louis Real Estate Exchange, and engaged in real estate, insurance and loan business, 437 Missouri Avenue, East St. Louis, was born at Lebanon, St. Clair County, Ill., August 19, 1872, a son of John M. and Maggie E. (Royse) Chamberlin. John M. Chamberlin, Sr., born at Lebanon, January 21, 1837, is a son of the Rev. David Chamberlin, a native of Vermont, and one of the pioneer residents of Lebanon and of St. Clair County. He was engaged in the mercantile business at Lebanon the greater part of his active life, but has retired. He has been one of the active supporters of McKendree College, of which institution he has been Treasurer for many years, his brother, Dr. M. H. Chamberlin, uncle of the subject of this sketch, being the President of the institution at this time. Mr. Chamberlin's mother, Maggie E. Chamberlin, whose death occurred in 1889, was a daughter of the late Rev. P. E. Royse. John M. Chamberlin, Jr., was educated in the Lebanon public schools and at McKendree College, at which latter institution he was graduated in the class of 1890. He was employed as a telegraph operator for a period of five years, and in 1896 established the "Lebanon Leader," a weekly paper which he edited for five years. He is at present engaged in the real estate, insurance and loan business, and is President of the East St. Louis Real Estate Exchange. In 1900 he was elected on the Republican ticket a member of the Forty-second General Assembly of Illinois, serving one term. He is a member of the Masonic fraternity, the Benevolent Protective Order of Elks, the Knights of Pythias and the Modern Woodmen. He was married to Lulu M. Farthing, of Odin, Ill., November 26, 1903. Mrs. Chamberlin is a daughter of W. D. Farthing, formerly State's Attorney of Marion County, a member of one of the best known families in that part of the State.

became a teacher, and subsequently was elected County Superintendent of Schools. At a later period, he was successively occupied as editor and publisher of a newspaper, and as General Agent for the American Book Company, and in both of these relations increased his reputation as a man of superior capacity and unusual energy. In 1892, he changed his residence from Falls City to Lincoln, Neb., and in 1897, moved from the latter place to East St. Louis.

The marriage of Mr. Faulkner occurred at Falls City, Neb., August 15, 1883, when he was united in wedlock with Sarah Agnes Abbey, who was born in Warren, Jo Daviess County, Ill., and is a daughter of Wallace W. and Alzina Abbey. Her father is a veteran of the Civil War. He has been prominent in the agricultural, political and business affairs of Nebraska, and has filled various city, county and State offices, serving in all with marked efficiency and fidelity. Mr. and Mrs. Faulkner are the parents of a son, Worthe Wallace Faulkner, born February 4, 1887.

In his early years as a voter Mr. Faulkner was a Democrat, but in 1888 became estranged from that party on the tariff issue, and since then has co-operated with the Republicans. In 1884 he was elected School Superintendent of Richardson County, Neb., on the Democratic ticket, but represented a Republican constituency at a later period, when serving as City Clerk of Falls City, same county. Religiously, Mr. Faulkner is inclined toward the Methodist faith, although his family are attendants of the Episcopal Church. Socially, he is a member of the St. Clair Country Club, of which he is Secretary. In fraternal circles, he is identified with the K. of P. and the B. P. O. E. With the former organization he has been affiliated since 1882, and is now officiating as Past Chancellor and Deputy at Large. He joined the Elks in 1901. He is a member of the Grand Lodge in both of these orders, and is very active in both. He has served as Secretary of the Illinois Elks Association two years, is District Deputy for the Southern Illinois district, and has been District Deputy at Large in the Knights of Pythias for three years. He is a man of versatile qualities, is generally known as a "good mixer," and has long taken an active and prominent part in social, fraternal and political affairs. Mr. Faulkner is very popular, and has both an extensive and cordial acquaintance.

FAUST, Nicholas (deceased), was born March 12, 1833, at Hesse-Darmstadt, Germany, son of Nicholas Faust, also a native of the Empire. At the age of five years he came with his parents to St. Clair County, and located in Stookey Township. After receiving a private school education he served an apprenticeship to the blacksmith trade, and in 1852 went to California, where he worked at gold mining for five years. He then returned to St. Clair County, rented a farm, and engaged in agriculture until 1864, in that year purchasing a place situated on the line between St. Clair and Clinton Counties and operating it for nine years, when he bought other land located two and a half miles south of Lebanon. This he cultivated and made his home for the succeeding twenty-nine years. He then invested in 148 acres on Section 4, Mascoutah Township, living here in retirement until his death, which occurred June 20, 1902. In politics, he was a supporter of the Democratic party, and in religion, a faithful adherent of the Catholic Church.

On June 5, 1858, Mr. Faust was united in marriage to Mary L. Pfeiffer, who was born February 12, 1840, in St. Clair County, where she received her education in private schools. Her parents were Sebastian and Catherine (Wetzer) Pfeiffer, both natives of France. Of the seven children born to them, Mary L. is the youngest. Mr. and Mrs. Faust became the parents of the following children: Mary, born March 20, 1859, who became the wife of Peter Rasp; George, born September 1, 1860, who married Annie Reiger, and is the father of four children; and Nicholas A., whose birth occurred October 20, 1865, and who has successfully conducted the farm since the death of his father.

FEKETE, Alexander, M. D., was born in Buda-Pesth, Hungary, and there received his preliminary education. He studied medicine at Vienna. He took an active part in the Hungarian Revolution (1848-49), fighting on the side of Louis Kossuth, whom he accompanied, in 1850, to America. He was graduated from the St. Louis Medical College in 1854. For three years during the Civil War he was Surgeon of the Fifth Missouri State Militia Cavalry. After the war he established himself in his profession in East St. Louis He has been Assistant County Physician, City Health Officer, and several times President of the Board of Health. Besides, he ably served his fellow townsmen as Postmaster of East St. Louis. His office is at 324½ Collinsville Avenue.

FEKETE, Thomas Louis, real estate, insurance and loan agent, 324 Collinsville Avenue, East St. Louis, was born at Aviston, Ill., April 7, 1856, a son of Dr. Alexander and Kate (Fisher) Fekete; was educated in the public schools of East St. Louis and at the Bryant & Stratton Commercial College, St. Louis, Mo., and has been engaged in his present business since 1875. Not only is he President of the Thomas L. Fekete Company, but also of the Modern Building & Savings Association and the St. Clair Turnpike Company, is also Vice-President of the First National Bank of East St. Louis and the Illinois Trust Company, and a Director in the East St. Louis & Suburban Railway Company. In politics, Mr. Fekete is a Republican, has served as President of the East St. Louis Board of Education (1894-95), and Postmaster of the city of East St. Louis from 1897 to 1901, retiring from the latter office by resignation. He was appointed aide-de-camp on the general staff of the Illinois National Guard, with the rank of Colonel, by Gov. Richard Yates, July 19, 1902, and served through Governor Yates' term. He is President of the One Hundred Thousand Club of East St. Louis, one of the governors of the Missouri Athletic Club, and a member of the Mercantile Club of St. Louis, Mo. Long a member of the Masonic Fraternity, Mr. Fekete is identified with East St. Louis Lodge, Tancred Commandery, Knights Templar of Belleville, the Oriental Consistory of Chicago, and Moolah Temple, Mystic Shrine, St. Louis, Mo. He is also an Elk, and a member of Eureka Lodge, Knights of Pythias. Mr. Fekete was married June 22, 1881, to Charlotte J. Le Beau, and they have six children, namely: Thomas L., Ophelia F., Robert A., Forest F., George E. and Josephine C. A study of the history of East St. Louis will show that Colonel Fekete has long been one of its foremost citizens, and that he has had as much to do with the promotion of its advancement as any other single individual. His residence is at 1018 Pennsylvania Avenue.

FELLNER, Peter, President and Manager of the Horn Dry Goods Company, of Belleville, this county, was born April 15, 1866, in Bavaria, Germany, and is the youngest in a family of two sons and three daughters born to George and Margaret (Zitzmann) Fellner. His parents were natives also of Bavaria—the father born December 11, 1827. His paternal grandfather was John Fellner, also of Bavaria. Mr. Fellner arrived in America with seventeen years to his credit, the possessor of good health and spirits, but of little capital, locating in Belleville whither a brother had preceded him six years before. Securing employment in the dry goods store of Kanzler Brothers, he remained with that firm for eleven years, afterward entering the employ of Horn & Rodenheiser. When Mr. Rodenheiser withdrew from the business in 1895, Mr. Fellner found that his business ability and faithfulness were appreciated by Mr. Horn, who made him the Manager of the store. Shortly after the death of Mr. Horn, in 1897, a corporation was formed of which Mr. Fellner became President and Managing Director, operating under the firm name of the Horn Dry Goods Company.

On November 22, 1887, Mr. Fellner married Katie Trenz, a native of Summerfield, Ill., and who was educated in the public schools. To Mr. and Mrs. Fellner have been born five children: Olive, Thekla, Othmar, Clothilda, and Alfonso.

FERNAU, August, for many years of his active life a cigar manufacturer of Belleville, and whose death, February 21, 1889, is recalled as a distinct loss to the community, was born in Kur Hessen, Germany, August 22, 1836, and when nine years old came to America with his parents, John and Elizabeth Fernau, also natives of Germany. Settling in Baltimore, Md., he attended the public schools of that city, in time being apprenticed to a cigar maker, and thereafter following the trade until coming to Belleville in 1857. Starting a cigar shop on West Main Street, he was successful beyond his expectations, the growth of the business necessitating larger accommodations. Manufacturing cigars, and dealing in pipes, tobacco, and general smoking accessories, Mr. Fernau finally accumulated a competence, and as a business men won the complete esteem and confidence of the home community. The wife, who survives him, was formerly Louisa Krauss,

192

completed. His reputation as sa master workman is by no means confined to Belleville, for evidences of his skill are seen in all of the towns of St. Clair County. At present he has under way a bank building at Freeburg, having previously erected in that town the Evangelical church, and the $4,500 residence of Mr. Reichert.

On November 4, 1880, Mr. Geyer married Sarah Meyer, who was born in Nashville, Ill., and is the mother of three children, of whom Rosa, born November 5, 1881, died in January, 1886. The living children are G. William, born September 12, 1883, and Ophelia, August 12, 1885. Mr. Geyer is a Republican, and in religion is affiliated with the Methodist Episcopal Church. He is a highly respected and thoroughly appreciated citizen, enjoying the advantages of an occupation which perpetuates him in the history of the community, and which enables him to encourage and employ a considerable number of high-class workmen.

GIESSING, Fred, one of the leading public men of East St. Louis, this county, and one of the most prominent merchants of Southern Illinois, was born at Iron Mountain, Mo., August 17, 1863, the son of Charles and Mary (Hoehn) Giessing. His father is a native of Germany, but removed to this country when quite a young man. He settled in Missouri in 1847, long before any of the railroads which now cross the State were projected. In fact, the number of houses was very limited, and the elder Giessing at first occupied a hut constructed of branches of trees, covered with the skins of wild animals, which were plentiful around Iron Mountain at that date. When Fred Giessing was three years of age, his parents removed to Valley Forge, Mo., where his father embarked in the milling business. From a small beginning, this mill became one of the largest and strongest in that section of the State. Fred Giessing attended the schools of his native place, and later pursued courses at the Farmington College and Johnston's Commercial College, St. Louis, from which latter institution he was graduated in 1883.

The family of Giessing consisted of seven boys and one girl. The boys, all of whom were active millers and mill owners, were called the Milling Brothers. Fred Giessing was the fifth member of the Milling Brothers, and, on account of his adaptability to the work, had particular charge of the books of the general store, while the other brothers managed the mill and farm. After his graduation Fred Giessing assumed charge of the books of Giessing & Sons, the milling firm, to which the general store and other interests were added in 1888. It was the mercantile department to which he paid particular attention. Mr. Giessing also took an active interest in the educational work of his section and acted as School Director for years, serving as Secretary of the Board. Later he was appointed Postmaster, under President Harrison, and held the position for six years.

Desiring a larger field of action, Mr. Giessing removed to East St. Louis, in 1894, and became connected with the Schaub Hardware and Iron Company, a leading firm of Southern Illinois. He was elected Secretary of the company in 1898, and the same year was chosen a Director of the Southern Illinois National Bank. Mr. Giessing represented the Third Ward in the City Council, having been elected to the place on the Citizens' ticket. He was also President of the East St. Louis Retail Merchants' Association for two years, and Vice-President of the Illinois State Retail Merchants' Association. He has been a member of the Board of Managers of the Protestant Hospital Association for eight years. In religion, Mr. Giessing is a member of the German Lutheran Church. In politics, he is an ardent supporter of Republican principles, following the precepts of his father, who, at an early date, was one of the three Republicans of his county in Missouri.

On June 14, 1894, Fred Giessing married Anna K. Schaub, daughter of George and Elizabeth Schaub, one of the oldest and most respected families of this city. Four children blessed the union, but only two are now living.

GITHER, Richard, grocer and meat merchant of East St. Louis, this county, is a native of Woodstock, Ill., and was born August 22, 1873. His parents were Jacob and Theresa (Speaker) Gither, and his maternal grandfather, William Speaker. The family came to Illinois at an early day, and Richard had few advantages of any kind, save those which he created for himself. At the age of nine he began to work for a butcher at Quincy, Ill., learned the trade in a thorough manner, and remained with his first employer for twelve years. With this practical experience, he came to East St. Louis in 1892, worked for Christ Rohn, Sr., for three years, for John Herman a short time, and for Charles Ketter about a year and a half. In March, 1903, he established a business of his own at No. 328 North Tenth Street, and now carries a full line of meats, vegetables, and general groceries.

Mr. Gither is a Democrat in politics, and is a member of the Royal Arcanum. On October 17, 1894, he married Celestine Dauer, who was born, reared and educated in East St. Louis, and who is the mother of four children—Edith, Richard, Rosalie and Jacob.

GOEDDE, Charles B., is a native son of East St. Louis, this county, and to say that he is one of its most progressive citizens would be stating a fact which past events have fully demonstrated. Mr. Goedde, who is now Treasurer of city, enjoys the distinction of being the youngest man ever elected to such an important place in East St. Louis. He was born within the limits of the town on May 27, 1865, when the city extended to Tenth Street on the east and when Illinois Avenue was the northern limit. He came of sturdy German stock, and, inheriting the progressive and tenacious characteristics of his father, soon after reaching his majority evinced those sterling qualities which only successful business men possess. His father, Bernhardt Goedde, was born in Prussia, but became a pioneer settler of this section. His mother, Adelaide (Wetterer) Goedde, a native of Baden, Germany, came to this country when quite young. His maternal grandfather was Henry Wetterer, a Nationalist of Baden, and his paternal grandfather, Ciemens Goedde, was also a friend of liberty in Prussia.

"Charlie" Goedde, as he is familiarly known in this part of the country, attended the local schools of East St. Louis until he was sixteen years of age, when he entered the lumber firm of B. Goedde & Company, which was established by his father. He remained in the office until 1892, when he became a manager of the company, and it was mainly through his efforts as such that it became one of the leading concerns of the kind in Southern Illinois. The firm has recently established a planing mill in connection with the great lumber yards.

Politically, Mr. Goedde is a Republican, but he was elected to the office of Clerk of the village of New Brighton, Clerk of Centerville Station Township, member of the Centerville Station Drainage Commission, Alderman from the Sixth Ward and Treasurer of the city of East St. Louis, successively, on a non-partisan ticket, by the votes of Democrats and Republicans alike. Fraternally, Mr. Goedde is a member of the A. F. & A. M., Knights of Pythias, B. P. O. E. and the Modern Woodmen. In June, 1901, he married Erna Ropiequet, of Belleville, who was born, reared and educated in that city. They have an interesting family of two children, Bernice and Gladys. Mr. Goedde is of a retiring disposition, but straightforward and scrupulously honest. At no distant day, it is understood, the people of this section will call him to a higher position than he at present holds. They claim that he would greatly advance the interests of East St. Louis if placed at the helm of the city as its Mayor.

GOTTSCHALK, Louis, President and Treasurer of the Gottschalk Grocery Company, Belleville, Ill., was born in Germany in 1860, came to America in 1881 and, in 1882, became connected with the old Gundlach grocery business. William A. Twenhoefel, Jr., Vice-President of the Gottschalk Grocer Company, was born of German parentage in Cincinnati, Ohio. Henry Stoltz, Secretary of the Company, is a native of Belleville. After selling groceries for the late Henry Gundlach during 1882-83, Mr. Gottschalk was, in 1883-85, a clerk in the First National Bank of Belleville. On August 4, 1885, he succeeded to the management of the grocery business of his former employer. In April, 1906, the store was removed from 200 East Main Street to the Rentchler Building, 116-118 East Main Street, its present location. Mr. Twenhoefel was a clerk for Mr. Gundlach and later for Mr. Gottschalk till the Gottschalk Grocer Company was incorporated, March 10, 1906, when he became a stockholder in the concern, and is now (1906) senior partner in the firm of William A. Twenhoefel & Sons, real estate dealers. Mr. Stoltz also clerked for both Mr. Gundlach and Mr. Gottschalk. Eugene Weingartner, another stockholder, had been for more than ten years a salesman in Mr. Gottschalk's employ. The Gottschalk grocery ranks as the most attractive establishment of its

member of the Democratic Central Committee of Christian County, and served two terms as City Clerk of that place. In his religious views, he is affiliated with the Baptist Church. Socially, he belongs to the Knights of Pythias. On February 25, 1893, Mr. Jordan was united in marriage to Lily May Murray, who was born in Collinsville, Ill., and attended the public schools of Pana. Two children have been born of this union: Irene Luellen and Will Fringer.

JOYCE, Maurice V., City Attorney, East St. Louis, was born in that city October 28, 1873. After gaining his primary education in the public schools in his native city, he entered St. Louis University, where he took the regular course, and gave so much special attention to German that he speaks the German language fluently. He completed a course in law at the Harvard University Law School and was admitted to the bar in 1896, and since that time he has been actively engaged in the practice of his profession. In April, 1903, he was elected to the office of City Attorney, re-elected in the spring of 1905, and in that position has won an enviable reputation as a public officer. In 1904 he was the candidate of the Democratic party for the office of State's Attorney of St. Clair County. Mr. Joyce married Miss Reine Jones, of East St. Louis, November 16, 1904.

JUNG, George, hotel proprietor, Shiloh, St. Clair County, was born in Germany in the year 1873, the son of George and Catherine (Doll) Jung, natives of the same country. Mr. Jung received his education in his native land, and when a youth emigrated to America, arriving in St. Clair County in 1891. Here for more than a year he found work in a coal mine, but on September 2, 1902, purchased the "Shiloh Hotel," which he has since conducted. In connection with this hostelry is a large and beautiful park, which, especially in the summer season, is in great demand for the use of picnickers and other devotees of pleasure. In 1893, Mr. Jung was married to Mary Lynder, a native of Germany, and of this union five children have been born: John, Freda, Tracy, Lizzie and Otto.

KALTWASSER, Louis F., grocer, was born in St. Louis, Mo., in 1864, a son of Fred Kaltwasser. When quite young he came with his parents to Belleville, where his father engaged in the trunk business, and in whose public schools he received his early education. About twelve years ago he opened a general grocery, glass and tinware business, in which he is still engaged. He is known as "The West End Grocer," and his store covers Nos. 201-7 North Silver Street, Belleville.

KAMINER, Reuben, was born in Russia in 1867 and educated in the common schools of his native country. In 1886 he came to the United States, and for three years worked in Massachusetts, at the same time studying hard and attending a night school in order to advance his knowledge of the English language. In 1889 he went to St. Louis, where he obtained employment as Clerk in a clothing store, but later removed to Mississippi, remaining there one year, then going to Little Rock, Ark. After staying there a short time he came to East St. Louis, locating on Broadway, where he established a clothing business in a little store, twelve by thirty-six feet, which he called the "Blue Front." There he remained until the disastrous cyclone, which caused so great a damage to business houses and residences in that locality, and in which he lost everything he possessed. Still later he opened another store on a somewhat larger scale at No. 330 Broadway, and there continued in business until the close of the year 1903. In that year he promoted and designed plans for the present building now occupied by him on Broadway, at the foot of Collinsville Avenue. It is a handsome building, fifty by one hundred feet, including basement, first floor, balcony, and second floor, all of which he occupies. Here he carries on a clothing business known as "Kaminer's Outfitters for Men and Boys," and through the medium of advertising and liberal treatment of customers, he has had the satisfaction of seeing the business grow until it has become the largest of its kind in the city. He has ten employes who are always kept busy.

Socially, Mr. Kaminer is affiliated with the fraternal organizations of the Elks, Knights of Pythias, Redmen of America, A. O. U. W., Foresters, and the Eagles. In 1895 he was married to Miss Pauline Lasker, who was a native of St. Louis, and two children have been born to them, Frieda and Blanche.

26

Albert, Oscar, Ida, Alfred, Arthur, Augusta, Elizabeth, Amelia (deceased). Mr. Keitel has served as School Trustee for a number of years. Politically, he is a Republican.

KERCHNER, (Dr.) F. W., a popular and progressive young physician of Millstadt, Ill., was born in Belleville, January 16, 1871, and there obtained his preliminary education in the public schools, after which he attended the State University of Chemistry, from which he received the degree of B. S. in 1894. He then took a four years' course in the Marion Simmes Medical College at St. Louis, where he held the position of Assistant Physician in the Female Hospital for fifteen months. Subsequently he moved to Belleville, where he practiced for a time, and in 1901 came to Millstadt, which he has since made his home and where he has established a lucrative practice. Owing to his superior abilities in his profession he was appointed a member of the Health Department of Millstadt. Socially, he is a member of the Modern Woodmen of America and the I. O. O. F. In 1898 he married Amelia Snyder, whose birth occurred in Belleville, Ill., and to them have been born one daughter, Cornelia. The parents of Dr. Kerchner are Frank and Adeline (Schmidt) Kerchner, the former of whom is a native of Germany, and the latter of De Sota, Mo. The father resides in Belleville, where he held the office of Mine Inspector.

KEYWORTH, Thomas, who for nine years has occupied the position of janitor of the public school building of Marissa, this county, was born in Yorkshire, England, in 1845. He is a son of William and Anna (Boyd) Keyworth, both of whom were born in Yorkshire in 1802. After attending the public schools of his native place until he was nineteen years old, he served an apprenticeship as hairdresser and wigmaker. In 1869 he came to America, and entered the employ of J. C. Elms, under the "Southern Hotel," in St. Louis, Mo. There he was employed as a hair dresser for more than three years. He subsequently worked in a like capacity for J. M. Campbell, corner of Fifth and Locust Streets, for about the same period, and then moved to Marissa, where he opened a barber shop. After conducting this for seventeen years, he sold out and entered the public service as school janitor.

Mr. Keyworth was married in 1867, to Alice Singleton, who was born in Tickhill, Yorkshire, in 1847, and received her early education in the public school of her native place. Mr. and Mrs. Keyworth have the following children: Fannie (Mrs. Morganthaler); Mary (Mrs. Wiltshire); Emma (Mrs. Gray); Nellie (Mrs. Brown); Blanche (Mrs. Landgraf); George and Alice.

KIRCHER, Henry Adolph, hardware merchant of Belleville, a machinist by trade, and holder of important political offices in St. Clair County, is a native of Cass County, Ill., and was born in 1841. After completing his education Mr. Kircher learned the machinist's trade, worked at the same for three years, and then enlisted in the Ninth Illinois Volunteer Infantry for three months. Re-enlisting in the Twelfth Missouri Volunteer Infantry, he served until the close of the war, and for meritorious service was commissioned Captain of Company E, Twelfth Missouri Independent Volunteers. Upon returning to Belleville, he was elected Clerk of the Circuit Court, an office which he retained four years. He then became interested in the hardware business which had been established by his father, Joseph Kircher, and Henry Goedeking, in 1848, and which is now operated under the firm name of Kircher & Son.

Mr. Kircher is independent in politics. He was Mayor of Belleville from 1877 to 1878, and has served as Recorder and member of the Board of Education. For twenty years he has been a Director in the Belleville Savings Bank, and since the death of Edward Abend, President of that institution. Through his marriage with Bertha Engleman, of Belleville, three children have been born into his family: Harry Bertram, Joseph Casimir and Theodore Englemann Kircher.

KIRK, James W., editor "East St. Louis Daily Journal," residence, 1117 Pennsylvania Avenue, East St. Louis, was Auditor of East St. Louis, 1872-78, and was for many years City Comptroller; was Librarian of the City Library, 1879-81, and is now one of the Directors of that institution. He was born at Byron, N. Y., and was first engaged in reporting and editorial work on the Batavia (N. Y.) "Spirit of the Times," and later on the "Union and Advertiser," Rochester, N. Y. He came to East St.

brick manufacturers of the county, was born at Belleville in March, 1873, a son of John and Katherine (Mueller) Kloess, natives of Kreutznacht, Germany. John Kloess came from Germany in 1849, and at once became identified with the business life of Belleville as an experienced baker. Becoming interested in the development of coal in the county, he operated in this direction at irregular intervals from 1857 until 1895, and in 1862 started the brick manufacturing business in Belleville. He was the fortunate possessor of sons who inherited his thrift, energy, and ability, and in 1899 transferred his business to William and Julius J., who continued together until the retirement of the latter in 1902. At that time John J. Kloess, another son, who had established a brick manufacturing business of his own, succeeded to the interest of Julius, consolidated his enterprise with that of his brother, and admitted J. J. Kohl, a brother-in-law, as Superintendent of the combination. William Kloess became President of the new company, and John J., Secretary and Treasurer. John Kloess, the elder, died May 22, 1904, his wife having preceded him July 31, 1896.

William Kloess began to assist his father in the coal business at the age of fifteen, and his education from that time was irregular, and the result of his willingness to combine work and study. In 1895 he turned his attention exclusively to brick manufacturing, and is now at the head of a concern which is able to ship 45,000 brick per day. He is possessed of energy, good judgment, and through knowledge of his business, and personally is popular and influential.

KNOBELOCH, George (deceased), who at the time of his death, in October, 1873, was a retired farmer, residing in Belleville, this county, was born in Hesse-Darmstadt, Germany, in 1825. He received his education partly in his native land and partly in the public schools of his adopted country. Politically, he was in harmony with the doctrines of the Republican party. In church membership he was a Lutheran, and altogether an upright man, enjoying the full confidence and respect of the home community.

In 1864 Mr. Knobeloch was married to Katherine Hage, a native of Germany, whose mental instruction was obtained in its public schools. Her parents, Philip and Elizabeth Hage, were also German-born. Mrs. Knobeloch came to the United States at the age of four years, with her parents, who settled in St. Clair County. She lived in the country until 1879, when she moved to Belleville and resided on North High Street until 1897. Since that year she has made her home with her daughter, Mrs. John E. Thomas.

Mr. and Mrs. Knobeloch were the parents of the following children, namely: Adolph, George, Mrs. John E. Thomas, Emma (Mrs. Davis) and Walter.

KNOEBEL, Thomas, Ph. G., pharmacist, 209 Collinsville Avenue, East St. Louis, was born in Belleville, August 30, 1859, the last but one in order of birth of ten children of Carl Knoebel. He was graduated from the Belleville High School in 1876. Accepting a clerkship under Adolph Finke, of East St. Louis, he entered the St. Louis College of Pharmacy, where he was graduated with honorable mention in 1880. Later he took a special course in microscopy in the same institution. In 1881, he bought the drug stock and fixtures of Mr. Finke and began his successful career as a pharmacist, in 1888 removing his stock to his present location at No. 209 Collinsville Avenue. He was prominent in securing the enactment of the pharmacy law of Illinois, is a member of the Illinois Pharmaceutical Association, of the American Pharmaceutical Association and of the St. Louis Club of Microscopists. Possessing marked literary talent, and having views on many subjects of interest to progressive people, he is a welcome contributor to the city and county press. He married Miss Minnie D. Eslaman, of Belleville, March 20, 1883.

KNOX, Charles Gordon, the controlling force of the great National Stock Yards, St. Louis, was born at Yonkers, New York, in 1852, and is, consequently, fifty-four years of age. He is the son of Isaac H. Knox, who is also a native of New York. Charles Gordon Knox was educated in the University of Bonn, Germany. After completing his education, he became connected with New York bankers and financiers who dealt extensively in foreign securities, and here laid the foundation for acquiring that knowledge which so admirably fitted him in after years to assume the management of the diverse interests which he controls so creditably at the great St. Louis National Stock Yards.

ary 22, 1846, the son of Nicholas and Marian Louis, natives of Lorraine (then France), who came to America when about nine years old, and located in St. Clair County with their parents. Mr. Louis secured his education in the parochial and public schools of his native county, and remained with his parents on the home place until he reached the age of twenty-five.

On October 18, 1869, Nicholas Louis was married to Elizabeth Damrich, of Millstadt, St. Clair County, and a daughter of Jacob and Eva Damrich, natives of Germany and early settlers in St. Clair County, and of this union six children were born: Eva, Mary Ann, Caroline, Lena, Jerome, Freda and Julius. After his marriage, for about nine years, Mr. Louis rented a farm, but in 1877 he moved to Section 3, of St. Clair Township. He now owns 145 acres on the Lebanon road three miles northeast of Belleville, beside three other farms in the township, where farm, garden and dairy produce are raised. In his political views Mr. Louis is a Democrat and is a member of the Catholic Church. He is well known and has a host of friends in St. Clair County.

LOVINGSTON, (Hon.) John B., was born in Sulzburg, Bavaria, Germany, February 17, 1840, and died in East St. Louis, July 31, 1897. He was a son of Franciscus Lovingston and his wife Crescencia (Maurer) Lovingston. He was educated in the common schools of his native village, studying Latin and Greek after school hours at the Gymnasium. His father died while he was in college, and when he had completed his education he came, with his mother and other members of the family, to the United States. They located in Wisconsin, where, for three months, young Lovingston attended a subscription school. Later he worked in a country store at a salary of fifty dollars a year. June 1, 1857, he entered the employ of Howe & Rablin, lumbermen, at Dunleith, Ill., later was promoted to general manager, and in 1864 became a member of the firm, which, in 1859, had established a branch at East St. Louis. In 1869, after the death of Lyman Howe, one of his partners, he purchased the interest of the other partner, Mr. Rablin, and from that time until his death was a leader in the lumber trade in East St. Louis. In 1867 he was elected Mayor of the city, and for a con-

siderable time was Treasurer of East St. Louis Township. He was also a Director and Vice-President of the East St. Louis Elevator Warehouse Company, a Director of the East St. Louis Bank (now the First National), the Workingmen's Banking Company (now the Southern Illinois National), the Franklin Housebuilding Association, the East St. Louis Railway Company, the East St. Louis and Carondelet Railroad Company, and the East St. Louis Rail Mill Company, and President of the East St. Louis Gas Light and Coke Company. He was a "Democrat of Democrats." In the Civil War period, he sided with the Union, and, when the Home Guards were organized at St. Louis, he became a member and, under Generals Lyons and Blair, helped to save St. Louis and Missouri to the Federal cause. He was born and reared a Roman Catholic, but sympathized with the liberal element of the church. He was identified with his partner, Mr. Howe, in the attempt to establish the Howe Literary Institute. Mr. Lovingston married, February 10, 1868, Miss Mary Chartrand, daughter of Joseph Chartrand, Esq., a descendant of one of the first French settlers at Cahokia.

MADDUX, William, was born in St. Clair County in 1863, son of John and Louisa (Tate) Maddux, the former a native of Cincinnati, Ohio, and the latter of St. Clair County. His education was obtained in the district schools and he subsequently followed farming for twenty years in St. Clair County, to which his father had come at an early day, being one of the well-known pioneer agriculturists. In 1886 Mr. Maddux became interested in coal mining and has since followed that vocation with every degree of success. In 1886 he was united in marriage to Harriet Carr, a native of St. Clair County, and to them have been born the following six children: Lee, Earl, Hazel, Rex, Flossie and Grace.

MANK, Nick, Treasurer and Manager of the Richland Foundry Company, Belleville, Ill., was born in St. Clair County in March, 1869, and has followed the trade of a molder since his early youth. He is a stockholder in the concern which he manages. Mr. Mank was married in 1895 to Lena Spaeth, who was born and schooled in Trenton, Ill. They are the parents of four children, namely: Oscar, Alvena, Lena and Adala.

who knew him, both in a social and business way. Charles Merck, Sr., and his wife, Louise (Knoebel) Merck, were both born in Germany, coming to this county at an early day. In 1835 the former started in the bakery business with a very small capital on South Illinois Street, but by careful management, energy and a desire to please, he soon overcame any obstacles which beset his path. In its early history this establishment was noted for its excellent quality of ginger-bread and cider with which Mr. Merck served the public, as many of the older inhabitants of Belleville well remember. In 1845 the elder Merck moved his establishment to No. 24 West Main Street, its present location, where he trained his son to be an excellent baker, and to maintain a high standard of cleanliness and purity.

Charles, Jr., developed practical business qualities, and upon succeeding to the bakery not only retained the old trade, but added greatly thereto. In the early 'sixties Charles Merck, Jr., was married to Margaret Kessler in Belleville. Of this, the first union, there were born eight children: Louise, now Mrs. Graf; William P., who died in October, 1903, leaving a widow and one child; Bernhardt; Bertha; George; Fredoline; and Ella and Freda (twins)—the former now the wife of Dr. Bechtold, of Freeburg, Ill. On March 10, 1881, he was again united in marriage to Eugenie Bechtold, who was born in Belgium, and of which union there were three children: Eugenia and Freda, who reside at home; and Herman, who is attending Washington University (dental department), at St. Louis, Mo. Politically, Mr. Merck was a Republican, and served two years as Alderman from what was then the Third Ward. Fraternally, he was an honored member of the Masonic order, and was also a member of St. Paul Evangelical Church. His death occurred October 13, 1901, and cut short a career still rich in promise. The bakery business at No. 24 West Main Street has since been very carefully and successfully managed by his widow, Mrs. E. C. Merck.

MERKER, Henry F., City Engineer of Belleville, this county, was born in that city in 1877. His father and mother, Louis P. and Anna (Schneider) Merker, were natives of St. Clair County. Louis P. Merker was toll-gate keeper on the Lebanon Road for twenty-eight years,

and served also as City Weighmaster and Marketmaster. Henry F. Merker was a pupil in the Belleville high school, from which he graduated, and subsequently pursued a course of study in the engineering department of the University of Illinois, from which he was graduated in 1898. He afterward followed railroad work, and was construction engineer for the St. Louis, O'Fallon & Lebanon Electric Railroad, when the line was being built. Since May 2, 1904, he has served as City Engineer of Belleville. Fraternally, Mr. Merker is affiliated with the A. F. & A. M., K. of P., and M. W. A.

MERTZ, Frank Frederick, was born April 10, 1876, in East St. Louis, a son of John and Catherine (Ammon) Mertz, both of whom were natives of Germany. His early education was obtained in the public schools, and at the age of fourteen he started to work in the rolling mills where he remained one year. He then became an apprentice in the tinner's trade, being employed by the C. Hauss Hardware Company, with whom he remained eight years. Later he became associated with the Barbour Hardware Company, in which he became a stockholder and was elected Vice-President. On September 15, 1904, the Barbour Company was merged with the Illinois Hardware Company, and since that time Mr. Mertz has served as Second Vice-President. He is a Lutheran in religious belief and, in politics, a Republican. On November 26, 1898, he was married to Miss Catherine Schmidt, who was born in Belleville, and there educated in the public schools. Their children are William Norman and Harvey.

MESSICK, (Hon.) Joseph B., one of the most able and prominent lawyers of Southern Illinois, and an honored and highly esteemed resident of East St. Louis, St. Clair County, was born in Macoupin County, Ill., January 29, 1847. He is a son of Joseph W. and Sarah E. Messick, natives of Kentucky. Joseph W. Messick was a farmer by occupation, and a man of notable industry, sound judgment and sterling character. In boyhood the son, Joseph B., made diligent use of the opportunities for instruction afforded by the public schools of his neighborhood, and spent his early youth on the home farm, assisting his father in its operation until he reached the age of twenty-one years. He

a good education is the first qualification of an American citizen.

RODENBERG, Charles F., Assistant Postmaster of East St. Louis, is a native son of Illinois. He received his early training in the public schools and later took a course at Greene's Business College, St. Louis. He is a son of Charles and Anna (Walters) Rodenberg, the former of whom is a native of Germany, while the latter was born in Illinois. Mr. Rodenberg's father emigrated to the United States and settled in Illinois. He was a Methodist minister, and during his pastorates inculcated ideas of frugality, industry and energy into the hearts and minds of his listeners, particularly the younger element. Charles F. Rodenberg was one of the young men who was influenced by the pastoral admonitions, as well as the fraternal guidance. He early evinced those qualities, which in after years, assisted him in the forward and upward path.

Mr. Rodenberg became interested in coal mining, and for fifteen years held the responsible position of Superintendent of the Consolidated Coal Company's mines in this section. In this position he enjoyed the absolute confidence of his employers, and the esteem and good will of those with whom he associated. At the conclusion of his fifteen years of honorable service with the company named, he came to East St. Louis, where he engaged in the coal business for himself. Later he associated others with him, and an organization known as the Contractors' Material Company, was formed. Mr. Rodenberg became the Secretary, Treasurer and Manager of this concern.

In the summer of 1889, when Thomas Fekete was appointed Postmaster of East St. Louis, he looked over the local field for a competent man as his assistant, and selected Charles F. Rodenberg to fill this place. Mr. Rodenberg has brought to the position all the vigor, ability and carefulness which he displayed in private business. He and Mr. Bader (who succeeded Mr. Fekete) work hand in hand for the purpose of giving East St. Louisans the best service possible for a department the size of the East St. Louis office.

Fraternally, Mr. Rodenberg is a member of the Knights of Pythias, Red Men of America, Mystic Circle, Modern Woodmen of America and D. O. K. K. In 1881, Mr. Rodenberg was married to Anna C. Busiek, a resident of Belleville, and four children—Nellie, Elmer, Ethor and Jessie—have blessed this union.

RODENBERG, (Hon.) William A., member of Congress from the St. Clair District, and lawyer, Postoffice Building, East St. Louis, was born at Chester, Ill., October 30, 1865, a son of Rev. Charles and Anna (Walters) Rodenberg, natives of Germany. His father, now retired, was for forty-two years an active minister of the German Methodist and Methodist Episcopal Churches. His ministerial work was confined principally to Southern Illinois and the city of St. Louis, and for four years he was Presiding Elder of the Belleville, Ill., district of the Illinois Conference. William A. Rodenberg was educated in the common schools, at Central Wesleyan College, Warrenton, Mo. (where he was graduated in 1884), and in the Law School of Washington University, St. Louis. For seven years he was a teacher, being employed for one year in St. Clair County, one year in Staunton, Ill., and five years as Principal of the public schools at Mt. Olive, Ill. He was a candidate for the office of County Superintendent of Schools of Macoupin County, Ill., in 1890, and was defeated, though he ran 1,700 votes ahead of the State ticket. Returning to St. Clair County in 1901, he was admitted to the practice of law. He has been four times elected Representative in Congress— first in 1898—was defeated for that office in 1900, and in 1901 was appointed United States Civil Service Commissioner by President McKinley, which office he resigned April 1, 1902, to again become a candidate for Congress. He was elected that year, re-elected in 1904 and again in 1906. His religious affiliations are Methodistic. He is identified with the Masonic Order, Elks, Knights of Pythias, the Modern Woodmen of America, the Ancient Order of United Workmen, the Improved Order of Red Men, the Tribe of Ben Hur, the Court of Honor, etc. Mr. Rodenberg was married, at Asbury Park, N. J., April 30, 1904, to Mary Grant Ridgway, a native of Shawneetown, Ill., and of Revolutionary stock in both her paternal and maternal lines, and they have one son, William Ridgway Rodenberg, born October 16, 1905.

RODENBERGER, Mabury Charles, was born May 4, 1844, at Reading, Pa., and was there

roads employing him while constructing new lines. On June 24, 1890, Mr. Sefert was married to Mary Richards, of Illinois, and of this union two children have been born—Edna and Vera.

SEHLINGER, Anton, a flour and feed merchant of Belleville, this county, was born in Baden, Germany, February 13, 1837, and was educated in the public schools of his native country. His father came to St. Clair County in 1851 and followed the industry of farming northeast of Belleville, but subsequently moved to Mascoutah, where he engaged in the milling business for some time. In 1886 he came to Belleville and became interested in grain and feed, a line which he and his son have since carried on in an extensiv way. On January 23, 1866, Mr. Sehlinger was married to Louise Faust, a native of Germany, and of this union the following six children have been born: Tony J., Mary C., Lena S., Anna Louisa, George N. and Edward J.

SEIBERT, Peter, farmer and stock-raiser, of Engelmann Township, this county, was born in Gross, Grand Duchy of Hesse-Darmstadt, Germany, April 24, 1844, the son of Balthazar and Katherine (Jost) Seibert, natives of that Empire, who came to St. Clair County and located on a farm near Belleville when Peter was but eight years of age. The boy attended the German and public and high schools near his home and assisted in the work of the farm, remaining with his parents until maturity.

On September 6, 1868, Peter Seibert was married to Katherine Eidmann, of St. Clair County, and of this union eight children were born—Louisa, who married Gustave Karch; Emily, the wife of Rudolph Joenk, who resides in St. Louis; Bertha, who married John Clemens, and also lives in St. Louis; Rudolph, who is practicing dentistry in St. Louis; Julius, Emma, Ella and Henry G., all of whom reside at home. After his marriage Mr. Seibert moved onto the old Dr. Wells farm owned by his sister, two and one-half miles east of Mascoutah, removing, in 1876, onto Section 30, Engelmann Township, where he has since resided, and where he makes a specialty of raising live stock and small grains. In his political affiliations, Mr. Seibert is a Democrat. He was elected State Senator from the Forty-sev-

enth District in 1890, serving in the Thirty-seventh and Thirty-eighth General Assemblies, also serving as the first Supervisor of Engelmann Township. In his religious connections, he is a Protestant.

SENG, Charles, owner and proprietor of the "Green Tree Hotel," East St. Louis, this county, was born in Summerfield, Ill., in 1865, and is a son of Charles and Margaret (Noll) Seng, natives of Germany. Charles Seng, Sr., a cooper by trade, located in East St. Louis in 1886, became proprietor of the "Green Tree Hotel," and conducted the same until his death in 1895. His son and namesake succeeded to both his trade and his business, and in addition learned to be a collar maker, coopering and collar making occupying several years of his early manhood. His long association with the elder man in the hotel business qualified him for assumption of the entire management in 1895, and in the meantime his hostelry has undergone many changes, having been modernized and enlarged as an increase of trade demanded. In 1905, with an increased and established business, Mr. Seng occupied his new and commodious building on the corner of Third Street and Missouri Avenue. It is needless to say that he has a practical knowledge of the hotel business, understands the advantages of courtesy and tact in dealing with the traveling public, and in consequence is known as one of the most successful in his line in East St. Louis. In 1897 he was united in marriage with May Kelley, of Chicago, Ill.

SEXTON, Henry D., President of the Southern Illinois National Bank, is a native of Illinois, having been born in East St. Louis, on November 18, 1854. His father, Daniel Sexton, was born in Rochester, N. Y., February 22, 1826, while his mother, Mary (Brundy) Sexton, was born in Ermschwerd, Germany, May 4, 1835. Both wings of the family were of sturdy, progressive and liberty-loving stock, and Henry D. Sexton, breathing this particular atmosphere, and being born into humble circumstances, could not but imbibe elements which have since brought him fame and respect as one of the leading financiers of Southern Illinois. His father was a hotel keeper by profession, but dabbled in politics long enough to become "recognized," and was consequently selected as the first Postmaster of East St. Louis. The elder Sexton ran the first large hotel on the East Side, at which the drovers of that early date, many of whom became the forerunners of the present beef barons, stopped for the night and awaited the first toot of the morning ferry in order to be first on the St. Louis market with their herds. The hotel at such an early date eked out but a poor competence for the proprietor, and the future banker consequently had slight prospects of a good start in the world when he began his education at the ramshackle local place of learning.

On account of an innate energy and desire on his part to "hustle," Henry D. Sexton at an early date entered the law and loan office of the late lamented John B. Bowman, the first Mayor of East St. Louis. Mr. Bowman, then in his prime and admittedly one of the best lawyers of the State, recognized the push, energy and absolute integrity of the youth whom he had selected as his private secretary. It was here that Mr. Sexton secured the training to which much of his later success must be attributed. John B. Bowman was an indefatigable worker, and he found in his secretary a worthy companion. Bowman burned the midnight oil, but young Sexton continued his studies and worked long after Bowman had retired, and his industry, coupled with his natural ability, laid the foundation of a career which has placed him far in advance of that class of financiers who only believe that they know the people of their section. He made a study of the values, the feelings, the standings, and the prejudices of men. He came to know where they worked, their condition and prospects of life, and whether they were inclined to pay moral as well as legal obligations. His intimate knowledge of men and affairs was of great value to him when he launched out for himself in business in October, 1879, and opened a real estate and insurance office. His success was immediate, and he later formed a co-partnership with his brother Stephen, known as H. D. Sexton & Brother, which became the largest real estate and insurance firm in the city.

As early as 1880, Mr. Sexton's knowledge of men, values and local conditions made him a valuable man to be connected with financial enterprises, and he was in that year elected a Director of the Workingmen's Banking Com-

pany. In 1881 he became Secretary, in 1886 Vice-President, and in 1898, when the Workingmen's Banking Company was changed to the Southern Illinois National Bank, he bacame the President of the new bank, and has since continued in that position.

Mr. Sexton now has the honor of being a leading factor in the following corporations, viz.: President of the Southern Illinois National Bank, the Citizens' Savings and Trust Company, Main Street Safe Deposit Company and State Savings and Loan Association, and Director of the Citizens' Electric Light and Power Company and East St. Louis and Carondelet Railway Company. He is also a member of many minor corporations. As a native of East St. Louis, Mr. Sexton has always manifested the greatest interest in the welfare of the city. He never for a moment lost confidence in the city, but on the contrary was ever ready to warmly uphold it. Even when the storms of adversity have overtaken East St. Louis, from whatever cause, Mr. Sexton at every turn has requested his friends to stand by the ship and assist in weathering the gale. When the city had reached a low plane, its financial condition being at its lowest ebb, Mr. Sexton, with other stout hearts called for a change. He was one of the active members of a committee which inaugurated a new financial system for the city. Its oppressive debt was arranged by an issue of $650,000 in long-time bonds, and since that time the former practice of issuing scrip, which was always of doubtful value, has ceased, and the city has been enabled to pay cash for all work and has since continued on a firm financial basis. For his leading part in this work, Mr. Sexton received the praise and commendation of the intelligent men of East St. Louis, and is entitled to the honor which posterity will accord him for the erection of the particular monument which he unconsciously reared for himself by lifting the city from the financial slough into which it had fallen.

While this work in the interest of the public, without remuneration, may be considered one of the crowning events of Mr. Sexton's life, all who know him appreciate the fact that he has performed many other services for his native place, which, on account of his unostentatious ways, few ever knew he planned or fathered. He was President of the first electric street railway, of the first safe deposit company, of the first electric light company and of the first savings and loan association ever organized in East St. Louis. He was always in the front rank when friends were needed for any local enterprise. He assisted in settling the Broadway Viaduct damage suits for $20,000 when the claimants wanted over $400,000, and it was his name which added weight to the scheme to build a $150,000 City Hall, when the available funds in the City Treasury amounted to but $8,000. In politics, Mr. Sexton affiliated with the Democratic party, and was recognized as a leader in the councils of that party up to 1896, when he refused to follow the Bryan standard.

On September 29, 1879, Mr. Sexton led to the altar Jennie F. Hake, daughter of ex-Mayor S. S. Hake, of East St. Louis. Mrs. Sexton was born at Aurora, Ill., and is a lineal descendant of General Webb, of Revolutionary fame.

SEXTON, Stephen Andrew Douglas, more familiarly known as Steve Sexton, the subject of this sketch, was born in East St. Louis, Ill., on November 19, 1860. His parents were Daniel Sexton, a native of Rochester, N. Y., and Mary (Brundy) Sexton, who was born in Germany but emigrated with her parents to this country when she was a child.

Mr. Sexton was not reared in luxury and, after acquiring the rudiments of an education in the schools of his native city, was compelled at an early age to begin to battle with the world for his own support. He was but sixteen years of age when his father died, and yet at that time he displayed those sterling qualities of honesty, push, energy and industry which were soon recognized by associates and the business public. From the very date of his entrance into a business life, Mr. Sexton began to climb the ladder of success. Being associated with his brother, Mr. H. D. Sexton—then the leading real estate and insurance agent in the city—he acquired a fund of information in those lines which have placed him at the head of the largest purely real estate company south of Chicago. After serving his brother, H. D. Sexton, in the capacity of confidential man, for a time, and when Mr. Sexton concluded to pay his undivided attention to banking and banking interests, the subject of this sketch organized the firm of Sexton & Company, the standing of which is now favorably

commented upon in all sections of Illinois. Friends of Mr. Sexton attribute to him the possession of more knowledge about East St. Louis land values and speculative features than any other citizen. He has made a careful study of every feature of the city's advantages, and can tell, to the fraction of a cent, the productive value of every foot of ground in any part of town. While every lot of the same dimensions in a city, may be said to be of equal value from a foreign point of view, it is now a well established fact that all may differ in producing income. It is this quality that creates value in a city, and this trait and condition is known to Mr. Sexton so thoroughly that a chart is superfluous.

Aside from Mr. Sexton's identification with real estate transactions, it seems that he also possesses many traits of character which have commended him to the people of his native town. He is affectionately called "Steve" by those with whom he is associated; and, although quiet and unassuming, is popular with the general public. This was fully demonstrated when he ran for the office of Alderman of the Seventh Ward some time ago. In that year there was a landslide for the opposition, but Mr. Sexton was elected by a handsome majority over one of the most popular men of East St. Louis. His time in the Council was faithfully devoted to the interests of the city, and since on frequent occasions, he has been importuned to become a candidate for the position of Mayor of his native town, and, on account of this growing sentiment, it is believed, if he would yield to the popular demand, he would be given an enthusiastic endorsement for the position.

On September 25, 1889, Mr. Sexton was united in marriage with Minnesota Closson, an accomplished young lady of East St. Louis, and of this union were born two sons: Henry D., born August 11, 1891, and Stephen D., born June 5, 1896. Socially, Mr. Sexton is a member of the Order of Elks and Modern Woodmen. In religion he maintains a membership in the Methodist Church; but whether in church, society or in business circles, he is always known as plain, honest Steve Sexton.

SIKKING, John B., Jr.—One of the best known and most important real estate and fire insurance firms which have had to do with the upbuilding of East St. Louis, is that of J. B.

Sikking & Sons, established in the early 'nineties by John B. Sikking, Sr., and now composed of the originator and his two sons, John B., Jr., and Robert W. Sikking. John B. Sikking, Sr., is a typical representative of that clean-minded, substantial, and morally high people who established New Amsterdam on the Atlantic coast in 1626, purchasing Manhattan Island from the Indians for twenty-four dollars, and thereafter laying the foundation for one of the greatest cities in the world— their descendants scattering to every part of the continent, the conservative, painstaking, and solid element in whatever community they elected to reside. Born in Holland, in 1836, Mr. Sikking came to America in 1845 with his parents, settling in St. Louis, which continued his home until he was eighteen years of age. What is now known as East St. Louis was then Illinois Town, and thither the lad traveled in 1855, entering the railroad shops, where he remained for eleven years or until 1866. In the meantime his thrift and energy had projected him into various channels of municipal life, and the growing settlement had need of his far-sightedness and conservatism, utilizing it among other ways as Postmaster of East St. Louis from 1868 until 1886. In the latter year he abandoned the town for country life, engaging in farming and dairying in Kansas for about four years, and upon returning to East St. Louis, entered the journalistic field as owner and proprietor of the "Signal" for a year, being ably assisted by his son, John B., Jr. Father and son soon after engaged in the real estate and fire insurance business, under the firm name of J. B. Sikking & Son, continuing thus until the retirement of John B., Sr., in 1889, and the entrance, as a partner, of Robert W. Sikking, a younger son. In early life Mr. Sikking married Sarah E. Cunningham, a native of Gallipolis, Gallia County, Ohio, and daughter of Israel and Catherine (Wise) Cunningham, also natives of the Buckeye State.

John B. Sikking, Jr., was born in East St. Louis, December 29, 1868, and was educated in its public schools and at Jones' Commercial College, St. Louis, Mo. As already intimated, his business life has run parallel to that of his pioneer father, and from the beginning of his wage-earning career he has profited by the wise council and sagacity of the older man. Mr. Sikking inherits the substantial Dutch traits of his ancestors, and to them adds the progressiveness and broad mindedness characteristic of the sons of America. At the age of thirteen, while still a school boy, he received his first business experience in managing a news stand connected with the postoffice, when his father was Postmaster, and in connection therewith developed a business for himself of printing visiting cards. When fifteen years old he served as a regular clerk in the postoffice, and in 1884 moved with the family to a farm in Kansas. He returned to East St. Louis in 1890, and managed the printing office of the "Signal," which was sold in June, 1891, when, with his father, he established a real estate business. They were the first to open up an exclusively two-story residence district of the city, known as the Lovingston Addition, and they have since been interested in developing Effinger Place, North Renshaw Place and Rebhan Addition, De Haan Addition and Trendley Heights, having carried through as many and important real estate deals as any other firm in the city.

A large share of the public services of Mr. Sikking have been of a political nature, for he is a stanch Republican, and has been recognized as a valuable adjunct to the local undertakings of his party. In 1899 he was employed by the Board of Review to make a readjustment of the assessment of East St. Louis, a task for which his extensive real estate knowledge made him singularly eligible, and in 1904 he was employed by the Sewer Commissioners as Chief Clerk in making out an assessment roll for a large outlet sewer. At the time of the flood of 1903 Mr. Sikking, with W. H. Hill, was chosen by Mayor Cook, to take charge of the sandbag dikes near the Relay Depot, where the miraculous task of holding back the Mississippi River with a dike built in seventy-two hours was accomplished. Mr. Sikking has been Vice-President of the Real Estate Exchange since 1902, and is largely responsible for the present efficiency of that organization. His firm erected the building it now occupies at No. 136 Collinsville Avenue, in 1898. Mr. Sikking is prominent fraternally, being connected with the Knights of Pythias and the Modern Woodmen of America, having served as District Deputy Grand Chancellor of the first named organization. For many years the Baptist Church Society has regarded him as one of its chief supporters, and he has been particularly active among the young people, serving as President of the City Sunday School Union for two years, and as Sunday School Superintendent. His married life dates from March 9, 1892, when he was united to Jessie L. Prince, daughter of Dr. L. F. Prince, of St. Louis, and who is now the devoted mother of four children: Emma, John B., Arthur L. and Raymond C.

SIMPSON, Joseph, who is the proprietor of a saloon in Belleville, was born in 1874, in Freeburg, Ill., his father, Robert Simpson, being a native of Durhamshire, England. For eight years Joseph Simpson was engaged in painting at the Harrison Machine Works, and in 1898, he established himself in his present business on West Main Street. In 1899, Mr. Simpson was married to Lillian Hargrave, who attended school in St. Louis, which was her native city. They have two children, Arleigh and Vernon. Socially, Mr. Simpson fraternizes with the Red Men, Good Samaritans, and Eagles.

SIX, George, proprietor of a well-equipped machine shop in Lebanon, St. Clair County, was born in this place December 7, 1860, and here attended the village school. He is a son of Frederick and Eliza (Roth) Six, natives of Saxony, Germany. Frederick Six came to the United States in 1853, and spent some years in Lebanon, Pa. In 1858, he moved to Lebanon, Ill., and started a general repair shop for machinery, which he operated until his death, September 7, 1893. Since that period George Six, the son has conducted the business. The shop is furnished with a full outfit of modern machinery, and does all kinds of machine repair work.

In 1887, George Six was married to Josephine Buscher, who was born in Lebanon, a daughter of John and Caroline Buscher, and three children—Flora, Arline and Fred—have resulted from their union. Politically, Mr. Six is identified with the Democratic party, and socially, is a member of the K. of P. and Modern Woodmen.

SLADE, James Park, the popular and efficient Superintendent of Schools in East St. Louis, St. Clair County, from August, 1890, to November, 1895; former State Superintendent of Public Instruction of the State of Illinois, and one of the most favorably known and highly reputed of Western educators, was born in Westerloo, Albany County, N. Y., February 9, 1837. He is a son of Leonard and Eliza (Park) Slade, natives, respectively, of New York and Connecticut. The birthplace of Leonard Slade, who was a farmer by occupation, was the same as that of his son James. The latter was reared on the home farm, passing his childhood years with his parents, brothers and sisters. In early youth he received his education in the public schools of his vicinity, and after finishing his rudimentary studies became a pupil at Fairfield (N. Y.) Seminary. He afterward supplemented this course by attending the Hudson River Institute, at Claverack, in the same State. His academic instruction having been completed, he applied himself to the task of teaching a country school for one year, boarding in the neighborhood of his work. He then removed to Belleville, Ill., near which place he taught school for another year.

In 1857, Mr. Slade commenced his career as a teacher in Belleville, where he was principal of one of the grammar schools until the summer of 1861. In that year he was elected principal of the Belleville High School, filling that position until 1867, when he was chosen County Superintendent of Schools. By election and appointment he acted in this capacity until 1878, in the fall of which year he was elected State Superintendent of Public Instruction. On retiring from this office, Mr. Slade received a letter, dated January 15, 1883, from Dr. Robert Allyn, President of the Southern Illinois Normal University, in which he wrote thus: "In most points, your administration of the office you now leave, in my opinion, excels any previous one, and equals almost the highest of Mr. Bateman, in his few best points. I am sure educators fully appreciate your work, and the whole people will have for it the highest regard, as time reveals to them its meritorious character." At the end of his term as State Superintendent, Mr. Slade became President of Almira College, at Greenville, Ill., remaining in this connection until 1890, when he accepted the position of City Superintendent of the Public Schools of East St. Louis. A State certificate was awarded to Mr. Slade in 1864, and in 1873 the honorary degree of A. M. was conferred upon him by Shurtleff College. He was appointed

STEPHENS, Malbern Monroe, for thirty-five years a conspicuous factor in the social, industrial and civic development of East St. Louis, St. Clair County, and a citizen whose career has been inseparably interwoven with the fabric of the county's wholesome and substantial growth, was born in Abington Centre, Luzerne County, Pa., February 7, 1847. He is a son of Ziba and Mary (Travis) Stephens, natives of Pennsylvania. His father was born in Wyoming County, in that State, May 15, 1822, and his mother, in Luzerne County, June 5, 1824. Ziba Stephens, successively a farmer, merchant and contractor by occupation, was a man of much force of character, sound intelligence and excellent reputation, and his and his wife's families were among the early settlers of Pennsylvania and New York, respectively.

In boyhood, Malbern M. Stephens attended the public schools of Providence, Pa., finishing his regular schooling at the age of twelve years. He then secured employment in a bolt factory at Fort Chester, N. Y., and subsequently in a grocery store in the same place, meanwhile devoting his intervals of leisure to the study of mechanics, for which line of work he had a strong inclination. When sixteen years old he obtained a position as brakeman on the Delaware, Lackawanna & Western Railroad, and was also employed in the machinery department of the Delaware & Hudson Canal and Railroad Company. He then worked one year as fireman on the road, and between three and four years as engineer. In September, 1866, he located at Murphysboro, Jackson County, Ill., and was for about three years engaged in superintending the installation of mine engines in the Big Muddy coal fields of Southern Illinois. In 1869 he became a locomotive engineer on the Ohio & Mississippi Railroad (now the Baltimore & Ohio Railroad), and at the same time established his residence in East St. Louis. He relinquished the pursuit of railroading in 1875, and purchased a hotel on the corner of Collinsville and Summit Avenues, in that city. On July 1, 1902, he leased his hotel property, moved to his present residence, No. 1010 Penn Avenue, and has since been engaged in dealing in real estate, stocks and bonds. Toward the close of the Civil War (in the fall of 1863), Mr. Stephens offered his service in defense of his country, but was rejected for the reason that he was too young.

Malbern M. Stephens was a Director in the East St. Louis Bank, and was instrumental in the reorganization of that institution when it became the First National Bank of East St. Louis, still remaining in the directorate. He organized, and was President of, the East St. Louis Trust and Savings Bank, and is Vice-President of the State Savings and Loan Association. He constructed the Belleville & East St. Louis, and Collinsville, Caseyville & East St. Louis electric railways. He was the organizer, and is President of, the East St. Louis Locomotive Machine Shop Co., and is a member of the Board of Directors of the St. Louis & Cairo Railroad Company. He holds the positions of President of the Marlborough Building and Realty Association of St. Louis, and of the "Four C." Coal Co., and is a Director in the Southern Coal and Mining Co. of Illinois, and in several gas and electric companies. Mr. Stephens secured the charter from Congress for the third bridge across the Mississippi River, and is President of the constriction company. It is but simple justice to him to record the fact that he has been prominently identified with more important industrial enterprises involving the progress and prosperity of East St. Louis and St. Clair County than any other resident of that section of the State.

Mr. Stephens has been twice married. On June 8, 1872, he was united with Mary E. Bean, of French nativity, who departed this life September 2, 1894. His second marriage occurred January 8, 1896, when Sarah J. Bolt, whose birthplace was Duquoin, Ill., became his wife. Two sons and a daughter resulted from the first union, namely: William Romain, who was born July 21, 1873, and died March 23, 1879; Ziba Jennings, born November 16, 1880, who died June 19, 1881; and Leonora Frances, born June 27, 1882.

In politics, Mr. Stephens is a steadfast and influential Democrat, although he dissented from the free silver theories of William J. Bryan during the latter's candidacy for the presidency. In 1878 he was elected Alderman in East St. Louis on the Citizens' ticket, and was again elected to that position in 1884, serving in all four years. He became Mayor of East St. Louis in 1887, and was re-elected in 1889, 1891 and 1893, discharging the duties of the mayoralty for eight years with marked efficiency and unswerving fidelity to the trust thus repeatedly imposed upon him by the people of that city. After serving as Postmaster of East St. Louis for one term by appointment of President Cleveland, he was again elected Mayor for three consecutive terms. The fact of his fourteen years' incumbency of this office is a signal attestation of the high estimation in which he is held by his fellow citizens, and their unreserved confidence in his ability and faithfulness. During his municipal administration, he settled the large indebtedness that placed the city on a solid financial basis; the city streets were raised from five to fifteen feet, and were sewered and paved; the Public Library and City Hall were erected; and ten public schools were built. In fraternal circles, Mr. Stephens is affiliated with the A. F. & A. M., being a member of the Mystic Shrine and of other societies in that order. He is also connected with the B. P. O. E.; K. of P.; Brotherhood of Locomotive Engineers, and various benevolent organizations.

STERNKOPF, Henry, of H. Sternkopf's Sons (Henry and Alfred), Eighth Street and Walnut Avenue, East St. Louis, proprietors of one of the largest planing mills in the county, was born in St. Louis, Mo., September 7, 1867, a son of Henry and Margaret (Renz) Sternkopf. The elder Sternkopf established the planing mill about 1875, but died in 1899. The son, Henry, was educated in the East St. Louis public schools, and has ever since been connected with the manufacturing enterprise. Mr. Sternkopf married Lena Adolph, a native of Millstadt, St. Clair County, and she has borne him a son, Henry, the third of his name in direct descent. Mr. Sternkopf is a Republican and a member of the German Evangelical Church. He is a member of the Order of Odd Fellows and Knights of Pythias, and also belongs to the East St. Louis Liederkranz, a German singing society.

STOLBERG, John M., a retired farmer and coal operator, was born April 24, 1829, in Saxony, Germany, son of Henry and Elizabeth (Hesse) Stolberg, natives also of that kingdom. In 1844 his parents emigrated to the United States, locating in St. Louis, where in the following spring, the father purchased a farm south of Belleville, on which he followed agriculture until his death in 1849. Mr. Stolberg resided on the home place for the succeed-

ing eighteen years and then purchased 320 acres four miles south of Belleville, where he resided until 1891, and then removed to the city, his residence now being at No. 600 East B Street. In 1858, in partnership with his brother, Andrew, he opened a mine on his farm, but five years later disposed of his interest to Andrew. He is a Lutheran in religion, and politically, casts his vote for the Democratic party. On March 24, 1851, Mr. Stolberg was united in marriage to Elizabeth Kremer, who was born in Byran, Germany, and there acquired her education in the public schools. Mr. and Mrs. Stolberg are the parents of the following children: Martin, Helene, Henry, John, Andrew, Liese and George.

STOLTZ, William J., was born in Belleville, this county, February 23, 1864, a son of William and Elizabeth (Demmerle) Stoltz, the former a native of New Swansea, Wales. He completed his education in the Belleville schools at the age of eighteen, after which time he became a molder, learning the trade with Guys & Broches, and working at it for nine years. He also mastered the various kinds of cement work, and followed this industry for seven years. For a time he traveled through the country selling health products, but since 1901 has resided in St. Louis, Mo. In his political views Mr. Stoltz affiliates with the Democratic party, and in his religious belief, is connected with the Catholic Church. On May 24, 1888, he was united in marriage to Sarah Jones, a native of Wales, who received her education in St. Clair County. The three children born of this union are Lulu, Mamie and Lillie.

STOOKEY, John D. (deceased), a resident of St. Clair Township, from his birth here, on November 22, 1835, until his death, May 10, 1906, was one of the best authorities of his time on the early history of this section, as well as one of the most successful and substantial of the men who developed its agricultural resources. Of old Virginia ancestry on the paternal side, his father, Moses, was born in the Old Dominion in 1779, his grandfather, Daniel, and his grandmother, Barbara (Whetstone) Stookey, being natives of the same State. His mother, Elizabeth (Anderson) Stookey, was born in Pennsylvania in

engaged, for the four years preceding December, 1903, in the manufacture of cigars. At that period he entered into the general merchandise business, under the firm name of L. Traband & Son. Joseph F. Traband is one of a family of four children. After attending the public schools and pursuing a course in McKendree College, he spent three years in the employ of William Kolb, after which he became associated with his father, as above stated. In 1902 Mr. Traband married Hulda Hoffman, who was born and educated in Lebanon.

TRAUTMANN, William Emil, lawyer, Postoffice Building, East St. Louis, was born at Caseyville, St. Clair County, August 16, 1872, a son of Frederick and Dorothea (Deck) Trautmann, natives of Hatten, Alsace, Germany, the former born November, 1838, the latter December, 1835. Frederick Trautmann settled in St. Clair County in 1858, and his wife, Dorothea Deck, in 1855. They were married at Caseyville, December 24, 1860. Mrs. Trautmann died February 7, 1902. Her husband became successful as a farmer and influential as a citizen, serving several years as Township School Trustee.

William E. Trautmann was educated in the Caseyville public school and at McKendree College, taking courses in both the scientific and law departments of that institution. His younger years were spent on the farm. He was admitted to the bar of the Supreme Court at Ottawa, Ill., in March, 1894, opened a real estate office in East St. Louis, July 1, 1895, and began the practice of his profession there in January, 1897. Politically, he is "a Republican all the time." He was elected Representative, successively, to the Forty-first, Forty-second, Forty-third and Forty-fourth General Assemblies, from the Forty-ninth District (St. Clair County), in 1898, 1900, 1902 and 1904, and on May 24, 1905, was appointed by President Roosevelt as United States District Attorney for the Eastern District of Illinois. He was a candidate for Mayor of East St. Louis in April, 1905, but defeated by Mayor Silas Cook by 249 votes. His religious affiliations are with the Methodist Episcopal Church. He is a Mason, an Odd Fellow, an Elk, a Knight of Pythias, a Modern Woodman and a member of the Ancient Order of United Workmen, the Tribe of Ben Hur and the Improved Order of Red Men.

32

"TRENDLEY, John.—Long identified with the interests of East St. Louis, during which time nothing of public moment was started but that had a share of his attention, Capt. John Trendley was looked upon as one of the fathers of the city. To adopt his language, he 'wore out in the service of ferryman five horse-boats.' He was born in the Black Forest, Germany, June 20, 1804. Came to America in 1817, landing first at Alexandria, Va. Two years after he came up the Mississippi from New Orleans, and located here. He was married, March 28, 1828, to Harriet Aberle, a Swiss lady, who died March 21, 1869. Captain Trendley preserved his faculties to a remarkable degree and delighted in living in the past, recounting the incidents of an active and well-spent life. His contributions to the upbuilding of his adopted city were notable." (Brink's History, 1881.)

TRIEB, John, was born in St. Clair County, April 14, 1872, a son of Philip and Anna E. (Lippert) Trieb, natives respectively of Germany and of this county. He received his education in the public schools and when about thirteen years of age began working in the grocery store of J. C. Koska, where he remained for over eleven years. In December, 1896, he established a business of his own, opening a grocery store at No. 408 East Main Street, where he is still located and carries a full line of groceries and provisions.

In his political affiliations, Mr. Trieb belongs to the Republican party, and in his religious belief is a member of St. Paul's Evangelical Church. On September 25, 1898, he was united in marriage to Emma Dittmann, who was born in Belleville, Ill., and there received her common school education. They are the parents of one child, Florence, who was born June 11, 1899.

TURNER, Lucius D., a prominent attorney of Belleville, St. Clair County, was born October 5, 1849, three and a half miles southeast of that city, on the old Turner homestead. He is a son of Lucius D. and Matilda Virginia (Stuntz) Turner. The Turner family originated in Ireland, and settled in Virginia before the Revolutionary War. Trump Turner, grandfather of Lucius D., was a planter and slaveholder, but liberated his slaves in Botetourt County, Va. In 1829, when thirty years old,

WISKAMP BROTHERS are proprietors of the St. Clair Laundry at Nos. 8 and 10 South Spring Street, with office on the northwest corner public square, Belleville, Ill. Louis C. Wiskamp was born in Prairie du Long Township, St. Clair County, in 1876, and Walter F., in 1879, the sons of Fred and Mary (Knebelkamp) Wiskamp. They established the St. Clair Laundry December, 1902, and by square dealing and strict attention to business have made it one of the leading industries of its kind in this part of the State. Their large plant is equipped with the most modern machinery, and by the employment of ample skilled help, they are able to keep pace with a large and constantly growing patronage.

WOELK, Robert D.—Among the dental surgeons of St. Clair County, Dr. Robert D. Woelk, of Belleville, takes high rank, his intelligent and conscientious practice having established a large and profitable trade, and gained him extended influence in matters pertaining to dental science. Born in Springfield, Greene County, Mo., in 1872, the Doctor was educated in the public schools primarily, and through his professional efforts was able to augment his previous training by a course at Washington University, from which he was duly graduated in the class of 1896. In all he has practiced dentistry for sixteen years, having begun at an unusually early age. Dr. Woelk is Past Chancellor and First Lieutenant of Uniform Rank of the Knights of Pythias and a member of the Benevolent Protective Order of Elks and the Modern Woodmen. He is a son of Edward A. Woelk.

WOLF, Philip, Sr., was born in Germany in 1841 and was educated in the public schools of that country. Coming to the United States in 1866, he located in St. Louis and worked at the baker's trade. For several years he had charge of a large ice plant in East St. Louis. From 1868 to 1871 he followed farming, which he abandoned to engage in the grocery business, continuing in that line of work for a number of years, but finally turning his store over to his son, who is now successfully conducting it. He built his present home, at No. 1100 Pennsylvania Avenue, in 1894, besides which he owns several other houses in the business and residence part of the city.

Politically, Mr. Wolf is a Republican and active in the interest of his party. For two years, 1890 to 1892, he held the office of City Treasurer, and in 1902 was elected County Treasurer of St. Clair County. In 1868 Mr. Wolf was united in marriage to Emma Plappert, a native of East St. Louis. The following children have been born to them: Anna (Mrs. A. J. Mote); Rosa (Mrs. Reimold), deceased; Valentine Wolf, deceased; Emma (Mrs. Rhodes); Lillian (Mrs. Boyer); Anna, Philip, Jr., Walter A. and Olivet.

Fraternally, Mr. Wolf is a member of the Elks and the Knights of Pythias.

WOLFORT, Louis, was born in 1876, in Belleville, Ill., a son of Philip Wolfort. He was educated in the public schools of his native town and at the Bryant & Stratton Business College, of St. Louis, and is a member of the firm of L. Wolfort & Co., who carry on an extensive business in the buying and selling of horses and mules all through the North, South and East. They have an extensive sales-stable in Belleville and another in Little Rock, Ark. The business first established by Neuburger & Wolfort in 1872, and in 1886, was known as the firm of Wolfort & Wohlgemuth. In 1894 Philip Wolfort died, and Louis Wolfort was taken into partnership, and in 1896 Mr. Wohlgemuth retired, after which the firm was known as L. Wolfort & Co. It is today one of the best known in its line in the State of Illinois. The firm does a wholesale and retail business, supplying the neighborhood as well as foreign markets.

Louis Wolfort is a member of two fraternal orders, the Knights of Pythias and T. P. Association.

WOLLESON, Anton M., Librarian, Public Library, Belleville, was born in Denmark, May 10, 1853, and was educated partly in Germany and partly in America. His childhood was passed amid the scenes of country life, and, in early manhood, he was engaged in teaching school in Germany. In 1872, when nineteen years of age, he emigrated to the United States, where for several years, he followed various occupations until 1878, when he obtained a position as teacher near New Haven, Mo. In 1879 he was chosen as teacher in the Belleville public

Endnotes:

(1) *History of St. Clair County, Illinois, with Illustrations: Descriptive of Its Scenery, and Biographical Sketches of Some of Its Prominent Men and Pioneers* (Philadelphia, PA: Brink, McDonough & Co., 1881); Wilderman and Wilderman, *Historical Encyclopedia of Illinois and History of St. Clair County* (Chicago: Munnell Publishing Co., 1907).

(2) *City Directory of East St. Louis, Illinois, and a Street Directory* (East St. Louis, IL: East St. Louis Publishing Company, 1912)

Chapter 4: City Directories

City directories and other sources that contain data normally found in city directories are gold mines of information. Directories are snapshots in time of the residents, the economic diversity, and social and cultural pulse of a town or city. In that sense, taken together these sources compose another form of historical information, and they act as indicators of urban and economic growth. City directories give residents and nonresidents an idea of suitability or affordability of homeownership or rental in different areas in town, the availability of jobs and professional services, the number and kinds of schools, churches, labor unions, and civic groups, and the names of local government officials. Oftentimes, city directories have a subject index listing of businesses and commercial enterprises. Directories convey to nonresidents whether the municipality is welcoming to newcomers, open to certain or many types of industry and commerce, and capable of sustaining quality of life attractive to families and middle-class life. Directories have many pages of local businesses advertising their products or activities. As a communication tool, city directories allow townspeople to glean information about their neighbors and other residents with whom they had little or no reason to engage in conversation. Directories also have been a highly preferred tool utilized by city boosters who constantly seek ways to encourage individuals, families, and industrial employers to move into town.

The *Directory of the City of East St. Louis, St. Clair County, Illinois, for 1893*, the 1887 *East St. Louis Directory*, and the 1901 *Standard Atlas of St. Clair County, Illinois* that are selected for this chapter are representative samples of East St. Louis city directory information. *(1)* Like city directories elsewhere, the East St. Louis directories were a multipurpose device. They primarily and simultaneously served as an alphabetical street guide and as a basic census, listing inhabitants, businesses, and other establishments in street number order.

Depending on the publisher, a directory might name at each residential address only the head of the household or both spouses, but rarely did the book enumerate or name other members of the household. The directory often listed a resident's occupation. Sometimes, they indicated if the head of the household is a homeowner. East St. Louis directories identified African American townspeople and their institutions with the designation "col." or "colored."

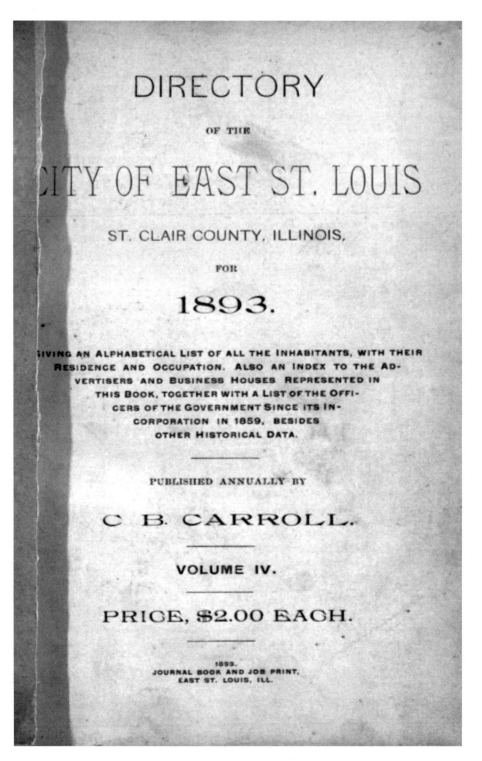

DIRECTORY

OF THE

CITY OF EAST ST. LOUIS

ST. CLAIR COUNTY, ILLINOIS,

FOR

1893.

GIVING AN ALPHABETICAL LIST OF ALL THE INHABITANTS, WITH THEIR RESIDENCE AND OCCUPATION. ALSO AN INDEX TO THE AD-VERTISERS AND BUSINESS HOUSES REPRESENTED IN THIS BOOK, TOGETHER WITH A LIST OF THE OFFI-CERS OF THE GOVERNMENT SINCE ITS IN-CORPORATION IN 1859, BESIDES OTHER HISTORICAL DATA.

PUBLISHED ANNUALLY BY

C. B. CARROLL.

VOLUME IV.

PRICE, $2.00 EACH.

1893.
JOURNAL BOOK AND JOB PRINT,
EAST ST. LOUIS, ILL.

INTRODUCTION.

The East St. Louis Directory has become an absolute necessity, not only on account of its worth to the local merchants and business men by furnishing them with an alphabetical list of all the inhabitants, but to the outside world who have learned to patronize it as well, and every merchant in St. Louis now desires to transact business with the people here, and as a means of becoming acquainted finds no easier method than a liberal use of the directory affords.

The whole country now treats East St. Louis as a great city, which must be dealt out in a business way. The old town methods will no longer suffice, as the change of conditions have also caused a wonderful change in business, and the manner of procuring it. A few years ago none of the great firms of St. Louis cared about working the field on this side, but now on account of an abundance of first-class houses at home, nothing but constant attention on the part of oursiders will give a footing in the commercial line here. All classes of business have progressed wonderfully and according to the opinions of men who have fortunes invested in East St. Louis, the city will continue to advance in all lines, until it reaches that position in the commercial and manufacturing world, which nature and the great work of financiers, railroad men and its staunch friends desire it to fill. Although it has progressed greatly in many branches, it seems to be specially favored as a manufacturing center, and long before the end of the next year, it will no doubt far surpass any city in the west of its size as a mart in this line. Elliot's Frog and Switch Works, Wuerpels, the Tudor Works, the Malleable Iron Works, the Western Forge Works, the Freeman Wire Works, the Todd Pulley Works, the Steel Post and in fact every other class of iron factory has almost doubled its capacity in the past year, and it is said all contemplate making more extensions to their plants. The great stock yards on the north end handled more stock last season than in any two former seasons. The cattle, hogs and sheep have not been sent to this place as a main watering station either. Vast herds, flocks and droves of the animals have arrived at the pens on foot, but in a short space of time were killed and cured in one or the other of the great packing and storage houses at the yards. In former years, many loads were merely transferred from one road to another after a day's feeding but now with the increased facilities for killing and packing, the owners of all consignments find a ready market at the place, and as a consequence the stock market here has become one of the leading industries of

Interestingly, directories can show which neighborhoods became racially segregated over the decades. As for nonresidential and noncommercial facts, some East St. Louis directories offer biographical sketches of prominent business owners and of key civic and political leaders and narratives of the history of the city. For example, they provide information on the ways East St. Louisans struggled to control the annual Mississippi floods, how railroads stimulated local economic growth, and the pride townspeople had for their schools, recreational facilities, and general improvements of the infrastructure. In short, city directories demonstrate the pride East St. Louisans had in their river city.

the country. The factories at the yards under new managements have taken on a new life and with the great Swift works in full blast will soon compare with any point in the country. Few cities now surpass us in this industry, and a less number equal us. A number of new railroads have been constructed with terminals here and many more will find yards in East St. Louis, before the close of the present year, all of which add new facilities to the town and assist in pushing it along in its career of success. No other city in the land possesses its advantages for all classes of manufacturing. The place offers cheap lands for sites, coal can be had at 4 cents per bushel, water almost free of charge, and the methods of shipment are excellent, either by water or rail. In point of railroads, East St. Louis is the second largest center in the world, and as they are all closely connected by belt lines a factory placed any where within its limits can transact business with ease and dispatch. But it is not alone in the manufacturing world that East St. Louis boasts of its particular advancement. Every line of business has progressed. Through the endeavors of the real estate and other financial interests she has spread out over territory which but a couple of years ago was barren, residences, business and manufacturing houses have sprung up as if by magic and the scene is one of progress and development. But of course the change had its cause. Capital never came here unsolicited. The work of Mayor M. M. Stephens and his government gave the city its start which effected the change and pushed it on its booming career. Internal improvements were commenced. The dangerous crossing at Broadway was eliminated by the building of the viaduct and the commencement of the elevated street system and thorough system of electric street railroads were the key notes which invited the men of means to our door. Front street, Collinsville avenue, Broadway, Main street, Third street and the Broadway extension, gave the world to understand that the government and the people of East St. Louis meant business and the tide of advancement followed. The McCasland opera house sprang up. The Deering's and McCormick's made this city their principal shipping point, the glass works and other industries which needed good roads located here, and as all kinds of protection is afforded them in the police and fire departments and their business has rapidly increased, they naturally feel more than satisfied with the location. But it would be useless to attempt to enumerate and name the factories, firms and kinds of business which have located and been developed in the past year or two. To any one who visited East St. Louis only five years ago, and then returned in the spring of '93 such a change would be noticed by him, that he could scarcely realize that the place he saw before occupied the same ground upon which the Queen City of Egypt stands. And yet it is believed by the leading men of East St. Louis, that what has been done, is but a trifle compared with the advancement which she will make this year and next. The energy and perseverance of the real estate men assisted by the excellent management of city affairs will no doubt invite many new great corporations to locate here.

TOWN AND CITY OFFICERS.

CATALOGUE OF THE TRUSTEES AND OFFICERS OF ILLINOISTOWN (NOW A
PART OF CITY OF EAST ST. LOUIS) AND OF THE MAYORS, ALDERMEN
AND OTHER OFFICERS OF THE CITY OF EAST ST. LOUIS, FROM THE
ORGANIZATION OF ILLINOISTOWN ON APRIL 4, 1859, TILL 1891, IN-
CLUSIVE.

ILLINOISTOWN.

(Incorporated 1859.)

1859—Trustees, W. J. Enfield, Samuel W. Toomer, Andrew Wettig, Henry Jackiesch,
ex-officio president, Wm. Hamilton; clerk and assessor, J. W. Kemp; treasurer, Daniel Sexton; police magistrate, Wm. Hamilton; marshal, George
Johnson; street commissioner, E. D. Walker. In the same year Hamilton's
bond, as president, being rejected, Daniel Sexton was appointed president.
Subsequently Sexton resigned and Samuel W. Toomer was appointed. He also
resigned and Henry Jackiesch was appointed president *pro tem.*, and S. W.
Toomer appointed treasurer.

1860—Trustees, B. B. George, Timothy Canty, R. C. Bland, Richard Hermann; ex
officio president, Daniel Sexton; clerk and assessor, J. W. Kemp; treasurer,
Henry Jackiesch; police magistrate, Daniel Sexton; marshal, E. D. Walker.
In the same year Mr. Jackiesch ceased to act as treasurer and Andrew Wettig
succeeded him. To fill vacancies, Richard Hennessey and Frederick Fye
were in the board of trustees

TOWN OF EAST ST. LOUIS.

(Charter, 1861.)

1861—Councilmen, John Monaghan, Florence Sullivan, Frank Karl, Samuel B.
Walker; president, Samuel W. Toomer; police magistrate, John B. Bowman;
marshal, John Hennessey; clerk, Samuel M. Lount; assessor, F. Hinze; assistant assessors, Louis A. DeLorme and E. D. Walker; collector, John Hennessey.

1862—Councilmen, Florence Sullivan, John Monaghan, Louis A. DeLorme and John
O'Connell; president, Samuel W. Toomer; police magistrate, John B. Bowman; marshal, John Hennessey; clerk, Samuel M. Lount; assessor, F. Hinze,
collector, John Hennessey. In that year John Monaghan resigned as councilman, and Henry Jackiesch was elected to fill the vacancy. John Hennessey
resigned as marshal and Timothy Canty succeeded him.

1863—Councilmen, Louis A. DeLorme, John O'Connell, Henry Jackiesch and Henry
Oebike; president, Henry Jackiesch; clerk John O'Reilly; police magistrate,
John B. Bowman; marshal, Timothy Canty; assessors John B. Bowman, F.
Hinze and Daniel Sexton; collector, Timothy Canty.

1864—Councilmen, Hy. Oebike, John O'Connell, L. A. DeLorme and Hy. Jackiesch;
president, H. Jackiesch, and in the same year S. W. Toomer; clerk, John
O'Reilly; police magistrate, John B. Bowman; marshal, Timothy Canty; as-
sessors, John B. Bowman, M. Millard and B. B. George; collector, Timothy
Canty. January 17, 1865, committee to draft a city charter: John B. Bowman,
Henry Oebike, Wm. G. Kase, M. Millard.

TOWN AND CITY OFFICERS.

CITY OF EAST ST. LOUIS.

(April 3, 1865.)

1865—Mayor, John B. Bowman; councilmen, First ward, John O'Connell and Michael Murphy; Second ward, Henry Schall and James Hazen; Third ward, John Trendley and John B. Lovingston; city clerk. John O'Reilly; city attorney, M. Millard; city treasurer, Francis Wittram; city marshal, Timothy Canty; city judge, Wm. G. Kase; calaboose keeper, Timothy Canty. On June 1⁰, this year, John O'Reilly resigned as city clerk and M. Millard was appointed to succeed him.

1866—Mayor, John B. Bowman; councilmen, First ward, M. Murphy and John O'Connell: Second ward, Henry Schall and James Hazen; Third ward, John B. Lovingston and John Trendley; city clerk, Wm. O'Neill, appointed December 10, 1866; city treasurer, Francis Wittram; city marshal, Tim Canty; city judge, Wm. G. Kase; calaboose keeper, Tim Canty; city attorney, M. Millard. Metropolitan police system attempted to be enforced against the mayor's and council's wishes in February, 1867.

1867—Mayor, John B. Lovingston, (amendment to city charter made term one year); councilmen, First ward, Michael Murphy and John O'Connell; Second ward, Jas. Hazen and Henry Schall: Third ward, Patrick McCormack and John Trendley; city clerk, Wm. O'Neil; city treasurer, Francis Wittram; city marshal, Tim Canty and H. Swigart; city attorney, M. Millard; city judge, Wm. G. Kase, Metropolitan police system contested.

1868—Mayor, John B. Bowman; councilmen, First ward, John O'Connell and Michael Murphy; Second ward, Henry Schall and Garrett Stack; Third ward, Patrick McCormack and John Trendley; city clerk, Wm. O'Neill; city treasurer, Francis Wittram; city marshal, Tim Canty; city judge, Wm. G. Kase; city attorney, L. H. Hite. Market house or city hall contracted for with Niemes & Mathews on Oct. 18, 1868. for $14,450. Metropolitan police system contested.

1869—Mayor, Vital Jarrot; (1869 charter and mayor's term made two years again); councilmen, Michael Murphy, P. W. Vaughan, Geo. W. Davis, Garrett Stack, John Doyle and Patrick McCormack; city clerk, Wm. O'Neil; city treasurer, Benedict Franz, succeed Mr. Wittram, Ju'y 8, 1869; city attorney, L. H. Hite; city marshal, Tim Canty; city judge, Joseph D. Manners; calaboose keeper, R. Hennessy. Metropolitan police system contested.

1870—Mayor, Vital Jarrot; councilmen, P. W. Vaughan, Michael Murphy, Geo. W. Davis, Garrett Stack, John Doyle and P. McCormack; city attorney, L. H. Hite; city clerk, Wm. O'Neill; city treasurer, Benedict Franz; city marshal, Tim Canty; city judge, J. D. Manners. September 27, mayor Jarrot, resigned, but subsequently withdrew his resignation. Metropolitan police system contested.

1871—Mayor, Dennis Ryan; councilmen, First ward, John B. Bowman and P. W. Vaughan; Second ward, George W. Davis and John McMullan; Third ward, John Doyle and Richard Gilchrist; Fourth ward, John V. Tefft and John Scullon; city clerk, Wm. O'Neill; city treasurer, Benedict Franz; city attorney, Luke H. Hite; city marshal, Mike Walsh; chief of police, Benj Godin; city judge, Joseph D. Manners; calaboose keeper, Richard Hennessey; city engineer, Daniel McGowan; assessor, P. M. Sullivan; collector, John M. Sullivan. Metropolitan police system declared unconstitutional, and force disbanded.

1872—Acting mayor, John B. Bowman; (Mayor Ryan died this year) councilmen, First ward, John B. Bowman and P. W. Vaughan; Second ward, John McMullon and John Benner; Third ward, John Doyle and Richard Gilchrist; Fourth ward, John V. Tefft and John Scullon; city clerk, Wm. O'Neill, city treasurer-

Benedict Franz; city auditor, James W. Kirk; city marshal, Mike Walsh; city attorney, Luke H. Hite; chief of police, John W. Renshaw; collector, John M. Sullivan; assessor, P. M. Sullivan; calaboose-keeper, Richard Hennessey; city engineer, T. M. Long; city judge, Joseph D. Manners.

1873—Mayor John B. Bowman; councilmen First ward, Anson Gustin and Cornelius Buckley; Second ward, John Benner and John Niemes; Third ward, John Doyle and Joseph Ryan; Fourth ward, John V. Tefft and John Scullon; city clerk, Wm. O'Neil; city treasurer, Benedict Franz; city auditor, James W. Kirk; city marshal, Mike Walsh; city attorney, Luke H. Hite; chief of police, John W. Renshaw; collector, John M. Sullivan; assessor, P. M. Sullivan; calaboose keeper, Richard Hennessey; market master, Daniel Sexton; city engineer, T. M. Long; city judge, Joseph D. Manners.

1874—Mayor, John B. Bowman; councilmen, First ward, Patrick W. Vaughan and Anson Gustin; Second ward, John Benner and John Niemes; Third ward John Doyle and Joseph Ryan; Fourth ward, John V. Tefft and John Scullon; city clerk, Wm O'Neill; city treasurer, Benedict Franz; city auditor, James W. Kirk; city marshal, Michael Walsh; city attorney, Luke H. Hite; chief of police, John W. Renshaw; collector, John M. Sullivan; assessor, P. M. Sullivan; market master, Daniel Sexton; city judge, Joseph D. Manners; city engineer, H. Koch; public librarian, L. D. Caulk; judge court of record, Daniel McGowan; clerk of court, Thos. Hanifan.

1875—Mayor, Samuel S. Hake; councilmen, First ward, P. W. Vaughan and Maurice Joyce; Second ward, John Benner and John Niemes; Third ward, John Doyle and Nicholas Colgan; Fourth ward, John V. Tefft and Christian Rohm; city clerk, Wm. O'Neill; city treasurer, Benedict Franz; city auditor, James W. Kirk; city marshal, Mike Walsh; city attorney, Charles Conlon; corporation counsel, John B. Bowman; chief of police, John W. Renshaw; collector, John M. Sullivan; assessor, T. J. Canty, Jr.; market master, Daniel Sexton; city judge, Joseph D. Manners; city engineer, H. Koch; public librarian, R. Lee Barrowman; judge court of record, D. McGowan; clerk of court, T. Hanifan.

1876—Mayor, Samuel S. Hake; councilmen, First ward, Maurice Joyce and E. W. Wider; Second ward, John Niemes and John Benner; Third ward, Nicholas Colgan and John Doyle; Fourth ward, Christian Rohm and John V. Tefft; city clerk, Wm. O'Neill; city treasurer, Benedict Franz; city auditor, James W. Kirk; city marshal, John W. Renshaw; corporation counsel John B. Bowman; chief of police, Mike Walsh; market master, Daniel Sexton; city judge, Joseph B. Messick; city engineer, H. Koch; public librarian, James W. Kirk; judge court of record, Daniel McGowan; clerk of court, Thos. Hanifan.

1877—Mayor, John B. Bowman; councilmen, First ward, E. W. Wider and Maurice Joyce; Second ward John Benner and John J. McLean; Third ward, John Doyle and Henry Sackman; Fourth ward, John V. Tefft and Jas. J. Rafter. In this year Tefft resigned and Levi Baugh was elected to succeed him. City clerk, first, V. H. Wettig; second. M. F. Tissier and third Benedict Franz; city treasurer, J. M. Sullivan; chief of police, Mike Walsh; city judge, J. B. Messick; city engineer, H. Koch; public librarian, J. W. Kirk; judge court of record Daniel McGowan; clerk of court, Thos. Hanifan.

1878— Charter, Mayor John B. Bowman; councilmen, First ward, Maurice Joyce and Anson Gustin; Second ward, John J. McLean and Henry Rowe; Third ward, Henry Sackmann and L. Lohrer; Fourth ward Jas. J. Rafter and Levi Baugh.

Subsequently in this year, in the charter council, E. W. Wider acted in Anson Gustin's place; Thos. Hanifan in Rowe's place, Louis Boismenue in L. Baugh's place. City clerk, M. F. Tissier; city treasurer, first, H. Jackiesch, Second, F. Hinze; chief of police, first Chas. M Carpenter, second, W. B. Walsh, third, J. W. Renshaw; city attorneys, Jesse M. Freels and others; judge court of record, Daniel McGowan; clerk of court, Thos. Hanifan.

General Law—Mayor, John B. Bowman; councilmen, First ward, Anson Gustin and V. B. Whitney; Second ward, Henry Roewe and P. J. Crotty; Third ward, L. Lohrer and John Doyle; Fourth ward, Levi Baugh and M. M. Stephens; city clerk, Benedict Franz; city treasurer, J. M. Sullivan; city marshal, M. J. Walsh; city attorney, W. H. Bennett.

1879—[Charter] Mayor, Maurice Joyce; councilmen, First ward, E. W. Wider and John Prottsman; Second ward, Thos. Hanifan and John J. McLean; Third ward, Henry Sackmann and P. H. O'Brien; Fourth ward Jas. J. Rafter and Louis Boismenue; city clerk, first, M. F. Tissier; second, Jas. Shannon; city treasurer, John O. Butler; chief of police, J. W. Renshaw; city attorneys, J. M. Freels and several others; judge court of record, Chas. T. Ware clerk of court, Thos. Hanifan. General Law—Mayor, Thos. Winstanley; councilmen, First ward, Anson Gustin and Maurice Bunyan; Second ward, Henry Rowe and P. J. Crotty; Third ward, L. Lohrer and John Doyle; Fourth ward, M. M. Stephens and Levi Baugh; city clerk, Benedict Franz; City treasurer, J. M. Sullivan; city attorney, W. H. Bennet; city marshal, M. J. Walsh. During this year the incorporation of city under general law was declared by supreme court invalid.

1880—Mayor, Maurice Joyce; councilmen, First ward, John Prottsman and E. W. Wider; Second ward, John J. McLean and Thomas Hanifan; Third ward, Henry Sackman and P. H. O'Brien; Fourth ward, Jas. J. Rafter and Levi Baugh; city clerk, James Shannon; city treasurer, George W. Dausch; city attorneys, Jesse M. Freels, A. Flannigen and others; chief of police, J. W. Renshaw; judge court of record, Chas. T. Ware; clerk of court, Thos. Hanifan.

1881—Mayor, John J. McLean; councilmen, First ward, E. W. Wider and Thos. T. Walsh; Second ward, Thomas Hanifan and Michael Healey; Third ward, Henry Sackmann and P. H. O'Brien; Fourth ward Levi Baugh and Jas. J. Rafter; city clerk, James Shannon; city treasurer, George W. Dausch; city attorneys, several; chief of police, J. W. Renshaw; judge court of record, Chas. T. Ware; clerk of court, Thos Hanifan.

1882—Mayor, John J. McLean; councilmen, First ward, Thos. T. Walsh and George Greer; Second ward, Thomas Hanifan and Michael Healey; Third ward, Henry Sackmann and P. H. O'Brien; Fourth ward, Levi Baugh and Jas. J. Rafter; city clerk, James Shannon; city treasurer, George W. Dausch; city attorneys, several; chief of police, Patrick Kerrigan; judge court of record, Chas. T. Ware; clerk of court, Thos Hanifan.

1883—Mayor, O. R. Winton; councilmen, First ward, George Greer, and P. M. Sullivan; Second ward, Thomas Hanifan and Wm. Shea; Third ward P. H. O'Brien and Robert Cunningham; Fourth ward, Levi Baugh and Frank Keating; city clerk, Dennis J. Canty; assistant clerk. T. A. Canty; city treasurer, John M. Sullivan; chief of police, John Holloran; city attorneys, Geo. F. O'Melveney and others; judge court of record, Wm. P. Launtz; clerk of court Thomas Hanifan.

1884—Mayor, O. R. Winton; councilmen, First ward, P. M. Sullivan and Wm. H. Hill; Second ward, Wm. Shea and John Niemes; Third ward, Robert Cunningham and Henry Sackman; Fourth ward, M. M. Stephens and Frank Keating; city clerk, first, D. J. Canty, second, T. A. Canty; city treasurer, Wm. P. Launtz; chief of police, John Holloran; city attorneys, Geo. F. O'Melveney and others; judge court of record, Wm. P. Launtz; clerk of court, Thos. Hanifan.

1885—Mayor, Maurice Joyce; councilmen, First ward, Wm. H. Hill and C. A. Haines; Second ward, Wm. Shea and John Niemes; Third ward, Henry Sackmann and Robert Cunningham; Fourth ward, M. M. Stephens and Garrett Stack; city clerk, T. A. Canty; city treasurer, Wm. P. Launtz; chief of police, John Holloran; city attorneys, Geo. F. O'Melveney and others; judge court of record, Wm. P. Launtz; clerk of court, Thos. Hanifan.

1886—Mayor, Maurice Joyce; councilmen, First ward, C. A. Haines and W. W. Russell; Second ward, Wm. Shea and Louis Menges, Jr.; Third ward, Robert Cunningham and Martin Egan; Fourth ward, Garrett Stack and Mark Bird; city clerk, T. A. Canty; city treasurer, Alex. Flannigen; chief of police, John Holloran; city attorneys, Geo. F. O'Melveney and others; judge court of record, Wm. P. Launtz; clerk of court, Thos. Hanifan.

1887—Mayor, M. M. Stephens; councilmen, First ward, W. W. Russell and David C. Marsh, Second ward, Louis Menges, Jr. and Dr. C. F. Strecker; Third ward, Martin Egan and Robert Cunningham; Fourth ward, Mark Bird and John V. Tefft; city clerk John Meyer; city treasurer, John W. Renshaw; city attorney, E. R. Davis; special counsel, F. G. Cockrell; city auditor, James W. Kirk; city engineer, Chas. L. Weber; street inspectors, Sam Lannighan and Mike Hurley; oil inspector, D. L. Marsh; city judge, B. H. Canby; clerk of court, Thos. May, Jr.; city marshal, Mike Walsh, superintendent fire alarm, Burt Sager.

1888—Mayor, M. M. Stephens; councilmen, First ward, David C. Marsh and Henry W. Hempe; Second ward, Dr. C. F. Strecker and G. H. Kemper; Third ward Robert Cunningham and Henry Sackman; Fourth ward, John V. Tefft and Wm. E. Hender; city clerk, Ed C. Schuetz; city treasurer, Martin Martell; city Attorney, E. R. Davis; special counsel, F. G. Cockrell; city auditor and comptroller, Jas. W. Kirk; city engineer, Chas. L. Weber; street inspectors Sam Lannighan and Mike Hurley; oil inspector, D. L. Marsh; city judge, B. H. Canby; clerk of court, Thos. May, Jr.; city marshal, Mike Walsh; lieutenant, Jas. L. Rodgers; superintendent fire alarm, Burt Sager.

On August 28, 1888, the city voted to organize under the general city corporation law of the state; the wards were increased to 7 and the number of aldermen to 14 The first election under the new law took place in April, 1889, when the mayor, all of the aldermen—14—the city clerk, treasurer and attorney were elected by the electors, as follows:

1889—Mayor, M. M. Stephens; councilmen, First ward, Robert Cunningham and Henry Sackmann; Second ward, David C. Marsh and Henry Hempe; Third ward, Henry Roewe and Robert Thomas; Fourth ward, Dr. C. F. Strecker and G. H. Kemper; Fifth ward, John Higgins and John Benner; Sixth ward, John V. Tefft and William E. Hender; Seventh ward, Thomas H. White and Christian Rohm; city comptroller, James W. Kirk; city clerk, Edward C. Schuetz; city treasurer, Martin Martell; city attorney, E. R. Davis; special counsel, F. G. Cockrell; city engineer, Chas L. Weber; street inspectors, Thomas Murphy and M. Schlattweiler; sidewalk inspector, J. L. Strider; city judge, B. H. Canby; court clerk, Thomas May; chief of police, M. Walsh; lieutenant of police, J. L. Rodgers; sergeant of police, Jeff. Langley; police clerk, Dennis Guihan; fire marshal, M. Walsh; superintendent fire alarm, Burt Sager; city hall janitor, M. Priester.

1891-92—Mayor, M. M. Stephens; councilmen, First ward, Robert Cunningham and Henry Sackmann; Second ward, David C. Marsh and Henry W. Hempe; Third ward, W. J. Eddinger and Louis Knauss; Fourth ward, G. H. Kemper and C. Hauss ; Fifth ward, J. Higgins, and W. H. Grupe; Sixth ward, T. J. Ganey, and T. J. Daniel; Seventh ward, T. H. White and Levi Baugh; city comptroller, James W. Kirk; city clerk. E. C. Schuetz; city treasurer, Phillip Wolf; city attorney, Charles B. Carroll; special counsel, F. G. Cockrell; city engineer, Chas. L. Weber; street inspectors, T. Murphy and M. Schlattweiler; sidewalk inspector, J. L. Strider; oil inspector, D. L. Marsh; city judge, B. H. Canby; clerk of court, Thos. May, Jr.; city marshal and superintendent of police, Mike Walsh; sergeants of police, John McGrath and G. W. Bowler; police clerk and turnkey, Dennis Guihan; superintendent fire alarm, I. B. Sager; city hall janitor, M. Priester.

EAST ST. LOUIS HISTORICAL DATA.

[COMPILED BY JAMES W. KIRK.]

First civilized settlement in the present East St. Louis, in 1765 by Richard McCarty, known as "English McCarty," being 400 acres on both sides of Cahokia creek.

Jacksonville laid out in 1815; changed to Illinois Town in 1817, or 1818.

Illinois Town laid out in 1817 or 1818; incorporated in 1859.

Illinois City laid out in 1817; plat recorded in 1825, made part of the city in 1875.

St. Clair laid out in 1837.

Bloody Island, the present First ward, made its appearance in 1800.

Town of East St. Louis incorporated in 1861; made city of East St. Louis in 1865, Ferry Division laid out in 1865 and made part of the city of East St. Louis.

Third Ferry Division laid out in 1865 and made a part of East St. Louis.

Second Ferry Division laid out in 1872.

First hotel, Western, or Brundy House, 1854.

First mill, Pensoneau mill, 1810 or 1812.

First plank sidewalk, 1862.

First steamboat on Mississippi river, 1811.

First bridge over Cahokia creek in 1795, by Captain Piggott.

First Ferry across the Mississippi here 1797, by Captain Piggott.

Wiggins ferry established in 1818.

Wiggins steam ferry, 1828.

Illinois and St. Louis bridge commenced in 1869; finished and opened in 1874, cost, including tunnel and approaches, $13,000,000.

A dike was partially erected near the present Vaughan dike in 1847 1851; destroyed by flood of 1851.

The dike, the present west Broadway, was built by St. Louis in 1851 1856, at a cost of $175,000.

First fire company, 1872.

First street railway, 1872.

Public library and reading room, 1872.

First cemetery was on survey 116, in old First ward, but destroyed by flood of 1844.

Second cemetery was an Indian mound, on Collinsville avenue.

Third cemetery, Catholic, just beyond the National Stock Yards.

Fourth cemetery, the city one, in Illinois City.

Fifth cemetery, St. Henry's, on the St. Clair county turnpike.

Sixth cemetery, St. Peter's, on the St. Clair county turnpike.

Seventh cemetery, Mount Carmel, on the Bluff.

First stock yards at Papstown, present New Brighton portion of city.

National Stock Yards established in 1873.

City court of record, established in August, 1874.

East St. Louis Gas Light and Coke Co., established in 1874.

East St. Louis Bank established in 1865.

Workingmen's Banking Company established in 1870.

First railroad—ground broken for the Ohio and Mississippi, near Broadway and Main streets, in 1852; the road in operation in 1857.

Earthquake in 1811.

Tornado, March 8, 1871.

First Masonic lodge, February 22, 1866.

First flood, in 1826; second, in 1844; third, 1851; fourth, in 1858; fifth, in 1862.

Lowest stage of water in 1832.

First brick house built here in 1810, by Etienne Pensoneau, corner Main and Menard streets.

The first railroad built in Illinois, from East St. Louis to the bluffs, in 1836, as a coal road.

The first school house built here was by Capt. John Trendley, in 1840.

The first church established here was of the Methodist persuasion, in 1845.

The Methodist Episcopal church of Illinois Town was organized in 1849; reorganized in 1868 as St. John's M. E. church; reorganized in 1887 as the Summit Avenue M. E. church.

St. Patrick's Catholic church organized in 1861, by Rev. John J. Brennan; church built in 1862.

St. Henry's Catholic church organized in 1866, by Rev. Father Rinkes.

Evangelical Lutheran church organized in 1863, by Rev. P. Buenger

The Presbyterian church organized in 1868.

Episcopalian church organized in 1870; reorganized by W. H. Tomlins, in 1886.

Howe Literary Institute, Baptist, organized in 1873-4.

The first duel on "Bloody Island" was on August 12, 1817, between Col. Thos. H. Benton and Charles Lucas; Lucas wounded.

Second duel, same place, between same parties, on September 27, 1817; Lucas killed.

Third duel, same place, between Thos. C. Rector and Joshua Barton, U. S. Dist. Attorney, on June 30, 1823; Barton killed.

Fourth duel, same place, between Maj. Thomas Biddle and Congress

PRESENT OFFICERS OF THE CITY GOVERNMENT OF THE CITY OF EAST ST. LOUIS.

1893.

MAYOR.
M. M. STEPHENS.

CITY CLERK.
JERRY J. KANE.

MEMBERS OF THE CITY COUNCIL.

First Ward,

ROBERT CUNNINGHAM,   HENRY SACKMANN.

Second Ward,

JOHN KICKHAM,   HENRY W. HEMPE.

Third Ward,

JOHN KOENIGSTEIN   R. A. SULLIVAN.

Fourth Ward,

G. H. KEMPER,   C. D. MORRISON.

Fifth Ward,

JAMES J. DONAHUE,   C. L. HORN.

Sixth Ward,

CHAS. HISSRICH,   T. J. DANIEL.

Seventh Ward

THOS. H. WHITE,   JAS. H. MEEHAN.

CITY OFFICERS.

City Comptroller ....James W. Kirk.
City Treasurer ....Henry Roewe.
City Attorney ....Charles B. Carroll.
Special Counsel...F. G. Cockrell.
City Engineer...A. E. Abend.
Street Inspectors........................Thos. Murphy and M. Schlattweiler.
Sidewalk Inspector ....J. L. Strider.
Oil Inspector...D. L. Marsh.
City Judge..B. H. Canby.
Clerk of Court ....J. G. Carr.
City Marshall and Superintendent of Police........................Mike Walsh.
Sergeants of Police ....John McGrath and G. W. Bowler.
Police Clerk and Turnkey..J. J. Driscoll.
Superintendent Fire Alarm ....I. B. Sager.
City Hall Janitor...M. Priester.

BOARD OF ELECTION COMMISSIONERS:

Gustav Horn,   J. M. Sullivan,   Patrick Flannery.
        Martin D. Baker....................................Chief Clerk.
Justices of the Peace, H. M. Wilson, B. P. Concannon, Patrick McKane, James White
                    and Jesse Gray.
Police Magistrate ....Thos Healey.
Constables...M. J. Lynch, B. T. Blythe, J. Lannigan Thos. Kinsella and Robt. Gray.
Township Supervisor...Patrick Kelly.
Assistant Supervisors....J. M. Boggemann, G. H. Trebbe, H. Mannle, M. Peppi and
                    Frank Kurrus.
Township Assessor ....John P. Enright.

SCHOOLS:

School Township Trustees.................M. F. Geary, Joe Dashner and Robert Gray.
School Township Treasurer...Dan. Sullivan.
Board of Education. First District—John J. Snowball, Forbes Davidson, A. L.
            Keechler, Thos. Hayes, Thos. Halpin and M. D. Baker.
President...T. L. Fekcte.
Secretary and School Superintendent...............................Prof. James P. Slade.
Principal of High School..C. L. Manners.
Principals—Arthur O'Leary, W. G. Padfield, Chas. Zittel, Richard Byron, B. Guithues
                    and T. C. Metz.
School Directors, Second District—J. Doyle, Henry Sackmann and R. Cunningham.
Principal...John Suess.

man Spencer Pettis, on August 27, 1830; both died from wounds received.

Dual government and municipal difficulties, 1877 and 1878.

City hall building and public library destroyed by fire in 1881; police station burned in 1883.

First city charter in 1865; amended in 1867; a new one in 1869; incorporated under General Law of State, August 28, 1888.

Ex-Mayor John B. Bowman assassinated on November 20, 1885.

Railroad employes' difficulties, 1886.

New registration and election law adopted by East St. Louis in November, 1886.

M. M. Stephens elected Mayor, April, 1887.

The new, progressive and prosperous era for East St. Louis, inaugurated in April, 1887.

East St. Louis Indebtedness Funded in 1888-9.

First granite pavement, Front street, 1887-8.

Streets commenced to be raised to new grade, 1889, starting with Broadway.

Population of East St. Louis, in 1870, 5,000; in 1880, 9,000; in 1888, 16,000.

FIRST OFFICERS.

First mayor, John B. Bowman, 1865; first city clerk, John O'Rielly, 1865; first city treasurer, Francis Wittram, 1865; first city marshal, Timothy Canty, 1865; first city auditor James W. Kirk, 1872; first chief of police, Ben Godin, 1871; first city engineer, Daniel McGowan; first police court judge, Wm. G. Kase; first city court of record judge, Daniel McGowan; first clerk of court, Thomas Hanifan; first city comptroller, James W. Kirk, 1888.

EAST ST. LOUIS JOURNALISM.

First newspaper, American Bottom *Gazette*, in 1842; Sunday *Herald*, in 1865; East St. Louis *Gazette*, 1866; People's *Gazette*, in 1871; *The Press*, in 1873; *National Stock Yards' Reporter*, in 1873; *Daily Press*, in 1874; *Tri-Weekly Press*, in 1875; *Daily Gazette*, in 1876; St. Clair *Tribune*, in 1875; East St. Louis *Herald*, in 1878; East St. Louis *Signal*, 1882; East St. Louis *Star*, in 1888; East St. Louis *Journal*, in 1889; East St. Louis *Daily Journal*, in 1890; East St. Louis *Truth*, 1892.

STREETS.

All streets of East St. Louis run north and south, or parallel with the Mississippi river, while avenues run east and west except Collinsville avenue, as follows:

Commencing at the river, are Front, A, B, C, Brooklyn, 1st, 2nd, 3d Main, Collinsville, 4, 5, 6, 7, 8, 9, 10, 11, (Pearl, Champa,) 12, (Euclid Fremont) and south of the Missouri avenue line commencing at 10th the streets are Chicago, Minneapolis, St. Paul, Omaha, Duluth, Salt Lake, Galveston, Tacoma, Seattle, Laredo, Pueblo, Birmingham, Ogden, Oklahoma, Portland, Manito, Cheyenne, Dallas; north of the Missouri avenue line beginning with the Belt line there are Webster, Madison, Brooks, Welton, Monroe, 14th, Cinabor, Elizabeth, Carolina, Josephine, Thomas Park, Ashland, Highland, Showman, Brockman. The streets running east and west commencing with Broadway south and west of 10th, are Walnut, Railroad Brady, Converse, Bond, Market, Trendley, Piggott, Valentine, Tudor, east of 10, Walnut, Balantine, Church, McCasland Boulevard, Fisk, Ernest, Bates, Porter, Yarnall, Baker and north of Broadway and west of 10th are Division, Missouri, St. Louis, Illinois, Ohio, Summit, Pennsylvania, St. Clair, Baugh, Bowman, Exchange, Winstanly, Lynch, Lake, east of 10th Grand, Missouri, Gaty, St. Louis, Illinois, Olive, Belview, Ridge, Gleyere Turnpike, Belmont, Ohio, College, Summit. Numbers on streets run north and south from Broadway while those on avenues run east and west from Cahokia creek.

CLASSIFICATION
OF
PROMINENT BUSINESS HOUSES
AND
PROFESSIONAL MEN,

As Shown by Advertisements in this Directory.

ABSTRACTS.

Donovan-Guignon Land Title Co, Jules B Guignon, manager, 419 Broadway

St Clair Title Office, F B Bowman, manager, 120 n Main street

ARCHITECTS.

Frankel Albert B, 636 n 8th street

Jaeger Fred, 555 Collinsville avenue

Pfeiffenberger L & Son, office First National Bank, Collinsville and Missouri avenues

Wilson George, 400 s Main street

ARTISTS.

Binnette Isaac Jr, 820 n 9th street

Lowry W J, 409 n 9th street

ATTORNEYS AND COUNSELORS AT LAW.

Baker Martin D, National Bank building, Collinsville and Missouri avenues

Bartholomew J W, 320 Missouri avenue

Bennett W H, 108 n Main street

Bowman F B, 120 n Main street

Canby B H, City Hall

Carroll C B, City Hall

Carroll M J, 638 n Third street

Chapin S P, Commercial Building

Cockrell F G, 21 n Main street

Cockrell & Moyers, 21 n Main street

Corliss Geo L, 121 n 3rd street, up stairs

Davis E R, 125 n 3rd street

Edwards & Corliss, 121 n 3rd street

Eggman E J, National Bank building

Belleville.

ESTABLISHED 1862.

OFFICE, COURT HOUSE.

St Clair Title Office,

Land Titles Furnished or Examined by

306

Eggman E W, National Bank building
Enloe S A, 110 n Main street
Flannigen A, 123 n Main street
Freels J M, Jackiesch Building
Hite L H, 130 n Main street
Howell E S, 336 Broadway
Launtz W P, 419 Missouri avenue
Marcoot L A, 121 n 3rd street
Messick J B, room 4, Jackiesch Building
Messick & Rhoads, room 4, Jackiesch Building
Millard M, 130 n Main street
Moore Henry W, 117 n 3rd street
Moyers W N, 21 n Main street
Neustadt Charles. 101 n 3rd street
Omelveny G F, 823 Pennsylvania avenue
Rafter James J, 119 n 3rd street
Rhoads E C, room 4, Jackiesch Building
Williams J W, 108 n Main street
Wise & McNulty, rooms 5, 6 and 7 Adele Building, Main street and Broad-
way

BAKERS AND CONFECTIONERS.

Ashner Emil, 409 Brady avenue
Beyerlein Christ, 352 Collinsville avenue
Militzer Ernst, 500 Missouri avenue
Parent Chas, Ohio avenue and 5th street
Schmidt George, 343 Broadway
Vollman John A, 21 Collinsville avenue
Wies Louis, 313 s Main street

BANDS.

Knights of Pythias, Geary's Hall
Queen City, 1303 Missouri avenue

BANKS.

First National Bank, cor Collinsville and Missouri avenues, Paul W Abt,
president; H C Fairbrother, vice president; J M Woods, cashier; J J
McLean, ass't cashier
National Stock Yards Bank, C G Knox, president; G H Bradford, cashier

---

307

Workingmen's Banking Co, cor 3rd street and Broadway, R J Whitney, president; A Isch, cashier; H D Sexton, vice president

BARBERS.

Brucker H, 212 s Main street
Burkhardt Frank, 603 Bond avenue
Costello D J. 26 n 3rd street
Daniels A, 923 Illinois avenue
Eckert Chas, 22 Collinsville avenue
Eisel Jacob, 505 Collinsville avenue
Ernst J C, 923 Illinois avenue
Gates C T, 26 St Clair avenue
Giles Lemuel, 411 Collinsville avenue
Greene G W, 411 Collinsville avenue
Grondenberg George, Main street and Division avenue
Jobe John T, 6 Collinsville avenue
Killian Geo W, 343 Collinsville avenue
Kleinhenn Aug, 305 Broadway
Koen J E, 343 Collinsville avenue
Kuehn F A, 1205 Missouri avenue
Kuntzman Henry, 314 n Front street
Lynch Chas, 203 Missouri avenue
Maddux Ira, 110 St Clair avenue
Maddux J N, 208 Missouri avenue
Mahkorn Rudolph, 128 s Front street
Mahkorn Paul, 128 s Front street
Martin E B, 314 Missouri avenue
McCullough S, 208 Missouri avenue
Metzger Wm R, 6 Collinsville avenue
Muehlfield Con, 205 Broadway
Osborn S, 117 n 3rd street
Record Ed, 1401 Walnut avenue
Riels Geo, cor Rockroad and Voss Lane
Rinehardt Bert, 117 n 3rd street
Sanders Wm, 1310 Missouri avenue
Schmidt Adam, 6 Collinsville avenue
Sherwood Jesse, 305 Broadway

308

Wenrick W D, 125 Missouri avenue
Williams Randolph, Relay Depot

BLACKSMITHS AND WAGONMAKERS.

Burns Patrick, 15 s 3rd street
Cashel Charles P, 223 n 1st street
Edlich Louis, Missouri avenue and Rockroad
Koenigstein John, cor 4th street and Railroad avenue
Ortgier Wm, 335 Collinsville avenue
Schwart Fred, 125 n 6th street

BOARDING HOUSES AND HOTELS.

Airens Mrs Mary, 214 n 3rd street
Baughan Mrs Hattie, 25 s Main street
Cody Mrs Maggie, 331 n 7th street
Copley Mrs M, 22 s Main street
Daley Mrs Emma, Pearl street and Grand avenue
Dawson Mrs Lucy, 12 s 3rd street
Gerold Geo, 36 St Clair avenue
Lynch M J, 3 n 2nd street
McCarren James, 20 St Clair avenue
McCarthy Thomas, 84 St Clair avenue
McHugh John, Locust street and St Clair avenue
Morton Mrs Elizabeth, 122 St Clair avenue
Schwald Mrs Mary, 608 s 6th street
Simpson Mrs Mary, 610 s 6th street
Vonnahme Joseph, 40 St Clair avenue
Woods Mrs J H, 430 s A street

BOOTS AND SHOES.

Beatty D B, 321 Broadway and 317 Missouri avenue
Fallan Matt, 327 Broadway
Hellbrueck Theodore, 515 Converse avenue
Irwin Geo, 306 Market avenue
Keese Aug, 406 Missouri avenue
Lange J C, 104 Collinsville avenue
Tracy M X, 325 Missouri avenue
Trebbe H H, 414 Collinsville avenue

309

Ziegenfuss Henry, 522 Collinsville avenue
Zornstein Jacob, 915 Illinois avenue

BREWERIES.

American Brewery, St Louis, F M Priester, agent
Heim Brewery, 10th street and Illinois avenue, Henry C Griesedick, manager, res 1125 Morrison avenue, St Louis
Wainwright Brewing Co, Henry Boselager manager, 121 s 5th street

BROOMMAKERS.

Kramer Henry, 1404 Rockroad
Neis Louis, 1404 Rockroad
Schlenker Henry, 1500 Rockroad
Schumacher Fred, 1218 Rockroad

BUTCHERS AND MEAT DEALERS.

Cole Frank, 742 Collinsville avenue
Davies D T, 742 Collinsville avenue
Gehrig Chas, 610 n 6th street
Glock Joseph, 356 Collinsville avenue
Huschel Wendlein, 1412 Rockroad
Leber Fred, 554 Collinsville avenue
Mann Mrs Louis, 354 Collinsville avenue
Rohm Christ, 114 Collinsville avenue
Sullivan & Cleary, Missouri avenue near 3rd street
Sullivan J M & Bros, 4th street and Railroad avenue
Wallace W J, Collinsville avenue near Illinois avenue

CARPENTERS AND BUILDERS.

Bosquit W C, 1715 Gaty avenue
Caldwell S H, 11th street and Division avenue
Chapin D O, 1495 Belmont avenue
Coats John T, 712 Division avenue
Eiskant Gus, 1403 Gaty avenue
Emery W S, 707 Pennsylvania avenue
Kiser L C, 102 n 5th street
Tojo R J, 816 St Louis avenue

310

CARPETS.

Koch F H, 619 Franklin avenue, St Louis

Behrens & Co, 216 Collinsville avenue

CHINA AND GLASSWARE.

Enterprise China Co, 520 Franklin avenue

Steger F J, 206 Collinsville avenue

CHURCHES.

American Catholic Episcopal, Rev W H Tomlins. pastor, 512 Ohio avenue

Baptist, colored, Duboc Albert, pastor, 525 Brighton Place

Baptist Sec, colored, Rev C Leonard pastor, 3 Collinsville avenue

Baptist Church, cor Brighton Place and Rockroad

Evangelical Lutheran, Rev H Meyer pastor, 8th street near Illinois avenue

First Christian Church, Rev H R Trickett pastor, 742 n 7th street

Methodist, Rev F L West pastor, 614 n 9th street

Presbyterian, Rev D L Temple pastor, 533 n 9th street

St Henry's Catholic, Rev C Koenig pastor, 6th street and Broadway

St Mary's Catholic, Rev John Harkins pastor, 4th street and Converse ave

St Patrick's Catholic, Rev P J O'Halloran pastor, 6th street and Illinois ave

CIGARS AND TOBACCO.

Adolph W H, 346 Collinsville avenue

Eisinger Mrs Lizzie, 210 Broadway

Kleinert John, 307 Missouri avenue

Knoll C F, 4th and Morgan streets. St Louis

Saeger Henry, 515 Railroad avenue

COAL AND ICE.

Beaird John Jr, 100 w Broadway

Bryden Coal Co, 440 s Front street

Bott Wm, 442 Railroad avenue

Consolidated Coal Co, 222 s Front street

Cooper E, 126 n B street

Drury John H, 38 Missouri avenue

Gartside Coal Co, 298 s Front street

Glendale-Maguire Co, s Front street near Short Line

Hill W H, 202 Broadway, warehouse 417 Railroad avenue

McKinley coal office, 300 s Front street

Sykes Orlando, 23 Missouri avenue

311

COLLECTORS.

Bauchens Adam, 312 Collinsville avenue
Chapin S P, Commercial Building
Deems Chas, 417 Missouri avenue
Duddleson Theo, 503 Illinois avenue
Wolfer Wm, cor 3rd street and Broadway

CONFECTIONERS.

Harman T J, 106 Broadway
Hughes A J, Opera House
Finke E J, 215 Collinsville avenue

CONSTABLE.

Blythe B T, 123 n 3rd street
Gray Robt, 214 n 2nd street
Kinsella T W, 119 n 3rd street
Lynch M J, 2nd street and Broadway
Oehler Moritz, 713 Broadway
Rowland W H, 110 n Main street

CONTRACTORS AND BUILDERS.

Aney A J, 418 n 5th street
Ard John J, 1105 Gaty avenue
Bosley Amos 319 n 8th street
Bosley G, 620 n 6th street
Caldwell S H, 11th street and Division avenue
Crow J W, 226 n 6th street
Davis W H, 416 n 8th street
Edinger Wm, 27 s Main street
Fraser Duncan, 602 Ohio avenue
Freeman J M, 416 Broadway
Forbes Rob, 418 Broadway
Gillham I, 422 n 8th street
Gray J W, 1008 St Louis avenue
Gray Mac, 301 Collinsville avenue
Grice R B, 711 Missouri avenue
Haeffner Geo, 1317 Gaty avenue
Hannifan Thos, 516 n 8th street

312

Harrington Chas, 206 s 4th street
Hemler E C, Belt road and St Louis avenue
Hewitt W H, 905 Pennsylvania avenue
Jimmerson E W, 511 Brighton Place
Joergenson Peter, 443 n 7th street
Lilves Francis A, 1136 Gaty avenue
McLean John A, 620 Collinsville avenue
Moucheront M & Son, 735 Baugh avenue
Moore J W, Maple street and Gaty avenue
Niemes & Reiman, 41 Missouri avenue
O'Brien P H, 716 n 9th street
O'Connell Patrick, 1211 Grand avenue
Ploudre John B, 338 Brady avenue
Reed E G, Rockroad and Voss Lane
Robinson & Galloway, 119 s Main street
Simons Geo, 1618 Division avenue
Stolle Casper & Son, 108 n Main street
Surber Gus, 1121 Gaty avenue
Thornton Charles, 717 Exchange avenue
Thrasher Frank, 814 Pennsylvania avenue
Trundell P N, 40 Missouri avenue
Voss Cawper, 118 n Main street
Voss & Hass, Belt Line and Rockroad
Welty Ed, 1604 Everest avenue
Winterman Henry, 1000 Rockroad

COOPERAGE.

Horn Ben F, Missouri avenue and 1st street
Springmeyer Henry, 15 n 2nd street

DENTISTS.

Boston Dental Co, 615 Olive street, St Louis
Canine R H, Commercial Building
Chase Dr, 9th and Olive streets

DRESSMAKERS.

Baughan Miss Millie, 224 n 6th street
Burke Miss Maggie, 130 s Main street

313

Clancy Miss Mary, 230 n 3rd street
Clancy Miss Nora, 230 n 3rd street
Conway Miss Mary, 101 n Main street
Eckert Miss Emma, 22 Collinsville avenue
Hamblen Mrs M E, 231 n 5th street
Kehoe Miss Annie, 316 Summit avenue
Leahy Mrs Patrick, 227 s Main street
Leitner Miss Julia, 411 St Louis avenue
McDonnell Miss Mamie, 13 n Main street
McHale Miss Margaret, 627 s 5th street
Scully Rilley, 705 Collinsville avenue
Tankersley Miss M O, 514 Missouri avenue

DRUGS AND MEDICINES.

Bader H F, 323 Broadway
Gain Jacob W, with T Knoebel, 209 Collinsville avenue
Heller George G, 10th street and St Louis avenue
Heller & Traubel, 5th street and Missouri avenue
Huggins M C, 654 Collinsville avenue
Knoebel Thomas, 209 Collinsville avenue
Kring A O, 116 St Clair avenue
Mootz Albert, 326 and 328 Missouri avenue
Schlott D C, 201 s 4th street
Schlueter A G, 401 Collinsville avenue
Traubel Robt, 501 Missouri avenue

DRY GOODS, ETC.

Becker Geo F, 308 Collinsville avenue
Becker J P, 310 Missouri avenue
Benas Samuel, 103 Collinsville avenue
Benton & Traub, 318 Broadway
Buerki Henry J, 339 Collinsville avenue
Dillon T E, 320 Broadway
Essermann M, 431 Collinsville avenue
Hogan Bros, 14 and 16 Collinsville avenue
Horn Gust, 400 Missouri avenue
Kaminer R, 304 Broadway
Meinsohn John, 503 Missouri avenue
Model Clothing Co, 200 Collinsville avenue

314

Meyers John, 1022 St Louis avenue

Traub Frederick, 318 Broadway

Way C H, 441 Collinsville avenue

Zwingmann Mrs Anna, 221 Collinsville avenue

ELECTRIC LIGHT.

Citizens' Electric Light and Power Co, H D Sexton, secretary, 21 n Main

Turner & Moore Electrical Co, Main street and Broadway

ELEVATORS AND WAREHOUSES.

Advance, H D Richardson, agent, Front street and Missouri avenue

Cresent, Michael Mahoney, foreman, Front street and Trendley avenue

East St Louis, C H Seamann, superintendent, 401 s Front street

Star Elevator, Gus Lindquist, foreman, 5th street and Railroad avenue

Union, H H Ghiselin, superintendent, 448 n Front street

Valley, Pittsburg Dump

EXPRESS.

Adams, Relay Depot, J H McKernon, agent

American, 15 n Main street, John Ruffner, agent

Morrison C D, 115 n 3rd street

Pacific, Relay, Thos Hyland, agent

Southern, Relay, Thos Hyland, agent

Spannagel John, 134 n 4th street

Deering Wm & Co, J T Morgan, manager, 208 Railroad avenue

Denverside Manufacturing Co, H H Smith, manager, 11th street and Walnut avenue

Freeman Iron & Wire Co, 3rd street and St Clair avenue

Elliot Frog & Switch Works, Main street and Bond avenue, H Elliot, president; res 3631 Washington avenue, St Louis; H Elliot Jr, vice president and secretary; res 3871 Washington avenue, St Louis

Kingman & Co, H P Farr, manager, 6th street and Walnut avenue

McCormack Harvesting Machine Co, A R Anderson, manager Illinois dep't and W A Winslow manager Missouri dep't, cor Railroad avenue and Main street

Missouri Malleable Iron Co, F S Taggart, Supt, Champa street and Air Line railroad

Murphy P H, Manufacturing Co, Division avenue and Belt railroad
Obear Glass Works, Joe Nester, supt, Belt and Air Line railroads
St Louis Cotton Compress, C F Fentress, supt, 6th street near Tudor Iron Works
Todd Pulley & Shafting Works, St Clair avenue near Vandalia railroad, D McCarthy, secretary
Tudor Iron Works, E C Hanpeter, manager, 6th street and Piggott avenue
Western Forge & Rolling Mills, John Wilson, secretary, Summit avenue and Voss Lane
Wuerpel Switch & Signal Co, Frank A Laphan, manager, Belt and Air Line railroads

FEED, HAY AND FLOUR.

Abraham & Gerdes, 622 Collinsville avenue
Freeman J M & Co, 416 Broadway
Gerdes & Shade, 725 Collinsville avenue
Kemper G H & Co, 106 and 108 Collinsville avenue
Lehan J E, 721 Valentine avenue
McHale John, 627 s 5th street
McHale T C, 627 s 5th street
Roewe Henry, 340 Broadway
Seppi Bros, 604 Missouri avenue
Shade John T, 725 Collinsville avenue
Sullivan M J, 422 Trendley avenue

FACTORIES, MILLS, ETC.

Hezel Mill Co, Charles Hezel, president, Division avenue near Broadway
Koehler's Mills, Front street
Seppi Bros, 128 Rockroad
St Louis Flour Co, George Hazen, manager, Front street and Trendley ave
Baxters Frame Works, s 3rd street St Louis, Clarence Richards, foreman
Cairo Short Line freight depot, E T Hilgard, agent, 318 s Front street
C & A freight depot, J S Lake, agent, Front street
C B & Q freight depot, Chas Keith, agent, 420 n Front street
C C C & St L freight depot, G W Benjamin, agent, 208 s Front street
J & S-E freight depot, W H Calvert, agent, near water works
L & N freight depot, J A Lindsay, agent, near Bridge approach

316

M & O freight depot, A L Pollard agent, Front street
O & M freight depot, J M Davidson, agent, Front street and Missouri ave
T St I. & K C freight depot, E J Linchey, agent, 606 n Front street
Wabash freight depot, T W Anderson, agent, 516 n Front street

FURNITURE.

Adam Chas, 400 Broadway
Mueller Bros, 328 Broadway
Walsh W B, 329 Missouri avenue
Willard W G, 302 Broadway

GROCERS.

Ax Fred, 801 s 5th street
Becker Louis, 427 s 4th street
Beeken D A, 213 Collinsville avenue
Beykirch Joseph, 523 Missouri avenue
Burke W P, 1305 Missouri avenue
Buxton J R, 102 Collinsville avenue
Callais Sylvester, cor Grand avenue and 11th street
Caughlan D W, 443 Collinsville avenue
Clasquin D, 516 Illinois avenue
Doehler Herman, 915 Collinsville avenue
Dooley Mrs Margaret, 125 n 2nd street
Gain John, 608 Missouri avenue
Ganey T J, 722 Ohio avenue
Gallenbeck A, 1300 St Louis avenue
Graebe H C, 600 s 6th street
Griffith A J, 136 s Main street
Hagner R W, Buesse street and Gaty avenue
Hempe John F, 38 St Clair avenue
Hempe H W, 301 s Main street
Hewett W C, 5th street and Ohio avenue
Hissrich C R, 471 Collinsville avenue
Hottes Fred, 623 Trendley avenue
Jalageas J C, 313 Broadway
Joyce Maurice, 316 Broadway
Kelley Patrick, 126 s Front street
Klingler Wm, 601 Mulliken avenue

317

Lain T M, 1020 Porter avenue
Lehman C, 719 Piggott avenue
Leveling Gehard, 6th street and Ohio avenue
Lotz Geo, 832 n 2nd street
Marks Louis, 347 Collinsville avenue
Mehan T P, Missouri avenue and B street
Mehring Chas, 10th street and Rockroad
Mehring H C, 312 n 8th street
Meints A M, 224 Missouri avenue
Moser Bros, 210 Missouri avenue
Oebike H, 329 Broadway
Oglesby N, 607 Missouri avenue
Oppliger & Derleth, 357 Collinsville avenue
Peters John, 500 Brady avenue
Querney Wm, 106 s Main street
Roe Richard, 545 n 6th street
Scheetz Iron, 700 Collinsville avenue
Schroeder ———, 316 Missouri avenue
Seim Jacob, 714 West Broadway
Smith Mrs C, 404 s A street
Strauss Wm, 601 Bond avenue
Strickler P J, 301 Collinsville avenue
Strothman H, 419 Broadway
Stoerger Phillip, 1140 St Louis avenue
Sullivan J M & Bros, 4th street and Railroad avenue and 721 Collinsville
   avenue
Sullivan P M, 424 Trendley avenue
Tissier M F, 101 n 3rd street
Vonnahme Joseph, 422 Missouri avenue
Waltman H J, 915 St Louis avenue
White C A, 500 Illinois avenue
Wies Louis C, 112 Collinsville avenue
Wolfer Anthony, 139 n B street

HARDWARE, ETC.

Bradford & Co, 521 Missouri avenue
Berkmeyer Chas, 216 Broadway
East St Louis Hardware Co, 216 Broadway

318

Flynt D H, 435 Collinsville avenue
Gutwald Frank, 435 Collinsville avenue
Gutwald & Flynt, 435 Collinsville avenue
Hauss Chas, 332 Missouri avenue
Jordan F B, 402 Co'linsville avenue
Mauer Chas, 222 Collinsville avenue
Schaub George, 312 Broadway

HARNESS AND SADDLES.

Boggemann J M, 353 Missouri avenue
Gutwald Frank. 309 Broadway
Pope J A, 337 Railroad avenue

HATS, CAPS, ETC.

Hager F P, 205 Collinsville avenue
Oppenheim M, 334 Broadway
Sulman M, 302 Collinsville avenue

HORSESHOEING, ETC.

Hayes Bros, 1010 Illinois avenue
Cashel & Burns, 3rd street near Broadway
Pennell M C, Rockroad near Broadway
Jones A, 6th street near Summit avenue

HOTELS.

Barnums Hotel, 6th street near Washington avenue, St Louis
Martell House. 2 Missouri avenue
National Hotel, St Clair avenue and 2nd street
Seng Chas, 2nd street and Broadway
Stephens Hotel, 555 Collinsville avenue
Trebbe G H, 204 Collinsville avenue
Tremont House, 6 w Missouri avenue
Van Hammen Mrs Kate, 930 Broadway

HOUSE MOVERS.

Dashney Jos, 1133 Division avenue
Hagemeyer ——, 1021 Lake avenue
Martin Chas, 702 St Louis avenue
Scott Daniel, 1115 Division avenue

319

HOSPITALS.

St Mary's, ten Sisters of St Francis, 810 Missouri avenue

LIFE INSURANCE.

Dubois F M, 123 s Main street
Johnson W E, 1224 Grand avenue
Kane H M, 13 n Main street
Killenberg John, 117 n 3rd street
Metropolitan, W E Arensmeyer, supt, 419 Missouri avenue
Niederfeldt C H, 106 n 5th street
Wood C H, 555 Collinsville avenue

JUSTICES OF THE PEACE.

Concannon P H, 102 Main street
Gray J T, 125 n 3rd street
McKane Patrick, 119 n 3rd street
White James, 26 n 3rd street
Wilson H M, 110 Main street
Wyatt James H, 123 n 3rd street

LAUNDRIES.

Dustin F W, 105 n 3rd street
Queen City, 305 Missouri avenue
Reliable, 413 Collinsville avenue

LIME, CEMENT, ETC.

Hill W H, office 202 Broadway, warehouse 417 Railroad avenue

LUMBER.

Butler John O, Broadway near Viaduct
Goedde B & Co, Missouri avenue near 10th street
Knapp Stout & Co, 3rd street and St Clair avenue
Maurer Joseph A, 8th street and Air Line railroad
St Clair Planing Mill, Converse avenue near Air Line railroad
Whitney Bros & Co, room 4, Adele Building

MEATS AND VEGETABLES.

Baries F, 535 n 6th street
Etzkorn G T, 317 Broadway
Geiler Ernst, 512 Missouri avenue
Hermann John A, 1307 Missouri avenue

320

Hubbard W, 400 s 4th street
Kastner Frank, 13 Collinsville avenue
Mann Mrs Mary, 356 Collinsville avenue
Sullivan & Cleary, 303 Missouri avenue
Schultz Wm, 433 Collinsville avenue
Staeger Phil, 1140 St Clair avenne
Traub Chas, 1307 Missouri avenue
Wallace & Schultz, 433 Collinsville avenue
Weigert Louis, 227 s 4th street

MILLINERS.

Harlan Mrs J M, 353 Collinsville avenue
McDonnell Miss Mamie, 13 n Main street
Ziegenfuess Miss Tillie, 552 Collinsville avenue

MUSIC STORES.

Lehman G, 211 Collinsville avenue
Estey & Camp, 916 Olive street, St Louis

MUSIC TEACHERS.

Carter T M, 327 Collinsville avenue
Chase Mrs L J, 1112 Pennsylvania avenue
Flaherty Miss Lizzie, 434 n 8th street
Gaudard Ernst, 212 n 5th street
Hirth Miss Josephine, 543 Collinsville avenue
Howel Miss Anna, 614 n 9th street
McHale Miss Ella, 627 s 5th street
Moyers Miss Rosalie, 533 Brighton Place
Sacks' High School, McCasland Opera House
Shone Miss Lizzie, 705 Collinsville avenue
Voltz Chas, 1117 Gaty avenue

OILS.

American Linseed, R D Kirkpatrick, manager, 301 Converse avenue
Standard Oil, J T Hinch, manager, Water street

OPTICIAN.

Mechin A J, 315 Broadway

321

ORGANS.

Estey & Camp, 916 Olive street, St Louis
Lehman G, 211 Collinsville avenue

PAINTERS.

Benwell John L, 415 Collinsville avenue
Blackburn A M, 1020 Division avenue
Caldwell J W, 800 Broadway
Caldwell W J, Grand avenue
Corell Fred, 1004 Gaty avenue
Corell F J, 1004 Gaty avenue
Ducray Justin, 9 s 4th street
Dusseau A, 415 Bond avenue
Knab John W, 17 s 4th street
Lingenfelter J, 511 n 8th street
McLean Stewart, 542 Collinsville avenue
Salmons J, 705 Ohio avenue
Schwarz Ferdinand, 318 Collinsville avenue
Sullivan John, 202 St Louis avenue
Traub Wm, 1204 Gaty avenue
Tucker John L, 1001 Broadway
Wilhelm G L, 1118 Illinois avenue
Zittel Andrew, 105 n 5th street

PHOTOGRAPHERS.

Blinn Gustav, 409 Missouri avenue
Central Photo Co, 816 n 6th street, St Louis
Killion Geo W, 343 Collinsville avenue
Shields C H, 208 Collinsville avenue, Commercial Building

PHYSICIANS.

Bates O C, 227 Collinsville avenue
Boswell W H, 208 Collinsville avenue
Carr M S, 320 Missouri avenue
De Haan H J, First National Bank
Doyle M R, 365 Missouri avenue
Dwyer J W B, 347 Missouri avenue

322

Eggmann J P, 410 Converse avenue
Fairbrother H C, 513 Missouri avenue, and 500 n 10th street
Fekete Alexander, 322 Collinsville avenue
Green Mc Q, 718 n 6th street
Gundlach George, 419 Missouri avenue
Harkins D, 419 Missouri avenue
Illinski A X, 320 Missouri avenue
Kirsch F, 358 Rockroad
McLean W H, 9 Collinsville avenue
Neagle Institute, 720½ Pine street, St Louis
Porter J H, 523 Trendley avenue
Stack J P, 617 Summit avenue
Strecker C F, 705 Illinois avenue
Teague T J, 612 n 7th street
Thompson Eugene, 320 Missouri avenue
Twitchell R A, 426 s 4th street
West E J, 453 Collinsville avenue
Wiggins J L, 18 n Main street
Wilhelmj C F, 13 n Main street
Woods Alexander, 501 Collinsville avenue

PIANOS, ETC.

Lehman G, 211 Collinsville avenue

PLANING MILLS, ETC.

St Clair Planing Mill Co, F Schafer, manager, 716 Converse
Wiegreffe Planing Mill, 4th street and Brady avenue

PLASTERERS AND CONTRACTORS.

Broderick Wm P, 214 n 5th street
Cashen Henry, 430 n 5th street
Forbes Wm, 7th street and Brady avenue
Gemmell James, 1318 Gaty avenue
Gilpin J H, Fremont street and Gaty avenue
Shaw George, 1318 Gaty avenue

323

PLUMBING AND GAS FITTING.

Blackburn John, 355 Missouri avenue
City Plumbing Co, John McIntyre, manager, 417 Missouri avenue

PROVISIONS, ETC.

East St Louis Packing & Provision Co, National Stock Yards
Nelson Morris & Co, G A Peck, superintendent, National Stock Yards
Swift & Co, National Stock Yards

REAL ESTATE, INSURANCE, ETC.

Bowman F B, 120 n Main street
Brooks C E, McCasland Opera House
Fekete Thos L, 333 Missouri avenue
Gross, Voss & Co, 108 n Main street
Guignon & Greenwood, 417 Broadway
Hart W L, McCasland Opera House
Horsey Chas, 604 Illinois avenue
McCasland C D, Opera House
McCasland C O, McCasland Opera House
McCasland J T, McCasland Opera House
McCasland W A, McCasland Opera House
McLean & Griswold, 303 Broadway
Mechin J, 716 n 6th street
Renshaw J W, 106 n Main street
Sage David S, 315 Missouri avenue
Sexton Henry D & Bro, 21 n Main street
Sikking J B & Son, 130 Collinsville avenue
Scherrer & Son, Main street and Broadway
Stone M T, Hagan Opera House, St Louis
Van Blarcom W D, 10 Collinsville avenue
Waddingham W, 321 Collinsville avenue
Wagner Philip H, Adele Building
Walrath C L, 3rd street and Broadway
Wood A B, 725 Walnut avenue

RESTAURANTS.

DeWolf D, 1 Missouri avenue
Erickson Mrs H, 322 Missouri avenue

324

Kenner Mrs Julia, 124 Broadway
Klipfel George, w Broadway
Mead Mrs Hannah, 127 n 3rd street
Silver Moon, B M Leady, 322 Broadway
Tuttle Frank, 204 Missouri avenue
Wies J J, Relay depot
Wilkins B D, race track
Wise J S, National Hotel

ROOFING.

Boughan H C, 19 s Main street
Columbia Corrugating Co, 119 n 2nd street
Cunningham Walter, 526 Converse avenue
Gilsonite Roofing & Paving Co, Wainwright Building, St Louis
Murphy P H, Division avenue near Belt railroad

SALOONS.

Adler Henry, 723 Valentine avenue
Bailey Eugene, 218 Missouri avenue
Bailey Homer, 458 Collinsville avenue
Bailey J D, 719 Collinsville avenue
Baldwin Patrick, 100 n B street
Baudendistel Ignatz, Brooklyn Road
Becker C J, 428 Brady avenue
Becker Louis, 427 s 4th street
Binder Louis, 1000 Rockroad
Bird Mark, 600 Collinsville avenue
Brew James T, 1009 n 10th street
Buecjmann D J, 724 w Broadway
Burke James W, 214 St Clair avenue
Burke Thomas, 2nd street and Missouri avenue
Burns J E, 310 n Front street
Cannavan Thos J, 601 Brady avenue
Carpenter C M, 716 s 6th street
Claes Mrs B, 130 s Front street
Clanton J W, 138 St Clair avenue
Clerer Conrad, 1214 Rockroad

325

Cloystein D G, 2034 Division avenue
Connolly Wm, 70 St Clair avenue
Connors James, 327 s 4th street
Cooper Wm, 1410 n 9th street
Coughlan Thomas, Church and Salt Lake streets
Craven John, 114 w Broadway
Dermody John, 113 Missouri avenue
Dittmer Gus, 337 Collinsville avenue
Ditzenberg Martin, 24 Collinsville avenue
Donahue James, 600 w Broadway
Donahue J T, 32 St Clair avenue
Duddleston W H, 518 Missouri avenue
Duffy Mrs B, 627 s 6th street
Eberhardt Fred, near Malleable Iron Works
Egler John, 357 Rockroad
Enright John, 113 n 3rd street
Erwin Frank, 2018 Broadway
Erwin Thos, 5th street and Illinois avenue
Fay P J, 440 s A street
Fietz Henry, 602 s 6th street
Foster N H, 405 Collinsville avenue
Frawley Con, 701 Bogy avenue
Fulner Mrs Mary, 432 n 3rd street
Geary M F, 126 n Main street
Gerard Chas, 100 s Main street
Geppert Henry, Pearl street and Broadway
Geppert Joseph, 1301 Missouri avenue
Geyer J P, 36 St Clair avenue
Giedeman T J, 129 Collinsville avenue
Gilligan & Erwin, 2018 Broadway
Gleason James, 207 Missouri avenue
Golden John, 312 n Front street
Griffin ———, 209 Broadway
Grimes Patrick, 3rd street and St Clair avenue
Halloran Eugene, Broadway and Front street
Halloran Pat, 100 St Clair avenue
Hellbruck John, 401 Brady avenue

326

Hempe John F, 38 St Clair avenue
Hempe Henry W, 301 s Main street
Hickey T J, 472 n Front street
Hicks & Vogle, 224 w Broadway
Higgins Wm, 530 Trendley avenue
Horrigan Terrence, 212 Missouri avenue
Huber N, 1024 Rockroad
Jackiesch H C, 318 Missouri avenue
James G H, Collinsville and Missouri avenues
Kneiley & Sweeney, 215 Brordway
Klinger Wm, 601 Mulliken avenue
Knaus Louis, 300 Broadway
Kincher Wm, 36 St Clair avenue
Kuntzmann Fred, 128 n B street
Laumann Ed, 727 s 6th street
Long C E, Rockroad and Voss Lane
Lynch James, 316 n Front street
Maddigan Con, 304 n Front street
Mahar Mrs J, 622 Winter avenue
Mannle Henry, 101 Collinsville avenue
Mannle Frank H, 1235 Missouri avenue
Martin Frank E, 120 St Clair avenue
Mathews J J, 1000 Porter avenue
Mayer Jack, 1800 Missouri avenue
McGlynn John W, 26 St Clair avenue
McGowan J T, 8 St Clair avenue
McGrath Joseph, 411 Missouri avenue
McKinley E H, 76 St Clair avenue
McLean R, 330 Broadway
McManus Wm E, 808 Lynch avenue
Meehan Bros, 1401 Walnut avenue
Mehlig Louis, 600 Pennsylvania avenue
Menges Mrs Caroline, 8 w Broadway
Mooney G H, 727 Valentine avenue
Muenteferring John, 420 Missouri avenue
Murray James, 22 St Clair avenue
Murphy J M, 201 s Main street

O'Hara Mrs, 704 w Missouri avenue
Parle John, 1201 Missouri avenue
Poole Wm, 212 Missouri avenue
Priester Fred, 128 w Broadway
Purden George, 324 Missouri avenue
Reeb Con, 319 Broadway
Reynolds Thos, 300 Collinsville avenue
Rial S E, cor 10th street and Illinois avenue
Rial T P, St Louis avenue and Rockroad
Ryan John J, Railroad avenue and Piggott Alley
Ryan & Baker, Railroad avenue and Piggott Alley
Ruff George, 154 Front street
Scheibe Frank E, 1221 Rockroad
Schneider Jacob, 121 n 3rd street
Sculley Bros, 304 Broadway
Seng Charles, 201 Broadway
Slawson J T, 116 s Front street
Smith James 474 n Front street
Stacy Frank, 400 s A street
Stack G E, 313 Missouri avenue
Starke! Wm, 601 Missouri avenue
Steger E A, Main street and Trendley avenue
Stoekel Mrs F E, 122 s Front street
Sullivan J M & Bro, 4th street and Rockroad
Surwald Casper, 2 St Clair avenue
Sweeney Ted, 215 Broadway
Traubel L, 301 Missouri avenue
Trebbe G H, 335 Missouri avenue
Tojo ———, 127 Missouri avenue
Turmes Ed, 335 Broadway
Vogt Theodore, 339 Missouri avenue
Wachtel Fred, Missouri avenue and 2nd street
Wallace E, Collinsville and Ohio avenues
Walsh T E, 110 Main street
Wyatt & Chamlin, 100 w Broadway *tolat 129*

SECOND-HAND STORES.

Fink J, 510 Collinsville avenue

(left margin, rotated text) The St. Clair Title Office, Est. 1862, Furnishes and Examines Land Titles. Office, Court House, Belleville.

328

Ford J P, 103 n 3rd street
Stone R J, 336 Broadway

SHORT HAND AND COMMERCIAL SCHOOLS.

Jones Commercial College, 309 n Broadway, St Louis
Schott J E, Odd Fellows Building, St Louis
Perkins & Herpel, 4th street and Washington avenue, St Louis

SEWING SCHOOLS.

Jameson A, 327½ Broadway
Singer Manufacturing Co, G W Hall, manager, 505 Missouri avenue

SLATE ROOFERS.

Robinson E J, 119 s Main street
Galloway E P, 119 s Main street

SOCIETIES.

Ancient Order of Hibernians, 417 Missouri avenue
A O U W, Geary's Hall
Progressive Council No 1117 A L of H, Launtz's hall
C K of I, Branch No 2, St Patrick's hall
C K of I, Branch No 44, St Mary's hall
Eureka Council Chosen Friends, Launtz's hall
Father Matthew's Temperance, St Mary's hall
McDowell Post G A R, Launtz's hall
I O O F, Jackiesch hall
Knights and Ladies of Honor No 481, Launtz's hall
Knights of Labor No 3835 Launtz's hall
Knights of Labor No 9125, Launtz's hall
Knights of Labor No 3976 Launtz's hall
Knights of Pythias, Geary's hall
Knights of Wisemen No 2, Launtz's hall
Knights of Labor D A, No 206 Launtz's hall
Woman's Relief Corps No 82, Launtz's hall
Masons, Beatty's hall
Sons of Veterans No 174, Launtz's hall
Switchman's Mutual Aid, Launtz's hall

329

Western Catholic Union, St Henry's hall
Y M C A, Association hall near Relay depot

SODA FACTORIES.

Auer Emanuel, 1606 Missouri avenue
Schroeder George, 919 Illinois avenue
Spannagel Soda Co, 12 s Main street

STAIR BUILDERS.

Stofiel Robt, 1207 Grand avenue
Speisbach Edward, 1200 Cleveland avenue

STENOGRAPHERS.

Caldwell Miss Bessie, City Hall
Flemming Samuel, Perkins & Herpel's school, St Louis

STOCK DEALERS.

Brown Bros Smith & Co, Exchange Building
Coddington Eugene, Exchange Building
Daly C C & Co Exchange Building
Daniel T J, Exchange Building
Dunn Wm, Exchange Building
Evans, Snyder, Buell & Co, Exchange Building
Hayes Matt, Exchange Building
Keys C M & Co, Exchange Building
Lindsay Rufus P, Exchange Building
Little & Broderick, Exchange Building
Malone John P, Exchange Building
Mannion Thos, Exchange Building
McCormack C A, Exchange Building
Means Z T, Exchange Building
Metcalf T A, Exchange Building
Metcalf James, Exchange Building
Metcalf West K, Exchange Building
Mills Hugh, Exchange Building
Moody James, Exchange Building
Owens C L, Exchange Building

330

Scaling & Tamblin, Exchange Building
Stewart & Overstreet, Exchange Building
Tarleton, Moody & Co, Exchange Building
Turpin Frank, Exchange Building
White C E, Exchangn Building
White T H, Exchange Building

SURVEYORS.

Abend A E. Adele Building and City Hall
Abry John D, 618 n 9th street
Cox H W, 1102 Illinois avenue
Weber C L, 555 Collinsville avenue

TAXIDERMIST.

Meamber Joseph, 815 Illinois avenue

TAILORS.

Brinkman Henry, 310 Broadway
Malmors A, 340 Collinsvile avenue
Scheibel John, 127 Collinsville avenue
Urban L W, 125 n 3rd street

TEAS, ETC.

Home Tea Company, 323 Collinsville avenue

UMBRELLAS.

Imbusch Claus, 310 n 10th street

UNDERTAKING AND LIVERY.

Benner Livery & Undertaking Co, 126 and 128 Collinsville avenue
Kurrus Joseph A, Livery Co, 104 n 3rd street
Walsh M J, 334 Collinsville avenue

VARIETIES, NOTIONS, ETC.

Barr Abraham, 118 St Clair avenue
Bergin Miss Ann, 220 Missouri avenue
Broughton Mrs Ruth
Collins Mrs M A, 1500 Church street

Flemming L M, 500 s 4th street
Horn Wm, 502 Missouri avenue
Keough Mrs N, 429 Collinsville avenue
Kollme Theodore, 701 Pennsylvania avenue
Kresse O F, 331 Missouri avenue
Meyers Mrs A E, 223 s Main street
Watson M W, 423 Missouri avenue
Wettig G A, 210 s Main street
Winne A R, 428 Trendley avenue
Winters Miss Mary, 620 w Missouri avenue

VETERINARY SURGEONS.

Armstrong F H, 602 Missouri avenue
Niederfeldt B H, 412 n 5th street
Niederfeldt Henry, 412 n 5th street

WAREHOUSES.

Esterley Harvester Co, J H Crandall, agent, 110 n 2nd street
Hackmann F W & Co, 101 n 2nd street

WATCHMAKERS AND JEWELERS.

Derleth Chas G, 355 Collinsville avenue
Eckhold Chas, 315 Broadway
Graves Chas, 214 Missouri avenue
Mechin A J, 315 Broadway
Mechin J & Son, 315 Broadway
Mengel W T, 355 Collinsville avenue
Sauer Chas, 100 Collinsville avenue
Wuille Mrs Arnold, 306 Broadway

WAGONMAKERS.

Gain Jacob, 1407 Missouri avenue
Koenigstein John, cor Railroad avenue and 4th street
Winkle Henry, 125 n 6th street

WOOD TURNING.

Sternkopf Henry, 306 Brady avenue

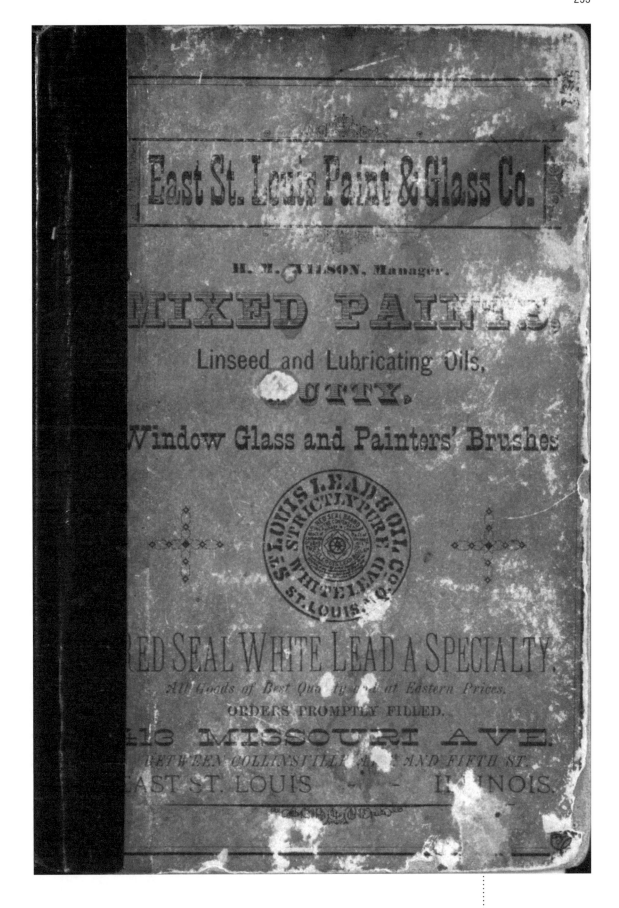

254

SALUTATORY.

is customary in this century of enlightenment when presenting
ilation of any description to the public, to add a nonsensical
lage in the shape of a preface or introductory extolling the con-
f the volume and giving in a succinct form the principal points
which the book or author seeks for fame. That the East St·
Directory shall not be an innovation, and that its compiler may
embered by those very particular individuals who continually
for the style of the day, the well trodden path of introduction
followed at a distance.

is useless to state that many difficulties stood in the way of a
ete classification of all the inhabitants of the city the great
bling block being the absence of numbers of the houses and the
gularity of the streets, which defects will undoubtedly be eliminated
future editions of the book.

Besides furnishing our citizens with a list of names and a first clas.
rtising medium,the author of this volume had another object when
onceived the idea of compiling it, that is to show to our people the
essity of petitioning the Post Office Department for a free delivery,
hich we are justly entitled. Other towns with a less population
we have are enjoying the delivery system, and why should East
Louis not put on airs and show to the world that she is the com-
cial and manufacturing metropolis of southern Illinois. The cen
taker has completed his labors and figures out a population of fif
thousand two hundred and seventeen, a number far less than a
ctory containing 5,000 names would indicate, owing perhaps to the
y enterprises operated by single persons. It is to be hoped
the leading citizens will take an active part in the project of se-
g the delivery and by such action attempt to add materially to
welfare of the city.

The delivery an assured thing and not a scheme on paper, and
city would rise like the Phœnix of old and command the respect
St. Louis that Brooklyn does from New York. Why should we
p? We have the advantages and should put on our armor. The

2

leading capitalists are now offering great inducements to foreign ca
to locate here and if all the citizens will take an active part in boo
the town, dealing at home and doing all in their power to support
representatives of the people we will undoubtedly succeed. The
enjoys a fine water works, which has a capacity of several millio
gallons per day, three influential newspapers, viz: the "Herald" I
pendent M. F. Tissier, editor and proprietor; the "Signal" Repub
H. D. O'Brien, editor and the "Gazette", Democratic, J.W.Kirk, ed
a first class school board consisting of Messrs J. M. Sullivan, presid
John A. Joyce, secretary; and John Cantillon, Dennis Rush, W
Dill, Thomas Cannavan. A council consisting of Mayor M. M. Steph
Aldermen John V.Tefft, M. Bird, Louis Menges, Dr. C. F. Strecker
C. Marsh, W. W. Russell, R. Cunningham, Martin Eagan; one of
finest police departments in the country under the command of C
Michael Walsh, and many large manufacturing establishments, wh
have been secured through the indefatigable efforts of some of our l
ing citizens.

We now conclude by thanking the many business men who assis
in the enterprize and landing the East St Louis Herald, and Mr. Tiss
ts proprietor, for the magnificent mechanical production of this volu
e earnestly hope that the delay will be excused, and faithf
promise to issue all future editions on time.

THE PUBLISHER,

STREET DIRECTORY.

——o——

NORTH AND SOUTH.

——o——

First street runs from Broadway, parallel with the Pittsburg railroad, to Railroad street.
Hamilton from Broadway, to Railroad street.
Main from Missouri avenue, to old bed Cohakia Creek.
Second, First Ward from Broadway, to old bed Cohakia Creek.
Third, First Ward, from Broadway to old bed Cohakia Creek.
Second, Second Ward, from Missouri avenue to St. Louis avenue.
New Second from Missouri avenue to City limits.
Third from Broadway Second Ward, to Illinois Avenue.
Fourth from Broadway, to St. Clair avenue.
Collinsville avenue, from Broadway to City limits.
Short street, Second Ward, from Missouri to Broadway.
Fifth from Broadway to intersection of Ohio and Collinsville avenues.
Sixth from Broadway to intersection of Pennsylvania and St. Clair avenues.
Seventh from Broadway to St. Clair.
Eighth from Broadway to St. Clair avenue.
Ninth from Broadway to St. Clair avenue.
Tenth from St Clair avenue to old bed Cohakia Creek.
Eleventh Missouri avenue to St Clair avenue.
Twelveth Missouri avenue to Rock road.
Front, Island parallel with river.
Second, Island, from Trendlay to Spring.
Third, Island, from Trendlay to Spring.
Fourth, Island, from Trendlay to Spring.
Brooklyn avenue, Illinois to Dyke avenue.

EAST AND WEST.

——o——

Commencing at southern limits of City the Streets West of Cohakia Creek are:

1. Piggott.
2. Menard.
3. Market.
4. Bond.
5. Converse.
6. Brady,
7. Railroad
8. Broadway.
9. Division Avenue.
10. Missouri Avenve,
11. St. Louis Avenue.
12. Illinois Avenue.
13. Ohio Avenue
14. Summit Avenve.
15. Pennsylvania Avenue.
16. St. Clair, and the boundary of Illinois City, Elysium avenve,

On the Island from the South.

1 Trendlay,
2 Pratte,
3 Boggy,
4 Dyke.
5 Mullikin,
6 Christy,
6 Wiggins,
8 Winter,
9 Spring.

CHURCH DIRECTORY.

————o————

St. Patrick's, English, Roman Catholic, Sixth and Illinois avenue. Low Mass 7:30, Childre[n] Mass 9:00, and High Mass, 10:30, Vespers 3:00, p m Very Rev. P. J. O'Halloran. V, F., Past[or] Rev William Grant Assistant.

St. Henry's, German, Roman Catholic, Broadway and Sixth street. Low Mass 8:00 and Hi[gh] Mass 10:00. a m Vespers 3:00 p m Rev. C. Koenig. Pastor.

First Presbyterian, Collinsville avenue, between St. Louis and Illinois avenues. Services [at] 11:00, a m, and 7:30, p m Sunday School at 2:00, p m Prayer meeting every Wednesday 7:30, p m. Rev. William Johnson Pastor.

St. John's M E, Seventh and Summit avenue. Services at 10:30, a m and 7:30, p m Sun [day] School 2 30 pm. Prayer meeting at 7:30 pm. Rev. S. D. Chapin, Pastor.

German Evangelical, Eighth between Illinois and St. Louis avenues. Services at 10:00 a[m] Rev Mr. Meyer, Pastor.

St Mary's Mission, Episcopalian, St Louis avenue near Eighth street. Services at 10:45 a [m] and 7:30 p m. Sunday School 2:00 p m. Rev W H Tomlins, M A, Pastor.

African Zion M E Church, Rock road, between Broadway and Railroad street. Services [at] 11:00 a m and 7:30 p m. Class meeting 3 00 p m. Sunday School 2:00 p m. Prayer meeting ever[y] Thursday at 7:30 p m. Rev W E Jackson, Pastor.

First Baptist Church, Colored, Converse near Third First ward. Services at 11:00 a m 3:0[0] and 7:00 p m. Sunday School 2:00. Sacrament second Sunday of each month. Prayer meeting every Thursday at 7 p m· Church meeting second Saturday of each month· Rev C W Carter pastor·

J A BEASLEY. Clerk

STANDARD ATLAS
OF
St. CLAIR COUNTY
ILLINOIS

INCLUDING
A PLAT BOOK
OF THE
VILLAGES, CITIES AND TOWNSHIPS OF THE COUNTY.
MAP OF THE STATE, UNITED STATES AND WORLD.
Patrons Directory, Reference Business Directory and Departments
devoted to General Information.
ANALYSIS OF THE SYSTEM OF U.S. LAND SURVEYS, DIGEST OF THE
SYSTEM OF CIVIL GOVERNMENT, ETC. ETC.

Compiled and Published
BY
GEO. A. OGLE & CO.
PUBLISHERS & ENGRAVERS.
134 VAN BUREN ST.
CHICAGO.
1901

PATRONS' REFERENCE DIRECTORY

OF

ST. CLAIR COUNTY, ILLINOIS.

EXPLANATION.—The date following a name indicates the length of time the party has been a resident of the county. The abbreviations are as follows: S. for Section; T. for Township; P. O. for Post-office address. When no Section Number or Township is given, it will be understood that the party resides within the limits of the village or city named, and, in such cases, the post-office address is the same as the place of residence, unless otherwise stated.

Abend, Edward, President Belleville Savings Bank, Belleville.
Abbott, L. D. & Co., Lumber, Coal, Builders' Supplies, etc., East St. Louis.
Adams, J William, Farmer, S. 11, T. Prairie du Long, P. O. Smithton, 1870.
Adele, August, Farmer, Sur.59, T.Centerville station, P.O. EastSt.Louis, 1872
Adelsberger, John F. Supervisor and Farmer, Sur. 192, T. Sugar Loaf, P. O. East Carondalet, 1885
Albrecht, H. & Co., Wholesale Liquors, Cigars, Wines, etc., East St. Louis.
Ahlheim, F. L., Farmer, S. 34, T. New Athens, P. O. New Athens, 1860.
Alexander, J. P., Farmer, S. 16, T. Shiloh Valley, P. O. Shiloh.
Alexander, W. M., Farmer, S. 21, T. Lebanon, P. O. Summerfield, 1850.
Ammel, N. E., Farmer, S. 36, T. Stookey, P.O Bell. ville, 1858.
Andel, A, County Treasurer, Belleville.
Andres, Jacob, Farmer and Stockraiser, S. 16, T. Engelmann, P. O. Mascoutah, 1863.
Arras, John, Farmer and Stockraiser, S. 13, T. Sugar Loaf, P. O. Columbia, 1839.
Atkinson, J. H., Farmer, S. 31, T. O'Fallon, P. O. O'Fallon, 1832.

Baer Bros., Horses, Mules and Farm Lands, Belleville.
Baer Bros., Breeders of Shorthorn Cattle and Berkshire Hogs, S. 34, T. Lebanon, P. O. Trenton, 1880.
Baer & Baer (Benj. D. Baer and Adolph G. Baer), Breeders of Aberdeen Angus Cattle, S. 26, T. Lebanon, P. O. Summerfield, 1871-75.
Baer, Albert, Farmer, S. 22, T. Lebanon, P. O. Summerfield, 1874.
Baer, Jacob B., Farmer, S. 23, T. Lebanon, P. O. Summerfield, 1855.
Baer, John C., Farmer, S. 26, T. Lebanon, P. O Summerfield, 1863.
Bach & Meyer (J. L. Bach & Geo. Meyer), Publishers, Belleville.
Bachmann, Jacob, Teacher, Mascoutah, 1860.
Baker, Martin D., States Attorney, Belleville.
Baltz, Anton, Farmer and Stockraiser, S. 12, T. Sugar Loaf, P. O. Columbia, 1872.
Baltz, F. L., Mayor and Supt. Millstadt Milling Co., Millstadt.
Baltz, F., Farmer, Mill Owner and Director St. Clair County Farmers' Mutual Fire Insurance Co., S. 7, T. Millstadt, P. O. Millstadt.
Baltz, W. N., Farmer and Supervisor, Millstadt.
Barbier, Edward, Farmer, S.15, T.Centerville station, P.O. EastSt.Louis, 1883
Barnard, H. L., Supt. Terminals L. E. & St. L. R. R., East St. Louis.
Barthel, August, Attorney at Law, Belleville, 1861.
Bartholomew, T. W., Attorney at Law, East St. Louis, 1890.
Beatty, James H., Engineer, Mascoutah
Becherer, Frank, Farmer, S. 16, T. Lebanon, P. O. Lebanon, 1855.
Becker, Rev. P. J., Rector St. Agatha Church, New Athens, 1896.
Becker, Wm., Farmer, Sur. 359, T. Sugar Loaf, P. O. East Carondolet, 1879.
Beckwith, Walter E. & Bro. (Walter E. Beckwith and Arthur M. Beckwith), Real Estate and Insurance, East St. Louis, 1881.
Begole, Hon. H. C., State Senator, Belleville.
Begole, C. S., Farmer, S. 22, T. Caseyville, P. O. O'Fallon.
Beerens, Clarissa, Farming, S. 27, T. O'Fallon, P. O. O'Fallon.
Belleville Advocate Printing Co. (J. F. Wassell, Pres.; J. A. Willoughby, Secy.), Publishers, Belleville.
Belleville Pump and Skein Works, Belleville.
Belleville Savings Bank, Belleville.
Belleville: St. Clair County Farmers' Mutual Fire Insurance Co.; George Schuerger, Pres.; Sophia E. Tindale, Secy.
Benner & Brichler, Livery and Undertaking, East St. Louis.
Berger, Adolph, Physician, Lebanon, 1850.
Bergmann, Ed., Farmer, S. 33, T. Caseyville, P. O. Caseyville.
Bergmann, F. H., Farmer, S. 28, T. Caseyville, P. O. Caseyville.
Bergman, F. H., Priest, Smithton, 1899.
Bergmann, Henry, Farmer, S. 16, T. Caseyville, P. O. Caseyville.
Bietel, Jos. E., Farmer, S. 34, T. St. Clair, P. O. Belleville, 1861.
Bitzer, C. H., Farmer, S. 6, T. Lebanon, P. O Lebanon, 1873.
Blum, Emil, Farmer and Stockraiser, S. 33, T. Mascoutah, P. O. Mascoutah, 1856.
Blum, Fred, Farmer and Stockraiser, S. 33, T. Mascoutah, P. O. Mascoutah, 1855.
Bodenberg Produce and Commission Co., East St. Louis.
Borders, M. W., Attorney at Law, Belleville.
Borders, W. E., Coal Operator, Marissa.
Bornman, L. C., Farmer, S. 28, T. St. Clair, P. O. Belleville, 1836.
Boyle, S. S., Merchant, Marissa.
Bowman, Frank B., Real Estate, East St. Louis.
Boyne, Geo. A., Justice of the Peace, East St Louis, 1860.
Brand, John J., Farmer, S. 23, T. Lebanon, P. O. Summerfield, 1865.
Brandenburger, F., Coal Operator, Belleville.
Brede, George, Farmer and Stockraiser, S. 11, T. Mascoutah, P. O. New Baden, 1836.
Brefeld, Rev. A., Rector St. Libory Church, St. Libory, 1879.
Brenner, Wm., Sr., Carpenter and Builder, S. 34, T. Smithton, 1846.
Brichler, John M., Farmer, S. 9, T. St. Clair; P. O. Belleville, 1865.
Brinkmann, J. H., Wines and Liquors, East Carondolet, 1880.
Brieinlinger, Rev. A., Priest, Millstadt, 1890.
Brown, Wm. R., Jr., Insurance and Real Estate, East St. Louis, 1901.
Burgard, Conrad, Justice of the Peace, Farmer and Veterinary Surgeon, S. 11, T. Fayetteville, P. O. St. Libory, 1848
Burr, J. C., Farmer, S. 27, T. Lenzburg, P. O. Baldwin.
Buescher, Prof H. Anton, Teacher and Farmer, S. 11, T. Fayetteville, P. O. St. Libory, 1883.

Campbell, J. M., Physician, Marissa.
Campbell, S. W., Farmer, S. 27, T. Marissa, P. O. Marissa, 1878.
Canning, Daniel, Farmer, S. 25, T. Marissa, P. O. Marissa
Canavan, Thomas J., Wines, Liquors, Cigars, etc., East St. Louis, 1866.
Carr, A. M. Town Clerk and Farmer, S. 35, T. Smithton, P.O. Smithton, 1861.
Carroll, C. B. Lawyer, East St. Louis, 1871.
Carroll & Mumme (C. B. Carroll and Jno. L. Mumme), Attorneys and Collecting Agents, East St. Louis.
Casperson, Wm., Supervisor and Cigar Manufacturer, Lenzburg.
Chamberlin, C. E., Attorney at Law and Supervisor, Lebanon, 1874.
Chamberlin, J. M., Editor "Lebanon Leader," Lebanon, 1872.
Chapin, S. P., Real Estate, East St. Louis, 1886.
Chenot, Augustus, Farmer, S. 24, T. St. Clair, P. O. Belleville.
Church, O. C., Teacher, S. 1, T. Millstadt, P. O. Belleville.
Cohen, L. B., Physician and Supt. G. S. S. & A. Association, East St. Louis, 1901.
Consolidated Coal Co., Coal Operators, Belleville.
Coulter, R. S., Publisher "Marissa Messenger," Marissa.

Danner, Alex., Wholesale and Retail Dairy Goods, East St. Louis, 1889.
Dare, J. James, Farmer, S. 6, T. Marissa, P. O. Lenzburg, 1844.
Darrow, Wm. A., Farmer, S. 27, T. O Fallon, P. O. O Fallon, 1837.
Davinroy, Felix, Farmer, S. 25, T. Centerville, P. O. French Village, 1843.
Day, John A., President St. Louis & Belleville Traction Co., Belleville, 1881.
Decker, Henry J., Hotel and Livery, Mascoutah, 1846.
Dohn, Louis, Township Clerk and Meat Market, Millstadt.
Demarse, John, Farmer, Sur.109, T.Centervillestation, P.O. EastSt Louis, 1852
Detharding, Geo. W., Public Administrator, Belleville, 1856.
Deutschmann, Henry, Saw Mill, Lenzburg.
Diehl, George, Proprietor Hotel Diehl, East St Louis, 1888.
Diesel, A. C., Farmer, S. 4, T. Millstadt, P. O. Millstadt.
Dickhaut, George, Farmer and Stockraiser, S. 9, T. Engelmann, P. O. Mascoutah, 1852.
Dickhaut, Gustav, Farmer and Stockraiser, S. 4, T. Engelmann, P. O. Mascoutah, 1864.
Dill, J. M., Attorney at Law, Belleville.
Dintelmann, Conrad, Farmer, S. 7, T. New Athens, P. O. New Athens, 1854.
Dintelmann, L. F., Nurseryman and Town Clerk, S. 33, T. St. Clair, P. O. Belleville, 1861.
Doerr, George, Farmer and Commissioner, S. 26, T. Sugar Loaf, P. O. Imbs, 1851.
Donovan Guignon Land Title Co., Abstracts and Loans, Belleville.
Dornhoff, John F., Undertaking and Livery, East St. Louis, 1893.
Draser, George, Jr., Lumber, Mascoutah, 1865
Dressler, Benj., Hotel "Okaw" and Saloon, Fayetteville, 1860.
Droit, C. W., Farmer and Nurseryman, East St. Louis, 1853.
Drummond, H. J., Supervisor and Insurance, East St. Louis, 1855.
Drury, John H., Ice and Coal, East St. Louis, 1865.
Dryer, Louis, Farmer and Stockraiser, S. 27, T. Sugar Loaf, P. O. Columbia, 1865.
Dunnavan, J. A., Farmer, S. 22, T. O'Fallon, P. O. O'Fallon, 1870.

East St. Louis Lumber Co.; M. C. Reis, Manager; Lumber, East St. Louis.
East St. Louis Stone Co., Stone, Brick, Cement, etc., East St. Louis.
Ebert, Wm. H., Farmer, S. 23, T. Caseyville, P. O. O Fallon, 1893.
Eckert, Charles, Jr., Farmer, S. 23, T. Millstadt, P. O. Millstadt.
Eggman, Horace J., Real Estate, Insurance, etc., East St. Louis.
Eggmann, E. J. & E. W., Lawyers, East St. Louis.
Eidmann, L. F., Farmer, S. 18, T. Engelmann, P. O. Mascoutah, 1847.
Elliott Frog & Switch Co., Manufacturers, East St. Louis.
Emg, Frank, Farmer, Z. 11, T. Stookey, P. O. Belleville, 1867.
Engea, Jos. J., Farmer, Sur. 359, T. Sugar Loaf, P. O. East Carondolet, 1876.
Engler, M. T., Farmer, S. 8, T. Millstadt, P. O. Millstadt.
Engelmann, W. B., Farmer and Town Clerk, S. 20, T. Engelmann, P. O. Mascoutah, 1847.
Enterprise Printing Co., Publishers, Millstadt
Euler, Andrew, Farmer, S. 33, T. Prairie du Long, P. O. Hecker, 1845.
Euler, John, Farmer, S. 18, T. Prairie du Long, P. O. Paderborn, 1855.
Eyman, Walter, Farmer, S. 36, T. Stookey, P. O. Belleville.

Feig, George, Farmer, S. 14, T. Caseyville, P. O. Collinsville.
Fekete Thos. L., Real Estate, Loans, Insurance, etc., East St. Louis.
Ferber, F., Priest, Paderborn, 1898.
Feurer, Martin, Farmer and Road Commissioner, S. 15, T. New Athens, P. O. New Athens, 1849.
Flannigen, Alex., Attorney, East St. Louis, 1871.
Fietsam, Chas. H., Farmer, Justice of the Peace and Director Farmers' Mutual Fire Insurance Co., S. 2, T. New Athens, P. O. Fayetteville, 1850.
Fink, Henry J., Insurance, Belleville, 1860.
Fink & Steinman (Henry J. Fink and E. W. Steinman), Real Estate and Loans, East St. Louis.
First National Bank, East St. Louis.
First National Bank, Belleville.
Fischer, Fred, Farmer, S. 9, T. New Athens, P. O. New Athens, 1877.
Fredericks, H. J., Mayor' Belleville.
Freisz, G. P., Farmer and Stockraiser, S. 15, T. Mascoutah, P. O. Mascoutah, 1872.
Friess, Phillip P., Farmer, S. 22, T. Shiloh Hill, P. O Belleville, 1863.
Freiss, Henry G., Farmer, S. 11, T. Freeburg, P. O. Mascoutah, 1867.
Frey, German, Commissioner, S. 4, T Mascoutah, P. O. Lebanon, 1872.
Fries, Adam, Farmer, Assessor and Creamery Operator, S. 12, T. Engelmann, P. O Mascoutah, 1862.
Foeller, Jos. P., Principal Belleville Commercial College, Bellville, 1858.
Fournie, Victor, Farmer, S. 9, T. St. Clair, P. O. Belleville, 1843.
Forman & Browning, Attorneys, East St. Louis.
Fox, Elmore, Postmaster, Sur. 113, T.Centerville, P.O.Centerville station, 1894
Fox, Frank P. & Co., Publishers "Daily Journal," East St. Louis.
Fuess-Fisher Co. (W. J. Fischer, Secy. and Treas; Joseph Fuess, Pres.), Dry Goods, Carpets, etc., Belleville.
Fuchs, A. J., Physician and Surgeon, Mascoutah, 1875.

Galle, William, Farmer, S. 23, T. Marissa, P. O. Marissa.
Gaskill, Isaac, Teacher and Farmer, S. 34, T. Sugar Loaf, P. O. Columbia 1858.
Gauch, Henry, Farmer, S. 34, T. Shiloh Valley, P. O. Belleville, 1853.
Gauss, Victor, Merchant, Belleville.
Gauss, George, Merchant, Belleville.
Gausz, Henry, Retired Farmer, Mascoutah, 1844.
Geiger, Martin, General Merchandise, New Athens, 1870.
Gibbs, H. P., Publisher "O'Fallon Progress," O'Fallon, 1889.
Gintz, Adam, Retired, Belleville.
Gouin, Edmond' General Merchandise, and Liquors, East Carondolet, 1873.
Godin, Isaac, Merchandise and Liquors, East Carondolet, 1887.
Goedde, B. & Co (B. Goedde, Edmund Goedde and Chas. Goedde), Lumber, East St. Louis, 1858-66 74.
Gough, James M, Rector St. Lukes Church, Belleville.
Graner, Louis, County Surveyor, Belleville, 1853.
Grey & Heller (C. L. Grey, Pres. Southern Ill. Construction Co.; Geo. G. Heller, Pharmacist), East St. Louis, 1887-17.
Griffin, Arthur, Farmer, S. 25, T. Freeburg, P. O. Mascoutah, 1877.
Griffin, John, Farmer, S. 25, T. Freeburg, P. O. Mascoutah, 1837.
Griffin Chas., Farmer, S. 14, T. Shiloh Valley, P.O. Grassland, 1845.
Grimmer, P. P. Farmer and Stockraiser, S. 26, T. Mascoutah, P. O. Mascoutah, 1861.
Gruenewald, Jacob, Farmer, S. 5, T. Millstadt, P. O. Millstadt.
Gruenewald, John, Farmer, S. 5, T. Millstadt, P. O. Millstadt.
Gundlach, B. A., Prop. Vinegar Factory, Belleville, 1870.
Gundlach, P. M., Prop. Grain Drill Works, Belleville, 1842.
Gundlach, Jacob J., Farmer, S. 24, T. St. Clair, P. O. Belleville, 1866.
Gundlach, Jacob Jr., Farmer, S. 3, T. Smithson P. O. Belleville, 1854.
Gundlach, Nic., Farmer, Sur. 375-76, T. St. Clair, P. O. Belville, 1856.
Gutherz, Louis Farmer, S. 5, Millstadt, P. O. Millstadt, 1867.

Haas, J. H. A., Farmer, S. 33, T. St. Clair, P. O. Belleville, 1867.
Hacker, J. George, Farmer, S. 15, T. Marissa, P. O. Marissa.
Hagemann, Simon Farmer, S. 15, T. O'Fallon, P. O. O'Fallon, 1855.
Halbert, Wm. U., Attorney, Belleville, 1873.
Halstead, A. S., Dentist, Belleville, 1853.
Hamilton, J. A., Banker, Marissa.
Hankamer, Wm., Farmer, S. 4, T. Millstadt, P. O. Millstadt, 1872.
Harbaugh, J. B., Assessor, Farmer and Breeder Poland China Hogs, S. 28, T. Prairie du Long, P. O. Hecker, 1882.
Harkins, Rev. J. B., Pastor St. St. Mary's Church, East St. Louis, 1889.
Harper Bros. (L. L. Harper, City Engineer; E. F. Harper, C. E.), Civil Engineers, East St. Louis.
Harris & Smith (M. L. Harris and L. G. Smith), Real Estate, Loans, etc., East St. Louis.
Harrison Machine Works (Hugh W. Harrison, Pres.; Cyrus Thompson, Secy.), Manufacturers Threshing Machinery, Belleville.
Hartman & Sons, General Contractors, Grading, Excavating, Wrecking, etc., East St. Louis.
Hartman, B., President Star Brewery, Belleville.
Haupt, Peter, Pres. Business Men's Association and Secy. New Athens Milling Co., New Athens, 1858.
Hauft, Wm., Brick Mfg. and Notary Public, New Athens, 1854.
Haupt, Louis, Farmer, S. 35, T. New Athens, P. O New Athens, 1857.
Heberer, Henry, Farmer, St. 15, T Freeburg, P. O. Freeburg, 1834.
Heil, Valentine, Jr., Farmer, S. 22, T. Marissa, P. O. Marissa, 1860.
Heiligenstein, Chris, Miller and Supervisor, Freeburg.
Heiligenstein, F. X., Saloon and Boarding House, Freeburg.
Heim Brewery, Robert Bethmann, Manager, East St. Louis.
Heimberger, Hon. H. R., Attorney, Belleville, 1870.
Helm, E. G., Civil Engineer, East St. Louis, 1896.
Helms, F., Farmer, Sur. 382, T. Smithton, P. O. Belleville, 1853.
Henrich, W. P. (Ph. G., M. D.), Physician and Surgeon, Mascootah, 1870.
Herold, Hugo, Physician and Surgeon, Mascoutah, 1869.
Herr, Louis J., Farmer, S., Farmer, S. 24, T. St. Clair, P. O Belleville, 1854.
Herrmann, Jacob, Farmer, S. 12, T. Millstadt, P. O. Millstadt.
Hermann, Peter, Retired Farmer, S. 18, T. New Athens, P. O. New Athens, 1841.
Herman, Philip, Saw Mill, Threshing Machine Operator and Farmer, S. 7, T. New Athens, 1844.
Hertel, Chas., County Supt. of Schools, Belleville, 1874.
Hessick, Henry, Farmer, S. 34, T. New Athens, P. O. New Athens, 1858.
Hilgard, G. F., Deputy County Surveyor, Belleville, 1835.
Hill (W. H.) Lime and Cement Co., Coal, Lime, Cement, Builders' Material, etc.; W. H. Hill, Pres.; H. R. Thomas, V.-P.; H. M. Hill, Secy; East St. Louis 1871-81-85.
Hill, S. B., Farmer, S. 10, T. Lebanon, P. O. Summerfield, 1857.
Hill, Wm. H., Farmer and Dairy, S. 35, T. Smithton, P. O. Smithton, 1848.
Hill, Samuel, Farmer, S. 30, T. Freeburg, P. O. New Athens, 1836.
Hirsch, John, Jr., General Merchandise, Millstadt.
Hirst, Agnes, Farmer, S. 33, T. Prairie du Long, P. O. Hecker, 1885.
Hite, L. H., Lawyer, East St. Louis, 1859.
Hock, Frank, Farmer, S. 24, T. Millstadt, P. O. Millstadt.
Hofstetter, Adam, Farmer, Sur. 774, T. Centerville station, P.O. Imbs Station, 1862.
Holdener & Co., Livery, Belleville.
Hollows, John, Farmer, S. 10, T. Centerville station, P O. East St. Louis, 1855
Holzapfel, Henry, Farmer, S. 11, T. Freeburg, P. O. Belleville, 1859.

Horner, F. M., Supt. City Water Co., East St Louis, 1885
Horner, R. H., Attorney, Lebanon, 1858.
Huddle, J. B., Principal Caseyville schools, Caseyville.
Hueckel, Wm. H., Merchant, Caseyville.
Hueckel, John, Farmer, S. 9, T. Caseyville, P. O. Caseyville, 1860.
Hummel, Jos ; Farmer and Stockraiser, S. 36, T. Smithton, P. O. Freeburg, 1852.
Hummert, Bernard, Farmer and Director Farmers' Mutual Fire Insurance Co., S. 4, T. Fayetteville, P. O. St. Libory. 1870.

Idoux, Chas., Farmer, S. 14, T. Centerville station, P. O. East St. Louis, 1868.
Isch, J. P., Farmer, S. 12, T. St. Clair, P. O. Belleville, 1854.

Janssen, Rt. Rev. John, Bishop of Belleville, 1888.
Janssen, J. B., Farmer, S. 26, T. Freeburg, P. O. Fayetteville, 1866.
Jones, C. T., Manager National Stock Yards, East St. Louis.
Jones & Co., Paul, Real Estate and Loans, St. Louis Mo.
Joseph, Edw., Farmer, S. 16, T. New Athens, P. O. New Athens.
Joseph, L. G., Farmer, S. 17, T. New Athens, P. O. New Athens, 1860.
Joyce, M. V., Attorney at Law, East St. Louis.
Juenger, Conrad, Creamery and Justice of the Peace, Darmstadt, 1861.
Jung, Joseph, Farmer and Stockraiser, S. 29, T. Engelmann, P. O. Mascoutah, 1860.
Junk, Hermann, Farmer, S. 29, T. Lenzburg, P. O. New Athens.
Justus, Fred, Merchandise and Collector, Mascoutah, 1854.

Kaempfe, Gottfried, Farmer, Sur. 498, T. Centerville, P. O. Millstadt, 1853.
Kammann, E. C., Hardware, Stoves, Paints, Oils, Cutlery, Sporting Goods, etc., Mascoutah, 1872.
Karr Supply Co. (Adam Karr, Pres.; Theo. Karr, Treas.), Belleville.
Keating, Frank, Contractor, Paving, Granite Walks, etc., East St. Louis, 1878.
Keck, Christian H., Farmer, S. 9, T. Millstadt, P. O. Millstadt.
Keck, Fred, Farmer and Supervisor, S. 30, T. St. Clair, P. O. Belleville, 1854.
Keck, John F., Farmer, S. 3, T. Millstadt, P. O. Millstadt, 1859.
Keitel, Frederick, Farmer, S. 30, T. Lebanon, P. O. Lebanon, 1867.
Kern, A. C., Wines, Liquors and General Insurance, Millstadt.
Kern, Fred J., Publisher "News-Democrat," Belleville, 1864.
Kern, Oswall, Farmer and Stockraiser, Stockraiser, S. 15, T. Engelmann, P.O. Mascoutah 1863.
Kersey, Wm. M., Township Assessor, Caseyville, 1866.
Kiefer, Anthony, Farmer and Commissioner, S. 14, T. Centerville, P. O. French Village, 1861.
Kickham, John, Sheriff, Belleville, 1887.
Kircher, W. F., Secy Commercial Club, Belleville.
Kirchhoefer, Wendel, Farmer and Collector, S. 35, T. Lenzburg, P.O.Lenzburg
Kleinschmidt, Ferd, Farmer and Stockraiser, S. 1, T. Sugar Loaf, P. O. Columbia, 1861.
Kleinschmidt, Wm., Collector and Farmer, S. 36, T. Sugar Loaf, P. O. Columbia, 1854.
Klotz, Lewis, Farmer S. 8, T. Millstadt, P. O. Millstadt.
Knapp Bros. (Philip Knapp and Joseph Knapp), Jewelers end Music Dealers, Belleville.
Knobeloch, Adolph, Farmer, S. 29, T. Shiloh Valley, P. O. Belleville, 1861.
Kraft, S. W., Publisher "Tageblatt" and "Arbeiter Zeitung," Belleville, 1863.
Kramer, Creighton & Shaefer, Attorneys at Law, East St. Louis.
Krebs, Philip, Village Clerk, Marissa.
Kreig, Jacob, Farmer, S. 16, T. Freeburg, P. O. Freeburg, 1871.
Koenig, Chr., Pastor St. Henry's Catholic Church, East St. Louis, 1869.
Koenitz, Fred, Farmer, S. 15, T. Lenzburg, P. O. Lenzburg.
Koerber, Louis W., Farmer and Town Clerk, S. 21, T. Prairie du Long, P. O. Hecker, 1871.
Kolb, Philip, Coal Operator, Mascoutah, 1848.
Koesterer, Louis, Sr., Farmer, S. 17, T. Freeburg, P. O. Freeburg, 1853.
Koesterer, Jacob, Farmer, S. 19, T. Freeburg, P. O. Freeburg, 1848
Kombrink, John, Farmer, S. 15, T. Caseyville, P. O. Caseyville, 1872.
Kreamer, John N., Physician and Surgeon, Lenzburg.
Kuhlman, Deidrick, Farmer, S. 32, T. Caseyville, P. O. Caseyville.
Kunze, Gustave, Farmer, Sur. 380, T. St. Clair, P. O. Belleville, 1851.
Kunze, Gustave, Jr., Farmer, S. 7, T. Mascoutah, 1886.
Kunze, Fred A., Farmer, S. 36, T. Freeburg, P. O. Fayetteville, 1847.
Kunze, G. W., Farmer, Marissa.
Kunze, F. E., Farmer, S. 16, T. Marissa, P. O. Marissa.
Kurrus, Joseph A., Livery and Undertaker, East St. Louis, 1861.

Lanter, Dominick, Farmer, Sur. 387, T. New Athens, P. O. Freeburg, 1853.
Lange, Henry, Farmer, S. 24, T. Fayetteville, P. O. St. Libory, 1871.
Latinette, E., Farmer, Sur. 128, T. Centerville station, P. O. Centerville station, 1856
Leopold, Joseph, & Bro., Wholesale Liquor Dealers, Belleville.
Liebig, Henry V., Farmer, Supervisor, Saw Mill and Threshing Machine Operator, S. 13, T. Engelmann, P. O. Mascoutah, 1865.
Liebig, John H., Collector and Farmer, S. 12, T. Engelmann, P. O. Mascoutah, 18 5.
Lienesch, G. W., Farmer, S. 6, T. Shiloh Valley, P. O. O'Fallon, 1864,
Lischer, C. J., Publisher, Mascoutah, 1856.
Lischer, Geo. W., Contractor and Dealer in Lime, Cement, Sand, etc., Mascoutah, 1867.
Little, E. H. and H. M., Physicians and Surgeons, East St. Louis.
Lorenzen, The Grocery Co., Merchants, Belleville.
Lortz, John, Farmer, S. 4, T. New Athens, P. O. Freeburg, 1839.
Lyons, W. M. K., Lumber, Marissa.
Malter, Geo. J., Farmer, S. 10, T. Caseyville, P. O. Collinsville.
Mann, John, Jr., Farmer and Stockraiser, S. 32, T. Mascoutah, P. O. Mascoutah, 1870.
Montag, Carl, Publisher, Mascoutah.
Marlin, Louis, Farmer, Sur.725, T.Centerville station, P.O. East St.Louis, 1875
Mascoutah Brewing Co., Brewery, Mascoutah.
May, Thomas, Jr., Circuit Clerk, Belleville, 1869.
Mayer, Prof. Nicholas, Teacher and Organist, St. Libory, 1879.
Mayo, S. (F. P. Brigham, Manager), Lumber and Builders' Supplies, East St. Louis.
McCasland, C. O., Real Estate, Insurance, Loans, etc., East St. Louis.
McCracken, R. X., Physician and Surgeon, East St. Louis, 1864
McIntyre, Thos. N., Farmer and Road Commissioner, S. 35, T. Marissa, P. O. Marissa.
McFerron, Wm. R., Farmer, S. 1, T. Lenzburg, P. O. Lenzburg.
McKindley, H. F., Farmer, Sur. 359, T. Sugar Loaf, P. O. East Carondolet, 1842.
McSweeney, Rev. Charles. Pastor St. Patrick's Church, East St. Louis, 1899.
Meek, A. J., Merchant Miller (Meek Milling Co.), Marissa.
Meckfessel, Fred., Farmer, S. 7, T. O'Fallon, P. O. O'Fallon, 1866.
Meckfessel, Wm., Farmer, S. 29, T. Caseyville, P. O. Caseyville.
Meifus, Rev. J. F., Priest, Sur. 105, T.Centerville station, P.O. Centerville station, 1883.
Merrills, Fred B., Attorney at Law, Belleville.
Metze, Valentine, Farmer and School Treasurer, S. 32, T. Prairie du Long, P. O. Hecker, 1869.
Metzen, John P., Real Estate ond Loans, East St. Louis, 1879.
Metzger, John, Farmer and Stockraiser, S. 26, T. Sugar Loaf, P. O. Imbs Station, 1854.
Metzler, A. O., Farmer, S. 35, T. Millstadt, P. O. Millstadt.
Meyer, Joseph, Farmer, S. 3, T. Mascoutah, P. O. Mascoutah, 1866.
Miller, A. A., Farmer, S. 29, T. Smithton, P. O. Smithton, 1859.
Miller, August F., Insurance, Belleville.
Miller, Chas. M., Farmer, S. 36, T. Prairie du Long, P. O. Hecker, 1859.
Miller, D. F., Farmer, S. 18, T. Shiloh Valley, P. O. Belleville, 1844.
Miller, H. W., Farmer and Threshing Machine Operator, S. 30, T. Prairie du Long, P. O. Hecker, 1869.
Miller, L. T. Physician and Farmer, Caseyville, 1855.
Miller, Louis G., Farmer and Supervisor, S. 32, T. Prairie du Long, P. O. Hecker, 1856.
Miller, J. O., Attorney at Law, Belleville, 1861.
Miller, Jacob L., Farmer, S. 17, T. Millstadt, P. O. Millstadt.
Miller, Philip L., Farmer, S. 17, T. Millstadt, P. O. Millstadt.
Miller, Peter, Farmer and Stockraiser, Sur. 389, T.Freeburg, P.O. Belleville, 1840.
Miller, Wm. J., Farmer, Sur. 389, T. Smithton, P. O. Belleville.
Milleson, C. D. & Co., Wholesale and Retail Hay, Grain and Coal, East St. Louis.
Mindermann, Chas., Postmaster and Merchant, East Carondolet, 1882.
Mitchell, James, Farmer, S. 12, T. Stookey, P. O. Belleville, 1849.
Moser & Karch, Attorneys, Belleville.
Moll, A. D., Farmer and Dairyman, S. 29, T. Mascoutah, P. O. Mascoutah, 1870.
Moll, Mary T., Mascoutah, 1849.

Mollman, A. J., Publisher, Mascoutah, 1874.
Monroe, Robert, Assessor, East St. Louis, 1890.
Morton, S. H. & Co., Real Estate, Lincoln Trust Bld., St. Louis, Mo.
Moser, J. W., Farmer and Engineer, S. 29, T. Shiloh Valley, P. O. Rentchler Station, 1863.
Mueller, Anton J., Farmer, S. 25, T. St. Clair, P. O. Belleville, 1864.
Mueller, B. A., Architect, East St. Louis, 1891.
Mueller, Friedrich L., Farmer and Stockraiser, S. 24, T. Sugar Loaf, P. O. Columbia, 1844.
Mueller, George, Farmer, S. 23, T. Freeburg, P. O. Freeburg, 1855.
Mueller, George A., Farmer, S. 8, T. Millstadt, P. O. Millstadt.
Mueller, George C., Farmer, S. 14, T. Freeburg, P. O. Freeburg, 1865.
Mueller, Henry, Farmer, S. 23, T. Freeburg, P. O. Freeburg, 1860.
Mueller, John, Farmer, S. 13, T. Millstadt, P. O. Belleville.
Mueller, Konrad, Groceries, Wines and Liquors, and Creamery, New Athens, 1878.
Mueller, Nicholas, Farmer, S. 24, T. Marissa, P. O. Marissa.
Mueller, Solomon, Retired Farmer, Belleville.
Mueller, Wm., Farmer and Stockraiser, S. 14, T. Sugar Loaf, P. O. Columbia, 1838.
Mulkey & McHale (W. C. Mulkey and J. G. McHale), Attorneys, East St. Louis, 1898-95.
Murphy, J. F., Publisher East St. Louis "Republican." East St. Louis
Muskopf, Geo. J., Farmer, S. 32, T. St. Clair, P. O. Belleville, 1890.
Needles, H. M., Real Estate, Belleville, 1863.
Newman & Probst, Stave Mill, New Athens.
Niebruegge, Henry, Farmer and Supervisor, S. 23, T. Caseyville, P. O. O'Fallon.
Niebrugge, Frank, Farmer S. 22, T.Caseyville, P.O.Caseyville, P.O.Caseyville
Niemeyer & Harris (Arthur Niemeyer and M. L. Harris), Real Estate, East St. Louis, 1866-97.
Niederer, John, Dairyman and Creamery Operator, S. 9, T. Centerville, P. O. East St. Louis.
Nichols, J. J., Farmsr and Road Commissioner, S. 4, T. Caseyville, P. O. Caseyville, 1868.
Noble, Louis, Farmer and Gardener, East Carondolet, 1856.

Oberberbeck, Fred, Foundry, New Athens, 1872.
Oberniefermann, Henry, Farmer, S. 13, T. Caseyville, P. O. O'Fallon.
Ochs, Randolph, Farmer and Highway Commissioner, S. 34, T.O'Fallon, P.O. O'Fallon, 1847.
Ogle, E. B., Farmer, S. 1, T. Stookey, P. O. Belleville, 1854.
Orth, Phillip, Hotel, Marissa.
Otten, Hermann, Postmaster and Prop. Green Tree Hotel, St. Libory, 1857.

Parker, James, Farmer, S. 33, T. Prairie du Long, P. O. Hecker, 1856.
Patterson, H. E., Farmer, S. 22, T. O'Fallon, P. O. O'Fallon.
Pellitier, B. E., Assessor, French Village, 1865.
Penn, John, Landowner, Belleville.
Perrin, Frank, County Judge, Belleville, 1858.
Perrin, J. N., Lecturer (Lyceum Bureau), Lebanon, 1855.
Perrottet, Louis, Farmer, S. 27, T. Shiloh Valley, P. O. Belleville, 1854.
Peter, C. E., Farmer, S. 17, T. Millstadt, P. O. Millstadt.
Pfeiffenberger, L. & Son, Architects, East St. Louis, 1890.
Pfeiffer Anthony, Farmer, S. 36, T. Caseyville, P. O. O'Fallon, 1872.
Pfeifer, Geo. C., Merchant and Assessor, Mascoutah, 1869.
Pieke, Rev. Anton, Priest, Mascoutah.
Pitzman, J., Real Estate, St. Louis, Mo.
Postel, Philip H., Merchant Miller, Mascoutah.
Priester, Frank M., Prop. Priester Park and Kneipp Sanitarium, Belleville.
Rausch, Adolph, Farmer, S. 33, T. Prairie du Long, P. O. Hecker, 1900.
Repham, Geo. C., Attorney, Belleville, 1870
Reibold, John, Farmer, S. 32, T. Lebanon, P. O. Lebanon, 1852.
Reheis, George, Farmer and Saw Mill Operator, S. 31, T. Prairie du Long, P. O. Hecker, 1887.
Reimann, Jacob; Farmer, S. 19, T. Lebanon, P. O. Lebanon, 1849.
Reinhardt, Ferd, Farmer, Dairyman and Creamery Operator, S. 32, T. Mascoutah, P. O. Mascoutah, 1842.
Reinhardt, Geo. S., Farmer, S. 8, T. Lenzburg, P. O. New Athens.
Reinhardt, Julius, Farmer, S. 27, T. Freeburg, P. O. Freeburg, 1855.
Reis, M. & H., Lumber Dealers, Belleville, 1862-66.
Reis, Val & Sons, Planing Mill, Lumber and Contractors, Belleville.
Reiss, W. A., Civil Engineer, Belleville, 1853.
Reiss, F. J., Farmer, S. 7, T. Prairie du Long, P. O. Floraville, 1841.
Renshaw, J. W. & Sons, Real Estate, Insurance, etc., East St. Louis.
Renth, William, Farmer and Stockraiser, S. 13, T. Mascoutah, P. O. New Baden, 1865.
Rentchler, H. L., Plumbing and Electrical Contracting, Belleville, 1869
Reuss, F. L., Farmer, S. 4, T. Shiloh Valley, P. O. Shiloh, 1862.
Rhein, Charlotte, Farmer, S. 4, T. Smithton, P. O. Belleville.
Rhein, Louis, Farmer, S. 4, T. Smithton, P. O. Belleville.
Rhein, Fred, Farmer, S. 4, T. Smithton, P. O. Belleville, 1870.
Rich, James P. & Son (James P. Rich and W. J. P. Rich), Real Estate, Loans and Insurance, Belleville, 1856-78.
Richardson, R. A., Real Estate and Capitalist, East St. Louis, 1900.
Rieder & Rieder (Jos. Rieder and Frank Rieder), Farmers, S. 35, T. O'Fallon, P.O. O'Fallon, 1863-67.
Richter, Charles, Farmer and Stockraiser, S. 14, T. Mascoutah, P. O. New Baden, 1852.
Richter, George, Farmer and Stockraiser, S. 14, T. Mascoutah, P. O. New Baden, 1855.
Richter, Louis E., Farmer and Supervisor, S. 29, T. Mascoutah, P. O. Mascoutah, 1849.
Richter, Philip, Farmer, S. 28, T. Mascoutah, P. O. Mascoutah, 1859.
Robertson, Nathan, Farmer, S. 3, T. Prairie du Long, P. O. Smithton, 1835.
Robertson, Deborah, S. 3, T. Prairie du Long, P. O. Smithton.
Roedler, Balthaser, Farmer and Stockraiser, S. 1, T. Mascoutah, P. O. Trenton, 1868.
Roedler, J. B., Farmer and Stockraiser, S. 1, T. Mascouta, P. O. Trenton, 1864.
Rodenberg, Hon. W. A., Civil Service Commissioner and Attorney, East St. Louis, 1877.
Romeiser, Clothing Co., Clothing, Furnishings, etc., Belleville, 1873.
Ropiequet, R. W., Attorney, Belleville, 1866.
Rose, F., Physician, Millstadt, 1893.
Roth, C. H., Farmer, S. 11, T. Freeburg, P. O. Mascoutah, 1870.
Roth, Henry, Farmer and Stockraiser, S. 11, T. Freeburg, P. O. Mascoutah, 1840.
Rueter, John, Farmer and School Treasurer, S. 14, T. Fayetteville, P. O. St. Libory, 1865.
Ruhl, John, Farmer, S. 10, T. Sugar Loaf, P. O. Columbia, 1842.
Rutter Bros. (Bernard Rutter and George Rutter), General Merchandise, St. Libory, 1849.
Ruth, Mary E., Farmer, S. 26, T. Lebanon, P. O. Trenton, 1855.
Rutledge (Wm. A.) Realty Co., Real Estate, Loans, etc., 1005 Chestnut St., St. Louis, Mo.

Sauter, Philip H., Farmer, Mascoutah, 1865.
Santhoff, Geo., Farm Implements and Blacksmithing, Millstadt.
Schaer, Carl, Dentist, Mascoutah, 1900.
Schaefer, Fred. Farmer, S. 1, T. O'Fallon, P. O. Lebanon, 1866.
Schafer, Chas. D., Butcher, O'Fallon.
Schaller, John, Farmer, S. 14, T. Lenzburg, P. O. Lenzburg, 1844.
Schatte, Wm., Farmer, Sur. 388, T. New Athens, P. O. New Athens, 1863.
Scherrer & Son, Real Estate, Insurance, etc., East St. Louis.
Schlensker, H. C., Broom Manufacturer, East St. Louis, 1878.
Schlottmann, Rev. J. B., Rector St. Augustine's Church, Hecker
Schmisseur, Eugene, Farmer, Sur. 381, T. Smithton, P. O. Belleville, 1848.
Schmisseurs, L., Farmer, S. 12, T. St. Clair, P. O. Belleville, 1854.
Schnur, Philip, Farmer and Stockraiser, S. 11, T. Engelmann, P. O. New Memphis, 1895.
Schoepp, Leonard, Agricultural Implements, Buggies, Wagons, etc., Mascoutah, 1867.
Schott, C. J. R., Farmer, S. 5, T. Shiloh Valley, P. O. Shiloh, 1835.
Scuubkegal, Emil R., Contractor, Mascoutah, 1865.
Schumacher, Louis, Farmer, S. 25, T. Lebanon, P. O. Trenton, 1898.
Schuetze, Edward C., Insurance, East St. Louis.
SSchwebel, Henry, Farmer, S. 30, T. New Athens, P. O. New Athens, 1851.
Schwinn, Fred A., Farmer, S. 11, T. Stookey, P. O. Belleville, 1852.
Scott & Faulkner (J. C. Scott and John J. Faulkner) Publishers' Agents, East St. Louis, 1900-1898.
Scott, S. W., Farmer, S. 28, T. Caseyville, P. O. O'Fallon.
Scottt, W. S., Farmer, S. 32, T. O'Fallon, P. O. O'Fallon, 1836.
Seewald, J. P., Farmer and Stockraiser, S. 3, T Mascoutah, P. O. Trenton, 1840.

Seibert, Adam, Farmer, S. 30, T. Shiloh Valley, P. O. Belleville, 1839.
Siebert, Ewald H. Farmer, S. 27, T. Shiloh Valley, P.O. Belleville, 1846.
Seibert, Charles, Farmer. S. 34, T. Shiloh Valley, P. O. Rentchler, 1851.
Seibert, Hon. Peter, Farmer and Stockraiser, S. 30, T. Engelmann, P. O. Fayetteville, 1852.
Seiter, H. & Co., Real Estate and Loans, East St. Louis, 1845.
Seitz, Jacob, Farmer and Stockraiser, S. 22, T. Englemann, P. O. Mascoutah, 1880.
Semmelroth, H., Publisher "Post Zeitung," Belleville, 1875.
Serth, Henry, Grain Dealer, Lenzburg.
Sewald, Philip, Farmer, S. 33, T. Lebanon, P. O. Lebanon, 1853.
Sexton, H. D. & Bro. (H. D. Sexton and S. D. Sexton), Real Estate, Loans, etc., East St. Louis.
Seifert, Wm. E. & Bro. (Wm. E. Seifert and Emil A. Seifert), Real Estate, Loans, etc., East St. Louis.
Siekmann, Theresa, Farmer, S. 26, T. Centerville, P.O. French Village, 1857.
Sheets, Louis, Farmer and Supervisor, S. 17, T. New Athens, P. O. New Athens, 1859.
Skaer, Charles, Farmer, Sur. 607, T. Prairie du Long, P. O. New Athens, 1862.
Skaer, Louis, Farmer, S. 32, T. Prairie du Long, P. O. Hecker, 1870.
Skaer, Philip, Jr., Farmer, S. 10, Prairie du Long, P. Smithton, 1861.
Skaer, Wesley, Farmer, S. 4, T. Prairie du Long, P. O. Smithton, 1853.
Smiley, Hon. S. C., Retired Capitalist, O'Fallon.
Smith, Leon G., Real Estate, Loans and Insurance, East St. Louis, 1875.
Snyder, L. P., Farmer, S. 30, T. St. Clair, P. O. Belleville, 1848.
Soucy, P. J., Real Estate, Insurance, etc., East St. Louis.
Southern Illinois National Bank, General Banking, East St. Louis.
Spitznass, Herman, Farmer, S. 6, T. Freeburg, P. O. Belleville, 1850.
Stannus, E. J., Real Estate, Belleville, 1898.
Stapf, Louis, Farmer, S. 2, T. Freeburg, P. O. Muscoutah, 1865.
Stapf, Geo., Farmer, S. 2, T. Freeburg, P. O. Muscoutah, 1871.
Star Brewery Co., Belleville.
Stanfenbiel, Frederich J., Librarian, Belleville.
Stein, Louis, Farmer and Stockraiser, S. 22, T. Mascoutah, P. O. Mascoutah, 1850.
Steger, Fred J., Real Estate, Loans, etc., East St. Louis, 1881.
Stephens, M. M., Mayor East St. Louis.
Stock, Chas., Town Clerk, Mascoutah, 1854.
Stoffel, J. W., Hardware, Stoves, Tinware, etc., Mascoutah, 1858.
Stookey, Charles A., Contractor, Belleville.
Stookey, M. M., Farmer, S. 32, T. St. Clair, P. O. Belleville, 1839.
Stuntz, Geo. O., County Recorder, Belleville.
Suemnicht, Herman, Farmer, S. 11, T. New Athens, P. O. Freeburg, 1859.
Suemnicht, Gustav, Farmer and Fruit Grower, S. 2, T. New Athens, P. O. Freeburg, 1860.
Suessmann, Jos., Farmer, S. 21, T. Centerville, P. O. East St. Louis, 1870.
Suever, Frank, Farmer, S. 28, T. Caseyville, P. O. Ridge Prairie.
Swarz, A. H., Prop. Thomas House, Belleville, 1870.

Tegtmeier, H., Merchant Tailor, Millstadt.
Thielemann, F. Justice of the Peace, East Carondolet, 1855.
Thomas, Fay F., Assessor, S. 35, T. Sugar Loaf, P. O. Columbia, 1870.
Thomas Ice & Coal Co., Ice, Coal, Feed, Grain, etc., East St. Louis.
Thomas, John E., Postmaster, Belleville.
Thomas, C. W., Attorney; Belleville, 1844.
Thomas, Edward L., Capitalist, Belleville.
Thompson, H., Farmer, Sur. 583, T. Caseyville, P. O. Collinsville.
Tiedemann, E., Merchant, O'Fallon, 1850.
Tiedemann, Charles, Milling Co. (Jennie Tiedemann, Pres.; C. E. Tiede-Tiedemann, V.-P.; Geo. W. Tiedemann, Treas.; L. F. Fischer, Secy. and Manager), Merchant Millers, O'Fallon.
Toupnot, August, Farmer, Sur. 99, T. Centerville station, P. O. Centerville station, 1848.
Trautmann, Hon. W. E., Attorney at Law, East St. Louis.
Turner, Young, Farmer, S. 26, T. O'Fallon, P. O. Lebanon, 1865.
Turner & Holder, Attorneys, Belleville.

Valerius, Jacob, Farmer, S. 7, T. Smithton, P. O. Belleville, 1867.
Vahlkamp, Stephen, Farmer and Stockraiser, and Breeder of Registered Short Horn Cattle, Fayetteville, 1848.
Van Hoorebeke & Louden, Attorneys, East St. Louis.
Van Riper, J. C., Manager Southern Illinois Loan & Trust Co., East St. Louis, 1901.
Voellinger, Adam, Farmer, S 23, T. Stookey, P. O. Belleville, 1849.
Voellinger Jacob, Farmer, S. 24, T. Stookey, P. O. Belleville, 1847.
Voellinger, Peter, Farmer, S. 19, T. St. Clair, P. O. Belleville, 1854.
Voellinger, Michael, Farmer, S. 1, T. St. Clair, P. O. Belleville, 1856.
Vonnahme, Joseph, Staple and Fancy Groceries, East St. Louis, 1872.
Wallace, J. A., Livery, Lebanon, 1866.
Walrath, Charles L. & Co.; Real Estate and Insurance, East St. Louis, 1880.
Webb & Webb, Attorneys, Belleville, 1895.
Wegmann, Rev. A., Priest, French Village, 1894.
Weil, Adolph, Farmer, S. 34, T. O'Fallon, P. O. O'Fallon, 1860.
Weil, Otto, Farm Implements, Wagons, Buggies, etc., Mascoutah, 1858.
Weilbacher, Henry, Farmer, S. 11, T. Sugar Loaf, P. O. Columbia, 1848.
Weiss, Edward, Farmer, S. 35, T. Freeburg, P. O. Freeburg, 1866.
Weiss, Wm., Farmer, S. 3, T. Freeburg, P. O. Freeburg, 1869.
West, E. W., Jr., Real Estate, Belleville.
Wehrle, J., Jeweler, Belleville.
Weigand Bros., Publishers "The New Athens Journal," New Athens.
Wiesenborn, H. F., Teacher, S. 6, T. Millstadt, P. O. Millstadt.
Wiggins Ferry Co., Ferry and Transportation East St. Louis
Willard, W. G., Manufacturer of Ranges, O'Fallon.
Wilderman, J. L., Farmer and Stockraiser, Sur. 772, T. Freeburg, P. O. Freeburg, 1863.
Wilderman, J. T., Farmer, S. 31, T. Freeburg, P. O. Freeburg, 1864.
Williams, H. E., Livery, Belleville, 1845.
Wilson, J. R., Real Estate and Loans, East St. Louis, 1900.
Winkelmann, Wm., Attorney, Belleville, 1862.
Winter, Geo. H., Farmer and Assessor, S. 20, T. New Athens, P. O. New Athens, 1867.
Wise & McNulty, Attorneys, 20 North Main St., East St. Louis.
Wittmer, Henry, Farmer, S. 26, T. Lebanon, P. O. Summerfield, 1859.
Wombacher, G. F., Attorney, Mascoutah, 1869.
Woods, H. F., Librarian, Public Library, East St. Louis.
Wuest, Michael. Farmer, Sur. 115, T. Centerville station, P. O. Centerville station, 1870.
Zeller, Valentine. Farmer and Stockraiser, S. 14, T. Sugar Loaf, P.O. Columbia, 1867.
Zent, M. F., Insurance Inspector, East St. Louis.
Zimbelmann, Louis J. General Merchandise.
Zimmerman, John, Farmer and Stockraiser, S. 1, T. Engelmann, P. O. Mascoutah, 1865.

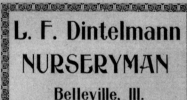

Endnote:

(1) *Directory of the City of East St. Louis, St. Clair County, Illinois, for 1893: Giving an Alphabetical List of All the Inhabitants, with Their Residence and Occupation: Also an Index to the Advertisers and Business Houses Represented in This Book, Together with a List of the Officers of the Government Since Its Incorporation in 1859, Besides Other Historical Data* (East St. Louis, IL: East St. Louis Directory Co., 1893); *East St. Louis Directory* (Herald Publishing, 1887); *Standard Atlas of St. Clair County, Illinois: Including a Plat Book of the Villages, Cities, and Townships of the County* (Chicago: George A. Ogle & Company, 1901).

Chapter 5: Ordinances and Statutes

In 1861, the majority of the inhabitants of Illinoistown, Illinois, incorporated their settlement as a city, annexed neighboring villages, and in the process renamed their town East St. Louis. With the founding of the city of East St. Louis, residents earned the right under Illinois law to enact ordinances, or local statutes, to govern the municipality. Indeed, townspeople saw the first ordinance stating the name of the new city as East St. Louis. Although the town had a population of fewer than five thousand during the 1860s, city politicians and business owners believed that in order for East St. Louis to have a great, prosperous, industrial future, they needed to ordinances to facilitate urban growth as well as to govern various aspects of urban life. Yet they started crafting various ordinances before the city reached a level of development that would justify having such ordinances, for example, the ones governing the grading of principal streets and buildings above flood stage. By the 1870s, city boosters thought that their town would grow rapidly largely because St. Louis, the giant metropolis and leading commercial powerhouse on the Missouri side of the Mississippi River, had become locked in economic competition with Chicago for leadership among Midwestern cities.

Unfortunately for St. Louis, before the end of the nineteenth century, Chicago moved into first place as the region's largest city in terms of population, industrial growth and productivity, and as the nation's largest railroad center. East St. Louisans remained undaunted by Chicago's besting St. Louis in part because they saw their city as Chicago's next and upcoming rival. By 1900, East St. Louis was the center of heavy industry in the St. Louis metropolitan region and its railroad center was the nation's second largest next to Chicago. East St. Louisan leaders knew that their expanding town needed ordinances to maintain order and reasonable development.

The selected images of ordinances

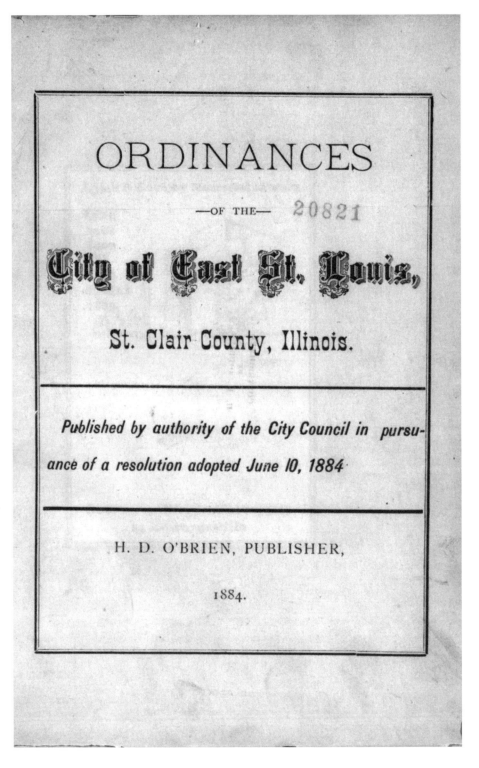

ORDINANCES

—OF THE— 20821

City of East St. Louis,

St. Clair County, Illinois.

Published by authority of the City Council in pursuance of a resolution adopted June 10, 1884·

H. D. O'BRIEN, PUBLISHER,

1884.

in this chapter come from the book, *Ordinances of the City of East St. Louis, St. Clair County.* (1) The municipal statutes are arranged by ordinance number order, which also means that the ordinances are in chronological order. Fortunately, one can access specific ordinances through the book's subject index. The ordinances cover a wide range of topics, including city indebtedness; the city seal; elections; houses; revenues; streets, alleys, and sidewalks; taxes; and wards. The book has a subject index that readers will find useful in locating ordinances, some of which are indexed under more than one

INDEX.

subject. More importantly, the range of subjects undergirds the fact that leading East St. Louisans establishing ordinances was a way to cope with as well as to encourage rapid urban and industrial growth. Unfortunately, the book does not reveal the debates and the struggles involved in the process of city hall enacting ordinances, but given the extreme fluidity of politics over the decades, the ordinances are a window to how townspeople sought the best way possible to make their city livable and attractive to current inhabitants, newcomers, and potential residents and industries.

2

3

4

5

6

7

8

9

11

12

3

tions in relation to his office as the public good may require.

SEC. 3. It shall be a breach of the Treasurer's official bond if he shall in any wise apply money belonging to the city to his own use.

SEC. 4. All orders drawn on the treasury by the City Council shall be paid by the City Treasurer on presentation, unless there shall be no money in the treasury; and he shall be liable to a fine and removal from office for any failure to comply with the requirements of this section, to be assessed by the City Council.

SEC. 5. The Treasurer shall take all necessary precaution to keep safe and secure from all danger, either of fire, robbery, larceny, or from other cause, all moneys or other things remaining in his hands as City Treasurer.

SEC. 6. He shall perform such other and further duties as are now or may hereafter be imposed on him by the City Council, and shall pay over and deliver to his successor, all moneys, papers, books and other things belonging to the city and pertaining to his office.

SEC. 7. The Treasurer shall discharge the duties of his office promptly, and endeavor at all times to correct abuses which may originate within the sphere of his own office, or in the offices of those with whom he may have official connection.

SEC. 8. He shall receive one per centum on sums disbursed by him, and two and a half per centum on all sums received by him from others than city officers, and no fixed salary.

SEC. 9. This ordinance shall be in force from and after its passage.

Passed May 1, 1865,   Approved May 1, 1865,
        JNO. O'REILLY, Clerk.   JNO. B. BOWMAN, Mayor.

[No. 3.]

An ordinance fixing the stated meetings of the City Council, and providing for special meetings of the same.

Be it ordained by the City Council of the City of East St. Louis:

SECTION 1. There shall be held twelve stated or regular meetings of the City Council in each year, one to be held at 3 o'clock P. M., on the first Monday of each and every month.

SEC. 2. Special meetings shall be called by serving written notices on the respective, members, or by leaving copies of such notice at the residence of members not personally served at least one day previous to such meeting. The Clerk or Marshal shall serve such notices as may be directed by the Mayor or two Aldermen calling the meeting.

SEC. 3. Nothing in this ordinance shall be construed to apply to or affect meetings pursuant to adjournment.

SEC. 4. Any member failing to attend the meetings of the Council without sufficient reason for absence may be fined by order of the Council in any sum not exceeding five dollars for each offense.

SEC. 5. This ordinance shall be in force on and after its passage and promulgation.

Passed April 24, 1865,   Approved April 24, 1865,
        JNO. O'REILLY, Clerk.   JNO. B. BOWMAN, Mayor.

[No. 4.]

An ordinance concerning the City Seal.

Be it ordained by the City Council of the City of East St. Louis:

SECTION 1. That the seal of said city be the same one used by the town of East St. Louis, with the following alterations, viz: that the word "town" be erased, and instead, the word "city" be put, so that it will read "City of East St. Louis, St. Clair County, Ill."

SEC. 2. The City Clerk is hereby directed to have the seal of the old corporation changed in conformity to the foregoing section. And he shall use all necessary dispatch and report at the next meeting of the Council the expenses incurred.

SEC. 3. This ordinance shall be in force on and after its passage and promulgation.

Passed April 24, 1865,   Approved April 24, 1865,
        JNO. O'RIELLY, Clerk.   JNO. B. BOWMAN, Mayor.

[No. 12.]

An ordinance in relation to numbering houses and buildings situated in the streets and avenues of this city.

Be it ordained by the City Council of the City of East St. Louis:

SECTION. 1. That all owners or occupants of houses, buildings and tenements, fronting on or near the line of the street or avenue on which they are situated, who shall desire to number such houses, buildings, or tenements, shall be governed by the rules and regulations hereinafter provided.

SEC. 2. Upon all streets or avenues leading directly back from the Mississippi river at right angles, or nearly at right angles from the river, or running parallel, or nearly so, with the longitudinal lines of the surveys of the common fields of Cahokia, it shall be the duty of all concerned to begin numbering the buildings, houses, or tenements on said streets or avenues at their terminus nearest the river, placing the number 1 (one) on the house or building on such street or avenue nearest to the river on the most northerly side of such street or avenue; and the number 2 (two) upon the building on the opposite side of such street or avenue nearest to the river, and so on alternately, placing the even numbers on the most southerly side and the odd numbers on the most northerly side of said streets or avenues.

SEC. 3. Upon all streets or avenues crossing or leading from Broadway or the Dyke, or leading from any street or avenue parallel (or nearly so) with Broadway or the Dyke, it shall be the duty of all concerned to begin numbering the houses, buildings, or tenements on said streets or avenues at Broadway or the Dyke, or nearest to the same as the case may be; placing the number 1 (one) on the house, building or tenement situated on the most northwesterly side of such street or avenue, or nearest to Broadway or the Dyke, and the number 2 (two) on the house, building or tenement on the opposite side of such street or avenue and nearest to Broadway or the Dyke, and so on alternately, placing the even numbers on the most southeasterly side, and the odd numbers on the most northeasterly side of said street or avenue. The provisions of this section shall apply only to streets or avenues leading or running northwardly from Broadway or the Dyke.

SEC. 4. Upon all streets or avenues crossing or running southwardly from Broadway or the Dyke, or any street or avenue parallel to either of them, it shall be the duty of all concerned to begin the numbering of houses, buildings or tenements on said streets or avenues at Broadway or the Dyke, or nearest to the same, placing the number 1 (one) on the building, house or tenement nearest to Broadway or the Dyke, and on the most southerly side of such street or avenue, and the number 2 (two) on the building, house or tenement on the opposite side of such street or avenue and nearest to Broadway or the Dyke, and so on alternately, placing the odd numbers on the most southerly side, and the even numbers on the most northerly side of said streets or avenues.

SEC. 5. This ordinance to be in force from and after its passage and promulgation.

Passed June 19, 1865.   Approved June 19, 1865.
         JOHN O'REILLY, Clerk.   JOHN B. BOWMAN, Mayor.

[No. 13.]

An ordinance in relation to the Calaboose Keeper.

Be it ordained by the City Council of the City of East St. Louis:

SECTION. 1. That there shall be appointed by the City Council a suitable person to keep the city calaboose, whose duty it shall be to attend at the calaboose, and receive and safely keep therein all persons committed to the same by any proper officer of the city, and to keep a register of such persons, the time of their commitment, the time and mode of their discharge, and the officer by whom they were committed, and to report to the City Council monthly the whole number of persons imprisoned during the month, for breaches of ordinances or other causes, together with the condition of the calaboose, with such other information as may be of value to the City Council.

20

SEC. 5. Boards and planks shall be classed as first-rate, common and refuse.

SEC. 6. The first rate shall comprise all boards, planks, joists and scantling, which contain no knots, which are square edged of equal thickness, in all respects sound and free from shakes, and which shall be half heart on the sap side.

SEC. 7. The common class shall comprise all boards, planks, joists and scantling, that are sound, free from shakes, and unsound or large knots, square edged, of equal thickness, in all respects sound, and which are one-fourth heart on the sap side.

SEC. 8. The refuse class shall comprise all boards, joists, scantling or plank not comprised in the first or common class.

SEC. 9. Should the planks, joists, scantling or boards, comprised in the first or common classes, be of unequal width at the end, they shall be measured at the narrow end and on the sap side: and the Lumber Master shall make such allowances as are necessary for straightening the same

SEC. 10. The refuse class shall be measured on the narrow side, and at the middle or average width, with the planks, joists or scantling.

SEC. 11. The measurement of all boards, planks, scantling and joists, and square timber, of less dimensions than one foot square, shall be by the foot of one hundred and fifty-four solid inches, except one and a quarter inch plank, which shall be measured as inch plank.

SEC 12. The measurement of all timber twelve inches square, or of that dimension which shall contain one hundred and forty-four square inches on the end, and all over that size shall be computed by the solid foot of seventeen hundred and twenty-eight solid inches.

SEC. 13. This ordinance to be in force from and after its passage.

Passed July 17, 1865,   Approved July 17, 1865,
  M. MILLARD, City Clerk.   JNO. B. BOWMAN, Mayor.

[No. 15.]

An ordinance to amend ordinance No. 5.

Be it ordained by the City Council of the City of East St. Louis:

SECTION 1. That section 1, of article 2, of ordinance No. 5, entitled "An ordinance in relation to licenses" be so amended as to read as follows: "No person shall, without complying with the provisions of this ordinance, use or cause to be used in the transportation of stone coal from places within to places without the city, or hire out or keep for hire or use, or cause to be used for hire in the transportation of persons or property from one part of the city to another, or from places within to places without the city, or from places without to places within the city, any hackney carriage, omnibus, dray, cart, wagon, or other vehicle."

SEC. 2. That paragraph No. 2, of section 2, of article 2 of said ordinance be so amended as to read, "On each hackney carriage, cab or cabriolet, baggage or express wagon, ten dollars."

SEC. 3. This ordinance to be in force from and after its passage.

  Passed Oct. 2, 1865,   Approved Oct. 3, 1865,
   M. MILLARD, City Clerk.   JNO. B. BOWMAN, Mayor.

[No. 16.]

An ordinance in relation to revenue from taxes.

Be it ordained by the City Council of the City of East St. Louis:

SECTION. 1. That an annual tax, including the year eighteen hundred and sixty-five, be levied and collected for city purposes, in a manner hereinafter provided for, on all real property within the limits of said city, and on all personal property within the same.

SEC. 2. The tax to be levied and collected as aforesaid, shall be at the rate of fifty cents on every one hundred dollars of the assessed valuation thereof; provided: No lower rate be determined upon by the City Council previous to the first Tuesday in the month of December each year.

SEC. 3. The term real property, as used in section one of this Ordinance, shall be construed to mean all lands within the said city, and all buildings or other things erected on or affixed to the same, and the term lands and lots, whenever they occur in this Ordinance, shall be construed as having the same meaning as real property.

SEC. 4. The term personal property as used in said section one, shall be construed to include all household furniture, goods and chattles, all moneys on hand and moneys loaned; all public stocks, stocks in turnpikes, bridges, insurance companies, and moneyed corporations, and also all commissions, and every species of property not included in the description of real estate.

SEC. 5. The following property shall be exempt from taxation: Every burial ground not exceeding five acres; every building erected for any literary, religious, benevolent, charitable or scientific institution, and the tract of land on which the same is situated, not exceeding five acres: Provided the said property shall not be exempt from taxation longer than the same is so used.

SEC. 6. The City Council shall, before the first day of December in each year, appoint a Board of Assessors, consisting of three residents of said city; at least two of whom shall be freeholders within the same at the time of their appointment. Each of which assessors shall before the fifth day next after their appointment, take, and subscribe the following oath before some person authorized to administer oaths:

'I do solemnly swear that I will fulfill my duties as one of the Board of Assessors of the City of East St. Louis, for the present year, fairly and impartially, to the best of my ability, so help me God," which said oath shall be delivered to the City Clerk, and by him filed in his office for safe keeping.

SEC. 7. The Board of Assessors shall in each year make an assessment of the taxable property aforesaid, according to their best judgments of the value thereof, and shall make out a list of the same, showing the names of the owners, where they can be ascertained; a description of the property, whether real or personal, assessed to each; the amount of taxes thereon, and the year or years for which the tax is levied. The description shall be in numerical order in case of real estate, as far as practicable, and in case the present owner of any real estate cannot be ascertained, the same shall be assessed in such numerical order to the last known owner thereof, but such last known owner thereof shall not thereby become liable, personally, for the taxes due thereon, and in case no owner can be found for any real estate within said city, the same shall be assessed—unknown.

SEC. 8. The Board of Assessors shall subdivide lots by correct description, when the same are owned in part by individuals, and when they can ascertain such ownership and descriptions, with reasonable certainty, and shall assess to each his part only.

Persons residing within said city, shall deliver to the Board of Assessors a list of his, her or their property, on or before the thirtieth day of December in each year; the said Board of Assessors shall also in such cases, when such list is not furnished, or is not satisfactory, call upon each taxpayer when practicable, and request a list of his or her property subject to taxation by the city, and assess the same.

SEC. 9. If the Board of Assessors cannot ascertain with reasonable certainty the taxable property of any person residing within the city, and such person shall neglect or refuse to give the said Board of Assessors, a list and statement in writing thereof, on demand made for the same; or if such list and statement be not satisfactory to said Board of Assessors, said Board or any member thereof, shall request such person to make out and subscribe in writing a list of his or her or their real estate within the city, and also a list of his, her or their personal property, with such person's oath or affirmation appended thereto, taken before the Police Magistrate or some other Justice of the Peace, within said city, that such list and statement contains all of his, her or their property aforesaid within said city, or deliver such sworn list to the Board of Assessors within three days after such request, and on demand made by any member of the Board of Assessors therefor, he or she shall forfeit or pay to the City of East St. Louis, not more than fifty dollars, to be recovered before the Police Magistrate of said city, or any Justice of the peace thereof, as other penalties are recovered by regulations of the City Ordinances, and in such case the Board of Assessors shall be governed by the best information they can obtain in regard to such person's property. The Police Magistrate shall make no charge for administering the oath or affimation to such person, and the same may be taken if such person prefer, before any person authorized to administer oaths.

SEC. 10. It shall be the duty of the Board of Assessors in making out the assessment list to assess all real property and the amount of taxes due thereon in columns separate and distinct from the personal property, and to assess all personal property and the amount of taxes due on the same in columns separate and distinct from the real estate, so that it may appear from said assessment list, the amount of real estate assessed to such person, and the amount of taxes due on the same, and the amount of personal property assessed to such person and the amount of taxes due on same, and in all cases under this ordinance, when taxes are assessed against the real estate of any person or corporation, and remain unpaid after the expiration of the time hereinafter limited for the payment of the same such real estate shall alone be liable to be sold to satisfy the taxes assessed against the same, and in no case shall the personal property of any person be liable to be sold to satisfy taxes assessed against the real estate of such person. And when taxes are assessed against the personal property of any person, and remain unpaid after the expiration of the time hereinafter limited for the payment of the same, the personal property of such person shall alone be liable to be sold to satisfy the taxes assessed against the personal property of such person, and in no case shall the real estate of any person be liable to be sold to satisfy the taxes assessed against the personal property of such person.

SEC. 11. The Board of Assessors shall make the assessment hereinbefore provided for before the twentieth of January in each year, and shall, on or before the last named day, return a complete list of assessment into the office of the City Clerk, there to remain for public inspection for a period of ten days, during which time all persons feeling aggrieved, may file with the city clerk their complaint in writing, briefly setting forth wherein they deem themselves aggrieved by said assessment, and describing the property of the assessment of which they complain. The Board of Assessors shall, upon such return being made, give notice thereof, by posting four notices in four of the most public places in said city, that is, one in each place, or by publication in some newspaper published in the city, or by both, that the assessment list for that year is completed and deposited in the City Clerk's office, and will there remain for the period of time aforesaid for public inspection, and requesting all persons feeling aggrieved, to file their complaints aforesaid before the expiration of the said ten days with the City Clerk. with the affidavit of the person aforesaid, that they were properly posted, said assessment shall be a lien on the personal property in the same described from and after the time said assessment list shall be returned by the Board of Assessors into the office of the City Clerk, for the city taxes due thereon, and no sale or transfer thereof shall effect the claim of the city thereto.

SEC. 12. Within ten days after the expiration of the time mentioned in section eleven of this Ordinance for inspection of said assessment list and filing complaints against the same, the City Council shall meet, and the City Clerk shall lay before the Council said assessment list, together with all complaints aforesaid touching the same, and the Council, together with the Board of Assessors, if practicable, shall carefully examine all complaints filed, and shall make such alterations and amendments in said assessment list as they shall deem just and equitable. They shall also cause any additions to be made to said list of property found to be omitted, or which may not have come to the knowledge of the Board of Assessors.

The Council shall cause all errors in said list to be corrected, the total amount of taxable property therein to be correctly ascertained, and also the total amount of taxes due thereon as appears by said list upon careful examination thereof, and the same to be set down at the end of said list, and they shall cause a record of the amount to be made.

SEC. 13. The said assessment list when examined and corrected as aforesaid, shall be certified to by the Board of Assessors, as near as may be in the following form.

"We do hereby certify that the foregoing assessment list for the City of East Saint Louis, for the year————, contains a true assessment of all the taxable property within said city for said year." Signed by the Board of Assessors.

And shall file the same with the City Clerk, and shall take from him a receipt therefor, showing the total amount of taxable property, and the total amount of taxes due thereon, which receipt said Board of Assessors shall file with the City Treasurer of said city.

SEC. 14. There shall be appointed by the City Council of said city, on or before the first Monday of February in each and every year, a collector to collect the taxes due said city, who shall, before entering upon the duties of his office, give a bond with security, to the satisfaction of the City Council, to the City of East Saint Louis, in a penalty of double the amount of taxes due for the year for which he is appointed, conditioned for the faithful discharge of his duties in the collection of the city tax, and for the payment of the amount thereof by him collected into the city Treasury, which bond shall be filed with the City Clerk.

SEC. 15. The City Clerk shall, within fifteen days after the filing of the assessment list in his office as provided in section thirteen of this Ordinance, make out a copy of said list and deliver the same to the city collector, with his certificate of authentication under the corporate seal thereto appended. The City Clerk shall take said collector's receipt for said assessment list, showing the total amount of taxable property, and the total amount of taxes due thereon as appears by said list, which receipt he shall file in his office.

The city collector shall, upon the receipt of said assessment list, forthwith proceed to the collection of the taxes therein specified.

SEC. 16. In the collection of the taxes, the collector shall call upon the resident taxpayers of the city respectively, or at the respective places of their business or abode, and make demand of the taxes due from them, or he may give notice by hand bills posted up in the city, or by publication in some newspaper published in said city, of the time and place where and when he will attend with the tax list and receive taxes.

Any person may pay taxes on any such portion of real estate as he may have claim to, provided he will furnish the collector with a plain and certain description thereof. Upon the payment of any tax to the collector, he shall first make an entry in his tax list of the name of the person paying, of the total amount paid and if payment is made on property of a different description, or in different parts or parcels, from the description thereof made by said Board of Assessors, and shown by said tax list, he shall enter a particular description thereof, after which he shall deliver, to the person paying, a receipt, stating the time of payment, by whom payment is made, a correct and plain description of the property paid on, the total amount paid, and the year or years for which the taxes are paid.

SEC. 17. The collector shall, at the expiration of seventy days from the time of the delivery of the tax list to him for collection, and after having complied with the provisions of section sixteen of this Ordinance, return said tax list into the office of the City Clerk, and take a receipt in duplicate from said Clerk, showing the amount of taxes paid on real estate, and the amount of taxes paid on personal property, also the amount of taxes remaining unpaid upon real estate, and the amount of taxes remaining unpaid upon personal property, as the same appears by said list, one of which receipts the collector shall file with the Treasurer of said city.

SEC. 18. The City Clerk shall at the expiration of twenty days from the delivery of said tax list to him by the collector as mentioned in the last section, make out a list of personal property upon which the taxes remain unpaid (as appears by said list,) with the amount of taxes and costs due on the same, and the name of the person against whom such tax is assessed, and shall append thereto a certificate under his hand, and the corporate seal of said city, that said list contains a true statement of the personal property within said city upon which the taxes due for the year therein set forth, remain unpaid, and deliver the same to the collector, and shall take from said collector a receipt therefor, showing the amount of personal property delinqent, with the amount of taxes due on the same as appears by said list, and file said receipt in his office.

24

SEC. 19. The collector shall immediately upon receipt of said last mentioned list, proceed to collect the taxes appearing due by the same, and may seize any personal property of the owner (or of any person having listed or consented to the listing in his name of any personal property upon which taxes may be due,) of sufficient value to satisfy the taxes and costs due from such person or his personal property, and may, from time to time, make such further seizures as may be necessary for that purpose; he shall cause any property so seized be advertised for sale for ten days, by posting notices of such sale in four of the most public places in said city, containing a description of the property to be sold, and of the time and place of such sale, and on the day of sale, shall sell the same at public vendue to the highest bidder, for cash, at the place named in said notice, and apply the proceeds as follows: First, to the satisfaction of the taxes, next to the satisfaction of the costs of seizure and sale, and after deducting ten per cent. of the whole amount of taxes and costs due as his fee for selling, shall pay the balance, if any, to the owner thereof on demand, and the said tax list shall be sufficient warrant for the collector to make seizure and sale: Provided, that if said collector or his successors in office shall not collect the taxes due on personal property within two years after having received said separate list, said city shall forever be debared from collecting the same.

SEC. 20. The City Council may, from time to time, call upon the collector to account for and pay over all moneys collected by virtue of the last section, and at the expiration of the time in which the same might be collected, or of the said collector's term of office, he shall deliver to the City Clerk said list, by him to be filed in his office, and shall take his receipt therefor, showing the amount remaining due and unpaid on said list.

SEC. 21. The City Clerk shall within twenty days after the assessment list is returned into his office as provided in section seventeen of this ordinance, make out from said assessment list, a list of all lands or real estate upon which the taxes remain unpaid and deliver the same to the collector and take his receipt therefor, showing the total amount of taxes yet due and unpaid as appears by said list, which receipt the Clerk shall record in his office.

The Collector shall within twenty days thereafter cause the real estate upon which the taxes remain unpaid, to be advertised for the taxes and costs due thereon, said advertisement shall contain a copy, as near as may be, of said delinquent tax list, with a notice thereto appended by the Collector as follows:

All persons are hereby notified that the foregoing is a list of lots and parts of lots within the City of East St. Louis, in the County of St. Clair and State of Illinois, upon which the taxes due to said city for the year therein set forth, remain due and unpaid, and that the said lots and parts of lots will severally and separately be sold at public vendue at the office of the City Clerk of said city, commencing on the   day of   , A. D. 18—, at 10 o'clock A. M., and closing at 5 o'clock, P. M., and continue from day to day until the same shall all be sold for the taxes and costs due on each lot and part of a lot respectively, to such person as shall bid the taxes and costs due on each lot and part of a lot separately for the least amount of each such lot or part of a lot.   Signed,   COLLECTOR.

Said notice and advertisement shall be published in some weekly newspaper printed and published in this city, for three weeks immediately preceding the day of sale, and when so published and printed, a copy of the advertisement shall be filed in the office of the City Clerk of said city, with the certificate of the printer and publisher thereto affixed or appended as near as may be in the following form:

I certify that the foregoing tax notice and advertisement was published in the a newspaper printed and published in the City of East St. Louis, County of St. Clair, State of Illinois, for three weeks immediately preceding the day of sale therein named.

Signed,   PUBLISHER OF PAPER.

SEC. 22. Any person may pay the taxes and costs due on any real estate to the Collector of said city at any time between the day the same is so advertised and the day of sale, and the Collector shall make an entry thereof in the delinquent list and shall deliver to the person so paying, a receipt stating the time of payment, by whom payment is made, a correct and plain description of the property paid on, the total amount paid, and the year or years for which such tax is paid.

25

Sec. 23. At the day named in the advertisement provided for in section twenty-one, the Collector, assisted by the City Clerk, shall offer the whole of each lot or tract for sale for the amount of taxes and costs thereon; and so much thereof as may be necessary to pay such tax and costs shall be struck off to the lowest bidder, that is, to the person who shall offer to pay the amount of taxes and costs due as aforesaid for the least quantity of ground. When a portion of a lot shall have been struck off on any such bid, it shall be taken off the east side of said lot extending the whole length thereof, should such lot have a northerly or southerly front, and from the north side of said lot extending the whole length thereof should such lot have an easterly or westerly front; and if no bids shall be made for any lot or part of a lot offered for the amount of taxes and costs due thereon, the same shall be struck off to the City of East St. Louis for the taxes and costs unpaid thereon, and the said city shall to all intents and purposes be the purchaser thereof. The Collector shall receive all moneys at such sale and shall execute to the several purchasers certificates of purchase, stating the name of the purchaser, the date of the purchase, the year or years for which the taxes accrued, the amount of taxes and costs on the tract purchased, and a plain description of the property purchased. Such certificate of purchase shall be assignable by indorsement, and an assignment thereof shall vest in the assignee, or his legal representatives, all the right and title of the original purchaser. The City Clerk shall keep a correct list of such sales, showing the name of the owner if known, the date of the sale, the year or years for which the taxes accrued, a plain description of the lots or parts of lots sold, the name of the purchaser and the amount paid, and shall also countersign and affix the city seal to all certificates of purchase executed by the Collector in pursuance of this section; all of which shall be kept in a book of the city in the office of the City Clerk as a public record.

Sec. 24. No sale of real estate for taxes by virtue of this ordinance shall be considered invalid on account of the same having been charged in any other name than that of the rightful owner, if the said real estate be in other respects sufficiently described, and the taxes thereon were due and unpaid at the time of such sale.

Sec. 25. Real property sold under the provisions of this ordinance may be redeemed at any time before the expiration of two years from the date of the sale by any one interested in such real estate by paying to the Collector of the City of East St. Louis double the amount for which the same was sold, upon the receipt of which it shall be the duty of the Collector to make out to such person so redeeming a certificate of such redemption; which certificate, countersigned by the City Clerk under the seal of the city, shall give a description of the land so redeemed, the amount paid to redeem the same. by whom paid and at what time; the said Collector shall note the land redeemed on the sale book and also by whom redeemed; the time the same was redeemed, the amount paid and by whom, and the amount paid shall be subject to the order of the person who may have purchased such real estate or his assigns, at the sale of the same for the taxes and costs due thereon, and such person shall deliver up to the Collector his certificate of purchase, who shall endorse on said certificate redeemed and file the same in the City Clerk's office.

Sec. 26. After the expiration of two years from the day of sale or any lot or part of a lot under this ordinance, the purchaser thereof, his heirs or assigns, shall be entitled to a deed therefor, provided the same shall not have been previously redeemed, and provided the purchaser, his heirs or assigns shall have complied with the provisions of the next section of this ordinance, and the Collector of the City of East St. Louis shall in such case, upon the surrender of the certificate of purchase thereof, execute to such purchaser, his heirs or assigns, a deed for such lot or part of a lot. The deed to be executed as aforesaid, shall for all purposes vest in the grantee therein named and his heirs a perfect title to the premises in such deed described, and all deeds executed under this ordinance by the Collector as aforesaid shall be *prima facie* evidence that all the proceedings had prior to such sale in regard to the listing, assessment and sale of the property described in said deed were regular. Excepting in the following cases, namely, when the party claiming in opposition to such tax-deed can show that the taxes on such real estate for the year for which the same was sold had been paid prior to the expiration of the time for redeeming the same.

26

Or can show that the same was not subject to taxation at that time.

And excepting in regard to the constitutional requirements of the next section, shall vest in the grantee in any such tax deed, his heirs and assigns, an absolute title in fee simple to to the premises in said deed described; and said deed shall be conclusive evidence that the provisions and requirements of this ordinance have been strictly followed and complied with, and that everything required by this ordinance to be done has been done regularly and properly. Provided said deed shall in no case be evidence that the requirements of the next section of this ordinance have been complied with, nor shall it affect the rights of parties claiming under a tax deed of later date, executed by the Collector of said city.

SEC. 27. No purchaser of real estate at a sale of the same held by virtue of this ordinance, shall be entitled to a deed for such real estate until he or she shall have complied with the following conditions, to-wit: such purchaser shall serve, or cause to be served, a written notice of such purchase, upon every person in possession of such real estate, three months before the expiration of the time of redemption on such sale, in which notice he shall state when he purchased such real estate, the description of the said real estate which he has purchased and when the term of redemption will expire, in like manner he shall serve on the person or persons in whose name or names such real estate is taxed, a similar written notice if such person shall reside in the county where such real estate is situated, and in the event that the person or persons in whose name or names such real estate is taxed, do not reside in the county in which the same is situated, he shall publish such notice in some newspaper published in said county, which notice shall be inserted three times, the last time being not less than three months before the expiration of one year from the time of the sale of such real estate. The purchaser, his heirs or assigns, shall before a deed is executed to him, by himself or agent, make an affidavit of having complied with this section, stating particularly the facts relied on as such compliance, which affidavit shall be delivered to the City Clerk and by him filed in his office and entered on the records thereof and preserved among the files of his office.

In case any person under this section shall be compelled to publish a notice in a newspaper, then before any person may have a right to redeem any such lot or part of a lot from any such tax sale, he shall pay to the Collector the printer's fee for publishing such notice and costs of having been sworn to such affidavit and of filing the same as aforesaid.

SEC. 28. In case any purchaser, his heirs or assigns, shall have lost or from any cause is unable to produce his certificate aforesaid, the City Clerk shall issue a duplicate certificate therefor, upon such person filing with him an affidavit of such loss or inability to produce the same, and that the same is his rightful property.

SEC. 29. If it shall appear to the City Clerk that the taxes for which any lot or part of a lot has been sold, has been paid previously to the sale of the same for such taxes, he shall present the case to the City Council at their next meeting and if it shall appear to the City Council that the same were so paid, an order shall be drawn on the City Treasurer in favor of the purchaser, his heirs and assigns, for the amount paid therefor and such sale shall be cancelled and if it shall appear that any moneys have been paid on such lot or part of a lot to the City Collector and have not been properly credited on the tax list and accounted for, the officer to whom the same was paid shall refund the amount thereof and costs to the city.

SEC. 30. It shall be the duty of the City Collector, and also of the City Clerk, to keep a list of all real estate within the city, which in the collection of the city tax they and each of them may discover to be omitted in the assessment list, and the same list shall be filed in the City Clerk's office, for the use of the Board of Assessors of the next year's revenue.

SEC. 31. In the case of the death of the City Collector while the tax books are in his hands, the City Clerk shall demand and take charge of the same and shall forthwith notify the City Council of the fact, who shall immediately appoint another collector, who shall, after filing his bond, proceed forthwith to collect the city taxes remaining unpaid, in the same manner as if he had been originally appointed.

SEC. 32. In all cases of assessment under this ordinance the fractions of a cent shall be rejected.

27

Sec. 33. There shall be allowed for collecting the city revenue from taxes the following fees, viz: To the Board of Assessors for making the annual assessment, two hundred dollars ($200); to the printer for publishing the delinquent tax list notice, on each lot and part of a lot, not more than twelve cents.

To the City Collector on all moneys by him collected and paid over, five per centum.

To the City Clerk for copying the assessment list, fifteen cents for each folio; for making out the delinquent list of real estate, fifteen cents for each description, and for making out the delinquent list of personal property, fifteen cents for each person.

To the Collector for making sale on each lot and part of a lot, five cents, and for each redemption certificate, twenty-five cents shall be paid to the Collector and ten cents to the City Clerk.

For each tax deed, fifty cents, and for filing and recording affidavit of purchaser at a tax sale, preliminary to obtaining a deed, twenty-five cents.

The three last charges shall be paid by the party demanding the service.

Sec. 34. All ordinances coming within the purview of this ordinance, or in any manner repugnant thereto, are hereby repealed, but all rights and liabilities accrued under any ordinance hereby repealed, are hereby vested and declared valid and binding, and may be enforced.

This ordinance to be in force from and after its passage and promulgation.

Passed Nov. 27, 1865.　　　　　　Approved Nov. 27, 1865.
　　M. Millard, City Clerk.　　　　　　JOHN B. BOWMAN, Mayor.

[No. 17.]

An Ordinance concerning Porters, Hotel Runners and others.

Be it ordained by the City Council of the City of East St. Louis:

Section. 1. That any person who shall within this city, make it his business or vocation, or part of his business or vocation, to solicit others, by going about from place to place, or otherwise, to take lodging, or be entertained, in or at any hotel, or other place where travelers or others are lodged, provided with food, or otherwise entertained; or shall solicit any person to take passage in any steamboat, or on any railroad, or in any omnibus, hackney carriage, cab, baggage wagon, stage, coach, or other public vehicle, or to have his or her trunk, carpet sack, valise, or other like property, transported for hire; and any person who shall pursue a like business shall be deemed a runner within the meaning of this ordinance.

Sec. 2. The provisions of this ordinance shall also be construed to apply to all proprietors of boarding houses, eating houses, hotels, saloons, restaurants, and to all owners of all vehicles referred to and mentioned in the preceding section, and to all persons controlling or driving the same; if any or either of them shall solicit, procure or obtain custom or patronage, either for themselves or others, in a manner similar to that usually practiced by persons generally called "runners" or others following like occupations; except, however, as may be hereinafter provided to the contrary.

Sec. 3. If any runner shall procure or attempt to procure, custom or patronage, either for himself or for another, under any false pretense, or by holding out any false inducement, or by using any false representation, or by practicing any deceit or any misrepresentation, or by using any unfair or fraudulent means in, at, or about any hotel, depot, wharf or landing, or other place within this city, he shall be deemed guilty of a misdemeanor, and subject to a fine.

Sec. 4. If any runner shall, within this city, take or obtain, or attempt to take or obtain, possession knowingly, either forcibly or otherwise, of any trunk, chest, carpet sack, traveling bag, valise, wearing apparel, or any other personal property carried by travelers and strangers, without first having the permission of, or being so requested by the owner thereof, he shall be deemed guilty of a misdemeanor, and subject to a fine.

30

placed on each side of the body or box thereof; on hackney carriages, cabs or cabriolets, the number shall be painted on the outer glass of the lamps, or on some other conspicuous place of such vehicle; on omnibus the number shall be painted on some conspicuous place on the outside of the body thereof, in numerals not less than three inches long, and on all vehicles not specially provided for, the number shall be cut on metallic plates and placed on some conspicuous place on such vehicle.''

SEC. 2. The word "painted" in the second section of said ordinance No. 11, is hereby repealed and stricken out.

SEC. 3. This ordinance to be in force from and after its passage and promulgation.

<table>
<tr><td>Passed March 5, 1866,</td><td>Approved March 5, 1866,</td></tr>
<tr><td>M. MILLARD, City Clerk.</td><td>JNO. B. BOWMAN, Mayor.</td></tr>
</table>

[No. 22.]

An Ordinance amending Ordinance No. 13, entitled "An Ordinance in relation to the Calaboose Keeper."

Be it ordained by the City Council of the City of East St. Louis:

SECTION 1. That section eight (8) of Ordinance No. 13, entitled "An Ordinance in relation to the Calaboose Keeper," be so amended as to read as follows: "The keeper of the city calaboose shall hold office during the pleasure of the City Council; he shall reside in the calaboose keeper's house rent free; he shall receive a salary of forty dollars per month; and during his absence from the city, or in case of his inability to act from sickness or otherwise, the functions of said office shall devolve on the Marshal of the city.

SEC. 2. This ordinance to be in force from and after its passage and promulgation.

<table>
<tr><td>Passed March 19, 1866.</td><td>Approved March 19, 1866.</td></tr>
<tr><td>M. MILLARD, City Clerk.</td><td>JOHN B. BOWMAN, Mayor.</td></tr>
</table>

[No. 23.]

An Ordinance concerning Elections.

Be it ordained by the City Council of the City of East St. Louis:

GENERAL PROVISIONS.

SECTION 1. That an election shall be held annually for one Alderman in each of the wards of said city, and biannually for Mayor and City Judge on the first Monday in April, at such place as shall be designated by the City Council, of which the City Clerk shall give written or printed notice on the Monday four weeks preceding such election. It shall be the duty of the Marshal to post such notices in three of the most public places in each ward, and it shall be the duty of the City Clerk to have such notices published in at least one newspaper published in said city.

SEC. 2. The City Council shall annually on the Monday five weeks preceding the charter election appoint three judges of election in and for each ward, of the electors thereof respectively, who shall make a register of the electors and preside at such election in their respective wards. The City Clerk shall make out, and the Marshal shall serve notices of their appointment in writing upon each of the persons so appointed.

SEC. 3. If any judge of election shall refuse or be unable to act, or fail to be present at the time for said judges to meet as a board of Registry as now required by law, the vacancy shall be filled by any qualified voter of the ward, to be selected by the remaining judge or judges. And if no judge shall be present, a full board may be selected from the qualified electors of such ward by the voters thereof. The judges shall have power to appoint two suitable persons to act as clerks of election.

SEC. 4. The judges and clerks shall severally before receiving any votes, take and subscribe an oath or affirmation which shall be attached to the Poll books and may be in the following form to wit: I————————do solemnly swear (or affirm) that I will perform the duties of judge of election (or clerk) according to law and the best of my ability and that I will studiously endeavor to prevent fraud, deceit and abuse in conducting the same.

31

Sworn to and subscribed before me at East St. Louis this————day of————18————

If no person shall be present at the opening of the polls authorized to administer oaths, it shall be lawful for the judges, or either of them to administer the same to each other and to the clerks. The oaths shall be certified by the person administering the same as in the form above given.

Sec. 5. At all elections the polls shall be opened at eight o'clock a. m., and continue open until seven o'clock p. m., of the same day. When opened proclamation shall be made that "the polls are now opened," and thirty minutes before closing the same, proclamation shall be made that "the polls will be closed in half an hour."

Sec. 6. A ballot box shall be provided for the use of the judges of each ward, with a lock and key, and in the top or lid an aperture not larger than shall be necessary to receive a single folded ballot. On opening the polls, the judges shall examine the ballot boxes, and have them closed and locked in the presence of the three judges.

Sec. 7. The City Clerk shall provide two poll books for each ward, and four blank register books for making a list of voters as required by law similar to those used in county and state elections. The poll books shall be kept by the clerks and the name of the voters shall be written and recorded therein in the order in which they vote: *Provided* that immediately prior to each vote being cast, the judges or a majority of them, shall be satisfied that the person offering to vote is a legal voter, when one of said judges shall endorse on the back of the ticket offered, the number corresponding with the number of the voter on the poll book, and put said ticket immediately in the ballot box.

Sec. 8. The mode of voting shall be by ballot. The ballot shall be placed by the judges (if received) in the ballot box, and shall consist of one slip of paper, on which shall be written, or printed, or partly both, the names of the person or persons voted for, with a pertinent designation of the office to which the person voted for is intended to be chosen; but no ballot shall contain a greater number of names than there are persons to be chosen for offices to be filled, and any ballot containing a greater number of names of persons designated for any office than there are persons to be chosen, or can be elected to that office shall be declared void so far as that office is concerned. It shall be unlawful for the judges to open, disfigure or examine any ballot offered until after the election shall be over and the polls closed; and then only as in the ordinance indicated.

Sec. 9. All persons who are entitled to vote for state officers, who shall have been actual residents of said city for at least three months, and of the ward wherein they may offer their votes, at least ten days, and who shall have been duly registered according to law, next preceding an election, shall be entitled to vote at such election, provided any qualified voter of the ward shall have a right to challenge, in common with the judges, and whenever any person shall be challenged, one of the judges shall administer to him the following oath: "You do solemnly swear (or affirm) that you are the age of twenty-one years; that you are a citizen of the United States (or was a resident of this state on the first day of April, 1848) and have been a resident of this state for one year last past, and an actual resident of this city for the last three months, and now have, and have had a permanent abode in this ward for the last ten days, and have resided at————————————————————in said ward for————————days last past, and have not voted at this election."

And in addition thereto, such voter so challenged shall be required to produce two witnesses, both of whom are personally known to said judges of said election, and residents in the ward, and each of whom shall take the following oath, to be administered by one of the judges of said election:. "You do solemnly swear (or affirm) that you are a resident of this election district and entitled to vote at this election, and that you have been a resident of this state for one year last past, and that you are well acquainted with the voter whose vote is now offered, and that he has resided in this state for one year last past, and in this city three months, next preceding this election, and has had an actual residence in this ward for the last ten days."

64

The City Council shall thereupon, by ordinance or resolution, levy such rate of tax as may be necessary or expedient for corporate purposes, not exceeding the authorized per centage.

Sec. 14. The City Clerk shall, within ten days after such confirmation, make out, in suitable books, a true copy of the assessment lists, with the tax assessed, with a warrant attached thereto for the collection thereof, and deliver the same to the collector, and take his receipt therefor, for the full amount of said assessments; and such warrant shall be signed by the Mayor, stamped with the corporate seal, and attested by the City Clerk, and may be in the following form:

STATE OF ILLINOIS, } ss
City of East St. Louis.

The people of the State of Illinois to the Collector of said City—greeting:

Whereas, the City Council of said city did, on the——day of——, levy and assess upon the assessed value, for the year——, of the (real or personal) property hereinbefore described, the several sums of money set opposite thereto, in the appropriate column, for the year ending——: now, therefore, you are commanded to make, levy and collect the said several sums of money set opposite to the (real or personal) property hereinbefore described as taxes thereon, for the year aforesaid, of the goods and chattels of the respective owners of said estate, and make return of this warrant on or before the——day of——, 18—.

"Witness———————, Mayor of said city, and the corporate seal thereof, this——day of——, 18—.   "————————————

"Attest: "Mayor.

———————————,
"City Clerk."

Sec. 15. The Collector shall, before proceeding to collect the annual revenue, execute a bond to the city in at least double the amount of tax to be collected, with two or more sureties, to be approved by the Mayor, and file the same with the City Clerk.

Sec. 16. On receiving the assessment lists from the City Clerk, and after filing his bond as aforesaid, the collector shall proceed, in the manner provided for county collectors by the general revenue laws of this State for the collection of general taxes, as near as may be, to collect the taxes charged in said lists; and he shall be authorized to levy on and sell the personal property of persons owing taxes, after having given three weeks' notice in the corporation newspaper that such taxes are due and payable in the same manner in which constables are required by law to sell property taken under execution, and shall be allowed the same fees.

Sec. 17. It shall be his duty to collect such taxes by the thirty-first day of December in each year; and if payment be not made by that time, it shall be his duty to make out, within ten days thereafter, a list of all lots and tracts of land upon which the taxes are unpaid, adding all costs, and enter such list in a suitable book, with an affidavit attached thereto, which may be in the following form:

"I,——————, collector in and for the City of East St. Louis, State of Illinois, do solemnly swear (or affirm) that the foregoing is a true and correct record of the delinquent lands and lots within said city, upon which I have been unable to collect the taxes due said city, as required by law, for the year therein set forth; that said taxes remain due and unpaid, as I verily believe."

Said affidavit to be at the bottom of such delinquent list.

Sec. 18. It shall be the duty of the collector to cause such delinquent list to be published, in some newspaper published in the city, as soon as practicable, with a notice appended at the foot of such list, specifying that application will be made to the County Court of St. Clair County, State of Illinois, for judgment against such delinquent lands and lots for the amount of taxes due and unpaid, and costs; and that on the first Monday subsequent thereto, the same will be sold at public vendue, for the payment of such taxes and costs; which delinquent list and notice shall be published at least thirty days previous to such application for judgment as aforesaid, and said notice may be in the following form:

65

STATE OF ILLINOIS,   } ss
  City of East St. Louis.   }

"All persons interested are hereby notified that I shall apply to the County Court of St Clair County, State of Illinois, on the——day of——, 18—, at the———term of said year, for judgment against the foregoing delinquent lands and lots for the amount of taxes and costs due thereon to said city, for the year therein named; and that on the first Monday succeeding the rendition of judgment against said lands and lots, I shall proceed to sell the same at the office of the City Clerk, at public vendue, commencing at 10 a. m., and continue, from day to day, until all are sold, as required by law.

      (Signed)   ———————————

                                  "City Collector."

SEC. 19. After having given notice as aforesaid, the collector shall apply to the County Court, on the day named in such notice, for judgment against said lands and lots. It shall be his duty to file a true copy of such delinquent list, and the printed advertisement of the same, with the printers certificate of publication attached with the County Clerk, at least five days before the first day of the term at which application for judgment will be made.

SEC. 20. On such application being made, the County Court shall proceed to hear and determine the same, and render judgment against such delinquent lands and lots in the same manner, and said judgment shall have the like effect as though said delinquent list had been returned to the County Court by the Sheriff or County Collector, in the collection of the State and County taxes; and the County Court shall issue its precept or order to the collector of said city of East St. Louis, directing him to sell said lands and lots at public auction, to pay said delinquent taxes and costs, in conformity to law.

SEC. 21. On receipt of said precept or order of sale, the collector shall proceed, at the proper time, to sell such delinquent lands and lots in the same manner as is provided by the general revenue laws for the collection of the State and County taxes.

SEC. 22. Within ten days after such sale the collector shall make out a minute and specific report of the sales made by him, and deliver the same to the City Clerk; and the City Clerk shall record such report in a suitable book for preservation and the inspection of all persons interested.

SEC. 23. The collector shall, when any lands or lots are struck off at tax sales, receive the money therefore forthwith; and if payment is not so made, he shall, before closing said sales, expose and sell the same again; and he shall execute to the several purchasers, certificates of purchase, stating the name of the purchaser, the date of the purchase, the year for which the taxes accrued, the amount of taxes and costs, and a description of the property purchased.

SEC. 24. If no bid shall be made for any lot or part of a lot offered at such sale, for the taxes and costs due thereon, the same shall be struck off to the City of East St. Louis, and the said city shall be considered, to all intents and purposes, the purchaser thereof.

SEC. 25. The taxes and costs charged against any land or lot may be paid at any time before sale, and such payment shall have the effect of canceling the taxes and costs so charged.

SEC. 26. The same rights of redemption from tax sales shall exist under this ordinance as under the general revenue laws of this state now in force or hereafter passed; and all persons interested in, or affected by said tax sales, shall have all the rights and be under the same obligations that now or may hereafter exist under said revenue laws in like cases, except as herein provided to the contrary.

SEC. 27. Redemption money shall be paid to the City Clerk; and whenever redemption is made, the City Clerk shall, thereupon, execute to the person redeeming, a certificate, stating the date of the sale, the year for which the taxes were due, to whom sold, the amount for which said lands or lots were sold, a description of the property sold and redeemed, the name of the person redeeming, and the amount paid thereon, and make a proper record of the same and pay such redemption money to the purchaser upon the surrender of his certificate of purchase.

66

SEC. 28. Conveyances, [in the usual form of tax deeds, shall be executed by the Mayor, under the corporate seal, and countersigned by the City Clerk, to all persons holding certificates of purchase, when they shall become entitled to the same by law; and such deeds shall have the same force and effect, as deeds executed under the general revenue laws of this State.

SEC. 29. It shall be the duty of the collector to pay over all moneys received for taxes to the City Treasurer, on every Monday; and make a final report and settlement with the City Council as soon as practicable after the tax sales shall have been concluded.

SEC. 30. All provisions of the general revenue laws of this State shall be adopted in levying and collecting the annual tax herein provided for, except where provision is made for such purpose in this ordinance.

SEC. 31. There shall be allowed for collecting the annual revenue from taxes the following fees:

To the Assessor, three hundred dollars, for making and returning the assessment.

To the City Clerk, for copying the assessment lists, three cents for each description in the real property list, and the same for each name in the personal property list.

To the Collector, on all moneys collected by him on the general tax lists, three per centum; for making out the delinquent list, ten cents for each tract.

To the Printer, for publishing the delinquent list, fifteen cents per tract.

To the County Clerk, for services under this ordinance, the same compensation he receives for like services under the general revenue laws.

To the Collector, for making sale and certificate, twenty-five cents for each tract.

(The last four items shall be charged and collected as costs.)

To the City Clerk, for each redemption certificate, fifty cents; for each tax deed, one dollar; (both charges to be paid by the party demanding the services;) and for recording the report of tax sales, ten cents for each description.

SEC. 32. All ordinances in conflict with this ordinance are hereby repealed; but all rights and liabilities accrued under any ordinance hereby repealed shall be valid and binding, and may be enforced; and this ordinance shall not be construed to affect, in any manner, the collection of the annual tax for the year 1866.

SEC. 33. This ordinance shall be in force and effect from and after its passage and promulgation.

Passed June 20, 1867,   Approved June 20, 1867,
  WM. O'NEILL, City Clerk.   JNO. B. LOVINGSTON, Mayor.

[No. 51.]

An Ordinance to amend Ordinance numbered forty-six (46) entitled "An Ordinance in relation to Licenses."

Be it ordained by the City Council of the City of East St. Louis:

SECTION 1. That section sixteen (16) of ordinance numbered forty-six (46) entitled "An ordinance in relation to Licences," be altered so as to read as follows: "Peddlers shall pay twenty-five dollars for each license for six months. Any person who shall sell, or offer to sell traveling from place to place in this city, any goods, wares, or other commodities, shall be deemed a peddler; provided, that the Mayor may authorize the issuing of licenses to such lame, old or infirm persons whom he may think deserving of charity, free of charge, or for any sum he may deem fit.

SEC. 2. That section numbered thirty-one of said ordinance be amended by striking out the word "twenty" and inserting in lieu thereof the word "five"

SEC. 3. This ordinance shall be in force from and after its passage and promulgation.

Passed July 1, 1867,   Approved July 2, 1867,
  WM. O'NEILL, City Clerk.   JNO. B. LOVINGSTON, Mayor.

avenue, alley, or other public thoroughfare or place, by a fence or otherwise, so as to hinder, or delay, or prevent passage or travel upon any part of the same is hereby declared a misdemeanor, subjecting each person engaged in causing such obstruction to a fine not less than 25 dollars for the first offense, and double the amount for any subsequent violation of this ordinance; provided, always, that for the purpose of depositing building materials, convenient to buildings in course of erection, permits may be granted by the city engineer, approved by the mayor, for the use of part of any street, avenue, alley, or other public thoroughfare or place, for a stated reasonable length of time, not exceeding eight weeks; and in no case to an extent preventing the free and safe passage of teams and persons.

SEC. 2. It is hereby made the duty of the proper officers, without delay, to arrest and bring or cause to be brought, before the city court, any person committing the misdemeanor defined in section one, of this ordinance; and to remove or cause to be moved, at once, all obstructions so made.

SEC. 3. This ordinance shall be in force and effect from and after its passage and promulgation.

Passed, October 30, 1867. Approved October 30, 1867.

WM. O'NEILL City Clerk. JOHN B. LOVINGSTON, Mayor.

[No. 60.]

An Ordinance fixing the Rate of Tax for the year A. D. 1867.

Be it ordained by the City Council of the City of East St. Louis:

SECTION 1. That one-half of one per cent. be, and is hereby levied, and shall be collected on the assessed value of all property, both real and personal, assessed for taxation for the year A. D. 1867.

SEC. 2. This ordinance shall be in force from and after its passage and promulgation.

Passed December 9, 1867, Approved December 9, 1867,

WM. O'NEILL, City Clerk. JNO. B. LOVINGSTON, Mayor.

[No. 61.]

An Ordinance in relation to the collection of the General Tax assessed for the year 1867.

Be it ordained by the City Council of the City of East St. Louis:

SECTION 1. That the collection of the general tax assessed for the year A. D. 1867, be postponed until the first Monday in April, A. D. 1868.

SEC. 2. Within ten days after said first Monday in April of said year, it shall be the duty of the City Clerk to make out a copy of the assessment lists, with the tax assessed for the year 1867, in the manner now provided by ordinance, and deliver the same to the collector of city taxes; and the collector shall proceed to collect the same in the manner now provided by ordinance for the collection of taxes, by the thirty-first day of December, 1868. And if any of such tax shall remain unpaid, it shall be his duty to make out a delinquent list of real estate, publish the same, make application for judgment against and sell such delinquent real estate at the time and in the manner and mode pointed out in the ordinance in relation to revenue from taxes, approved June 20, 1867. And the collector shall have the same power and be governed by the provisions of said ordinance (so far as applicable) in the collection of the taxes for the year A. D. 1867. as herein directed, as though the collection of said tax had not been postponed.

SEC. 3. The annual assessment for the year A. D. 1867, is hereby declared valid and binding in all respects, and shall so remain and be considered to all intents and purposes.

81

tinct and express understanding, on the part of the company accepting the same, to liquidate and to satisfy all damages accruing to any and all property owners by reason of the appropriation of Crooks street and Christy avenue, or either of them, for the purpose of the bridges of the said respective companies, or for approaches to said bridges; and that any failure, on the part of said companies, or either of them, to satisfy such damages, upon their being legally ascertained. shall work a forfeiture of all rights and privileges extended under said ordinance to the company and companies so in default, with the same force and effect and to the extent described in section 8 of said ordinance No. 62.

Sec. 2. That the word "north" in section 5 of said ordinance No. 62, be stricken out, and the word "south" be substituted therefor.

Sec. 3. This ordinance shall be in force form and after its passage and promulgation

Passed December 31, 1867,   Approved, January 2, 1868,
    Wm. O'Neill, City Clerk.   JOHN B. LOVINGSTON, Mayor.

[No. 65.]

An Ordinance in relation to City Indebtedness.

Be it ordained by the City Council of the City of East St. Louis:

Section 1. That upon the surrender of the city warrant, issued to Messrs Bischoff and O'Callahan, for macadamising certificates of indebtedness. payable one year after date, and bearing ten per cent. interest, may be issued to the holder thereof. Such certificate of indebtedness to be negotiable and payable without defalcation or discount and issued under the corporate seal, signed by the Mayor, and attested by the City Clerk.

Sec. 2. That upon the indebtedness of the city to Thomas Winstanley being ascertained, a like certificate of indebtedness be issued to said Winstanley, for the amount found to be due him.

Sec. 3. This ordinance shall be in force from and after its passage and promulgation.

Passed, January 9, 1868.   Approved January 10, 1868.
    Wm. O'Neill City Clerk.   JOHN B. LOVINGSTON, Mayor.

[No. 66.]

An Ordinance vacating a part of Second Street, of the platted town of East St. Louis.

Whereas, A public street, seventy feet in width, has been platted and dedicated in this city, the southeasterly line of which is located as follows—viz., commencing the survey thereof on the northeast line of survey No. 626 (the city limits) opposite the most westerly corner of block numbered one, of the platted town of Illinois City, in St. Clair County, Illinois; thence running southwestwardly, at right angles, to said survey line, to the northwesterly boundary of the machine shop tract of the Ohio and Mississippi railway company (part of said survey 626); thence on along said boundary to the most westerly corner of said tract; thence continuing southwestwardly, at right angles, to St. Louis avenue to said St. Louis avenue: and

Whereas, said new street makes useless that part of Second street, of the platted town of East St. Louis, in this city, lying between St. Louis avenue and Illinois avenue: therefore.

Be it ordained by the City Council of the City of East St. Louis:

Section 1. That, in consideration of the dedication of the above described new street, so much of said Second street, of the platted town of East St. Louis aforesaid, not included in said new street, and located between St. Louis avenue and Illinois avenue, of said platted town of East St. Louis, is hereby vacated.

Sec. 2. This ordinance shall be in force and take effect from and after its passage and promulgation.

Passed January 23, 1868,   Approved January 24, 1868,
    Wm. O'Neill., City Clerk.   Jno. B. LOVINGSTON, Mayor.

90

[No. 75.]

An Ordinance amendatory to Ordinance No. 14, approved July 17, 1865, entitled "An Ordinance in relation to measuring Lumber, and defining the duties of the Lumber Master."

Be it ordained by the City Council of the City of East St. Louis:

SECTION 1. That the lumber-master be authorized to charge, and shall be entitled to collect, for his own use, the following sums: to-wit., for measuring, inspecting, counting and marking boards, planks, scantling and joists, if in one class altogether, or divided into two classes, fifteen cents per thousand feet; if divided into three classes, twenty cents per thousand feet; on timber, more than twelve inches square, fifteen cents per thousand feet; on shingles, laths, rails, wagoners and coopers' stuff, two cents per thousand; on posts of all kinds and dimensions, five cents per hundred.

SEC. 2. The charges collected by the lumber-master, under the preceding section, shall be in full, and his only compensation, for the performance of the duties of his office.

SEC. 3. This ordinance shall be in force and effect from and after its passage and promulgation.

Passed, July 7, 1868.   Approved July 9, 1868.
[SEAL]   WM. O'NEILL City Clerk.   JOHN B. BOWMAN, Mayor.

[No. 76.]

An Ordinance in relation to City Indebtedness.

Be it ordained by the City Council of the City of East St. Louis:

SECTION 1. That upon the surrender of city warrant No. 480, bearing date the 7th day of May 1867, issued to Messrs Bischoff & O'Callaghan, for macadamizing, five certificates of indebtedness (four for $1,000 each and one for $867.42) payable two years from May 7, 1867, and bearing ten per cent. interest per annum, shall be issued to the holder thereof; such certificates of indebtedness to be made negotiable and payable without defalcation or discount, and to be issued under the corporate seal, signed by the Mayor and attested by the City Clerk.

SEC. 2. That upon the indebtedness of the city to Thomas Winstanley being ascertained, certificates of indebtedness, executed in like manner, bearing date from the acceptance of the work for which said indebtedness accrued, shall be issued to him for the amount found to be due him; no certificate thus to him issued to be for a greater sum than one thousand dollars.

SEC. 3. Ordinance No. 65, entitled "An ordinance in relation to the city indebtedness," is hereby repealed.

SEC. 4. This ordinance shall be in force from and after its passage and promulgation.

Passed July 9, 1868,   Approved July 9, 1868,
[SEAL]   WM. O'NEILL, City Clerk.   JNO. B. BOWMAN, Mayor.

[No. 77.]

An Ordinance in relation to Nuisances.

Be it ordained by the City Council of the City of East St. Louis:

SECTION. 1. It shall be the duty of the owner, occupant or person in charge of every dwelling, house, tenement, premises or place of business to provide the same with a suitable privy, the vault of which shall be sunk at least seven feet under ground, and walled up in a good and substantial manner; said privy shall be at least fifteen feet from any street and five feet from any alley, and as far as practicable from any adjoining tenement—not less than five feet, however, without the owner's or occupant's permission, and so constructed and situated as

95

Sec. 2. It shall be the duty of every person using weights, measures or other instruments in the sale or purchase of any article or commodity within this city, to have such weights, measures or other instruments tested, stamped or sealed, and the accuracy thereof certified to by the inspector of weights and measures, as herein provided, at least once in each six months; and any person refusing or failing to do so shall be deemed guilty of a violation of ordinance, and subject to a fine of not less than three nor more than one hundred dollars.

Sec. 3. The inspector of weights and measures shall be entitled to receive the following fees as compensation, in full for the duties of his office, and no more:

For every steelyard or beam, ground floor, platform or counter scales, weighing two hundred pounds or under, with the weights thereof, which he shall test, stamp and certify correct, 50 cents;

For scale and beam of every description, weighing over two hundred pounds, $1;

For any yardstick, dry or liquor measure or instrument used for weighing or measuring, which he shall test, stamp and certify, 25 cents.

For each nest or set of measures, 35 cents.

Sec. 4. This ordinance shall be in force form and after its passage and promulgation.

Passed December 7, 1868,   Approved, December 8, 1868,

[SEAL] WM. O'NEILL, City Clerk.   JOHN B. BOWMAN, Mayor.

[No. 84.]

An Ordinance extending the time for payment of General Tax due for the years 1867 and 1868.

Be it ordained by the City Council of the City of East St. Louis:

SECTION 1. That the time for the payment of the general tax assessed for the year A. D. 1867, be extended until the first day of February, A. D. 1869, and the time for the payment of the general tax for 1868 be extended to the first day of March 1869; and if any such taxes shall remain unpaid upon said 1st day of February and the first day of March 1869, it shall be the duty of the collector to make out respectively delinquent lists of the real estate, publish the same, make application for judgment against, and sell such delinquent real estate in the manner and mode pointed out in the ordinance in relation to revenue from taxes, approved June 20, 1867; and the collector shall have the same power and be governed by the provisions of said ordinance (so far as practicable) in the collection of taxes for the years A. D. 1867 and 1868, as herein directed, as though the time for the collection of said taxes had not been extended.

SEC. 2. Nothing in this ordinance shall be deemed to change the time, manner or mode of collecting the annual revenue for the taxes, except for the years A. D. 1867 and 1868, and this ordinance shall apply to the collection of taxes for said years only.

SEC. 3. This ordinance shall be in force from and after its passage and promulgation.

Passed January 7, 1869.   Approved January 8, 1869.

[SEAL] WM. O'NEILL City Clerk.   JOHN B. BOWMAN, Mayor.

[No. 85.]

An Ordinance in relation to City Indebtedness.

Be it ordained by the City Council of the City of East St. Louis:

SECTION 1. That certificates of indebtedness, in sums of five hundred dollars each, payable two years after date, and bearing ten per cent. interest per annum, be issued to the following named persons, viz:

To John Dwyer, two certificates, to wit, Nos. 10 and 11:

To Patrick Holloran, three certificates, to-wit, Nos. 12, 13 and 14.

To John M. Sullivan, seven certificates, to-wit, No. 15, 16, 17, 18, 19, 20 and 21, for balance

96

due them on their contracts; such certificates of indebtedness to be made negotiable and payable, without defalcation or discount, to be. receivable for all dues to the city, and to be issued under the corporate seal, signed by the Mayor, and attested by the City Clerk.

SEC. 2. This ordinance shall be in force from and after its passage and promulgation.

Passed, January 7, 1869.   Approved, January 8, 1869.
[SEAL]   WM. O'NEILL, City Clerk.   JNO. B. BOWMAN, Mayor.

[No. 86.]

An Ordinance amending Ordinance No. 2, entitled ''An Ordinance in relation to the City Treasurer,'' approved May 1, 1865.

Be it ordained by the City Council of the City of East St. Louis:

SECTION 1. That section 1, of said ordinance be amended so as to read: Before entering upon the discharge of the duties of his office, the Treasurer shall give a bond to the city, with two or more sufficient securities, to be approved by the City Council, in the sum of twenty-five thousand dollars, conditioned according to the requirements of the charter and this ordinance.

Passed, January 7, 1869.   Approved, January 8, 1869.
[SEAL]   WM. O'NEILL, City Clerk.   JOHN. B. BOWMAN, Mayor.

[No. 87.]

An Ordinance to amend Ordinance No. 83, entitled "An Ordinance in relation to Weights and Measures;'' approved December 8, 1868.

Be it ordained by the City Council of the City of East St. Louis:

SECTION 1. That section 2, of ordinance No. 83, entitled 'An ordinance in relation to Weights and Measures," approved December 8, 1868, be amended so as to read as follows: "To examine and test the accuracy of all weights and measures, instrument or thing, used for weighing or measuring within the city, for wholesale or retail, or in which any other person than the owner thereof is interested in its accuracy.

SEC. 2. To amend the third clause of section 3, so as to read: "For scale and beam of any description, weighing over 200 pounds, and under one ton, $1; and on all scales weighing over one ton, $2.''

SEC. 3. Dry measures shall consist of half bushel, peck, half-peck, quarter-peck, and eighth-peck measures; liquid measures shall consist of gallon, half-gallon, quart, pint, half-pint, and gill measures.

SEC. 4. This ordinance shall be in force from and after its passage and promulgation.

Passed February 2, 1869,   Approved February 6, 1869,
[SEAL]   WM. O'NEILL City Clerk.   JNO. B. BOWMAN, Mayor.

[No. 88.]

An Ordinance fixing the Salary of the Mayor and Council for the past year.

Be it ordained by the City Council of the City of East St. Louis:

SECTION 1. That the salary of the members of the City Council, for the year ending the first Tuesday of April, 1869, be and the same is, hereby fixed at the sum of one hundred dollars each.

SEC. 2. That the salary of the Mayor, for the same period, be one thousand dollars.

SEC. 3. This ordinance to be in force from and after its passage and promulgation.

Passed, April 23, 1869.   Approved, April 23, 1869.
(SEAL)   WM. O'NEILL, City Clerk.   JOHN B. BOWMAN, Mayor.

112

[No. 107.]

An Ordinance establishing a directrix for the City of East St. Louis.

Be it ordained by the City Council of the City of East St. Louis:

SECTION 1. That the level of the established directrix for the City of St. Louis, Missouri, carried across the Mississippi, produced and perpetuated on Front street, of the ferry division of this city, be and hereby is adopted as the directrix of the City of East St. Louis.

SEC. 2. That the City Engineer, with all possible dispatch, cause to be erected a permanent monument on said Front street, near Dyke avenue, establishing and displaying the level of said directrix.

SEC. 3. That the City Engineer, after the establishment of such monument, report the fact under his hand as such (giving a correct description of the location of such monument and of the mark thereon indicating such directrix) to the City Clerk, by him to be spread verbatum upon the records of the minutes of the City Council and for preservation with the archives of the city.

SEC. 4. This ordinance shall take effect and be in force from and after its passage and promulgation.

Passed, November 12, 1869.   Approved, November 13, 1869.
[SEAL]   WM. O'NEILL, City Clerk.   VITAL JARROT, Mayor.

[No. 108.]

An Ordinance ordering plank sidewalks along Fourth street, of the platted town of East St. Louis.

Be it ordained by the City Council of the City of East St. Louis:

SECTION 1. That plank sidewalks, 8 feet wide, be built along the curb lines of Fourth street, of the platted town of East St. Louis, from Missouri avenue to Division avenue, on both sides of the street.

SEC. 2. This ordinance shall be in force and take effect from and after its passage and promulgation.

Passed, November 1, 1869.   Approved, November 4, 1869.
[SEAL]   WM. O'NEILL, City Clerk.   VITAL JARROT, Mayor.

[No. 109.]

An Ordinance to grade a part of Main street and its extention.

Be it ordained by the City Council of the City of East St. Louis:

SECTION 1. That Main street and its extension to Missouri avenue be filled up and graded from the center line of Railroad street to said Missouri avenue.

SEC. 2. This ordinance shall take effect and be in force from and after its passage and promulgation.

Passed, November 21, 1869.   Approved, November 23, 1869.
[SEAL]   WM. O'NEILL, City Clerk.   VITAL JARROT, Mayor.

[No. 110.]

An Ordinance vacating part of an alley in block 173, town of East St. Louis.

Be it ordained by the City Council of the City of East St. Louis:

SECTION 1. That all that part of an alley running from Division avenue, through block 173, of the platted town of East St. Louis, to an alley in said block running from Fourth street to Collinsville plankroad, not taken by the extension of Main street from Broadway to Missouri avenue, be, and the same is, hereby vacated.

SEC. 2. This ordinance shall be in force and take effect from and after its passage and promulgation.

Passed November 1, 1869.   Approved, November 4, 1869.
[SEAL]   WM. O'NEILL City Clerk.   VITAL JARROT, Mayor.

123

(No. 142.)

An Ordinance ordering a plank sidewalk built on Jackiesch street.

Be it ordained by the City Council of the City of East St. Louis:

SECTION 1. That a plank sidewalk, five feet four inches wide, be built along the east side of First or Jackiesch street, between Broadway and Railroad street.

SEC. 2. This ordinance shall take effect and be in force from and after its passage and promulgation.

Passed, December 6, 1870. . Approved, December 8, 1870.

[SEAL] WM. O'NEILL, City Clerk. VITAL JARROT, Mayor.

[No. 143.]

An Ordinance to amend Ordinance No. 135, entitled ''An Ordinance authorizing the East St. Louis railway company to establish and maintain a street railway upon streets therein named,'' approved October 12, 1870, and to re-enact the same as amended.

Be it ordained by the City Council of the City of East St. Louis:

SECTION 1. That in section No. 1, of ordinance No. 135, entitled ''An ordinance authorizing the East St. Louis railway company to establish and maintain a street railway upon streets therein named,'' approved October 12, 1870, the words ''ninety days'' be, and the same are, hereby stricken out, and the words ''five months'' substituted therefor.

SEC. 2. That the said ordinance No. 135, thus changed, be, and hereby is, re-enacted for the purposes therein stated.

SEC. 3. This ordinance shall be in force and effect from and after its passage and promulgation.

Passed, January 7, 1871, Approved January 7, 1871,

[SEAL] WM. O'NEILL City Clerk. VITAL JARROT, Mayor.

[No. 144.]

An Ordinance to establish the Fourth Ward.

Be it ordained by the City Council of the City of East St. Louis:

SECTION 1. All that part of the Second ward, as now established by ordinance, lying north-eastwardly of the center line of Illinois avenue, is hereby constituted, and shall be known as the Fourth ward; and all that part of the Second ward, as now established, not embraced in he foregoing limits, shall constitute the Second ward, and hereafter be known as such.

SEC. 2. An election for two aldermen from the Fourth ward, as hereby established, shall be held in accordance with the charter and existing ordinance; and said aldermen, upon taking their seats in the City Council, shall determine by lot which one of them shall hold his office for two years and the other shall hold his office for one year, so that an alderman shall be elected from said ward annually, as in other wards of the city.

SEC. 3. The aldermen now representing the Second ward in the City Council shall continue to hold office for their respective terms as aldermen from the Second ward, as herein constituted and established.

SEC. 4. This ordinance shall be in force and take effect from and after its passage and promulgation.

Passed, March 6, 1871. Approved, March 6, 1871.

(SEAL) WM. O'NEILL, City Clerk. VITAL JARROT, Mayor.

126

[No. 150]

An Ordinance ordering Main Street Macadamized.

Be it ordained by the City Council of the City of East St. Louis:

SECTION 1. That Main street be paved with limestone rock, 18 inches thick, between a line 10 feet each way from the center line—the top 3 inches to be broken as ordinary macadamizing—from Missouri avenue to Menard street.

SEC. 2. This ordinance to be in force and take effect from and after its passage and promulgation.

Passed, May 1, 1871.   Approved, May 4, 1871.

(SEAL)   WM. O'NEILL City Clerk.   DENNIS RYAN, Mayor.

[No. 151.]

An Ordinance establishing and regulating the Police Department.

Be it ordained by the City Council of the City of East St. Louis:

SECTION 1. That there shall be, and is hereby established a police department, to consist of a Captain, Lieutenant, and such policemen as may be appointed by the City Council from time to time.

SEC. 2. All officers and members of the department must be citizens of the United States, and actual residents of the City of East St. Louis, and shall be able to speak, read and write the English language; and shall not be interested nor engaged, either directly or indirectly, in the keeping of any coffee-house, tavern, saloon, inn or dramshop.

SEC. 3. All members of the police department shall hold office during good behavior, and during the pleasure of the City Council, and subject also to the provisions of this ordinance, hereafter contained.

SEC. 4. The Captain shall be *ex-officio* Chief of Police, and the Lieutenant shall be acting Chief of Police, and whenever any vacancy shall occur in the office of Captain, it shall be filled by the Lieutenant.

SEC. 5. Every member of the police department is hereby authorized, and it is made his duty, to arrest, without warrant or process, all persons found in the act of committing any violations of any law or ordinance, or found aiding or abetting in any such violation.

SEC. 6. The Mayor, City Marshal, and his deputies, the Captain, Lieutenant, and every member of the Police Department, are hereby severally authorized to call upon any male inhabitant of city to assist in quelling any riotous or disorderly conduct; or to aid in arresting or safe-keeping any person accused of any crime, or violating any law or ordinance; and any inhabitant so called on who shall neglect or refuse to give such aid and assistance, to the best of his ability, shall be subject to a fine of not less than three nor more than one hundred dollars.

SEC. 7. When any member of the Police Department shall arrest any person for any criminal offense, or any offense against any ordinance, if the judge of the city court, or other proper judicial officer, before whom such person is to be tried, is absent from the city, or if it shall be impossible from any cause, for such person so arrested to have a trial at the time, it shall be the duty of the officer making such arrest to commit the person so arrested to the city jail to await the first session of the said court: provided, he may give bail; and provided also, that it shall be lawful in all cases where a continuance may be had for the person under arrest to enter into reconizance for his or her appearance, with such securities as may be approved by the officer before whom trial is to be had, or in his absence by the acting chief of police:

SEC. 8. In case of any alarm of fire, it shall be the duty of any member of the Police Department to proceed with the utmost dispatch (unless some emergency requires his services at some other place) to the place of the fire, and to be active in preserving order and protecting property.

129

SEC. 27. The policemen shall receive sixty dollars per month; and the Lieutenant sixty-five dollars per month.

SEC. 28. The Mayor is hereby authorized to detail one or more policemen to perform special duty at the railroad depots in the city limits. Such policemen to be paid by the company at whose depot he or they may be detailed.

SEC. 29. In case any railroad company shall desire to avail themselves of the benefit of the foregoing section, they shall designate to the Mayor some fit and proper person, with whom they shall agree to pay such salary as may be stipulated between them; and if the Mayor approve of such person being appointed, he shall recommend to the City Council that such person be commissioned as a special policeman.

SEC. 30. All policemen so appointed shall have all the authority conferred by the provisions of this ordinance on other policemen; and shall be governed by the rules and regulations found in the same; and shall obey all orders, promulgated by the Mayor, for the efficiency and good conduct of the police generally, so far as consistent with their duty as special policemen.

SEC. 31. It shall be the duty of special policemen to remain on duty at and about the places to which they are assigned; and they shall give their whole time and attention to the interest of those employing them, except in cases of fire, riot, or other emergency, when it shall be their duty to join the regular police and give such aid as the public good may require.

SEC. 32. Special policemen shall be subject to removal at any time by the person or persons employing them, or by the City Council; and such removal shall operate as a revocation of all authority conferred upon them; and the Mayor shall have power to suspend special policemen for any of the causes authorizing a suspension of other members of the department, or for any other cause.

SEC. 33. The provisions of the foregoing sections relating to special policemen shall extend to the Wiggins Ferry Company, and any other corporation desiring the same.

SEC. 34. The Mayor is hereby authorized to have the watchmen of the railroad companies, ferry company, or other persons, sworn in as special policemen: provided, he shall deem such person or persons fit; and such watchmen shall have power to exercise all the authority conferred on policemen generally, and shall be governed by the rules and regulations governing special and general policemen.

SEC. 35. The Mayor shall have supervision of the Police Department, and be held responsible for the efficiency and good government of the same; he shall have power to appoint temporary policemen in all cases of emergency; he shall have power to suspend any member of the department, but shall report such action to the City Council at the first meeting; and he shall have power in all cases where vacancies occur, from any cause, to appoint suitable persons to fill the same; and such persons shall hold office until the City Council shall fill such vacancies by regular appointment, or by such other action in the matter as they shall deem proper.

SEC. 36. All orinances and parts of ordinances in conflict with this ordinance, are hereby repealed.

SEC. 37. This ordinance to be in force from and after its passage and promulgation.

Passed, May 23, 1871. Approved, May 26, 1871.

(SEAL) WM. O'NEILL. City Clerk. DENNIS RYAN, Mayor.

[No. 152.]

An ordinance to fund the floating debt of the City of East St. Louis.

Be it ordained by the City Council of the City of East St. Louis:

SECTION 1. That fifty-six bonds of the city, numbered consecutively from No. 47 to No. 102, both inclusive, of the denomination of five hundred dollars each, bearing ten per cent. interest per annum, to be paid annually, the first twenty-eight, bearing the numbers from No. 47 to 74 both inclusive to mature in five years, and the other twenty-eight, bearing the numbers

130

from No. 75 to 102, both inclusive, to mature in eight years, shall be issued, negotiated and sold as hereinafter provided. Said bonds shall be stamped with the corporate seal, signed by the Mayor, City Clerk and Treasurer; and the interest and principal thereof shall be payable at the National Park Bank of the City of New York.

Sec. 2. It shall be the duty of the City Treasurer to cause a notice to be published in the East St. Louis *Gazette*, the corporation Newspaper of East St. Louis, and in the Missouri *Republican* and Missouri *Democrat*—two leading daily newspapers of the City of St. Louis, Missouri—setting forth in such notice a description of said bonds, the time and place, when and where he will receive bids and proposals for the purchase of the same. Said advertisement shall continue to be published for at least thirty days before the day set for disposing of the bonds; and shall also state that the City Council reserves the right to reject any and all bids for the purchase thereof.

Sec. 3. On the day appointed by said notice, the City Treasurer shall examine the bids and proposals received, and submit the same to the City Council at their first regular meeting thereafter; and if the council decide to accept any one or more of such bids, whether the same be more or less than the par value of such bonds, then said bonds shall be awarded to the highest bidder or bidders; and the money realized from the sale of said bonds shall constitute a fund for the liquidation of the claims of any of the creditors of the city.

Sec. 4. There is hereby levied a direct annual tax of one mill and one-half of a mill on the dollar upon each annual assessment made for general purposes, for the purpose of paying the interest on said bonds as the same falls due; and also to pay and discharge the principal thereof when due. And whenever there shall be more money in the fund so created than shall be necessary to pay accruing interest on outstanding bonds, or to liquidate bonds falling due, such surplus money may be used in purchasing and retiring such bonds as can be bought on terms favorable to the city.

Sec. 5. This ordinance shall take effect and be in force from and after its passage and promulgation.

Passed, May 5, 1871.   Approved, May 26, 1871.
[SEAL]   WM. O'NEILL, City Clerk.   DENNIS RYAN, Mayor.

[No. 153.]

An Ordinance ordering plank sidewalks built on certain streets therein named.

Be it ordained by the City Council of the City of East St. Louis:

SECTION 1. That a plank sidewalk, five feet four inches wide, be built along the northwesterly side of the curb line of Seventh street, from St. Louis avenue to Summit avenue.

Sec. 2. That a plank sidewalk, eight feet wide, be built along the northeasterly side of the curb line of Summit avenue, from Sixth street to Seventh street.

Sec. 3. That a plank sidewalk, eight feet wide, be built along the northeasterly side of the curb line of Ohio avenue, from Collinsville plank road street to Ninth street.

Sec. 4. This ordinance shall be in force and take effect from and after its passage and promulgation.

Passed, July 6, 1871.   Approved, July 7, 1871.
[SEAL]   WM. O'NEILL, City Clerk.   DENNIS RYAN, Mayor.

[No. 154.]

An Ordinance ordering the paving of Front street from Pratte street to Bogy street.

Be it ordained by the City Council of the City of East St. Louis.

SECTION 1. That Front street, from the north line of Pratte street to the south line of Bogy street, be paved its full width, side walks along the east side excepted, with limestone rock, set on edge, not less than 12 inches high, and the top broken so as to have a surface of at least 3 inches macadamized rock of the usual size.

westerly line of said street, from the north line of Dyke avenue to the north line of the depot grounds used by the Chicago and Alton railroad company, be graded up to the established grade at the expense of the city.

Sec. 2. That said carriage-way, so graded, be paved with limestone rock set on edge fifteen inches deep, the top three inches broken into ordinary macadamizing after paving, under the direction of the City Engineer, and that the cost thereof be assessed upon and collected from the owners of property benefited thereby in proportion as near as may be to such benefit.

Sec. 3. That this ordinance be in force from and after its passage and promulgation.

Passed, January 16, 1873.　　　　Approved, January 16, 1873.

(SEAL)　　　WM. O'NEILL, City Clerk.　　　JOHN B. BOWMAN, Acting Mayor.
By JAS. H. WYATT, Deputy.

No. 209.)

An Ordinance ordering Menard and Fourth streets of the First ward improved.

Be it ordained by the City Council of the City of East St. Louis:

SECTION 1. That Menard street (in the First ward) from the macadamizing on Main street, to Fourth street, and Fourth street, from the north-east side of Menard street to the railroad embankment of the St. Louis, Alton and Terre Haute railroad company (Belleville branch) be graded upon a temporary grade so as to prepare it for a double track plank road at the expense of the city.

Sec. 2. That a double-track plank road be laid upon Menard and Fourth streets aforesaid so graded—that is to say, one track on each side of the middle line of said street, from Main street to said railroad, each track to be eight feet wide, and to be constructed of best white oak boards, three inches thick, laid upon stringers 3 inches by 8 inches, and that the details of such superstructure conform to the instructions of the City Engineer in the premises, and that this work be done at the cost of the owners of the property benefited thereby.

Sec. 3. This ordinance to be in force and effect from and after its passage and promulgation.

Passed, January 22, 1873.　　　　Approved, January 23, 1873.

[SEAL]　　　WM. O'NEILL, City Clerk.　　　JOHN B. BOWMAN, Acting Mayor.

(No. 210.)

An Ordinance in relation to grades.

Be it ordained by the City Council of the City of East St. Louis:

SECTION 1. That all ordinances establishing grades by the city directrix, are by the city directrix of East St. Louis, upon the understanding that the plane of said directrix is on the same level with the point in height, known in the City of St. Louis, Missouri, as the city directrix of that city.

Sec. 2. This ordinance shall take effect from and after its passage and promulgation.

Passed, January 22, 1873.　　　　Approved, January 23, 1873,

[SEAL]　　　WM. O'NEILL, City Clerk.　　　JOHN B. BOWMAN, Acting Mayor.

[No. 211.]

An Ordinance to allow the Illinois and St. Bridge Company to erect the superstructure of the eastern approach of said bridge over Crooks street and other streets upon certain conditions.

WHEREAS, The Illinois and St. Louis Bridge Company desire to be allowed to raise the super-

177

SEC. 7. Every contract entered into by the engineer, as aforesaid, shall contain a clause stating that the same is entered into, subject to existing ordinances of the city and to the power of the engineer to suspend and annul the same for a failure on the part of the contractors to fulfil the same; but that such suspension or annulment shall not affect the rights of the city to all damages and penalties claimable by it on account of the contractor's failure.

SEC. 8. All bids for sidewalks shall be for so much per lineal foot; for macadam or making streets, so much each square of one hundred square feet, and for all other work, in the manner directed by the council.

SEC. 9. All ordinances and parts of ordinances in conflict with this ordinance shall be and the same are hereby repealed.

SEC. 10. This ordinance shall be in force from and after its passage and promulgation.

Passed. September 17. 1874.   Approved. September 17, 1874.

[SEAL]   WM. O'NEILL, City Clerk.   JOHN B. BOWMAN, Mayor.

[No. 243.]

An Ordinance to provide for lighting the streets of the City of East St. Louis with gas.

Be it ordained by the City Council of the City of East St. Louis:

SECTION 1. That a contract is hereby authorized and directed to be made and entered into by and between "The City of East St. Louis" of the first part and "The East St. Louis Gaslight and Coke Company" of the second part, as follows, to-wit:

This contract and agreement made and entered into this——day of October, A. D. 1874, by and between "The City of East St. Louis" as first party and "The East St. Louis Gas-Light and Coke Company" as second party. Witnesseth:

That said company shall and will extend its street main pipes within the present and future limits of said city whenever and wherever said city shall order public lamps to be erected upon connecting lines, not less than one lamp for every 125 feet of street-main;

That said company shall and will. at its own cost, erect iron lamp-posts and lamps, with foot burners along its street-mains. with necessary service-pipe, wherever ordered by said city, in conformity with the provisions of this contract, and label the lamps at street corners with names of intersecting streets:

That said company shall and will furnish gas for all public lamps of the city, to be kept burning from one hour after sunset to one hour before sunrise each day, except when the moonlight shall render it unnecessary;

That said company shall and will light, extinguish, clean and keep in repair said lamps, with lettering thereon as aforesaid; and

That the said city, on its part, covenants and agrees to require said company to furnish, from and after the execution of this contract, and as soon thereafter as lamps can be erected, not less than two hundred lamps, along the present street main-pipes of the company, as may be directed by the chairman of the Committee on Ways and Means, whose directions, in writing shall be conclusive in the premises; and

That said city will pay, in monthly installments, upon bills thereof, rendered by the company for the use of lamp-posts and lamps. for gas, furnished for lighting, extinguishing cleaning and repairing, and every other charge for maintaining said lamps, the sum of $35.20 per lamp per year—the lamp-posts, lamps and service pipes to be and remain the property of the company.

The standard of gas to be furnished shall not be less than of 14-candle power: a failure to furnish gas of that power for three days in succession after notice thereof by the city, shall subject said company to a forfeiture of $50.00 per day for every day they shall continue, after said three days, to furnish gas of less than 14-candle power.

In laying, relaying or repairing pipes for the conducting of gas for private or public consumption, the said company shall neither cause to be done nor suffer to be done any permanent injury to any of the streets, avenues, alleys, embankments, levees or public places in the city through which said company shall or may so lay, relay or repair its said pipes.

187

(No. 259.)

An Ordinance ordering a sidewalk on Third street.

Be it ordained by the City Council of the City of East St. Louis.

SECTION 1. That a plank sidewalk, eight feet wide, be constructed next the curb line on the south-easterly side of Third street, from Missouri to Division avenue.

SEC. 2. That said work to be done as directed by the charter and ordinances, and at the cost of the property benefited thereby.

SEC. 3. This ordinance shall be in force from and after its passage and promulgation.

Passed, March 16, 1875.　　　　　Approved, March 17, 1875.

[SEAL]　　　WM. O'NEILL, City Clerk.　　　JOHN B. BOWMAN, Mayor.

[No. 260.]

An Ordinance placing the revenue into certain funds.

Be it ordained by the City Council of the City of East St. Louis:

Section 1. All moneys received by the city treasurer shall be by him distributed to and kept in different funds which shall be known as "the general fund," "the interest fund," "sinking fund," and "the library fund."

SEC. 2. 1st. That hereafter of all moneys which shall be paid to the City Treasurer from general taxation, he shall at once pay into the library fund one-eleventh of the sum received: 2d he shall pay six-elevenths into the general fund; 3d the balance, four-elevenths, he shall pay two and one-half into the interest fund, and one and one-half into the sinking fund.

SEC. 3. All other moneys which shall be paid into the treasury, whether coming from special assessments, licenses, or other sources shall be by the treasurer at once placed in the general fund.

SEC. 4. Such parts of Ordinance No. 251, and all ordinance or resolutions, or parts thereof, in conflict with this ordinance are hereby repealed.

SEC. 5. This ordinance to be in force from and after its passage and promulgation.

Passed, March 16, 1875.　　　　　Approved, March 20, 1875.

[SEAL]　　　WM. O'NEILL, City Clerk.　　　JOHN B. BOWMAN, Mayor.

[No. 261.]

An Ordinance establishing the office of corporation counsel, and in relation to the office of City Attorney.

Be it ordained by the City Council of the City of East St. Louis:

SECTION 1. That from and after the passage of this ordinance, there shall be a city officer known as "Corporation Counsel"—who shall be appointed annually; who shall hold his office for one year and until his successor is appointed and shall have qualified.

SEC. 2. The Corporation Counsel shall have been regularly licensed to practice law in the courts of this State, at least two years before the appointment, and be of good standing in the legal profession.

SEC. 3. It shall be the duty of the Corporation Counsel to conduct all the law business of the corporation, and in which the city is, or in which, in the opinion of the Mayor, the city may be interested; to advise the Mayor, City Council or any committee thereof on all such legal questions as may arise in relation to the business of the city, and to give his opinion, in writing, on all questions of law when called upon by the Mayor or Council for that purpose; to draft ordinances, draw up contracts, and all legal papers in which the city may be a party, or in which, in the opinion of the Mayor, the interest of the city may be involved, and to perform all such other duties, not inconsistent with his profession, as the interests and welfare of the city may require.

any new bonds be issued or delivered except as old bonds, and past due coupons are surrendered or other of said legal and subsisting indebtedness is cancelled or satisfied therefor, but such new bonds may be sold as provided by said act for the purpose of raising money to liquidate any of said indebtedness.

SEC. 2. Upon the surrender of any bonds or matured coupons or other evidences of indebtedness the same shall be cancelled and, from time to time, be destroyed under the direction of the city council, if it shall be deemed necessary, and upon the issuing of any new bonds in lieu of bonds or other indebtedness the city clerk shall make a registration thereof in a book to be kept in his office for that purpose, showing the date, amount, number, class, date of maturity, date of interest and place of payment of such new bonds, and the description of the bonds coupons or other evidence of indebtedness for which or in satisfaction of which the same was given as nearly as practicable.

SEC. 3. The city clerk of said city is hereby directed to give notice as prescribed in the third section of the act aforesaid for an election to be held in the several wards in said city on the 20, day of July, 1880, as follows, viz:

At Patrick Kerrigan's house, in the First ward, on Second street, between Brady and Railroad street. Thomas C. Walsh, Patrick Kerrigan and Vincent B. Whitney, Judges.

At Thomas Graney's office, in the Second ward, George Kehoe, Thomas Graney, and John Benner, Judges.

At R. L. Barrowman's house, in the Third ward; Lee B. Mitchell, Frank Bisson and R. L. Barrowman, Judges.

At Samuel McCullough's shoe shop, in the Fourth ward; Samuel McCullough, W. J. McBride and Ambrose Jones, Judges.

The ballots used at such election shall read as follows: "For issuing the bonds" or "Against issuing the bonds."

SEC. 4. This ordinance shall take effect and be in force from and after its passage and promulgation.

Passed June 8, 1880.

[SEAL]   JAMES SHANNON, City Clerk.

At a regular meeting of the city council of the city of East St. Louis, held June 21, 1880, the following proceedings were had, to wit:

The Mayor returned ordinance No. 351, providing for funding the outstanding bonded and other legal subsisting indebtedness of the city of East St. Louis, which was passed by the council on June 8, 1880, with his veto thereto.

The question being put, 'Shall this ordinance pass, nevertheless the veto?' The council voted thereupon as follows.

Ayes—Messrs. Hanifan, McLean, O'Brien, Sackmann, Baugh, jr. and Rafter.

Nays—Mr. Wider.

Absent—Mr. Prottsman.

The ordinance having received a majority vote of all the aldermen elected was duly passed, nevertheless the veto.

[SEAL]   JAMES SHANNON, City Clerk.
Published in East St. Louis HERALD, June 26.

[No 352.]

Be it ordained by the City Council of the City of East St. Louis:

SECTION 1. That section seven (7) of ordinance number 332 entitled, "An Ordinance in relation to Market Master," be amended so as to read as follows: The Market Master, shall

Endnote:

(1) *Ordinances of the City of East St. Louis, St. Clair County, Illinois: Published by Authority of the City Council in Pursuance of a Resolution Adopted June 10, 1884* (East St. Louis, IL: H.D. O'Brien, 1884).

Epilogue

Almost all of the original source materials used to create this anthology is from the Bowen Archives of the Lovejoy Library at Southern Illinois University Edwardsville. The Bowen Archives extends an open invitation for all researchers of East St. Louis history to make use of the vast holdings found there.

In addition to the historic volumes reproduced here, visitors to the Bowen Archives will find mayoral administration papers, studies and reports, historic artifacts and souvenirs, photographs, bound newspapers, films and videos, recorded music, and much more. The special collections are always growing, and donations of historic materials are welcome. Also, the SIUE Institute for Urban Research is another campus resource for those seeking to learn more about East St. Louis, Illinois.

www.siue.edu/lovejoylibrary
(618) 650-2665

www.siue.edu/iur
(618) 650-5262